"Applying science to everyday life can be a challenge, especially when it comes to child development. But Maria's presentation of the literature helps to consolidate key insights and offer clear research-backed guidance."

Lara Aknin, *Distinguished Professor, Simon Fraser University*

"Maria Kalpidou takes a fresh approach in brilliantly weaving together theory, research evidence, and the voices of children and adolescents themselves to deepen understanding of the development of happiness and success. Each chapter begins with an illustrative vignette or quote and ends with practical suggestions for parents and other caregivers."

Paula Fitzpatrick, PhD, *Director of the Center for Well-Being at Worcester Polytechnic Institute, Certified Koru Mindfulness Teacher, Professor of Psychology*

The Development of Children's Happiness and Success

This engaging book is a comprehensive exploration of children's happiness and success covering a wide range of factors influencing positive functioning. It offers a holistic view of children's well-being, identifying both threats and catalysts to happiness and success, as well as evidence-based strategies that promote optimal functioning.

The first section of the book delves into the science of happiness, discussing the role of early social relationships, the importance of experiencing positive emotions and flow, spirituality, and physical health. The second section focuses on the science of success, exploring topics such as mindsets, self-control, and executive functions. Finally, the book explores individual and contextual factors explaining why character matters, the influence of media and technology, and the critical role of disadvantaged environments. Presenting happiness as an ongoing journey, intertwined with the pursuit and achievement of personal goals, the book concludes by proposing a new conceptual framework which identifies pivotal contributors to children's happiness and success such as relationships, self-regulation, and competence.

Suited to upper-level undergraduate and graduate courses in child development, family studies, education, and positive psychology, this book is also an invaluable resource for caregivers, educators, and child practitioners. It is a must-read for anyone interested in cultivating a fulfilling, well-lived life for children and adolescents.

Maria Kalpidou, PhD, is a psychology professor at Assumption University in Massachusetts with 25 years of teaching experience in child development, a parent of three, and an advocate of equal opportunities for all children to discover and develop their full potential.

The Development of Children's Happiness and Success

The Science of Optimizing Well-Being Across the Lifespan

Maria Kalpidou

Routledge
Taylor & Francis Group
NEW YORK AND LONDON

Designed cover image: Getty Images

First published 2024
by Routledge
605 Third Avenue, New York, NY 10158

and by Routledge
4 Park Square, Milton Park, Abingdon, Oxon, OX14 4RN

Routledge is an imprint of the Taylor & Francis Group, an informa business

Library of Congress Cataloging-in-Publication Data
Names: Kalpidou, Maria, author.
Title: The development of children's happiness and success : the science of optimizing well-being across the lifespan / Maria Kalpidou.
Description: Abingdon, Oxon ; New York, NY : Routledge, 2024. | Includes bibliographical references and index.
Identifiers: LCCN 2023034173 (print) | LCCN 2023034174 (ebook) | ISBN 9780367405014 (hardback) | ISBN 9780367404994 (paperback) | ISBN 9780429356414 (ebook)
Subjects: LCSH: Happiness in children. | Success in children.
Classification: LCC BF723.H37 K36 2024 (print) | LCC BF723.H37 (ebook) | DDC 155.4/1242—dc23/eng/20230815
LC record available at https://lccn.loc.gov/2023034173
LC ebook record available at https://lccn.loc.gov/2023034174

ISBN: 978-0-367-40501-4 (hbk)
ISBN: 978-0-367-40499-4 (pbk)
ISBN: 978-0-429-35641-4 (ebk)

DOI: 10.4324/9780429356414

Typeset in Times New Roman
by Apex CoVantage, LLC

To my family

for giving me happiness,

and to my parents and grandparents

for their stories

of hope, perseverance, and courage.

Contents

Preface

The inspiration for this book comes from decades of studying and teaching child development and from parenting three daughters, all of whom are now young adults. Like every parent, my goal was to raise happy and successful children who would also become happy and successful adults. In my parenting, I applied the latest research on child development, while being cognizant of the multiple factors that would work against my best efforts, like work-related stress and experience with loss. Contemplating how to optimize my children's well-being led me to the realization that most of the knowledge we have about child development centers on what typical development is and what is wrong with our children, including psychopathology and risk factors for normative development. Furthermore, this is also the knowledge that we tend to teach students of child development. For several years, I have taught a developmental psychology course to graduate clinical counseling students, who were eager to identify atypical behaviors and learn ways to fix them. As part of the course requirement, these future mental health counselors had to create a hypothetical child of any age and describe their optimal functioning. Needing more clarification, my students would often ask me if they simply needed to focus on listing the developmental milestones of that specific age. When I retorted that children may meet developmental milestones but not function optimally, my students became perplexed. They then thought that the child should also be free of any mental health problems or disabilities. To their dismay, I replied that even such a child may not be functioning optimally and asked them to contemplate whether a child with an anxiety disorder could be happy and successful or whether a child with childhood adversity could become a happy and successful adult. Meeting my students' confused faces, I would then ask: "Is your goal as a counselor to just treat the anxiety or to help your clients reach their optimal level of functioning?"

From my experiences as a parent and teacher, I came to believe that achieving happiness and success is a life-long process that can be cultivated in children. Achieving happiness and success is not simply living a life that is free from any problems, of any nature, free from anything that causes misery, helplessness, and failure. But rather, life challenges are framed in a context of positive well-being where the focus is the optimization of human potential under difficult circumstances. To use the analogy of "swim or sink," success is not just keeping your head above the water but having the skills to swim in all kinds of waters, no matter how turbulent they are, no matter how murky they can be, no matter what is under the waters, to always keep floating, to always enjoy swimming. While positive psychology has shed light on the happiness and success of adults, very little is known about what makes children happy and successful and most importantly how to teach children to achieve both, at any point in their lifetime. In this book, I take the perspective that happiness and success are life-long processes and that adults play an important role in teaching these processes by emphasizing a holistic view of the developing child. For optimizing the well-being of children, adults need to address their physical, emotional, social, intellectual, moral, and spiritual needs. Drawing from the most recent psychological research and other disciplines, as well as the children's perspective, I emphasize the role of relationships, positive emotions, flow, spirituality, self-control, cognitive control, mindsets, physical health, personality, intelligence, and character values on achieving happiness and success. Lastly, I consider the importance of contextual factors such as consumerism, digital media, poverty, and the physical environment.

Acknowledgments

I want to thank all those who have inspired this work, beginning with my three daughters, Tatiana, Natalia, and Nicole Karadimitriou, who willingly participated in experiments and classroom demonstrations when they were little. I joined the field of developmental psychology because of how intriguing I found the human capacity to adapt and flourish. No other field in psychology better reveals the remarkable commonalities we share as humans, as well as our unique individual traits. Seeing my daughters grow, overcome difficulties, unravel talents, learn to love, make principled decisions, appreciate beauty, search for purpose, and care for the world, was most rewarding and inspiring. I also want to thank my students of child development who shared my passion for children's well-being and kept me motivated throughout the years. I am grateful to my husband, Kosmas Karadimitriou, for his inspiring drive to live life to the fullest. I also want to thank my graduate fellow, Rylee Ferguson, who provided invaluable assistance with literature research and editing. Her meticulousness and promptness are much appreciated. Lastly, I am indebted to Hellen Pritt for believing in me and giving me this awesome opportunity to write this book and to Molly Selby and the production team for bringing this book to fruition.

Introduction to Happiness and Success

"Happiness is an activity of the soul in accordance with perfect virtue."

Aristotle
(Ross et al., 2009, p. 19)

The modern Greek words for happiness and success are respectively ***ευτυχία*** (eftychía) and ***επιτυχία*** (epitukhía). The reader may notice that the two words, seemingly referring to two different concepts, share a common root. The root word *τύχη* (túkhē), which means *luck, fate, or an unknown outcome*, is combined with the prefix *ευ* (eû) which means good, to create the word for happiness (*ευτυχία)*. The root word *τύχη* (túkhē) is also combined with the prefix *επι* (épi), which means *near*, to create the word for success (*επιτυχία)*. Therefore, the Greek word for happiness means to have a good fate while success means to realize a good fortune. Both terms share the element of the unknown, which is fate, an uncharted path, and imply a desire to pursue it. The similarity in these terms reveals how interconnected they are. One is happy when the path in life is appraised to be a good one, and one is successful when the end goals of the path in life are reached. Happiness and success are parts of a larger theory of well-being that includes the augmentation of positive outcomes such as supportive relationships and the minimization of negative outcomes such as mental and physical health problems. The position of this book is that when happiness and success are aligned our lives are optimized. Furthermore, while there are factors that contribute to one or the other, there are also dynamics that influence both, thus informing us of their strong interconnectedness. This book follows the science of happiness and success as well as the individual and contextual factors that optimize happiness and success. But let's begin at the beginning, by tracing the conceptualizations and measurements of happiness and success, identifying developmental and contextual considerations, and lastly revealing the main objectives of this book.

A discussion of well-being cannot begin without a reference to Aristotle, who is credited for being the first in ancient Western culture to develop a theory of well-being. According to Aristotle, the ultimate goal of life is to achieve "eudaimonia" a state of "good spirit," or intense *ευτυχία*, the modern Greek word for happiness. Aristotle did not think of happiness as a mental state or a feeling but rather as a

DOI: 10.4324/9780429356414-1

product that is built by the way life is lived. It is reached by achieving good health, wealth, knowledge, and virtues of friendship, honesty, justice, and honor. In other words, happiness and success are interconnected. Aristotle considered that only humans can achieve the highest level of well-being because only they possess the ability of rational thinking and contemplation that are needed to intentionally make decisions to live a virtuous life. According to Aristotle, children do not achieve happiness unless they acquire the intellectual faculties of rational and contemplative thinking. However, parents and teachers can engender the pursuit of the highest goal of happiness through direct teachings and modeling. Consequently, happiness is not inborn but something that is learned (Ross et al., 2009).

Modern conceptualizations of happiness in the field of positive psychology are highly influenced by Aristotle's views. According to Martin Seligman (2002), a pioneer of positive psychology, happiness is an outcome of experiencing positive emotions including pleasures, hope, and gratitude; developing and applying good character; and, leading a meaningful life. Seligman's most recent model is known as PERMA plus for identifying Positive emotions, Engagement, Relationships, Meaning, and Accomplishments as the main pillars of happiness (Seligman, 2011). For adults, seeking happiness means nurturing relationships; pursuing the experience of hope, optimism, and gratitude; maintaining a healthy and active lifestyle; practicing mindfulness; exploring spirituality; acquiring virtues such as courage and temperance; discovering personal strengths and talents; and putting them into good use to optimize personal potential and benefit others (Seligman, 2002, 2011).

Current research on children's happiness has applied the adult model offered by Seligman and other positive psychologists to promote children's happiness. For example, Christine Carter in her book *Raising Happiness* applies some of these principles to create advice for parents on how to foster their children's happiness. According to her, a "happy life is one that is full of different types of positive emotions" (Carter, 2010, p. x). Emotions of the past, such as gratitude; emotions for the present, such as contentment; and emotions of the future, such as hope, are central in directing actions and relationships to create happiness. In agreement with Aristotle, the contemporary view is also that happiness can be discovered, taught, and rediscovered if lost. Unlike Aristotle, however, Seligman (2002) views young children as being naturally inclined to be happy because of the adaptive value of happiness. Children experience and exhibit positive emotions because evolutionarily positive emotions are important for growth and adaptation. The sunny disposition of children elicits more caring behavior and resources necessary for development. In turn, children who feel safe, explore the opportunities opened to them and achieve their potential. On the other hand, children who experience negative affect may be prone to developing anxiety and depression. Indeed, while happy people experience more positive emotions than negative ones, depressed individuals experience an equal number of positive and negative emotions. Despite the adaptive value of a sunny disposition, happiness is considered an outcome of the interaction between nature and nurture. Twin studies with adults reveal that our biology determines 50% of subjective happiness, while 10% is explained by life circumstances (e.g., marriage, income) and 40% is shaped by intentional choices.

Most caregivers consider it their primary job to raise happy children. Therefore, it is this 40% that parents and child practitioners can help children optimize. In adulthood, the construction of happiness, at least in individualistic societies, is a matter that lies within the person. In other words, people are responsible for their own happiness. Hence, identifying the factors that contribute to happiness and success is crucial in raising children who can become happy and successful adults.

There is currently no systematic examination of whether the application of the adult model of happiness and success on children is supported by research. Such examination is necessary before it is possible to advise parents and child practitioners. Do the things that make adults happy also make children happy? In general, when children are asked about the things that make them happy, they provide responses that are congruent with adult views of happiness. Even young children, whose reasoning abilities are far less developed, agree that family, friends, pets, and having nice things make them happy (Uusitalo-Malmivaara, 2012). However, there are several other factors, constitutional or environmental, that affect happiness and success, and even though children and adolescents may not necessarily identify, they are linked to their well-being.

Childhood adversities such as neglect, abuse, poverty, and domestic violence, are significant threats to well-being, especially when the relationship between adversity and psychological dysfunction appears to be dose dependent. Retrospective adult studies have well documented that the cumulative number of adverse experiences increases symptoms of psychopathology (Kalpidou et al., 2021) and the likelihood of severe health problems that shorten the life span (Felitti et al., 1998). Adversity that causes chronic stress alters the physiological responses in the brain leaving the child in a state of constant arousal, prone to emotion dysregulation, and difficulty in making and executing appropriate plans of action. Children with unstable family life, who experience or witness violence, who lack support from their caregivers, and who have limited resources are more likely to fall behind at school and eventually drop out of high school. Success in the face of adversity builds resilience, a psychological phenomenon that is observed when protective factors outweigh risks, thereby allowing adaptive functioning. Showing resilience is not the same as living a happy and successful life, however. Learning to be happy and successful allows the child to move beyond adaptive functioning to their optimal zone of functioning.

Moreover, there are developmental trends in happiness and success to consider. There is some evidence to suggest a decrease in happiness from 12 to 15 years, although not in a homogeneous manner. Finnish adolescents who reported a decline attributed it to poor peer relationships and increased academic challenges. However, some students perceived an increase in their happiness due to improved friendships and romantic relationships, and others thought their happiness remained stable (Uusitalo-Malmivaara & Lehto, 2013). Morgan (2014) too showed that happiness was lower for 14-year-olds in a sample from England. Changes in the happiness of younger children have not been systematically reported, but Holder and Coleman's research showed that 90% of 9- to 12-year-olds perceived themselves as being happy, and this was in general agreement with parent ratings of happiness

(Holder & Coleman, 2009). Another perspective in the field of positive psychology is that each person develops a set point of happiness that remains fairly stable throughout the life span and at which people return after strong emotional experiences like loss or winning a lottery ticket (Cummins, 2003; Lyubomirsky et al., 2005). Such a set point of happiness is then a significant contributor to well-being. A theory of a set point of happiness implies that there may be fluctuations in assessments of happiness due to external factors and developmental adaptations (e.g., school transitions, puberty) because they have the potential to upset the set point.

Children's perceptions of success also develop over time. Children as young as 6 years old have subjective experiences with success that somewhat coincide with research assessments of success. They perceive that completing a task, continued engagement in an activity, overt expressions of contentment with an activity, positive feedback from teachers, parents, and peers, and getting good grades count as experiences with success (Määttä et al., 2016). As children get older their expectations for success become more aligned with performance, in other words, they heed the feedback from their performance, thus influencing their motivation and self-regulation on achievement activities such as exams. Based on research, beliefs about competence and expectations for success decline during middle childhood as children move from elementary to middle school and this applies to both academic and non-academic domains. Therefore, as children become better at self-evaluations, they may also begin to view themselves more negatively. In addition to their own views, several other factors help shape children's own expectations for success. Teachers, parents, and peers can provide feedback that affects children's achievement-related attributions and how they approach future challenges (Wigfield & Eccles, 2002). Personal qualities like optimism and cognitive and behavioral control also contribute to achievement in multiple domains.

Taking a developmental, contextual, and holistic approach, this book examines how ideas from current science on adult happiness can be applied to understand and then improve children's well-being. However, the book answers the question of what children think makes them happy instead of relying on adult accounts of children's happiness. Therefore, the research that is cited throughout the book is mostly based on children's and adolescents' views either in self-reports or experimental evaluations. Researchers have used different approaches to measure happiness and success. Most consider happiness to be equivalent to subjective well-being which is defined as the manifestation of three factors; global life satisfaction, the presence of positive affect, and the absence or reduced presence of negative affect (Diener, 1984; Holder, 2012). Life satisfaction includes cognitive self-appraisals of one's life that go beyond the present life conditions or emotions. Therefore, a person may perceive high life satisfaction but may currently experience more negative than positive emotions. The term subjective well-being with its emphasis on living a satisfied life is in line with Seligman's view of happiness. A popular measure of life satisfaction is the Student's Life Satisfaction Scale (Huebner & Gilman, 2002) which is often used along with the Scale of Positive and Negative Experiences (Diener et al., 2009) that accesses how frequently children experience negative (e.g., sad, bad) and positive emotions (e.g., happy, joyful). Another commonly used scale is the Oxford Happiness Questionnaire (Hills & Argyle, 2002), which measures well-being beyond concurrent contentment as it includes questions about attitudes towards the future, satisfaction with life, and level of engagement with life. In conjunction with one of the aforementioned scales, researchers often rely on the Subjective Happiness Scale (Lyubomirsky & Lepper, 1999) which is used to measure the global sense of happiness with four statements, such as rating how happy one is compared to peers. Lastly, researchers who are interested in the global perception of happiness as an affective state use the Faces Scale, where children choose among faces that progress from sad to happy (Holder & Klassen, 2010). Unlike the aforementioned scales which are largely adaptations of adult measures of happiness, the Children's Happiness Scale (Morgan, 2014) was developed based on children's own perceptions of what makes them happy. Morgan identified 20 statements that describe happiness, such as having friends, feeling safe, not having problems, not being bullied, and learning from mistakes. Morgan also found that children tended to agree more on what makes them unhappy than happy and that children considered multiple sources of happiness. Except for the Face Scale, all self-report measures have been used with children older than 8, leaving a gap in research assessing the happiness of very young children. Lastly, researchers have measured children's success primarily in the academic domain and used grades, standardized tests, attitudes toward school and learning, academic motivation, high school graduation rates, and college enrollment as indicators of success.

The book reviews the literature that focuses on positive functioning; therefore the dependent variables in the studies included here are measures of subjective well-being as identified earlier. Other variables of positive functioning such as self-esteem and prosocial behavior are also included. Reference to psychopathology such as internalizing (e.g., anxiety, depression, fear) and externalizing symptoms (e.g., aggression, bullying) are mentioned when research on positive outcomes is lacking or when studies include both positive and negative indices of well-being. Furthermore, the book incorporated studies from various countries and the latest meta-analytic reviews that often include international studies. The content of the book focuses on how experiencing healthy relationships; being grateful, hopeful, and optimistic; engaging in mind-absorbing activities; being in good physical health; and using individual strengths to benefit the self and others associate with well-being measures. Having a growth mindset, healthy development of executive function, and self-control not only contribute to academic achievement but support the pursuit of any goal in life. Success further depends not only on education but also on personal qualities of perseverance and grit. The book additionally examines individual, constitutional, and contextual factors that contribute to, or threaten, both happiness and success. Children's success and happiness are influenced by personality and intelligence, personal character strengths, the culture of consumerism and digital media, poverty, and the physical environment.

The book is organized into three parts. PART 1 follows the science of happiness and includes five chapters on the topics of relationships, positive emotions, flow, spirituality, and physical health.

Chapter 1: Relationships is dedicated to the role relationships with parents, peers, and teachers play in children's and adolescents' subjective well-being and discusses possible changes in the relative importance of these relationships as children get older. The chapter traces the children's own perceptions of the impact of their relationships, identifies relevant methodological issues, and offers suggestions on how to optimize children's healthy relationships.

Chapter 2: Feeling Good is dedicated to the role of positive emotions that enhance subjective well-being. It begins with the definition and developmental trajectory of gratitude, hope, and optimism and explores the ways that these positive emotions may protect children's and adolescents' well-being. The chapter also includes the topic of emotional intelligence as a way to enhance positive emotions while regulating negative ones. Lastly, ways that parents and other adults can promote and teach gratitude, hope, optimism, and emotional intelligence are proposed.

Chapter 3: Solitude and Flow aims to provide a comprehensive understanding of how children perceive and experience solitude and flow, and the potential benefits these concepts may offer in terms of their well-being and development. It addresses questions regarding the age at which children can identify constructive solitude and flow experiences and reviews potential environmental and personal factors that influence these experiences. Furthermore, the chapter provides suggestions to encourage flow experiences in children.

Chapter 4: Spirituality explores children's spirituality by examining theoretical perspectives as well as contemporary research on children's ability to ponder existential matters and their capacity for mindfulness. The chapter also examines research-supported relationships between spirituality and/or religiosity and personal happiness in children of different ages. Questions such as when children are more open to spiritual teachings, what aspect of spirituality is more meaningful to children and adolescents, and how to nurture spirituality and mindfulness are also addressed.

Chapter 5: Sound Body, Sound Mind is about the connection between physical activity, health, and being overweight with reports of happiness and life satisfaction. Being physically active is also associated with academic performance, cognitive skills, and other positive indices of well-being such as self-esteem and self-control. The chapter also reviews the literature on the connection that sleep duration and quality have with positive and negative affect. Evidence from cross-sectional and intervention studies, conducted in different parts of the world, is examined throughout the chapter, and recommendations for parents and child practitioners are made.

PART 2 of the book is focused on the science of success and the topics of mindsets and grit, self-control, and executive functions.

Chapter 6: The Power of Thinking Right is an exploration of children's attitudes towards ability and learning that influence academic outcomes. It describes the concepts of growth and fixed mindset, their relationship with grit, and the evidence that links mindsets and grit with successful outcomes in school and broader psychological well-being. The development of a growth mindset is discussed along with other motivational findings to reconcile positive affirmations with the theory of mindsets. A review of guidelines for fostering a growth mindset is also provided.

Chapter 7: Self-Control offers an understanding of self-control as a reflexive, fast, and stimulus-dependent system that has its origins in temperament. This type of control is different from cognitive control which has origins in executive function although the two are intertwined. The chapter traces the development of self-control and highlights its importance in achieving personal goals and protecting well-being in childhood, adolescence, and adulthood. The chapter discusses the unique role of self-control in predicting academic outcomes in comparison to IQ and explains the difficulties some adolescents have with impulse control. It concludes with general recommendations that enhance self-control in children of all ages.

Chapter 8: Cognitive Control discusses the important role that executive functions play in children's success. The developmental trajectory of executive functions is closely tied to changes in the prefrontal cortex, which becomes more specialized with age. Research indicates that stress, poverty, trauma, and family dysfunction have negative effects on the development of executive function and academic performance. The chapter traces the development of executive functions and their biological underpinning before it discusses the relationship that executive functions have with academic achievement and mental health. The chapter also reviews the threats to executive functions and offers ideas for family and school interventions.

PART 3 is dedicated to individual and contextual factors that influence both happiness and success. The topics cover personality and intelligence, character virtues, consumerism, digital media, poverty, the physical environment, and discrimination.

Chapter 9: Individual Differences Matter explores how individual differences in personality traits and IQ support children's ability to become happy and successful. It begins with an exploration of the links between childhood and adult personality by associating main temperament characteristics with the Big Five Factors of personality. The chapter reviews how personality traits predict childhood outcomes and foretell success in adulthood. The role of intelligence in school success and adult outcomes is also explored. Lastly, the chapter offers a discussion of how to enhance traits in children that are mostly linked with success.

Chapter 10: Character Matters describes the role of a virtuous life in happiness and success from a contemporary psychological perspective. The chapter traces the early character strengths in childhood in expressions of sharing and acts of kindness. It discusses the Values in Action (VIA) strengths and reviews their links to happiness, life satisfaction, risky behaviors, and academic success throughout childhood and adolescence. The chapter also discusses the effectiveness of character education programs and concludes with suggestions for parents and teachers to promote the development of character strengths.

Chapter 11: Consumerism, Materialism, and Digital Media is dedicated to the effects of consumerism, materialism, and digital media on children's well-being. It discusses how children become consumers and embrace materialism as a value system that leads to happiness and success. The chapter reviews the research that links consumerism and materialism with well-being and offers suggestions to protect well-being. The chapter also provides a review of current uses and misuses of digital media, the positive and negative outcomes on well-being, conceptual ideas to better understand the connection between digital media use and well-being, and recommendations to promote the adaptive use of digital media.

Chapter 12: Poverty, Physical Environment, and Discrimination focuses on the effects that poor contexts have on well-being and the capacity to live a healthy, happy, and successful life. Negative outcomes associated with poverty include poor self-regulation, deficits in executive functions, altered neurodevelopment, increased psychopathology, and disparities in academic achievement and educational attainment. Although inter-related to poverty, special emphasis is given to the physical environment (e.g., toxins and pollutants), the role of nature, and the association of racial discrimination with children's well-being. Lastly, the chapter presents some ideas about how to protect the well-being of children raised in poor contexts.

The book concludes with a discussion of the research evidence in this book and the proposal of a new conceptual framework, the INSPIRE model of happiness and success, to better conceptualize the findings and draw strategies for parents, educators, and child practitioners that promote children's optimal functioning.

In closing, happiness is not considered as a static mental state but a holistic cognitive and affective appraisal of one's way of living at any point in life. A happy life is a life well-lived. A well-lived life is full of positive emotions, good deeds, a sense of personal growth, health, and wisdom. From this point of view, the ability to succeed or meet personal expectations and goals is intimately related to happiness when such goals add purpose and meaning to life. Achieving one's goals increases happiness by increasing a sense of self-worth and self-efficacy. Like happiness, success is a journey and a process. Children need to develop skills and personal characteristics that allow them to "live in success," face adversity, and capitalize on failure.

References

Carter, C. (2010). *Raising happiness: 10 simple steps for more joyful kids and happier parents*. Ballantine Books.

Cummins, R. A. (2003). Normative life satisfaction: Measurement issues and a homeostatic model. *Social Indicators Research, 64*(2), 225–256. https://doi.org/10.1023/A:1024712527648

Diener, E. (1984). Subjective well-being. *Psychological Bulletin, 95*(3), 542–575. https://doi.org/10.1037/0033-2909.95.3.542

Diener, E., Wirtz, D., Biswas-Diener, R., Tov, W., Kim-Prieto, C., Choi, D.-W., & Oishi, S. (2009). New measures of well-being. *Social Indicators Research: Assessing Well-Being, 39*, 247–266. https://doi.org/10.1007/978-90-481-2354-4_12

Felitti, V. J., Anda, R. F., Nordenberg, D., Williamson, D. F., Spitz, A. M., Edwards, V., Koss, M. P., & Marks, J. S. (1998). Relationship of childhood abuse and household dysfunction to many of the leading causes of death in adults. *American Journal of Preventive Medicine, 14*(4), 245–258. https://doi.org/10.1016/S0749–3797(98)00017–8

Hills, P., & Argyle, M. (2002). The Oxford happiness questionnaire: A compact scale for the measurement of psychological well-being. *Personality and Individual Differences, 33*(7), 1073–1082. https://doi.org/10.1016/S0191-8869(01)00213-6

Holder, M. D. (2012). *Happiness in children: Measurement, correlates, and enhancement of positive subjective well-being*. Springer Science & Business Media.

Holder, M. D., & Coleman, B. (2009). The contribution of social relationships to children's happiness. *Journal of Happiness Studies, 10*, 329–349. https://doi.org/10.1007/s10902-007-9083-0

Holder, M. D., & Klassen, A. (2010). Temperament and happiness in children. *Journal of Happiness Studies, 11*, 419–439. https://doi.org/10.1007/s10902-009-9149-2

Huebner, E. S., & Gilman, R. (2002). An introduction to the multidimensional students' life satisfaction scale. *Social Indicators Research, 60*, 115–122. https://doi.org/10.1023/A:1021252812882

Kalpidou, M., Volungis, A. M., & Bates, C. (2021). Mediators between adversity and well-being of college students. *Journal of Adult Development, 28*(4), 286–298. https://doi.org/10.1007/s10804-021-09372-6

Lyubomirsky, S., & Lepper, H. S. (1999). A measure of subjective happiness: Preliminary reliability and construct validation. *Social Indicators Research, 46*, 137–155. https://doi.org/10.1023/A:1006824100041

Lyubomirsky, S., Sheldon, K. M., & Schkade, D. (2005). Pursuing happiness: The architecture of sustainable change. *Review of General Psychology, 9*(2), 111–131. https://doi.org/10.1037/1089–2680.9.2.111

Määttä, E., Mykkänen, A., & Järvelä, S. (2016). Elementary schoolchildren's self-and social perceptions of success. *Journal of Research in Childhood Education, 30*(2), 170–184. https://doi.org/10.1080/02568543.2016.1143418

Morgan, R. (2014). *The children's happiness scale: Scale and data for children in care, receiving social care support, and living away from home in boarding or other residential schools or colleges*. Retrieved April 29, 2023, from https://dera.ioe.ac.uk/20502/1/The%20Children's%20Happiness%20Scale.pdf

Ross, W. D., Aristotle, & Brown, L. (2009). *Nicomachean ethics (Oxford world's classics)*. Oxford University Press.

Seligman, M. E. (2002). *Authentic happiness: Using the new positive psychology to realize your potential for lasting fulfillment*. Simon and Schuster.

Seligman, M. E. (2011). *Flourish: A visionary new understanding of happiness and well-being*. Simon and Schuster.

Uusitalo-Malmivaara, L. (2012). Global and school-related happiness in Finnish children. *Journal of Happiness Studies, 13*, 601–619. https://doi.org/10.1007/s10902-011-9282-6

Uusitalo-Malmivaara, L., & Lehto, J. E. (2013). Social factors explaining children's subjective happiness and depressive symptoms. *Social Indicators Research, 111*, 603–615. https://doi.org/10.1007/s11205-012-0022-z

Wigfield, A., & Eccles, J. S. (2002). The development of competence beliefs, expectancies for success, and achievement values from childhood through adolescence. In A. Wigfield & J. S. Eccles (Eds.), The *development of achievement motivation* (pp. 91–120). Academic Press.

Part 1

The Science of Happiness

1 Relationships

> "For one human being to love another human being: that is perhaps the most difficult task that has been entrusted to us, the ultimate task, the final test and proof, the work for which all other work is merely preparation."
>
> Rainer Maria Rilke (2011, p. 25)

Humans are raised in relationships with others and as such, relationships are powerful in shaping identities, values, life goals, and ways to accomplish them. The influence of close and intimate relationships on happiness and general well-being is widely supported in the adult literature. Relationships offer companionship, support, and opportunities to experience positive emotions. Most importantly relationships protect from feeling loneliness which in great measure causes depression. Relationships are also the training ground for skills needed to expand interpersonal connections with people in various contexts, spaces, and times. The pursuit of gratifying relationships or the termination of unhappy ones is at the power of everyone. Adults maintain relationships that fulfill their emotional needs for intimacy, support, and trust, and they abandon relationships that cause stress and harm. In children, relationships are considered the source of a healthy emotional life although there is not a systematic approach to understanding how relationships contribute to their subjective well-being, especially when children do not have full control of their relationships. For example, they cannot terminate a conflictual relationship with a parent or sibling.

A few considerations arise when we contemplate how children's relationships influence their happiness. Their understanding of relationships changes as they develop emotionally, socially, and cognitively. The central features of friendships change over time with shared interests and common characteristics in preschool, giving way to trust and dependency in middle childhood, to intimacy and emotional connectedness in adolescence. Moreover, friend and peer relationships are the only horizontal relationships children have and can control. The extent to which they can influence their relationship with their parents depends on how accommodating or restrictive the parenting style is. Democratic parents allow more input from the children, while authoritarian parents have one-way relationships with their

DOI: 10.4324/9780429356414-3

children. Lastly, relationships with other adults such as teachers and coaches may leave a much smaller room for children's input in the quality of the relationship.

This chapter considers the children's perspective about how relationships contribute to their subjective sense of well-being, including life satisfaction which is the cognitive appraisal of how satisfied with the life they are, and the affective appraisal of their emotional states and moods, which is indicated by perceived overall happiness and the experience of positive and negative affect. It begins with an exploration of infant attachment and synchronous interactions with caregivers as the foundations for subjective well-being. It then traces the developmental changes in children's understanding that relationships can be a source of happiness, revealing that this emerges in the preschool period. The chapter delves more into the role of parenting and the associations between parents' and children's happiness. The roles of peers, friendships, teachers, and the school context in promoting subjective well-being are also discussed. The review highlights that parental relationships may contribute more to life satisfaction, but friends and peers may be a source of positive affect or subjective happiness. A discussion of the ways that parents and teachers can support healthy relationships ensues. Given that young children have limited introspective abilities the review of relevant studies occasionally includes other informants of children's well-being, especially in the early years.

Early Relationships and Happiness

The roots of healthy relationships are found in infant attachment, a prototypic relationship the infant experiences with the primary caregiver. Under optimal conditions, infants develop a secure emotional bond with one or multiple caregivers, who have consistently shown sensitivity and timely responsiveness to their needs. A secure attachment is not only a source of experiencing positive emotions but also the ground for learning the elements of a good relationship: trust, responsiveness, emotional availability, regulated emotions, and effective communication.

Extensive research has linked a secure attachment to optimal outcomes in childhood and adolescence, whereas insecurity has lingering negative effects on development. It is well established that children with a history of secure attachment demonstrate better social competence in preschool, are likely to be popular in middle childhood and experience more positive friendships in adolescence. Infants with inconsistent or rejecting parents are more likely to experience negative feelings of anxiety and insecurity that inhibit social exploration and the development of independence. The relationships of children with a history of insecure attachment are marked by anxiety and avoidance. The link between attachment quality and outcomes is theoretically explained by the construction of a relationship model based on these early experiences. Infants as young as 12 months old internalize characteristics of their first relationship in a working model that applies to future relationships. Such a model can potentially be revised and shaped as further social relationships expand through childhood and adolescence. Future relationships can potentially become a source of comfort or stress and anxiety, and thus contribute to perceived happiness accordingly. An alternative explanation of the long-term effects of infant attachment on well-being is based on the consistency and quality of parenting with some contributions from the child's temperament (Deiner & Deiner-McGavran, 2008). Positive parenting that effectively responds to the child's temperamental characteristics (e.g., emotionality) as the child develops explains the positive outcomes that are attributed to early attachment.

The direct association between happiness and attachment in the early years is difficult to assess. Psychologists have primarily made inferences about the infants' well-being by associating the quality of attachment with the presence or absence of internalizing (e.g., anxiety, fear) and externalizing (e.g., noncompliance, aggression) problems. However, even in infancy, it is possible to examine the experience of positive emotions in the context of attachment. Babies with responsive parents learn to become attuned with others, share their feelings, initiate and terminate interactions, and feel competent interactional partners. Furthermore, infants, as young as 5 months of age, not only perceive different emotions but also are capable of synchronous matching of others' emotions (Tronick, 1989). Relying on these infant skills, research shows that the overall family expressiveness of positive and negative emotions (i.e., the level of emotion expressed by all family members) is readily matched at 9 months, thereby emphasizing the important role of the family environment in experiencing and understanding positive emotions (Ogren et al., 2018). There is also evidence that experiencing positive emotions in a context of a secure attachment is also evident much later. Pre-teens who were classified as secure, based on interviews about their childhood, also reported experiencing more zest, gratitude, hope, and love. Security indicators in this study accounted for 12–19% of the variance in positive emotions (Obeldobel & Kerns, 2020). The foundation of well-being in infancy can be traced to the early synchronous interactions with caregivers where babies begin to make meaning of the world and the people and things in it (Tronick & Beeghly, 2011).

Relationships and Happiness: Developmental Changes in Children's Perceptions

While children benefit from consistency in supportive and positive parenting throughout childhood and adolescence, questions arise about their own perceptions of happiness in relation to others. Do children think of their parents and other relationships as sources of their happiness, and what age are they able to say so? In an interesting study, and perhaps the only one that provided insight into how 4- and 5-year-olds experience happiness, Adachi and Trehub (2011) asked preschoolers to create happy and sad songs by offering them a prompt of a rabbit that displayed the targeted emotion. The majority of Canadian children produced new songs which then allowed the researchers to examine the lyrics. Happy songs featured family and friends being with the main character, whereas sad songs described the rabbit being with no family and friends or not being able to get what it wanted (Adachi & Trehub, 2011). Sibling relationships as a specific source of happiness are not mentioned by children until the school-age period although negative relationships with siblings in the preschool period predict internalizing and externalizing problems

(Deiner & Deiner-McGavran, 2008). On the other hand, positive sibling relationships are related to increased prosocial behavior and better psychological adjustment of 4- to 8-year-olds, at least as rated by parents (Coldwell et al., 2008). These findings highlight that children begin to think about how others, including family members and friends, contribute to their emotional states sometime in the preschool period. They further suggest the importance of succeeding in fulfilling personal desires and likes, hinting that the need for an independent agency is an important aspect of happiness.

In early middle childhood, children's understanding of how their happiness is influenced by their activities, and who they spend their time with, appears to expand. They identify social activities such as play, as sources of happiness. Using an ethnographic approach, researchers asked 6- to 8-year-olds from Ireland to draw what made them happy. The researchers also interviewed the children in small focus groups and gave them cameras to take pictures of things that brought happy feelings, over three to four days. The children then looked at their data and organized them into themes such as activities and relationships. Not surprisingly, playing was one of the activities that made children happy especially when they needed to be cheered on when they played. In addition to providing fun, children considered play as a way to be healthy and energetic. Children also identified environmental restrictors (e.g., rain) or facilitators (e.g., park) for engaging in play, indicating that at this age, children can identify not only the sources of their happiness but also extraneous factors that influence them. Spending time with family in fun activities such as baking and cooking was a main source of happiness as well. In addition to activities, relationships with friends, family members, teachers, and animals were central to children's responses (Moore & Lynch, 2018). Other studies showed that friends and siblings are a source of fighting. Indeed, sibling rivalry can interfere with the well-being of children as noted earlier. In the context of differential treatment of siblings, those feeling unfavored experience more behavior problems, according to parental reports (McGuire et al., 1995).

Being perceived as a valuable family member and having to meet family expectations contribute to perceived happiness among 9- to 12-year-olds. Also, having many friends, spending time with friends, and feeling popular are factors that predict happiness (Holder & Coleman, 2009). And among 15-year-olds, relationships with family, positive friendships, negative friendships, relationships with other adults, being bullied, and being treated unfairly by adults, predicted a total of 40% in the variance of life satisfaction (Goswami, 2012).

Cross-sectional data with a broader range in age also confirm the preceding findings. Chaplin (2009) sought to assess developmental changes in children's happiness (8–18) by directly asking them what made them happy. Content analysis of the children's responses revealed the following categories in order of frequency: people and pets, achievements, material things, hobbies, and sports. All age groups considered people and pets as their number one reason that made them happy. There was a noted shift from hobbies to material things to achievements as children progressed from middle childhood to late adolescence. The results were replicated in the second study where children were given lexical items from the aforementioned categories and were asked to put together a happiness puzzle. The results indicate age-related changes in the paths leading to happiness but relationships with people (parents, friends, and teachers) and pets were most important. In addition, boys emphasized sports more than girls did and girls emphasized relationships with people and pets more than boys did.

Using the method of experience sampling, Csikszentmihalyi and Hunter (2003) asked 828 students from grades 6, 8, 10, and 12 to report their activities and emotional states for a week. The students received eight signals a day at random times to log in their information. Socializing with friends had the highest happiness score while school-related activities had the lowest score. Conversely, being alone had the lowest score, followed by being with teachers, then classmates, and then friends. Spending time with parents received average scores of happiness and were lower than being with siblings. Interestingly, happiness decreased with age with the lowest score at age 16 and then picked up by age 18. The results showed no gender or race differences. Solitary activities such as reading a book for pleasure were negatively correlated with happiness at the person level, presumably because it took away time from being with friends. Lastly, feelings of happiness were correlated with being excited, feeling good about the self, being proud, sociable, and feeling active and strong.

Throughout childhood, the level of support in children's relationships is a key reason for their well-being. A meta-analysis of 246 studies that utilized samples ranging from 3- to 20-year-olds revealed a small but positive association between social support from parents, teachers, or friends and well-being variables such as positive self-concept, psychological adjustment, and absence of behavior problems. Interestingly, perception of available support was a better predictor than actual support and the association with well-being became stronger from early childhood to adolescence. The relationship between social support and well-being was lower for teachers followed by families, and friends. Moreover, the association was stronger for female than male participants (Chui & Wong, 2016).

These findings suggest that children's and adolescents' understanding of how their own happiness is influenced by others is not very different from that of adults. Preschoolers recognize that relationships with family members and spending time with friends and pets contribute to their happiness. As they get older, there is a more sophisticated understanding of the elements of relationships that make them happy. In middle childhood, the number of friends and being popular becomes considerable factors. Throughout middle childhood and adolescence perceived social support from family, friends, and teachers is a strong predictor of psychological adjustment. Beginning with the preschool period, children highlight the need to fulfill needs and achieve personal goals. This raises the question of how close relationships can support the need to feel successful, thus contributing to life satisfaction and happiness. It is, therefore, worthwhile to examine specific relationships to uncover children's understandings of the elements of various relationships that contribute to happiness and the relative influence of specific relationships (e.g., are relationships with parents more important than peer relationships in influencing happiness?).

Parents' and Children's Happiness

As noted earlier, perceived support from parents is very important, at least in adolescence. More specifically, adolescents benefit from parents who emphasize their children's strengths and encourage them to apply their strengths to improve their lives. This strength-based parenting has been found to directly predict subjective well-being as measured by adolescents' own reports of life satisfaction, the presence of positive affect, and the absence of negative affect (Jach et al., 2018). Furthermore, research suggests that a parenting style that promotes autonomy also supports children's well-being during adolescence. Evidence for this comes from a Finnish longitudinal study that followed children as they transitioned to middle school, high school, and then post high school. Children whose parents promoted their autonomy reported fewer depressive symptoms during all three transitions and higher self-esteem as they left middle school and high school. Importantly, perceived maternal and paternal autonomy had equal effects (Duineveld et al., 2017). The parenting style of mothers and fathers may predict different outcomes, however. High schoolers with authoritative and permissive fathers reported higher scores in happiness and life satisfaction than those with authoritarian fathers. Having a mother with an authoritative or permissive style increased life satisfaction and having an authoritative mother increased positive emotions compared to the authoritarian style (Raboteg-Saric & Sakic, 2014). Studying preschoolers' perception of their parents' parenting may be difficult, but studies that relied on pictorial assessments of perceived maternal acceptance report favorable links with higher self-esteem and positive relationships with peers (Önder et al., 2021).

In addition to supportive parenting, researchers have considered whether happy parents have happy children and vice versa. The correlation between the parents' and children's happiness may be expected because of the idea that people have a set point of happiness that is partially passed on to the children by the parents. The set point of happiness is maintained throughout life regardless of fluctuations in perceived happiness. According to the Subjective Well-being Homeostasis theory (Cummins, 2003), such a set point is influenced by highly inherited personality traits such as optimism, extraversion, and neuroticism. It is argued that if the heritability of these traits is roughly 40% and the parents and children are genetically similar by 50%, then the correlations between parents' and children's happiness should not be less than .20. However, parents and children share the same environment and even though the effect of shared genetics and environment may not be additive, one should expect a strong correlation between the subjective well-being of parent and that of the child (Casas et al., 2012). In a sample of 9–12-year-olds, researchers found significant correlations between self-ratings of life satisfaction of children with their mothers (.26) and fathers (.29), supporting the idea that happiness runs in families. Moreover, there was no statistical difference in the strength of the relationship with mothers and fathers (Hoy et al., 2013).

A critique of such studies is that they use different scales to assess parents' and children's well-being and therefore they correlate apples with oranges. Casas et al. (2012) approached this problem by using scales with similar items, namely the Personal Wellbeing Index (PWI; Cummins & Lau, 2005) and the Brief Multidimensional Students' Life Satisfaction Scale (BMSLSS; Seligson et al., 2005). The results showed significant parent-child correlations but lower than what was expected to support previous research. The weakest parent-child correlations were about how friends and a sense of belonging to a group contributed to subjective well-being while the highest correlation was regarding how standards of family living contributed to happiness. Parents and children rated items of subjective well-being differently in terms of their importance. In addition, adolescents (12–16 years) reported higher subjective well-being than their parents did. The shared family environment influenced the subjective well-being of both parents and children, but the low correlations indicate a limited genetic effect on subjective well-being, thereby providing weak support to the Subjective Well-being Homeostasis theory.

In conclusion, the review highlights the importance of supportive parenting styles, such as strength-based parenting and promoting autonomy, in fostering adolescents' subjective well-being. Parenting styles of both mothers and fathers contribute to adolescents' life satisfaction and happiness, with authoritative and permissive styles having a more positive impact than authoritarian styles. Assessing preschoolers' perceptions of parenting styles can be challenging, but pictorial assessments have shown a favorable link between perceived maternal acceptance, self-esteem, and positive relationships with peers. While there is evidence to suggest that happiness runs in families, the correlations found in the studies mentioned are lower than expected in adolescent samples. A pattern may emerge, according to which, as children move onto adolescence, parental happiness may contribute less to children's happiness. The findings leave open questions about the role of friends and school context on adolescents' subjective well-being. The newly found independence may lead adolescents to explore sources of happiness outside of the family environment that are not controlled by the parents.

Peers and Happiness

Developmental research shows that high-quality friendships promote self-worth, strengthen social competence, and support school adjustment. Further, positive peer experiences that include peer support, being the recipient of prosocial acts, and low levels of peer victimization associate with life satisfaction (Bagwell et al., 2015). Spending time with friends, having positive friendships, and feeling supported are all linked with experiencing positive affect. Specifically, being liked by friends is directly related to the self-reported happiness of 16–18-year-olds and is a moderator in the relationship between gender and happiness. Girls report more happiness than boys when they also perceive that they are well-liked by peers (Chen & Furnham, 2002). Girls also consider better looks as a means to be better liked and popular with peers which in turn makes them happy (Uusitalo-Malmivaara, 2012). Friendships also buffer negative affect, loneliness, and depression, particularly in socially anxious teens (Bagwell et al., 2015). In contrast, negative relationships with peers and specifically being victimized by peers, as is the case with bullying, have been related to self-reported unhappiness (Rigby & Slee, 1993). In line with the preceding findings, Chui and Wong (2016) found that friendships predicted happiness in a large sample of 10- to 19-year-old adolescents from Hong Kong. However, friendships did not predict life satisfaction.

Noting that friends share similar personality traits and behavioral characteristics, including externalizing problems and risk behaviors, van Workum et al. (2013) explored the role of friend similarities in positive development. They expected to find an emotional contagion between friends because children expose their positive emotional states and moods to each other and overtly engage in a positive or negative reappraisal of their own emotional reactions. In a Dutch sample of 10th graders, who reported their own subjective happiness as well as their number of friendships, it was revealed that indeed the level of happiness became more like the average level of happiness of their friends over a year. Moreover, while adolescents did not exclude friends based on their happiness level, they tended to deselect friends if they were unhappy. Interestingly, the happier adolescents nominated fewer friends as if they were more selective in their friendships, in general.

While many studies support that peer connectedness, including friendships, contributes to happiness, it is unclear whether happiness is the antecedent or the consequence of adolescents' friendships. Are happy adolescents more likely to invest in building better relationships or are the relationships with peers the source of happiness? Moreover, the characteristics of friendships that contribute to happiness are largely understudied, especially from a developmental and cultural perspective. Research, based on reports of 34,000 children, ages 10 to 12 years, from 15 countries, indicates that 57% of the variance in children's well-being is explained by satisfaction with freedom, followed by appearance and possessions. Friends did not contribute much to well-being suggesting that any predictive model of happiness may be specific to each country. The only factor that seemed to be consistent among countries was satisfaction with personal freedom and with family life (Bradshaw & Rees, 2017).

Positive peer relationships and friendships create opportunities to experience positive emotions and buffer children and adolescents from negative emotions, but research suggests that they do not necessarily contribute to life satisfaction. In addition, friends may affect emotional states through emotion contagion and teenagers actively select or deselect friends based on how similar they are on perceived levels of happiness. Future longitudinal research could further study both the quality and quantity of friendships on life satisfaction, expand the definition of friendship to include friends on social media, and understand the role of mediators such as age, gender, and culture (Bagwell et al., 2015).

Teachers and Happiness

During childhood and adolescence children spend 6–8 hours a day in school, hence how the school context relates to their happiness is worth examining. Children's self-reports, as well as parent and teacher evaluations, revealed that primary school-age children reported higher subjective well-being than middle schoolers did. The transition to middle school is possibly responsible for this decline in happiness in the school setting. Moreover, learning and behavioral difficulties were associated weakly with the well-being of the younger children but significantly predicted the well-being of the older children. The reasons why children with such difficulties experience less happiness than their peers as they get older is worth studying further in the future. Moreover, girls and boys differed in their sources of well-being with girls reporting better relationships with teachers and boys reporting better relationships with peers (Tobia et al., 2019). This finding, if replicated, has important implications on how to support children's happiness in schools.

While the relationship with teachers may be more important for girls' happiness, teachers play an important role in all students' lives. As authority figures, they express expectations for academic achievement, provide emotional support, and communicate their opinions about students' behaviors and personal qualities. Therefore, teachers have the potential to influence the children's subjective well-being. Evidence for the importance of teachers' support comes from Tennant et al. (2015), who demonstrated that among 7th and 8th graders, perceived emotional support from teachers related to the positive adjustment of both boys and girls. Adolescents who experienced support from a teacher reported more happiness, higher self-esteem, and greater hope and optimism. Such research highlights the importance of children feeling safe enough to reach out for help from a caring and supportive teacher. Tennant et al. (2015) also showed that happy adolescents had teachers who showed their support by meeting their psychological needs of autonomy, relatedness, and competence. This effect increased with every increasing grade in high school, but it was weaker for African American students, pinpointing that there may be alternative pathways to happiness for students based on their racial and ethnic identity (Froiland et al., 2019).

Relative Importance of Different Relationships

Researchers are also beginning to address which type of relationship is a greater contributor to children's subjective well-being. Friends safeguard children from behavior difficulties, victimization, adjustment to new situations, and life transitions such as the birth of a sibling. They also offer opportunities to explore emotional topics where children stretch their ability to regulate behaviors and learn new ways of coping. But the long-term effect of friendships has been questioned because of their fleeting nature, especially among younger children, and the fact that many children maintain a high level of subjective well-being, while between friendships (Laursen & Mooney, 2005). Does this mean that parents may contribute more to their children's happiness than peers or friends do?

In a sample of 5,026 Canadian 4th graders, Gadermann et al. (2016) showed that the relationships with parents and peers were equally significant predictors, explaining 41% and 39% of the variance in life satisfaction, respectively. Connectedness with teachers was also a significant predictor but to a lesser degree, contributing 12% to the variance. Other studies reveal somewhat conflicting results. Researchers reported that the quality of friendships was a better predictor of self-reported happiness than parenting styles were. However, parenting was a stronger predictor of life satisfaction. Moreover, the interaction effect of parenting style and quality of friendship was not significant, indicating that peer relationships do not moderate the effect between parenting style and subjective well-being, and thus peer relationships may not buffer children from the effects of bad parenting on happiness (Gadermann et al., 2016).

Studies examining the contributions of multiple relationships at the same time also reveal some gender differences. In a sample of 700 Finn adolescents, there were no gender differences in levels of happiness and both genders identified family relationships as a source of happiness. However, for girls, having relationships with many people (parents, friends, teachers) was more important to their happiness, whereas for boys it was more important to have a few close friends (Uusitalo-Malmivaara & Lehto, 2013). Taking a different approach to adolescents' well-being, Kok et al. (2015) analyzed responses of Malaysian adolescents and young adults about what is a meaningful life. A thematic analysis revealed that female participants emphasized being around happy people and male participants focused on having good relationships with family and friends. These results highlight that boys view relationships as a source of happiness more selectively than girls do.

In summary, the review suggests that the roles of friendships and parental relationships in children's subjective well-being are complex and potentially differ by gender. Moreover, the quality of friendships may be a better predictor of self-reported happiness than parenting styles, while parenting is a stronger predictor of life satisfaction. Further research is needed to explore the relative contributions of each type of relationship and any potential gender differences.

Conclusions

There are two themes identified in the literature about subjective well-being from the perspective of children and adolescents. Children first begin to identify relationships with family and friends as important for their well-being during the preschool period. As children get older, they expand their relationships to include teachers, friends, and the peer group. In middle childhood, they are better able to describe relationship characteristics that make them happy. Being able to fulfill parental expectations and feeling supported are specific elements they emphasize. The second theme is relationships that encourage the agency to achieve personal goals and autonomy. Such findings support the self-determination theory according to which autonomy, competence, and support are important for the well-being of children (Ryan & Deci, 2000). It is noteworthy that while preschoolers recognize the need to pursue what they like, it is not until later in middle childhood that children speak about how this need is nurtured in relationships with parents, friends, and teachers.

Research has also examined the relative importance of different relationships in children's well-being. During childhood, both parents and peers explain similar amounts of variance in happiness, but parents' contributions seem to diminish while friendship influences appear to increase. There is some evidence to suggest that friendships are the source of the emotional ups and downs that affect a sense of happiness, but parents may contribute to perceptions of life satisfaction. Interestingly, the interaction effect between parenting style and friendships is not significant, further highlighting the unique contributions of these relationships.

Understanding how relationships are associated with perceived happiness is compounded by several factors. All studies are correlational; therefore, the existing associations may be bidirectional. Results make it clear that authoritarian or strict parenting is the least effective style that promotes happiness, life satisfaction, and self-esteem and that children benefit from mothers and fathers who are either authoritative or permissive. However, children's positive views about themselves may allow them to better adjust to the parenting style or create higher quality friendships (Raboteg-Saric and Sakic (2014). Conversely, negative affect could lead to rejection of others just as unfulfilling relationships could lead to negative feelings such as depression (Holder & Coleman, 2009).

There is a lack of longitudinal research to examine age-related trends, but cross-sectional studies indicate that happiness decreased during middle school and increased after the transition to high school. This coincides with the finding that as children move onto adolescence, parental happiness may contribute less to children's happiness. It appears that the newly found independence may lead adolescents to explore sources of happiness outside of the family environment that are not controlled by the parents.

Lastly, while there are no gender differences in the overall level of happiness, the fact that boys and girls emphasize different factors that make them happy at different ages further complicates our understanding of how relationships may contribute to perceived well-being. With the exception of the Malaysian study (Kok et al., 2015), a possible trend that is outlined in the current state of the literature is that girls emphasize more relationships (Chaplin, 2009); they value more support from families, friends, and teachers (Chui & Wong, 2016; Tobia et al., 2019); and they consider being popular as a stronger predictor of happiness than boys do (Cheng & Furnham, 2002). Boys, on the other hand, consider activities and relationships with peers as more important. There is an agreement in the literature, however, that there are no gender differences in how negative peer experiences such as victimization and bullying negatively associate with self-perceived happiness and well-being.

Supporting Relationships

Based on the research linking children's relationships with happiness, several recommendations can be made for parents. Fostering positive relationships begins with the development of a secure infant attachment. Parents are encouraged to be consistently sensitive and responsive to the child's needs from infancy. This helps establish trust, responsiveness, emotional availability, regulated emotions, and effective communication, which form the foundation of a good relationship. With consistent positive parenting, happy babies become happy children and adolescents. Parents may promote the experience of positive emotions such as gratitude and hope (see Chapter 2), create opportunities for children to feel valued and appreciated, and support their children's sense of agency. Parents need to foster a family environment that promotes the expression of positive emotions. This helps children learn to understand and experience positive emotions from an early age. Spending quality time together by engaging in fun activities with the children, such as baking, cooking, or playing, strengthens the parent-child bond and contributes to their happiness. Parents should promote positive sibling relationships because such relationships contribute to increased prosocial behavior and better psychological adjustment. The authoritative or democratic style is, unsurprisingly, the optimal parenting style that enhances the life satisfaction of children and adolescents. Children and adolescents benefit from parents who respect them, identify their strengths, and support their autonomy. And if we are to follow the anecdotal evidence from the practices of Dutch parents, who are considered among the happiest people in the world (Veenhoven, 2004), children tend to be happier when provided with opportunities to foster their self-confidence and independence. These opportunities often take the form of unsupervised play and encouraging children to bike to school in all weather conditions. Dutch parents also encourage children to form trusting relationships with other adults in the community, to have open communication with their parents, and spend more family time together with their parents. Based on the Dutch perspective, parents should strive to build relationships with their children, beginning in early childhood, that are characterized by authenticity, low stress, empathy, cooperativeness, and trust (Alexander & Sandahl, 2016).

Friends and a sense of belonging to a group contribute to subjective well-being. Positive friendships can promote self-worth, social competence, and school adjustment. Parents can directly support their children's friendships and positive peer relationships. Knowing the critical aspect of friendship at each developmental age could aid parents in finding ways to support their children. In preschool, having fun with friends can be encouraged by explicitly teaching the social skills of sharing, taking turns, and negotiating. In middle childhood, parents may promote their children's ability to be dependable, trustworthy, helpful, and kind. In adolescence, as emotional intimacy becomes important, parents may offer guidance about how to emotionally communicate difficult topics, how to respect privacy, and how to respond to rejection. Such parental guidance should also take into consideration the social networks that children have created in online settings (see Chapter 11). Parents who discuss challenging topics about relationships, including romantic relationships, support their children, and especially adolescents, in asserting their boundaries and easing their anxiety about experiencing intimacy with other people. Negative peer relationships can have a detrimental impact on a child's happiness and therefore parents should encourage open communication, monitor the child's school environment, and address bullying and peer victimization. Lastly, one piece of advice would be for parents to be happy themselves. While the correlation between parents' and children's happiness is lower than expected, there is still evidence that happiness runs in families. Prioritizing their own well-being would facilitate their children's happiness to some extent.

Teachers too play an important role in students' lives and their subjective well-being. Teachers should provide emotional support, communicate positive expectations, and foster a caring and inclusive environment. Teaching healthy relationships may also become part of a social and emotional learning curriculum. Roffey (2017) discusses a pedagogy for relationship education where children learn with others in group interactions about agency (i.e., learning to make decisions and rules on their own so they can live together in harmony), safety (i.e., learning to discuss issues that matter to all instead of personal incidents), positivity (i.e., learning their own and others' strengths), inclusion (i.e., learning to take perspectives of each other), respect (i.e., learning that respect is a right, not conditional regard), and equality (i.e., learning that all voices are heard). While the effectiveness of implementing such pedagogy belongs in future research, evidence from Argentina shows that such interventions improve collaboration among 6- and 7-year-olds, reduce stress, and improve social relationships in 7–9-year-olds (e.g., children are likely to choose more peers to play with). Moreover, practicing gratitude in the classroom decreased negative interactions among 4th graders (Lozada et al., 2017). Because children value their relationships as a source of their happiness, modeling positive relationships and openly discussing what a high-quality relationship looks like safeguard children's subjective well-being.

In closing, fostering positive relationships is vital for a child's well-being. Secure attachment and an authoritative parenting style promote healthy relationships and life satisfaction. By modeling positive relationships and openly discussing the characteristics of high-quality relationships, parents can help safeguard children's subjective well-being. Parents may provide developmentally appropriate support for children to build strong friendships, while educators may integrate relationship education into social-emotional learning curricula. Ultimately, children's happiness is deeply intertwined with the quality of their relationships. It is helpful for adults to recognize the unique contributions of different relationships and work together to create a relationship support system for children.

References

Adachi, M., & Trehub, S. E. (2011). Canadian and Japanese preschoolers' creation of happy and sad songs. *Psychomusicology: Music, Mind and Brain, 21*(1–2), 69. https://doi.org/10.1037/h0094005

Alexander, J. J., & Sandahl, I. (2016). *The Danish way of parenting: What the happiest people in the world know about raising confident, capable kids*. Penguin.

Bagwell, C., Kochel, K., & Schmidt, M. (2015). Friendship and happiness in adolescence. In M. Demir (Ed.), *Friendship and happiness*. Springer. https://doi.org/10.1007/978-94-017-9603-3_6

Bradshaw, J., & Rees, G. (2017). Exploring national variations in child subjective well-being. *Children and Youth Services Review, 80*, 3–14. https://doi.org/10.1016/j.childyouth.2017.06.059

Casas, F., Coenders, G., González, M., Malo, S., Bertran, I., & Figuer, C. (2012). Testing the relationship between parents' and their children's subjective well-being. *Journal of Happiness Studies, 13*(6), 1031–1051. https://doi.org/10.1007/s10902-011-9305-3

Chaplin, L. N. (2009). Please may I have a bike? Better yet, may I have a hug? An examination of children's and adolescents' happiness. *Journal of Happiness Studies*, *10*, 541–562. https://doi.org/10.1007/s10902-008-9108-3

Cheng, H., & Furnham, A. (2002). Personality, peer relations, and self-confidence as predictors of happiness and loneliness. *Journal of Adolescence*, *25*(3), 327–339. https://doi.org/10.1006/jado.2002.0475

Chui, W. H., & Wong, M. Y. (2016). Gender differences in happiness and life satisfaction among adolescents in Hong Kong: Relationships and self-concept. *Social Indicators Research*, *125*(3), 1035–1051. https://doi.org/10.1007/s11205-015-0867-z

Coldwell, J., Pike, A., & Dunn, J. (2008). Maternal differential treatment and child adjustment: A multi-informant approach. *Social Development*, *17*(3), 596–612. https://doi.org/10.1111/j.1467-9507.2007.00440.x

Csikszentmihalyi, M., & Hunter, J. (2003). Happiness in everyday life: The uses of experience sampling. *Journal of Happiness Studies*, *4*, 185–199. http://dx.doi.org/10.1023/A:1024409732742

Cummins, R. A. (2003). Normative life satisfaction: Measurement issues and a homeostatic model. *Social Indicators Research*, *64*(2), 225–256. https://doi.org/10.1023/A:1024712527648

Cummins, R. A., & Lau, A. (2005). *Personal wellbeing index–school children*. School of Psychology, Deakin University.

Deiner, M., & Deiner-McGavran, M. (2008). What makes people happy? A developmental approach to the literature on family relationships and well-being. In M. Eid & R. J. Larsen (Eds.), *The science of subjective well-being*. Guilford Press.

Duineveld, J. J., Parker, P. D., Ryan, R. M., Ciarrochi, J., & Salmela-Aro, K. (2017). The link between perceived maternal and paternal autonomy support and adolescent well-being across three major educational transitions. *Developmental Psychology*, *53*(10), 1978–1994. https://doi.org/10.1037/dev0000364

Froiland, J. M., Worrell, F. C., & Oh, H. (2019). Teacher–student relationships, psychological need satisfaction, and happiness among diverse students. *Psychology in the Schools*, *56*(5), 856–870. https://doi.org/10.1002/pits.22245

Gadermann, A. M., Guhn, M., Schonert-Reichl, K. A., Hymel, S., Thomson, K., & Hertzman, C. (2016). A population-based study of children's well-being and health: The relative importance of social relationships, health-related activities, and income. *Journal of Happiness Studies*, *17*(5), 1847–1872. https://doi.org/10.1007/s10902-015-9673-1

Goswami, H. (2012). Social relationships and children's subjective well-being. *Social Indicators Research*, *107*(3), 575–588. https://doi.org/10.1007/s11205-011-9864-z

Holder, M. D., & Coleman, B. (2009). The contribution of social relationships to children's happiness. *Journal of Happiness Studies*, *10*(3), 329–349. https://doi.org/10.1007/s10902-007-9083-0

Hoy, B. D., Suldo, S. M., & Mendez, L. R. (2013). Links between parents' and children's levels of gratitude, life satisfaction, and hope. *Journal of Happiness Studies*, *14*(4), 1343–1361. https://doi.org/10.1007/s10902-012-9386-7

Jach, H. K., Sun, J., Loton, D., Chin, T. C., & Waters, L. E. (2018). Strengths and subjective wellbeing in adolescence: Strength-based parenting and the moderating effect of mindset. *Journal of Happiness Studies*, *19*(2), 567–586. https://doi.org/10.1007/s10902-016-9841-y

Kok, J. K., Goh, L. Y., & Gan, C. C. (2015). Meaningful life and happiness: Perspective from Malaysian youth. *The Social Science Journal*, *52*(1), 69–77. https://doi.org/10.1016/j.soscij.2014.10.002

Laursen, B., & Mooney, K. (2005). Why do friends matter? Essay review of children's friendships: The beginnings of intimacy by Judy Dunn. *Human Development*, *48*, 323–326. https://doi.org/10.1159/000086878

Lozada, M., Carro, N., Kapelmayer, M., Kelmanowicz, V., Czar, A., & D'Adamo, P. (2017). Fostering positive changes in health and social relationships in children. In C. Proctor (Ed.), *Positive psychology interventions in practice* (pp. 143–161). Springer International Publishing.

McGuire, S., Dunn, J., & Plomin, R. (1995). Maternal differential treatment of siblings and children's behavioral problems: A longitudinal study. *Development and Psychopathology*, *7*(3), 515–528. https://doi.org/10.1017/S0954579400006660

Moore, A., & Lynch, H. (2018). Understanding a child's conceptualization of well-being through an exploration of happiness: The centrality of play, people, and place. *Journal of Occupational Science*, *25*(1), 124–141. https://doi.org/10.1080/14427591.2017.1377105

Obeldobel, C. A., & Kerns, K. A. (2020). Attachment security is associated with the experience of specific positive emotions in middle childhood. *Attachment & Human Development*, *22*(5), 555–567. https://doi.org/10.1080/14616734.2019.1604775

Ogren, M., Burling, J. M., & Johnson, S. P. (2018). Family expressiveness relates to happy emotion matching among 9-month-old infants. *Journal of Experimental Child Psychology*, *174*, 29–40. https://doi.org/10.1016/j.jecp.2018.05.003

Önder, A., Gülay Ogelman, H., & Göktaş, İ. (2021). Examining the correlations between the self-perception of preschool children and their levels of being liked by their peers. *Early Child Development and Care*, *191*(14), 2260–2268. http://dx.doi.org.lib.assumption.edu/10.1080/03004430.2019.1700239

Raboteg-Saric, Z., & Sakic, M. (2014). Relations of parenting styles and friendship quality to self-esteem, life satisfaction and happiness in adolescents. *Applied Research in Quality of Life*, *9*(3), 749–765. https://doi.org/10.1007/s11482-013-9268-0

Rigby, K., & Slee, P. T. (1993). Dimensions of interpersonal relation among Australian children and implications for psychological well-being. *The Journal of Social Psychology*, *133*(1), 33–42. https://doi.org/10.1080/00224545.1993.9712116

Rilke, R. M. (2011). *Letters to a young poet*. Penguin.

Roffey, S. (2017). Learning healthy relationships. In C. Proctor (Ed.), *Positive psychology interventions in practice* (pp. 163–181). Springer International Publishing.

Ryan, R. M., & Deci, E. L. (2000). Self-determination theory and the facilitation of intrinsic motivation, social development, and well-being. *American Psychologist*, *55*(1), 68–78. https://doi.org/10.1037/0003-066X.55.1.68

Seligson, J. L., Huebner, E. S., & Valois, R. F. (2005). Validation of a brief life satisfaction scale wit elementary school students. *Social Indicators Research*, *73*, 355–374. https://doi.org/10.1007/s11205-004-2011-3

Tennant, J. E., Demaray, M. K., Malecki, C. K., Terry, M. N., Clary, M., & Elzinga, N. (2015). Students' ratings of teacher support and academic and social–emotional well-being. *School Psychology Quarterly*, *30*(4), 494. https://doi.org/10.1037/spq0000106

Tobia, V., Greco, A., Steca, P., & Marzocchi, G. M. (2019). Children's wellbeing at school: A multi-dimensional and multi-informant approach. *Journal of Happiness Studies*, *20*(3), 841–861. https://doi.org/10.1007/s10902-018-9974-2

Tronick, E., & Beeghly, M. (2011). Infants' meaning-making and the development of mental health problems. *American Psychologist*, *66*(2), 107. https://doi.org/10.1037/a0021631

Tronick, E. Z. (1989). Emotions and emotional communication in infants. *American Psychologist*, *44*(2), 112. https://doi.org/10.1037/0003-066X.44.2.112
Uusitalo-Malmivaara, L. (2012). Global and school-related happiness in Finnish children. *Journal of Happiness Studies*, *13*(4), 601–619. https://doi.org/10.1007/s10902-011-9282-6
Uusitalo-Malmivaara, L., & Lehto, J. E. (2013). Social factors explaining children's subjective happiness and depressive symptoms. *Social Indicators Research*, *111*(2), 603–615. https://doi.org/10.1007/s11205-012-0022-z
van Workum, N., Scholte, R. H., Cillessen, A. H., Lodder, G. M., & Giletta, M. (2013). Selection, deselection, and socialization processes of happiness in adolescent friendship networks. *Journal of Research on Adolescence*, *23*(3), 563–573. https://doi.org/10.1111/jora.12035
Veenhoven, R. (2004). World database of happiness. In W. Glatzer, S. VonBelow, & M. Stoffregen (Eds.), *Challenges for quality of life in the contemporary world: Advances in quality-of-life studies, theory, and research* (pp. 75–89). Springer.

2 Feeling Good

Chloe is having a hard time finding good friends in her 3rd-grade class. The girls that she likes find excuses and continue to rebuff her best efforts to join their group. They are the dance girls on a competition team while Chloe does gymnastics for fun. They get more positive feedback from the teacher whereas Chloe simply gets indifference. They are treated as being the smartest, and Chloe does not understand why. Chloe can talk about her experiences to her parents, who coach her to see the positive qualities in other children, the things that make someone a good friend, and ways to cope with her disappointment. Chloe is by nature an optimistic and hopeful child and can overcome the year-long rejection, find happiness in other relationships, and preserve a positive self-image.

Rejection is a common human experience that undermines relationships and leaves a sense of loss, and often negative thoughts about the self; thus, it is a threat to subjective well-being. Children and adolescents may experience rejection from their parents and unfortunately, for some, rejection comes early and consistently. Rejection may also be experienced by peers, friends, teachers, and romantic partners. Point in case is the concept of fear of missing out (FOMO), an outcome of implicit or unintentional rejection from social media, that has attracted a lot of attention in research and popular media. Nowadays, youth is preoccupied with FOMO which seems to associate with increased depression, lower mindfulness, and physical health in young adults (Baker et al., 2016). How can one choose to experience joy in the presence of negative experiences such as rejection? Children and adults can learn to manage their feelings and thoughts to experience positive emotions that allow them to flourish. This chapter first offers an understanding of the functionality of positive emotions and then explores how gratitude, hope, and optimism may protect children's and adolescents' well-being. These positive emotions are defined, and their developmental trajectory is traced. Research evidence from both correlational and intervention studies, linking gratitude, hope, and optimism to happiness is presented. The chapter also includes the topic of emotional intelligence as a way to enhance the experience of positive emotions, while regulating negative ones. Lastly, the chapter provides ideas for parents and teachers to promote gratitude, hope, optimism, and emotional intelligence.

DOI: 10.4324/9780429356414-4

The Functionality of Positive Affect

As discussed in the introduction, experiencing positive affect is a component of subjective well-being. But what exactly is a positive affect? Positive affect is often conceptualized in three ways; as an attitude reflecting a belief about how satisfactory a specific experience is (e.g., experiencing pride when passing an exam), a mood reflecting an ephemeral and diffused affective state of being well (e.g., a sense of euphoria with no apparent reason), and an emotion, reflecting a discrete emotional state specific to a situation (e.g., joy in response to watching a beautiful sunset; Ramsey & Gentzler, 2015). Researchers have studied the effects of positive affect in the form of love, gratitude, pride, interest, laughter, and amusement (Ramsey & Gentzler, 2015).

Positive affect is considered to have functional value because it mobilizes people to engage in actions and thoughts that increase their sense of well-being. According to the *broaden and build* model (Fredrickson, 2001), such actions and thoughts result in growing social and other resources that increase the likelihood of experiencing positive affect in the future. For example, a joyful child is likely to share a toy with a peer; such an act of sharing strengthens the relationship with the peer, which can then be viewed as a social resource. In the future, said peer may offer comfort or reciprocate sharing a toy, thus becoming a source of positive affect. Experiencing gratitude in response to receiving a benefit from another may make one more aware of the qualities of the benefactor and more likely to engage in prosocial acts towards that person and others. Sharing pride in accomplishments, such as when a child shares with a parent a good grade on a hard test, strengthens the bond between the parent and the child. A spark of interest in another person, especially one that brings amusement and laughter, initiates the creation of new relationships. It appears that positive affect is likely to be experienced in the context of relationships, lead to the creation of relationships, or enhance the quality of existing relationships. Such relationships can then be a source of further positive affect, thus contributing to happiness and subjective well-being.

Empirical support for the broaden and build theory of positive affect is provided by Griffith et al. (2021) who evaluated the bi-directional effect and change in positive affect and the quality of the peer and parent-child relationships among 3rd, 6th, and 9th graders, who were followed for 3 years. The results of this study showed that an increase in positive affect was accompanied by an increase in the reported quality of positive relationships with peers and parents, which in turn predicted an increase in future positive affect. The connection between experiencing positive affect and positive relationships appeared like an upward spiral over the 3 years. Moreover, this was not true for negative affect. The results suggest that bolstering the experience of positive affect or enhancing social relationships contributes to the subjective well-being of children and adolescents.

In summary, positive affect can be conceptualized in three ways: as an attitude, a mood, or an emotion, and is a key component of subjective well-being. The broaden and build model posits positive affect fosters actions and thoughts to enhance social relationships, leading to a reciprocal upward spiral of increased positive affect and improved relationships, ultimately contributing to happiness. In the field of positive psychology, a good life is one filled with positive emotions of gratitude, hope, and optimism. These emotions and their connection to well-being are discussed next.

Gratitude

Gratitude is felt as a combination of thankfulness and joy in response to a benefit offered by another, or in response to a peaceful experience, like being in nature (Emmons & McCullough, 2004). Some consider it a virtue, or a dispositional trait, and others see it as a complex positive affect, that entails an attitude of appreciation combined with a discrete emotion of joy and calmness (McCullough et al., 2002). Adults who practice feeling gratitude report higher levels of happiness, and intervention strategies, such as keeping a gratitude journal, appear to increase levels of subjective happiness (Froh & Bono, 2008). However, there is limited research on how the experience of gratitude may enhance children's own happiness. Hence how children come to recognize it and describe it is of important consideration. The developmental trajectory of feeling and expressing gratitude is unclear, however. While children as young as toddlers are taught to say thank you, experiencing gratitude requires an understanding of different perspectives and complex emotions. With the mastery of theory of mind between the ages of 4 and 5, children can perceive that others may have beliefs different from their own. In the case of gratitude, children must understand the thoughts and motivations of the giver or benefactor. They should also be capable of experiencing empathy and reason morally about the benevolence of the act of giving. Such complex emotional understanding is evident in late preschool but increases during middle childhood (Froh & Bono, 2008). During that period, children are capable of recursive thought, which allows them to think about what their benefactor may believe about the beneficiary's thoughts and emotions. This understanding then permits a full appreciation of the prosocial act and its ramifications to all involved. It also possibly motivates the child to express thankfulness and act prosocially towards the giver or another person. It is, therefore, safe to say that the ability to recognize and express gratitude develops around the age of 7 years although there is some evidence that some 5-year-olds can draw things they are grateful for (Owens & Patterson, 2013). It is further implied that the connection between gratitude and happiness would not be evident unless the gratitude is genuine, and it would become stronger as children develop (Layous & Lyubomirsky, 2014). Indeed, when parents provide descriptions of the qualities of their 3- to 9-year-old children, the connection between gratitude and happiness is not present before the age of 4. Additionally, among 9- and 11-year-olds, those with increased perspective-taking ability expressed a stronger connection between performed acts of kindness and happiness. The link between gratitude and subjective well-being is clearly shown in older children and adolescents. Results from a meta-analytic examination of correlates of gratitude indicate a positive association with happiness, positive outlook, and positive self-appraisal. Results also reveal a negative association with negative affective states, depression, and somatic symptoms

(Renshaw & Olinger Steeves, 2016). Most recently, among 16-year-olds from South Africa, self-reported gratitude was positively correlated with life satisfaction and happiness and negatively associated with negative affect. Female adolescents reported higher dispositional and state gratitude and did not differ from male adolescents in overall life satisfaction and happiness (Guse et al., 2019).

Evidence for the benefits of gratitude in children from intervention studies is currently sparse with the exception of the Froh et al. (2008) study, where adolescents were asked to write down five things that they were grateful for, each day for two weeks. This simple counting of blessings was associated with increased reported gratitude and life satisfaction and decreased negative affect. Moreover, adolescents who experienced more gratitude also reported more school satisfaction and this association persisted three weeks after the intervention. Furthermore, gratitude in relation to counting incidents for receiving assistance related to positive affect, and this was still the case at the three-week follow-up. These findings suggest that simple gratitude interventions in the school setting can enhance the well-being of adolescents. Froh et al. (2014) designed a gratitude curriculum that involved teaching children how to recognize the intentions of the giver, the cost incurred by giving, and the benefits to the recipient. The intervention also included expressing gratitude in the form of writing thank you notes. The result was not only an increase in recognizing and experiencing gratitude among 8–11-year-olds but also an increase in positive affect. Designing interventions for even younger children is open for experimentation.

Parents may support the development of gratitude by acknowledging acts of gratitude, discussing the impact of gratitude, encouraging children to show gratitude in appropriate ways, and modeling acts of gratitude. Research supports a positive association between mothers' and children's gratitude among 9–11-year-olds. This association was not significant for fathers indicating perhaps that fathers may be less overt in their expression of gratitude, or that children spent more time with their mothers and imitated them more, or that mothers took over the role of socializing their children to express gratitude (Hoy et al., 2013). Rothenberg et al. (2017) shed some light on how this socialization process takes place. They discovered that parents who rate high on gratitude intentionally chose activities (e.g., playing sports, volunteering) that promoted the experience of gratitude in their children (6–9 years). This niche selection process is a form of emotional socialization and mediated the relationship between parental gratitude and parent-reported gratitude of the children. One thing that parents and teachers need to avoid, however, is forced demonstrations of gratitude that can potentially destroy the children's intrinsic motivation to express thankfulness. Children should be allowed to express gratitude freely on their own so that they can begin to view these acts as evidence of their own competence and as ways to make connections with other people (Layous & Lyubomirsky, 2014).

Optimism as a Disposition and an Attributional Style

Optimism is a complex construct that has been viewed in more than one way. As a trait or a relatively constant disposition, optimism is the expectation that good rather than bad things are going to happen. These expectations about the future can influence the actions and thoughts of children (Carver & Scheier, 2014). A child in a quest to find a playmate asks to join a group of children with the expectation that the request will be accepted. Dispositional optimism is usually assessed via self-reported measures designed for children older than 8 years. A commonly used measure for optimism is the Life Orientation Test (Scheier et al., 1994) which consists of six statements that assess expectations about future outcomes. The 2009 Gallup Student Poll (GSP) shows a downward trend in optimism during late middle childhood and the transition to high school among US students (Marques et al., 2014). Häggström Westberg et al. (2019) too found a decrease in optimism from 11 to 16 years of age, among Swedish adolescents, and Zou et al. (2016) showed that optimism scores followed a slightly negative linear pattern with age, with 5th graders reporting higher scores than the 6th, 7th, 8th, and 10th graders from China. Dispositional optimism has also been related to subjective well-being. The relationship between self-reported optimism and happiness was found among Korean preteens (Park & Kim, 2012). Others found that the link between dispositional optimism and subjective well-being was partially mediated by increased self-esteem. A positive outlook from being optimistic also casts a kinder view of the self thus experiencing more positive affect and life satisfaction (Duy & Yıldız, 2019).

In addition to being a dispositional trait, optimism is considered an explanatory style, specifically, the type of attributions one makes to understand personal experiences. In this view, optimism helps to form expectations about the future, based on the causes of current events. In the aforementioned example, how a child understands a rejection from a group of peers shapes the likelihood of asking again in the future. Evidence from neuroscience shows that different parts of the brain are activated in response to dispositional optimism and optimism that requires cognitive control, thereby supporting the theoretical differentiation of these concepts (Rosenfeld, 2019). Martin Seligman in his signature book, *The Optimistic Child* (2007), explains that children make attributions along the dimensions of permanence, pervasiveness, and personalization. An optimistic child believes that good things happen because of their traits and abilities that are permanent and global—qualities that children own and cannot be taken away. In contrast, bad events are attributed to transient and specific causes such as temporary moods and one-time events that are not likely to be repeated. The opposite pattern is seen in the attributions of a pessimistic child. Bad events are attributed to permanent, unchangeable traits and generalized conditions while good events are explained in terms of provisional and unpredictable causes. Optimistic children explain acceptance to a peer group in terms of their personal qualities of being friendly, likable, and interesting, characteristics that they tend to exhibit quite consistently. Pessimistic children would believe that their peers just happened to be in a good mood or that they really needed one more person to play the game, as reasons for acceptance. When faced with rejection, pessimistic children are likely to believe that there is something wrong with them; that they possess something that consistently appalls other children. Optimistic children will not give it a second thought, because they view rejection as a single-time event that will not be repeated. The optimistic child may reason that other children already were having fun and did not want to change their game or that there was no need for another partner at that specific time.

Optimistic children believe that good events happen because of personal qualities they possess and take responsibility for the undesirable outcomes without chastising themselves. Pessimistic children, on the other hand, tend to attribute positive outcomes to external factors such as luck and tend to blame themselves for bad things that happen to the extent that it hurts their self-esteem. If the rejection was seen as something that the child has caused, the optimistic child would take accountability and try to rectify the situation in the future, perhaps by apologizing. The pessimistic child, however, will experience self-blame and feel worthless. According to Seligman, the attributions of the pessimistic child create a path toward helplessness and depression. Failing to take credit for the good things that happen and believing that the causes of bad things are unchangeable, out of control, and unpredictable, take away any chance of hope.

Understanding the origins of optimism as an explanatory style is limited. Seligman and his colleagues have suggested that young children learn how to appraise situations and themselves from their parents who either model such interpretations or help their children interpret their experiences. However, the evidence about the correlation between parents' and children's explanatory styles is not clear. Some findings show that maternal pessimism is positively related to children's pessimism and negatively related to children's optimism (Hasan & Power, 2002). Interventions to increase optimism in children have been designed and implemented, primarily to battle a pessimistic explanatory style, that has long been linked with depression in children and adults. Children demonstrate low self-esteem in association with depression at age 8 and hopelessness in relation to depression at age 10. During middle childhood, children develop a global sense of self-worth as well as a sense of worth in different domains (e.g., academic, social, and physical appearance). These cognitive self-appraisals about the self, if negative, lead to low self-esteem but can be altered with appropriate cognitive behavioral interventions. In general, there is a lack of research about preschoolers' attributional styles, so interventions have focused on children who are 8 years and older.

An intervention to promote optimism and safeguard from pessimism is to change the way children think about their failures. Children are taught to attribute their failures to internal and changeable causes, such as effort, to empower them and give them a sense of agency. A full-scale cognitive behavioral approach engages children in thinking about alternative explanations and testing assumptions through trains of thought. Seligman and colleagues developed the Penn Optimism Program to teach children cognitive restructuring and social problem-solving skills. In this 12-session program, children learn that emotions and behaviors are generated by thoughts and that thoughts can be altered when one considers alternate ways to explain experiences. Children are exposed to the optimistic and explanatory styles and practice recognizing them in skits they play. Using cartoon worksheets, children rewrite their interpretations to reflect an optimistic explanatory style. Seligman and colleagues also use a detective analogy to help children identify automatic catastrophic thoughts and solve problems. Like Sherlock Holmes, who lists all possible suspects and looks for all possible clues, children list possible causes for their experience and examine the evidence carefully. The intervention is complemented by teaching children emotional coping skills, relaxation, and social skills like assertiveness and negotiation strategies. This program applies to middle school and high school students, and research demonstrates effectiveness in reducing depressive symptoms, although the long-term effects of the intervention are not clearly established (Gillham et al., 2001). Meta-analytic data demonstrate retention of the benefits of the intervention for at least a six-month follow-up (Ma et al., 2020). It is worthwhile to note that no research has linked such interventions to measures of happiness and life satisfaction. Future research should address this gap as well as the role of parents' attributional styles in shaping their children's explanatory styles. If there is a relationship between the two, interventions to teach optimism should also include parents and even teachers.

Hope

According to *hope theory*, hope is the belief that positive results will happen via one's planning and motivation. A hopeful child, therefore, is the agent in creating the pathways that lead to the attainment of personal goals (Snyder et al., 2002). Hope is commonly assessed by the Children's Hope Scale (Snyder et al., 1997) which includes six items that tap into children's beliefs about their current state of being (e.g., I think I am doing pretty well) and their ability to take matters in their own hands and find solutions. There are currently no appropriate assessments for younger children, but some evidence suggests that 4- to 7-year-old children understand the concepts of hope similarly to how adults would define it (Vorkapić & Šikić, 2019). Based on the GSP, half of the American students, ages 10 to 18 years, rated themselves as hopeful, meaning that they had plans and goals for the future, they had ideas about how to accomplish them, and they were motivated to do so. The remaining half reported that they were either discouraged, felt stuck, or did not believe they had the means to succeed (Marques et al., 2014). It is unknown if there are any age-related changes in hope like the ones observed in dispositional optimism.

Experiencing hope has been linked to a preference to attend to positive information which then predicts perceived happiness and lower anxiety and depression among adolescents (Yeung et al., 2015). Studies also reveal correlations between high levels of hope and life satisfaction among adolescents (Merkaš & Brajša-Žganec, 2011). High hope is also related to other factors that contribute to well-being such as high perceived competence and self-worth (Marques et al., 2011), high self-esteem, increased family cohesion, greater social support (Merkaš & Brajša-Žganec, 2011), and higher purpose in life (Feldman & Snyder, 2005). Lastly, hope is related to academic success as indexed by scores in achievement tests and GPA, explaining a 12% of improvement in academic performance (Marques et al., 2014).

In addition to correlational evidence, intervention studies reveal that hope can be increased over a five-week intervention program for middle-school-age children, and such improvement is accompanied by increases in life satisfaction and self-worth. Moreover, these effects were maintained over 18 months (Marques et al., 2011). Because of the associations between hope and academic performance, researchers have focused on creating interventions for increasing hope among American students. Based on Snyder's *hope theory*, children can be taught to set goals and learn how to prioritize them. Such goals could be either something they should work towards or avoid. Students then learn to break down goals into smaller objectives that are easier to accomplish. This process of setting steps essentially creates pathways toward the goals. To enhance the student's sense of agency, students would set goals that are personal and meaningful to them, and as such they would be more motivated to pursue them. Providing models of individuals who faced adversity may also act as a motivator. Lastly, a school environment where there is trust and predictable relationships with teachers assists in engendering hope among students (Gillham et al., 2001).

Hope and optimism are conceptually similar constructs, and both are associated with well-being. One may wonder what their relationship is and what unique contribution each construct makes to well-being. Wong and Lim (2009) addressed these questions using the earlier-mentioned scales to assess hope and dispositional optimism among Singaporean adolescents. They reported a correlation of .45 between hope and optimism. Both constructs predicted depression and life satisfaction but when considered at the same time, only optimism had a unique contribution in explaining the variance in life satisfaction and depression (Wong & Lim, 2009). The origins of hope and optimism may stem from temperamental characteristics such as early positive mood, tolerance to environmental stimulation, and flexible thinking. Evidence from twin studies demonstrates a level of heritability in dispositional optimism ranging from 25% to 30%. Correlations between parents and children imply a genetic similarity as well as socialization processes in the development of dispositional optimism. For example, the dispositional optimism of South Korean fathers was significantly correlated with their children's optimism and was mediated by paternal expressiveness (Yu & Ko, 2013). Therefore, it is implied that fathers not only passed their genes for optimism to their children but they also modeled or taught optimism by the way they expressed and regulated their emotions.

The relationship between hope and optimism, their roots, and their development are all subjects of future research. A note of caution about the extent to which optimism can influence well-being is also warranted. It is evident in adult literature that humans have several cognitive biases that make them think more favorably about the self and act optimistically contrary to reality. For example, adults tend to think that more positive than negative events are likely to happen to them, they take more credit for successes than failures, and believe that things are better here and now than in other places and other times. Such unrealistic optimism may endanger children, especially adolescents by taking miscalculated risks thus threatening their well-being (McGuire-Snieckus, 2014). Therefore, as parents and teachers strive to raise hopeful and optimistic children, it is important that children also develop a sense of realism and the ability to scrutinize beliefs using evidence and logic. This can be achieved by children who can master their emotional experiences and responses, a skill that is part of a general concept of emotional intelligence.

Raising Grateful, Optimistic, and Hopeful Children

There are several ways that parents can foster gratitude in their children. Encouraging perspective-taking and discussing the intentions behind acts of kindness or generosity help children understand the thoughts and motivations of the giver or benefactor. Promoting empathy encourages children to consider the feelings and emotions of others, which will help them morally reason about the benevolence of giving and receiving. Parents may engage children in age-appropriate gratitude activities. For younger children, it may be simple activities such as drawing things they are grateful for or reading books with examples of gratitude. For older children and adolescents, keeping a gratitude journal, writing thank you notes, or keeping a jar with grateful things that happen, are great ways to practice gratitude. Parents also can intentionally choose activities that promote the experience of gratitude in their children, such as playing sports or volunteering. Modeling gratitude regularly makes it more likely that children will adopt these behaviors as well. Parents should foster genuine expressions of gratitude and avoid forcing children to demonstrate gratitude, as this can undermine their intrinsic motivation to express thankfulness. Lastly, parents should engage their children in discussions about the impact of gratitude. These talks should include the benefits of gratitude, its connection to happiness, a positive outlook, and positive self-appraisal. This can help children better understand the importance of expressing gratitude. Teachers can easily adapt these recommendations as well and particularly focus on ways to integrate experiences with gratitude in the curriculum through literature and community service.

To support optimistic thinking, parents and teachers should display optimistic explanatory styles in their daily lives, to influence their children's interpretations of events. Parents need to encourage children to attribute positive events to their traits and abilities and view negative events as temporary and specific. They should teach children to attribute failures to internal and changeable factors, such as effort, rather than external and unchangeable factors. This approach empowers them and gives them a sense of agency.

With older children and adolescents, adults can explicitly explain the concepts of permanence, pervasiveness, and personalization, to help them understand the differences between optimistic and pessimistic attributions. Parents and teachers may promote problem-solving and cognitive restructuring by teaching children to think about alternative explanations and test assumptions through trains of thought. Children need to be encouraged to analyze situations carefully and consider various possibilities before arriving at conclusions. Equipping children with techniques to manage their emotions, such as relaxation, deep breathing, or mindfulness will help them better cope with challenging situations and maintain a positive and optimistic outlook. Encouraging children to learn assertiveness, negotiation strategies, and other social skills can boost their self-esteem and improve their ability to navigate social situations optimistically.

Parents and teachers can model and teach hope by encouraging goal setting. With the parents' support, children can set personal and meaningful goals and then break them down into smaller, achievable objectives. This process will create clear pathways toward their goals and instill a sense of hope. Encouraging children to take responsibility for their goals and be actively involved in achieving them fosters a sense of agency and autonomy. To be more successful, adults should help children identify and prioritize personal goals because children will be more motivated to pursue them. Parents and teachers may provide role models by sharing stories of individuals who have faced adversity and achieved success, as these can serve as powerful motivators for children and inspire hope. For many, these models can be found in family histories and local communities, in addition to fiction and nonfiction literature. While fostering hope and optimism, it is important to also teach children to scrutinize their beliefs using evidence and logic. This will enable them to develop a sense of realism and avoid taking miscalculated risks, especially in adolescence. Adults who cultivate trust and establish predictable relationships at home and school offer a nurturing environment that engenders hope in children, thus promoting their happiness, well-being, and academic success.

Emotional Intelligence

Emotional intelligence is an umbrella term that refers to a range of emotional and cognitive abilities that ultimately allow the individual to adapt effectively and flexibly to changing environmental demands. Based on its original conceptualization, emotional intelligence is "The ability to monitor one's own and other's feelings and emotions, to discriminate among them, and to use this information to guide one's thinking and actions" (Salovey & Mayer, 1990, p. 189). Specifically, emotional intelligence skills fall into four branches, each of which follows its own developmental path: "(a) perceive emotions in oneself and others accurately, (b) use emotions to facilitate thinking, (c) understand emotions, emotional language, and the signals conveyed by emotions, and (d) manage emotions so as to attain specific goals" (Mayer et al., 2008, p. 506). A discussion of emotional intelligence is relevant because this ability allows children to manage negative emotions and experience more positive ones. Moreover, the concept is promoted among parenting experts to increase children's happiness.

Despite the hypothesized link between emotional intelligence and subjective well-being (Carter, 2010), there is little research to support this connection in a direct way. One exception is a study from Spain, where the general intelligence of high-school students (14- to 18-year-olds) positively predicted happiness and optimism (Tejada-Gallardo et al., 2020). Additionally, emotional intelligence is negatively related to psychological dysfunction. In a large study involving 12- to 18-year-old adolescents from Spain, Balluerka et al. (2013) demonstrated an association between emotional intelligence and depression. Emotional intelligence was assessed by *attention to emotion* which allows the individual to notice negative moods and rebound from them, *clarity* which refers to confidence in identifying emotions, and *emotion repair* which involves positive thinking to correct negative feelings and moods. Emotional clarity and repair predicted lower levels of depression (22% of variance), rendering value to the skill of discriminating emotions and managing them. Moreover, interventions to increase emotional intelligence seem to associate with decreased clinical symptoms. Ruiz-Aranda et al. (2012) twice applied a six-month long intervention for two years to teach emotional intelligence in a group of 11- to 16-year-old adolescents. The results showed significant reductions in anxiety, depression, stress, and negative affect.

Another approach to finding supportive evidence for the association between emotional intelligence and subjective well-being is to examine how specific emotional intelligence components, namely understanding and regulating emotions, may relate to the positive functioning of children. Both processes begin to develop in the preschool years and contribute to the overall social and emotional competence of children and adolescents. Preschoolers can perceive the emotional body language of others, can differentiate emotions such as being happy and sad, can understand the causes of emotions, and can predict emotional reactions based on how one feels. Language skills are critical in emotional understanding because children must rely on words to express how they feel and why. Although children may be able to understand that breaking a toy would make someone sad, they may not always be able to spontaneously consider someone else's perspective unless prompted by an adult. Older children's emotional understanding becomes more sophisticated as they begin to comprehend and accept ambivalent and conflicting emotions and can consider multiple causes of emotions, including thoughts. The relationship between emotional understanding and subjective well-being has not been studied in children, but there is some evidence connecting emotional understanding and mental health. In a longitudinal study involving 1,840 adolescents, slow recognition of happy facial expressions predicted the onset of depressive symptoms 11 years later. Slow identification of happy emotions and fast identification of sad emotions predicted symptoms of anhedonia (i.e., absence of positive emotions) but not sadness (Vrijen et al., 2016).

Emotion regulation strategies have widely been studied and linked to psychological functioning. According to Gross' (1998) model of emotion regulation, there are several processes involved in emotion regulation of positive and negative emotions. One may choose situations that promote positive emotions or reduce/avoid negative emotions (situation selection) or may attempt to actively change the situation to produce desirable emotions (situation modification). Other coping processes include directing attention to aspects of the situation that change the experienced emotion (attention deployment) and reappraising the situation to alter its effect (cognitive change). Lastly, one may modify their own response (response modulation). The first four processes take place before one generates a response, and they are part of a coping strategy known as *cognitive appraisal*. The last step of response modulation aims at inhibiting emotional expression (i.e., emotional masking) and is generally referred to as *suppression*.

Research shows how children come to master suppression and cognitive appraisal and how useful these strategies are for well-being. Preschoolers have trouble controlling emotional displays. They are still learning rules for displaying emotions, such as masking disappointment in response to a less desired gift. This ability to modify or suppress the experienced emotion and allow a subdominant response to be enacted is almost nonexistent in children younger than 4. In a classic disappointing gift task, children's ability to express happiness or gratitude was observed in response to an undesired toy/gift. Even when children were promised rewards to mask their disappointment, 4-year-olds were not able to deceive observers who were blind to the study's instructions. Children between the ages of 6–8, however, were able to fake happiness (Kromm et al., 2015). To fully master the regulation of emotional displays, children must be able to understand and engage in the following processes: minimize the emotional display to appear less emotional, for example, less frightful; intensify the emotional display, for example, appear happier about a less desired outcome; neutralize facial expressions so as to appear unaffected; and, express an entirely different emotion from the experienced one, for example, demonstrating happiness while feeling sorrow. It is expected that children master these rules by 5th grade. Indeed, a study following 1st, 3rd, and 5th graders from Japan revealed that children tended to control the expression of happiness regardless of grade, but 5th graders were better at faking or dissimulating feelings of sadness by projecting happiness (Tamura, 2009).

Preschoolers also have trouble managing the intensity of their feelings as their coping strategies are limited. Preschoolers generally rely on caregivers and teachers for emotional comfort, support, and assistance in solving a problem. While individual differences exist, one could say that preschoolers' emotional intelligence while emerging is far from developed. School-age children develop more independent coping strategies, particularly problem-focused strategies, as well as an ability to consciously change the way they think about an emotionally provoking situation, which they have no control over. At the same time, children and more so adolescents have better introspective thinking and can consider various perspectives at the same time. Both skills are important for effective coping. Essentially, older children and adolescents grasp the relationship between emotions and thoughts and engage in cognitive appraisal.

Research with older children shows the effect of suppressing emotions in contrast to the effect of cognitive appraisal. Chervonsky and Hunt (2019) examined the role of reappraisal and suppression in predicting satisfaction with friends and family as well as victimization, depression, and anxiety in adolescents from 7th to 8th grade. Participants evaluated statements that demonstrated suppression such as, "When I am feeling negative emotions, I make sure not to express them" and statements that demonstrated reappraisal such as, "When I want to feel fewer negative emotions, I change what I'm thinking about." In a sample of 3,500 adolescents, ages 12–15 years, Chervonsky and Hunt (2019) found an inverse association between suppression and satisfaction with friends and family in 8th grade. At the same time, the relationship between suppression and depression, anxiety, and victimization was positive. Appraisal, on the other hand, correlated positively with family satisfaction and negatively with depression. The researchers reported no gender differences in the use of these strategies, but suppression appeared to influence boys' satisfaction with friends. In general, both boys and girls who relied more on reappraisal and less on suppression reported stronger satisfaction with family in grade 8. Moreover, suppression in grade 7 predicted lower friendship satisfaction in grade 8.

The aforementioned findings were replicated by Ng et al. (2018) with 6th graders who found that life satisfaction decreased as the use of cognitive reappraisal decreased and the use of expressive suppression increased. Both strategies mediated the path linking stressful life events and life satisfaction, showing that these strategies are activated in response to stressful events and predict life satisfaction. In addition, the authors revealed that young adolescents did not rely on cognitive reappraisal much when faced with uncontrollable situations. Therefore, adolescents would benefit from interventions teaching them how to cope with overwhelming stressful events. The connection between suppression and lower life satisfaction is not universal, however. In a meta-analytic review, Hu et al. (2014) found that emotional suppression was positively related to positive indicators of mental health such as positive affect, infrequent negative affect, and overall life satisfaction in China and other Eastern cultures, where reserved emotional expressions are highly valued. Therefore, the value of suppression in influencing life satisfaction is culturally determined.

In addition to life satisfaction, cognitive emotion regulation strategies are also linked to experiencing more positive affect and increased perceived happiness. How one chooses to process information influences which emotions are evoked. When children (6–13 years old) are instructed to ruminate, they experience less happiness and more sadness. However, when they are instructed to distance themselves or think about positive outcomes, they report more happiness and less sadness. Furthermore, when the sadness decreases, the children's way of paying attention broadens. They tend to take a more global perspective on the situation instead of focusing on bits of upsetting or saddening details (Davis, 2016). Among preteens, perceived effectiveness for emotional regulation positively correlated with happiness and hope and negatively associated with sadness and depression (Fry et al., 2012). In adolescence, emotion regulation is considered critical for positive functioning. Emotion strategies such as reappraisal aim at down-regulating negative affect and up-regulating positive affect. Up-regulating or elevating positive affect contributes to well-being. Challenges in down-regulating negative affect are linked with distress and dysfunction. Adolescents who are so overwhelmed by their emotions that they have difficulty engaging in goal-directed behaviors, tend to experience less positive affect, lower life satisfaction, and greater negative affect (Shourie & Kaur, 2017). More to the point, dysregulation may decrease academic performance, and increase tolerance to deviance and risky behaviors, leading to psychopathological symptoms. Emotion dysregulation has also direct links to internalizing and externalizing symptoms (Wills et al., 2016).

In conclusion, reappraisal and suppression are two commonly researched emotion regulation strategies. Both have been linked to the overall well-being of adolescents, but only cognitive appraisal appears to be beneficial. Suppression is not associated with the well-being of children in Western cultures. While children are expected to control their emotional displays, caution is warranted to not confuse this with emotional suppression as a coping strategy. It is clear in the literature that emotional suppression is not adaptive. The relationships between emotional intelligence and specifically emotion regulation and subjective well-being in children younger than 11 years old is not well studied. Furthermore, the research that exists lacks a developmental perspective. The relationship between emotional intelligence and well-being should be understood in the context of what emotional intelligence capabilities exist and are adaptive at each age group. Lastly, the pathways between emotion regulation and subjective well-being have not been sufficiently researched, particularly in different age groups, and in the face of stressful events.

Strengthening Emotional Intelligence

In preschool years, emotional intelligence is supported when parents encourage emotional awareness by teaching children to identify their own emotions and the emotions of others. Parents may help children understand the causes of emotions and how to predict emotional reactions based on situations. Language plays a crucial role in emotional understanding and therefore adults should encourage children to express their feelings and thoughts using words and engage them in conversations about emotions. For older children, helping them understand the perspectives of others and consider the feelings of those around them will improve their ability to understand and manage emotions in themselves and others.

Parents should aim to enhance emotion regulation strategies that up-regulate positive emotions and down-regulate negative affect, based on children's developmental level. Down-regulation, however, should be primarily through cognitive and attentional control although there is room in exploring how changing a stressful situation (e.g., situation selection and modification) may promote subjective well-being (Quoidbach et al., 2015). Because suppression of emotional expression has a negative association with well-being, children should be taught to recognize emotions and accept them, and to modulate the intensity of the emotions instead of trying to eliminate or replace them. Effective coping strategies for school-age children and adolescents are problem-solving cognitive reappraisal and attention deployment. Parents should help children understand that it is natural to experience a range of emotions and that it is important to address them rather than ignore them.

A popular approach to teaching emotional intelligence is called *emotion coaching*, a several-step process developed by Gottman et al. (1997). Emotion coaching aims at enhancing children's emotional intelligence by developing the ability to recognize emotions appropriately, consider their effects on self and others, harness impulsiveness, and regulate the experience and expression of emotions. Emotion coaching refers to parenting efforts specific to the children's emotions, but it is not limited to parents, as any adult working with children can become an emotional coach. Adults who engage in emotional coaching are encouraged to be good listeners so they can understand the emotional experience of the child. They consider any occasion as an opportunity to intimately connect and teach children how to recognize their emotions, how to label them, and how to cope with them by finding age-appropriate strategies. To be successful, effective emotion coaches must be in tune with their own emotions, separate them from the children's emotions, and model acceptance of emotions by validating the children's feelings. Emotion coaches are contrasted with dismissing and disapproving parents who brush off emotional reactions, minimize their importance, and shut down any communication channels. They are also contrasted with laissez-faire parents who accept their children's emotions but fail to clarify them, explain them, and help children cope with them. According to Gottman et al. (1997), emotion coaching is something that all parents can learn to do. Moreover, the steps of emotion coaching need not all take place in one interaction. For example, an older child may recognize emotions but may have a hard time coping. A younger child may need support with clarifying and labeling as well as managing emotions.

Building emotional intelligence can be particularly helpful when supporting children who are coping with significant adversities. Traumatic experiences can potentially change the neurochemistry and functionality of the emotional brain. While the exact neurophysiology of emotion regulation is not known, trauma appears to leave the individual in a state of hyperarousal. This state is caused by ineffective pathways between the structures of the limbic system, where emotions are registered, and the prefrontal cortex, where executive decisions are made about behavioral responses. Children exposed to trauma tend to have poor emotion regulation and therefore are at an increased risk for mental health problems. To support the well-being of these children, interventions should focus on building emotional intelligence by relearning emotional responses; reliving trauma safely in a form of play where trauma can be repeated in a less anxiety-provoking situation (Goleman, 2005). In this context, adaptive outcomes can be explored replacing the previous traumatic responses. Essentially, these interventions aim at creating cognitions that help regulate the intensity and appropriate expression of negative emotions, a significant process in improving children's well-being.

All children should have access to emotional comfort, support, and assistance when needed. All children need encouragement to focus on positive outcomes and maintain an optimistic and hopeful outlook when faced with emotionally challenging situations. Adults need to keep an eye on the child's emotional development and tailor coaching to the child's age and needs. Their support helps increase happiness and reduce negative affect.

References

Baker, Z. G., Krieger, H., & LeRoy, A. S. (2016). Fear of missing out: Relationships with depression, mindfulness, and physical symptoms. *Translational Issues in Psychological Science*, *2*(3), 275. https://doi.org/10.1037/tps0000075

Balluerka, N., Aritzeta, A., Gorostiaga, A., Gartzia, L., & Soroa, G. (2013). Emotional intelligence and depressed mood in adolescence: A multilevel approach. *International*

Journal of Clinical and Health Psychology, *13*(2), 110–117. https://doi.org/10.1016/S1697-2600(13)70014-0
Carter, C. (2010). *Raising happiness: 10 simple steps for more joyful kids and happier parents*. Ballantine Books.
Carver, C. S., & Scheier, M. F. (2014). Dispositional optimism. *Trends in Cognitive Sciences*, *18*(6), 293–299. https://doi.org/10.1016/j.tics.2014.02.003
Chervonsky, E., & Hunt, C. (2019). Emotion regulation, mental health, and social wellbeing in a young adolescent sample: A concurrent and longitudinal investigation. *Emotion*, *19*(2), 270. https://doi.org/10.1037/emo0000432
Davis, E. L. (2016). An age-related mechanism of emotion regulation: Regulating sadness promotes children's learning by broadening information processing. *Child Development*, *87*(5), 1617–1626. https://doi.org/10.1111/cdev.12552
Duy, B., & Yıldız, M. A. (2019). The mediating role of self-esteem in the relationship between optimism and subjective well-being. *Current Psychology*, *38*(6), 1456–1463. https://doi.org/10.1007/s12144-017-9698-1
Emmons, R. A., & McCullough, M. E. (Eds.). (2004). *The psychology of gratitude*. Oxford University Press.
Feldman, D. B., & Snyder, C. R. (2005). Hope and the meaningful life: Theoretical and empirical associations between goal–directed thinking and life meaning. *Journal of Social and Clinical Psychology*, *24*(3), 401–421. https://doi.org/10.1521/jscp.24.3.401.65616
Fredrickson, B. L. (2001). The role of positive emotions in positive psychology: The broaden-and-build theory of positive emotions. *American Psychologist*, *56*(3), 218. https://doi.org/10.1037/0003-066X.56.3.218
Froh, J. J., & Bono, G. (2008). The gratitude of youth. In S. J. Lopez (Ed.), *Positive psychology: Exploring the Best in People* (Vol. 2, pp. 55–78). Praeger Publishers/Greenwood Publishing Group.
Froh, J. J., Bono, G., Fan, J., Emmons, R. A., Henderson, K., Harris, C., Leggio, H., & Wood, A. M. (2014). Nice thinking! An educational intervention that teaches children to think gratefully. *School Psychology Review*, *43*(2), 132–152. https://doi.org/10.1080/02796015.2014.12087440
Froh, J. J., Sefick, W. J., & Emmons, R. A. (2008). Counting blessings, I early adolescence: An experimental study of gratitude and subjective well-being. *Journal of Social Psychology*, *46*, 213–233. https://doi.org/10.1016/j.jsp.2007.03.005
Fry, M. D., Guivernau, M., Kim, M. S., Newton, M., Gano-Overway, L. A., & Magyar, T. M. (2012). Youth perceptions of a caring climate, emotional regulation, and psychological well-being. *Sport, Exercise, and Performance Psychology*, *1*(1), 44. https://doi.org/10.1037/a0025454
Gillham, J. E., Reivich, K. J., & Shatté, A. J. (2001). Building optimism and preventing depressive symptoms in children. In E. C. Chang (Ed.), *Optimism & pessimism: Implications for theory, research, and practice* (pp. 301–320). American Psychological Association. https://doi.org/10.1037/10385-014
Goleman, D. (2005). *Emotional intelligence*. Bantam.
Gottman, P. D. J., Declaire, J., & Goleman, D. (1997). *Raising an emotionally intelligent child: The heart of parenting*. Simon & Schuster.
Griffith, J. M., Young, J. F., & Hankin, B. L. (2021). Longitudinal associations between positive affect and relationship quality among children and adolescents: Examining patterns of co-occurring change. *Emotion*, *21*(1), 28. https://doi.org/10.1037/emo0000682
Gross, J. J. (1998). The emerging field of emotion regulation: An integrative review. *Review of General Psychology*, *2*(3), 271–299. https://doi.org/10.1037/1089-2680.2.3.271

Guse, T., Vescovelli, F., & Croxford, S. A. (2019). Subjective well-being and gratitude among South African adolescents: Exploring gender and cultural differences. *Youth & Society*, *51*(5), 591–615. https://doi.org/10.1177/0044118X17697237

Häggström Westberg, K., Wilhsson, M., Svedberg, P., Nygren, J. M., Morgan, A., & Nyholm, M. (2019). Optimism as a candidate health asset: Exploring its links with adolescent quality of life in Sweden. *Child Development*, *90*(3), 970–984. https://doi.org/10.1111/cdev.12958

Hasan, N., & Power, T. G. (2002). Optimism and pessimism in children: A study of parenting correlates. *International Journal of Behavioral Development*, *26*(2), 185–191. https://doi.org/10.1080/01650250114300003

Hoy, B. D., Suldo, S. M., & Mendez, L. R. (2013). Links between parents' and children's levels of gratitude, life satisfaction, and hope. *Journal of Happiness Studies*, *14*, 1343–1361. https://doi.org/10.1007/s10902-012-9386

Hu, T., Zhang, D., Wang, J., Mistry, R., Ran, G., & Wang, X. (2014). Relation between emotion regulation and mental health: A meta-analysis review. *Psychological Reports*, *114*(2), 341–362. https://doi.org/10.2466/03.20.PR0.114k22w4

Kromm, H., Färber, M., & Holodynski, M. (2015). Felt or false smiles? Volitional regulation of emotional expression in 4-, 6-, and 8-year-old children. *Child Development*, *86*(2), 579–597. https://doi.org/10.1111/cdev.12315

Layous, K., & Lyubomirsky, S. (2014). Benefits, mechanisms, and new directions for teaching gratitude to children. *School Psychology Review*, *43*(2), 153–159. https://doi.org/10.1080/02796015.2014.12087441

Ma, L., Zhang, Y., Huang, C., & Cui, Z. (2020). Resilience-oriented cognitive behavioral interventions for depressive symptoms in children and adolescents: A meta-analytic review. *Journal of Affective Disorders*, *270*, 150–164. https://doi.org/10.1016/j.jad.2020.03.051

Marques, S. C., Lopez, S. J., & Pais-Ribeiro, J. L. (2011). "Building hope for the future": A program to foster strengths in middle-school students. *Journal of Happiness Studies*, *12*(1), 139–152. https://doi.org/10.1007/s10902-009-9180-3

Marques, S. C., Lopez, S. J., Rose, S., & Robinson, C. (2014). Measuring and promoting hope in schoolchildren. In M. J. Furlong, R. Gilman, & E. S. Huebner (Eds.), *Handbook of positive psychology in schools* (pp. 55–68). Routledge.

Mayer, J. D., Salovey, P., & Caruso, D. R. (2008). Emotional intelligence: New ability or eclectic traits? *American Psychologist*, *63*(6), 503–517. https://doi.org/10.1037/0003-066X.63.6.503

McCullough, M. E., Emmons, R. A., & Tsang, J. A. (2002). The grateful disposition: A conceptual and empirical topography. *Journal of Personality and Social Psychology*, *82*(1), 112. https://doi.org/10.1037/0022-3514.82.1.112

McGuire-Snieckus, R. (2014). Hope, optimism, and delusion. *The Psychiatric Bulletin*, *38*(2), 49–51. https://doi.org/10.1192/pb.bp.113.044438

Merkaš, M., & Brajša-Žganec, A. (2011). Children with different levels of hope: Are there differences in their self-esteem, life satisfaction, social support, and family cohesion? *Child Indicators Research*, *4*(3), 499–514. https://doi.org/10.1007/s12187-011-9105-7

Ng, Z. J., Huebner, E. S., Hills, K. J., & Valois, R. F. (2018). Mediating effects of emotion regulation strategies in the relations between stressful life events and life satisfaction in a longitudinal sample of early adolescents. *Journal of School Psychology*, *70*, 16–26. https://doi.org/10.1016/j.jsp.2018.06.001

Owens, R. L., & Patterson, M. M. (2013). Positive psychological interventions for children: A comparison of gratitude and best possible selves approaches. *The Journal of Genetic Psychology*, *174*(4), 403–428. https://doi.org/10.1080/00221325.2012.697496

Park, S. R., & Kim, K. S. (2012). The Relationship among savoring, happiness, and optimism of elementary school children. *The Korean Journal of Elementary Counseling*, *11*(3), 465–484.

Quoidbach, J., Mikolajczak, M., & Gross, J. J. (2015). Positive interventions: An emotion regulation perspective. *Psychological Bulletin*, *141*(3), 655–693. https://doi.org/10.1037/a0038648

Ramsey, M. A., & Gentzler, A. L. (2015). An upward spiral: Bidirectional associations between positive affect and positive aspects of close relationships across the life span. *Developmental Review*, *36*, 58–104. https://doi.org/10.1016/j.dr.2015.01.003

Renshaw, T. L., & Olinger Steeves, R. M. (2016). What good is gratitude in youth and schools? A systematic review and meta-analysis of correlates and intervention outcomes. *Psychology in the Schools*, *53*(3), 286–305. https://doi.org/10.1002/pits.21903

Rosenfeld, A. J. (2019). The neuroscience of happiness and well-being: What brain findings from optimism and compassion reveal. *Child and Adolescent Psychiatric Clinics*, *28*(2), 137–146. https://doi.org/10.1016/j.chc.2018.11.002

Rothenberg, W. A., Hussong, A. M., Langley, H. A., Egerton, G. A., Halberstadt, A. G., Coffman, J. L., Mokrova, I., & Costanzo, P. R. (2017). Grateful parents raising grateful children: Niche selection and the socialization of child gratitude. *Applied Developmental Science*, *21*(2), 106–120. https://doi.org/10.1080/10888691.2016.1175945

Ruiz-Aranda, D., Castillo, R., Salguero, J. M., Cabello, R., Fernández-Berrocal, P., & Balluerka, N. (2012). Short-and midterm effects of emotional intelligence training on adolescent mental health. *Journal of Adolescent Health*, *51*(5), 462–467. https://doi.org/10.1016/j.jadohealth.2012.02.003

Salovey, P., & Mayer, J. D. (1990). Emotional intelligence. *Imagination, cognition, and personality*, *9*(3), 185–211. http://citeseerx.ist.psu.edu/viewdoc/download?doi=10.1.1.385.4383&rep=rep1&type=pdf

Scheier, M. F., Carver, C. S., & Bridges, M. W. (1994). Distinguishing optimism from neuroticism (and trait anxiety, self-mastery, and self-esteem): A reevaluation of the life orientation test. *Journal of Personality and Social Psychology*, *67*(6), 1063.

Seligman, M. E. (2007). *The optimistic child: A proven program to safeguard children against depression and build lifelong resilience*. Houghton Mifflin Harcourt.

Shourie, S., & Kaur, H. (2017). Subjective well-being and difficulties with emotion regulation among adolescents. *Journal of Psychosocial Research*, *12*(1). https://web.p.ebscohost.com/ehost/pdfviewer/pdfviewer?vid=0&sid=15aff42c-7b59-4505-89c1-4ce6477976eb%40redis

Snyder, C. R., Hoza, B., Pelham, W. E., Rapoff, M., Ware, L., Danovsky, M., Highberger, L., Ribinstein, H., & Stahl, K. J. (1997). The development and validation of the children's hope scale. *Journal of Pediatric Psychology*, *22*(3), 399–421. https://doi.org/10.1093/jpepsy/22.3.399

Snyder, C. R., Rand, K. L., & Sigmon, D. R. (2002). Hope theory. In C. R. Snyder & S. J. Lopez (Eds.), *Handbook of positive psychology* (pp. 257–276). Oxford University Press.

Tamura, A. (2009). Developmental changes of strategies to regulate emotional expression in childhood. *Psychologia*, *52*(4), 245–252. https://doi.org/10.2117/psysoc.2009.245

Tejada-Gallardo, C., Blasco-Belled, A., Torrelles-Nadal, C., & Alsinet, C. (2020). How does emotional intelligence predict happiness, optimism, and pessimism in adolescence?

Investigating the relationship from the bifactor model. *Current Psychology*, 1–11. https://doi.org/10.1007/s12144-020-01061-z

Vorkapić, S. T., & Šikić, A. B. (2019). What pre-school children think about happiness, hope, gratitude, wisdom, justice, and optimism? The positive conceptual thinking development study. *Journal of Positive School Psychology*, *3*(1), 1–25. Retrieved May 1, 2023, from www.journalppw.com/index.php/JPPW/article/view/59

Vrijen, C., Hartman, C. A., & Oldehinkel, A. J. (2016). Slow identification of facial happiness in early adolescence predicts onset of depression during 8 years of follow-up. *European Child & Adolescent Psychiatry*, *25*(11), 1255–1266. https://doi.org/10.1007/s00787-016-0846-1

Wills, T. A., Simons, J. S., Sussman, S., & Knight, R. (2016). Emotional self-control and dysregulation: A dual-process analysis of pathways to externalizing/internalizing symptomatology and positive well-being in younger adolescents. *Drug and Alcohol Dependence*, *163*, S37–S45. https://doi.org/10.1016/j.drugalcdep.2015.08.039

Wong, S. S., & Lim, T. (2009). Hope versus optimism in Singaporean adolescents: Contributions to depression and life satisfaction. *Personality and Individual Differences*, *46*(5–6), 648–652. https://doi.org/10.1016/j.paid.2009.01.009

Yeung, D. Y., Ho, S. M., & Mak, C. W. (2015). Brief report: Attention to positive information mediates the relationship between hope and psychosocial well-being of adolescents. *Journal of Adolescence*, *42*, 98–102. https://doi.org/10.1016/j.adolescence.2015.04.004

Yu, J. J., & Ko, Y. K. (2013). Paternal family expressiveness as a mediator between father's dispositional optimism and child's dispositional optimism. *The Journal of Genetic Psychology*, *174*(6), 677–695. https://doi.org/10.1080/00221325.2013.783548

Zou, R., Zhang, D. J., Niu, G. F., Xie, X. C., Fan, C. Y., Tian, Y., & Zhou, Z. K. (2016). Cross-sectional age differences in dispositional optimism in Chinese children and adolescents. *Personality and Individual Differences*, *102*, 133–138. https://doi.org/10.3389/fpsyg.2020.01955

3 Solitude and Flow

Four-month-old Sophia cannot sit on her own yet, but she has begun controlling her "reach and grasp." She is already interested in animal books that her mother has been reading to her for a few weeks now. If she could talk, she would be able to make all animal sounds, her mother often thought. Right now, Sophia is pinned between two couch pillows in a sitting position, staring at a local coupons magazine that her mother is holding in front of her. The brightness and contrast of colors in the pictures and the print catch her attention. She reaches out and clumsily attempts to turn the pages. Her mother is impressed by her extended attention span. Sophia's focus becomes more intense and soon begins to make a soft humming sound. She seems to enjoy herself, totally absorbed in her visual, vocal, and motor exploration. The only time she looks at her mother is when she is done, 10 minutes after she first encountered the intriguing newspaper insert.

Four-year-old Dimitra, like other children of her age, loves imaginative play. Sometimes she is part of the play, especially when she is dressed like a princess and other times, she orchestrates a play for the little people from her doll house or the animals from the jungle, the farm, the ocean, and the sky. Her parents cannot tell what the story is as she mostly plays silently with the occasional interruption of an enthusiastic monologue. What they notice is that she spends hours in this manner, oblivious to what is happening around her. Her parents enjoy that she plays independently and look forward to seeing the state of the family room after she is done as it provides hints to what went inside her head. Frequently they find the little people and animals in interesting assortments and arrangements. Afterward, Dimitra appears content, calm, and ready for a snack.

Sixteen-year-old Amelia is different from her two older sisters. She often hears her parents murmuring about how she does not share their love for reading books. Amelia prefers to think that she is more selective about what she reads and that when the book captures her, she can forget that she is actually reading. The problem is, her parents tell her, that she cannot know whether a book will capture her unless she gives it a chance. When her mother passes to her Trevor Noah's Born in Crime, *Amelia is skeptical, but soon finds that it is hard to put the book down. She admits to her mom that her experience reading this book was as immersing as making fashion designs.*

DOI: 10.4324/9780429356414-5

Children, like adults, engage in solitary activities, such as the ones just described, that they find entertaining, absorbing, and even creative. Being alone, also known as solitude and its benefits to well-being have primarily been noted for adults, but there is developmental research illuminating how children come to understand solitude as a positive experience. The concept of *flow* has garnered significant interest within and beyond the scientific community. Psychologists use the term flow to describe a mental state where the person is absolutely absorbed in an enjoyable professional or recreational activity. Such a state in turn boosts creativity, enhances commitment to higher personal goals, and creates happiness in adults. This chapter addresses the question of when children differentiate aloneness from solitude and recognize the benefits of solitude in relation to happiness and success from a developmental perspective. The chapter answers questions about when children are capable to recognize flow experiences and it reviews potential environmental and personal factors that affect it. In addition, the chapter explores whether the positive effects of flow apply to children as they do to adults and provides suggestions that promote flow experiences in children.

How Children Understand Solitude

Investigating flow in children begins with an exploration of how children understand and experience solitude because flow is most likely to be experienced in a solitary state. Humans, as social creatures, naturally spend a significant portion of their lives in the company of others. Larson (1990) found that the amount of time spent alone varies across different age groups. For instance, children between the ages of 9 and 12 reported spending 17% of their time alone, while high school students spent around 26% of their time in solitude. The percentage of time spent alone increased to 29% for adults and further rose to 48% during late adulthood. Interestingly, this linear trend experiences a temporary decline during the child-rearing years, because the responsibilities of raising children restrict opportunities for solitude. As for younger children, they typically spend less time alone due to the need for adult supervision, although they may still engage in solitary activities while in the presence of adults or with adults nearby.

How do children learn to discern between the positive and negative aspects of solitude? In other words, how do they come to differentiate various states of being "on your own" and recognize that being alone is not inherently negative? A comprehensive examination of solitary states comes from Galanaki (2004), who explored how 2nd, 4th, and 6th graders differentiate and understand aloneness, loneliness, and solitude in themselves and others. Galanaki defined aloneness as the state of being physically alone, which may or may not lead to feelings of loneliness. Loneliness, on the other hand, is an undesirable emotional state that arises from unmet desires for intimacy and belonging. It is often accompanied by sadness and boredom and can stem from poor relationships, loss, or physical separation. Notably, loneliness can also be experienced in the presence of others when emotional needs for support, companionship, and communication are unfulfilled. In this case, a person may not be alone but still feel lonely. Solitude, in contrast, is a state of aloneness that can be associated with either loneliness or positive feelings of engagement. Negative solitude tends to be involuntary, while constructive solitude is typically a voluntary choice. In other words, individuals do not actively seek out negative solitude, but they deliberately create opportunities for positive solitude. This desired form of solitude closely relates with the concept of flow.

Across grades and genders, most children reported experiencing painful loneliness. Galanaki (2004) found an upward linear trend in understanding loneliness as distinct from aloneness, with older children being less likely to equate the two. With increasing age, more children recognized that people can feel lonely even in the company of others. Similarly, there was an age-related increase in understanding that one can be alone without feeling lonely, with girls reporting this more often than boys. Children who successfully distinguished between aloneness and loneliness believed that people can be alone without feeling lonely if they have satisfying relationships, pets, or favorite possessions; engage in enjoyable activities; are used to being alone; or use their alone time to reflect, daydream, and meditate. Conversely, children believed that people feel lonely in the presence of others if they are unhappy with their relationships, feel excluded or disliked, are among unfamiliar people, have a dispositional tendency towards loneliness or shyness, or harbor negative thoughts and emotions like guilt. These responses suggest that children develop a sophisticated understanding of solitary states and their accompanying emotions during their school years.

Galanaki (2004) also investigated when children begin to view solitude as a constructive experience and recognize the benefits that may result from positive solitude. Overall, less than half of the children had a positive view of solitude, but this attitude increased with age. Among 2nd graders, only 16.7% had a positive understanding of solitude. The percentage increased to 38.3% in 4th grade and 60% in 6th grade. Younger children (2nd grade) associated solitude with solitary activities like reading, occasions to focus on high-achievement tasks, and punishments meant to reflect on bad behavior. These findings are not surprising as they reflect the personal experiences that younger children have. They read alone, work on problems in the classroom by themselves, and receive time-outs for misbehaviors. Older children (4th and 6th graders) reported that solitude provides peace, quietude, and relaxation. It is also an opportunity to de-escalate negative feelings like anxiety and anger, reflect upon one's own problems and shortcomings, find solutions, make plans, develop a sense of mastery, daydream, and seek privacy.

Most children (62%) believed that people may voluntarily seek out aloneness, with this belief increasing significantly over time. However, younger children held negative views about those who voluntarily pursue aloneness. Older children provided several explanations as to why people might seek solitude, including personality traits, preferences, occupation requirements (e.g., scientists), or necessity (e.g., living in remote areas). All age groups recognized that being alone could be a result of peer rejection or a need for privacy. The understanding of privacy as a state of voluntary aloneness varies with age and develops over time. Seven-year-olds consider privacy to be a state of aloneness where one can control the degree of contact with others and the amount of information they desire to receive.

Nine-year-old children consider privacy as something people desire, and 11-year-olds consider privacy a state of being alone without being bothered (Galanaki, 2013). The understanding that people desire privacy is not evident in preschool.

Positive experiences of solitude typically emerge as preadolescence transitions into adolescence. Adolescents accept that aloneness may be constructive because it provides much desired privacy and a space to concentrate but at the same time, they also believe that aloneness is potentially painful. Viewing solitude as a positive experience may be supported by advanced reasoning skills that enable constructive use of time alone. It may also be influenced by the identity status and the attachment style of the adolescents. Those who have resolved identity issues and have a secure attachment style are more likely to accept solitary time as a positive experience. In conclusion, there is agreement in the literature that preference for solitude increases during adolescence, but aloneness is not always pleasant. In fact, adolescents associate aloneness with loneliness more so than adults do, especially on weekend nights (Long & Averill, 2003). Experience sampling studies show that adolescents often perceive solitude as lonely, even when they are engaged in productive or leisure activities (Larson, 1997).

Benefits of Solitude

Theoretically, solitude can be beneficial as it offers opportunities for creativity, self-improvement, reflection on self and others, spiritual connections, and even intimacy (Long & Averill, 2003). Winnicott (1958) famously argued that a person who has learned to be alone will never truly feel alone, as they can consider meaningful relationships and experience closeness and connectedness while in solitude. For adolescents, solitude aids in dealing with developmental tasks like individuation, autonomy, and identity formation (Larson, 1990). However, do these opportunities for renewal, growth, and focus contribute to broader psychological well-being?

Evidence supporting the importance of solitude in young children remains scarce. Developmental research on solitary passive activity among preschoolers, such as working on puzzles or drawing alone, may improve task persistence and emotion regulation (e.g., constructive coping to deal with social anxiety) but extended use of it predicts poor performance on social tasks like *show and tell* (Hane et al., 2008). Self-reported preference for solitary play among kindergarteners and 1st graders was associated with peer rejection if the children engaged in antisocial behaviors (Ooi et al., 2018). Moreover, solitary activity predicted poor acceptance, particularly in school age (Hane et al., 2008). This converges with the finding that children as young as 5 years of age perceive loneliness as being alone and sad and peers are likely to shun those who show preference for something that is considered negative.

During middle childhood, peers continue to view the preference for solitude as deviant and therefore there is a risk of peer rejection. Based on a large longitudinal study, a preference for solitude and not social inhibition (i.e., shyness) increased the risk for peer victimization and peer rejection from age 6 to age 10. Preference for solitude appears to be influenced by genetic factors as the aforementioned patterns appeared in genetically related children like twins (Morneau-Vaillancourt et al., 2019). Furthermore, preference for solitude among 9–12-year-old boys predicted peer problems and loneliness when solitude was displayed in the form of socially withdrawn behaviors, such as non-social behaviors in school and solitary activities after school (Coplan et al., 2015). However, the preference for solitude does not become more maladaptive with age despite the greater age-related demands for social interaction with peers. Additionally, the negative evidence is not always consistent. For example, among 9- to 12-year-olds, a preference for solitude did not necessarily lead to greater internalizing symptoms of anxiety and depression (Coplan et al., 2015). Lastly, the examination of the positive correlates of solitude preference is largely neglected in the literature.

In response to these findings, researchers have begun identifying children who consider solitude a positive experience and studying their psychological adjustment. Using a person-centered approach, Corsano et al. (2019) distinguished three clusters of adolescents. Most preadolescents fell into a cluster that had an aversion to being alone and reported adaptive functioning marked by low loneliness in their relationships with parents and peers. Two other clusters were of interest: one characterized by a high affinity towards solitude but reporting low loneliness, and the other characterized by a high affinity towards solitude but reporting high loneliness. Only the latter group experienced maladaptive functioning. In contrast, the cluster with positive attitudes towards solitude had high self-esteem and high-quality friendships. Another person-centered analysis revealed that a group of preadolescents (9–12 years) with high affinity for aloneness, but low social anxiety did not differ from those with low affinity for aloneness and low social anxiety in various psychological outcomes, such as quality of friendships, self-esteem, and depressive symptoms (Daly & Willoughby, 2020). Therefore, there may be other reasons why children with high tendencies for aloneness experience negative outcomes. Some children who prefer solitude may have social and communication difficulties that lead to peer problems and loneliness, while others can experience gratifying close relationships with family and friends.

As affinity for solitude increases from early to middle and late adolescence, there may be a corresponding increase in socially accepting peers who prefer solitary activities. However, evidence supporting the benefits of solitude for well-being during this period remains limited. Adolescents aged 13–16 continue to report more loneliness when alone compared to being with family, friends, or classmates. These feelings of loneliness often persist when transitioning from solitude to family time, but not to time spent with friends, highlighting contextual influences on solitude experiences (Van Roekel et al., 2015). Hipson et al. (2021) attempted to unravel some of this complexity by examining the quantity and quality of time spent alone in relation to the well-being of 15- to 19-year-olds. Based on self-reported activities, students were classified as *Engaged* (31.7%) if they spent their time interacting with technology, hobbies, or homework; *Thinking* (15%) if they spent their alone time in mental activities, such as planning and daydreaming; and, *Passive* (53.33%) if they were passive recipients of information, such as watching TV. Across all clusters, time spent alone was related to a greater preference for solitude, negative affect, loneliness, and lower positive affect. While preferences for solitude did not differ between groups, the Passive Media group spent the most time alone. The Thinking group experienced the highest negative affect and loneliness, with no significant difference from the Passive group. Interestingly, the Engaged group reported more positive affect than the Thinking group, suggesting that engaging in activities while alone is more beneficial than merely thinking.

These findings present a complex picture of the actual benefits of solitude in childhood and adolescence, with conceptualized advantages remaining largely theoretical. Children who hold a positive attitude towards solitude, feel comfortable in social situations, and experience low levels of loneliness in close relationships may benefit from actively engaging in solitary activities. However, it is unclear how many children fit these criteria. Most strikingly, there is a lack of research examining the direct association between experiences of solitude and positive indices of well-being. More research is needed to understand the motivation for solitude and what children and adolescents do while "alone but not lonely." Some children may even experience negative emotions if they do not spend constructive time alone. For instance, a child might need an hour of alone time in their room after school. It is crucial to examine how rewarding solitary activities are for children and adolescents. Flow experiences, as rewarding and integral parts of positive well-being, can be experienced by young children engaging in solitary activities, even if not entirely or voluntarily alone. This may be a starting point for appreciating solitude.

In conclusion, empirical evidence supporting the positive impact of solitude on children and adolescents remains sparse. The complexity of factors influencing solitude experiences and outcomes makes it challenging to pinpoint its overall contribution to psychological well-being. For some children, active engagement in solitary activities can be constructive, especially when accompanied by a positive attitude towards solitude and low levels of loneliness in close relationships. However, further research is needed to understand the motivations behind solitude-seeking behavior, how children and adolescents spend their time in solitude, and the potential role of flow experiences in enhancing well-being during solitary activities. By exploring these areas, we can better understand the intricate relationship between solitude and well-being in childhood and adolescence and ultimately guide the development of interventions and strategies to foster positive experiences and outcomes.

Is Flow Possible?

Psychologist Mihaly Csikszentmihalyi (1990) posits that individuals experience flow when they are deeply focused on a single activity, losing awareness of their surroundings and the passage of time, yet maintaining control over the task. As a result of this immersion, emotions become unnoticeable, and a person in flow does not experience feelings of loneliness even if they are alone. Upon reflection, individuals find the activity highly rewarding and exhilarating. During flow, the mind is active, controlled, and creative. Engaging in flow typically involves challenging activities, which may demand some effort initially. Csikszentmihalyi identified several characteristics that define a flow state, including a balance between challenge and skill, action-awareness merging, clear goals, unambiguous feedback, focused concentration, a sense of control, loss of self-consciousness, altered perception of time, and an autotelic experience (i.e., intrinsically rewarding, engaging in the task for its own sake). Flow can be achieved in both solitary and social settings, but the intensity of the experience is often greater during solitary engagement. The satisfaction derived from flow contributes to adult happiness. While in flow, individuals use feedback from their activities to improve, resulting in personal growth. Following flow experiences, people report increased motivation and dedication to pursuing higher goals, suggesting that flow also contributes to success.

Before investigating the relationship between flow and subjective well-being in children, it is crucial to explore how flow can be measured and the age at which children become aware of being in a flow state. Flow is a universal phenomenon that can be experienced at any age, as demonstrated by the vignettes at the beginning of the chapter. However, children cannot articulate the concept of flow until they develop the ability for self-reflection and introspection. In the preschool years, children's understanding of mental states is limited to recognizing some emotions and their causes, such as saying, "Drawing makes me happy" or "I like playing with my Legos." As children enter the school-age period, their ability to discuss mental states improves, and they gradually begin to connect emotions and thoughts to explain behaviors. They start to comprehend that emotions can be triggered by thoughts, for example, "Thinking about playing with Legos makes me happy." Metacognitive skills, such as recognizing cognitive strengths and weaknesses and regulating mental processes to achieve goals, also progress during this period. While individual differences exist, it is expected that most 8-year-olds possess the capacity to recognize flow states in themselves and others. This is consistent with the fact that an increasing number of children understand the benefits of solitude after the 2nd grade (Galanaki, 2004, 2013).

Consequently, the study of flow in young children has primarily relied on observation, while interviews and self-reports are used for late middle childhood and adolescence. The experiential sampling method developed by Csikszentmihalyi and Larson (2014) is also commonly used. Typically, children are paged electronically eight times a day for a week. At each response, children report their location, activity, thoughts about the activity as well as their level of concentration, interest, and engagement. Researchers use these data to determine the state of flow and its correlates. Qualitative accounts of flow have been provided for toddlers, preschoolers, and school-age children engaged in musical activities, such as singing songs or taking violin lessons (Akutsu, 2018; Custodero, 2005). However, these studies tend to be case studies or have small sample sizes. Following the experiential sampling paradigm by Csikszentmihalyi and Larson (2014), Custodero (2005) designed an observational protocol called the Flow Indicator in Musical Activities (FINA). This protocol has three categories of flow indicators consistent with those found in adults and older children: *challenge-seeking*, *challenge-monitoring*, and *social context indicators*. *Challenge-seeking* behaviors include initiating intentional acts, correcting an activity, and gestures that demonstrate focus and control. *Challenge monitoring* behaviors involve efforts to find the next step, transforming an activity to make it more difficult, and continuing the musical activity even after the teacher finishes the lesson. *Social context* behaviors consist of attempts to interact with others such as gazing and head-turning. Despite the small sample size, Custodero observed an increase in several challenge-seeking behaviors. Specifically, self-initiated activities increased from toddlerhood to preschool but declined in school-age children, presumably because at this age children are expected to heed more the teachers' instructions. Corrections increased from toddlerhood to school age. Deliberate gestures in response to the rhythm, pitch, and structure of music were observed across all age groups. Recently, Akutsu (2018) applied Custodero's FINA to observe the flow experience of a 2-year-old Japanese child playing the violin. The child demonstrated self-assigned tasks, self-corrections, and deliberate gestures. Notably, awareness of others appeared to facilitate flow. Akutsu suggests that the violin specifically provided the necessary range of difficulty to promote flow. These findings emphasize that even young children can experience flow in a context that supports their autonomy, offers suitably challenging materials and resources, and provides the necessary support.

In addition, there is some evidence that school-age children may find flow while playing video games. Inal and Cagiltay (2007) invited 7–9-year-olds to play computer games for 1 hour per week, for six weeks, and used both interviews and observational measures to assess flow states. The children were provided with descriptions of flow experiences to help them think about and articulate their own experiences. The researchers found that flow experiences lasted only 1–2 minutes but occurred three to four times per session. During these moments, the children appeared absorbed in the game, focused on progressing through levels, and less aware of their surroundings. Boys were more likely to experience flow than girls, possibly because girls' games did not present challenges such as level advancement. Interestingly, flow experiences also occurred in the presence of other children, which is common when children participate in sports or other physical activities—a topic that has garnered more research attention. A recent review of 39 studies from 16 countries, most of which used Csikszentmihalyi's theoretical framework, revealed that boys experienced slightly more flow than girls, that flow was beneficial, and that personality and contextual factors facilitated the experience of flow (Jackman et al., 2020). In a school setting, adolescent flow is often seen as a form of student engagement. For example, high school students, who responded to the experiential sampling and interviews, reported higher engagement (e.g., increased concentration, interest, and enjoyment) when they felt a balance between high task difficulty and their skills, they had a sense of control of the learning environment and believed the instructions of what to achieve were clear (Shernoff et al., 2014).

Flowing Into Happiness and Success

Flow, as a positive experience that leaves individuals feeling content and accomplished, is expected to contribute to children's well-being. Furthermore, it is believed that during flow, individuals reach their peak performance which leads to personal growth. Children can potentially develop better self-regulation and a love for life-long learning through flow experiences (Rathunde, 2015). However, there is little direct evidence that youth who experience more flow also report being happier or that children with more flow have greater accomplishments. This does not imply that these associations do not exist, but rather that they have not been extensively studied. Existing evidence suggests several positive outcomes. Csikszentmihalyi and Csikszentmihalyi (1988) found that high-flow teenagers reported higher levels of self-esteem and engagement in hobbies, sports, and homework. However, they believed that they did not have as much fun as low-flow peers who spent their time socializing and playing games. Csikszentmihalyi and Csikszentmihalyi (1988) theorized that a preference for low-flow activities might contribute to low self-esteem and depression. Another study demonstrated that high school students who experienced flow also reported a greater sense of self-control, higher self-esteem, and improved positive mood (Shernoff et al., 2014). Additionally, adolescents who experience flow in sports exhibit a heightened sense of accomplishment, superior objective performance, a stronger self-concept, commitment to physical activity, and reduced stress (Jackman et al., 2020). Lastly, Ceci and Kumar (2016) demonstrated that finding enjoyment and challenge in creative pursuits was associated with increased positive affect, life satisfaction, and decreased negative affect. Evidence of flow's benefits in younger children is understandably scarce, given our limited knowledge of how children experience flow. One potential direction for future research is to investigate the benefits of flow in the context of art therapy, where flow experiences and healing may intersect.

Although the full spectrum of flow's benefits has yet to be fully uncovered, it is essential to examine the factors that encourage and hinder the frequency and intensity of flow states. Researchers have investigated personality traits, qualities, and contextual factors such as family and school dynamics to understand these influences better. According to flow theory, children are more likely to enter flow when they perceive a balance between their abilities and task demands, can shield themselves from negative emotions like sadness and anger, and can protect themselves from distractions such as conversations with others or their own thoughts. A longitudinal study involving 8th graders found strong correlations between self-control and flow at both the beginning and end of the school year. Interestingly, self-control at the beginning of the year predicted flow at the end, while early flow did not predict later self-control (Kuhnle et al., 2012). Additionally, children aged 9–12 who placed a high value on their sports and believed they were skilled were more likely to experience flow in their sport (Drane & Barber, 2016). This connection between flow and confidence in athletic ability has been demonstrated in multiple sports (Jackman et al., 2020). In addition to self-control and confidence, personality may also affect how children approach challenging activities that have the potential for flow. Csikszentmihalyi (1990) proposed that individuals with an autotelic personality actively seek or create flow-inducing opportunities. These individuals are confident and secure to embrace challenges that result in self-actualization or discovering one's own potential.

Furthermore, Csikszentmihalyi expected that children raised in the emotional security of unconditional love would likely develop an autotelic personality. Csikszentmihalyi (1990) argued that the optimal family environment for youth to achieve flow is one of unconditional love. Feeling trust and security in their surroundings allows children to explore tasks that interest them without preoccupation. Unconditional love is the characteristic of authoritative or democratic parenting style. Such parents are warm, supportive, and encouraging while setting limits to foster self-control in their children. They scaffold children's experiences when facing challenges and offer positive experiences. On the other hand, strict parents who exert psychological control through manipulations, threats to remove affection, and invasions of privacy create an environment that is not conducive to flow. The threat of negative consequences and parental disapproval prevents children from exploring their own interests and taking on new challenges. Mesurado and de Minzi (2013) explored the associations of parenting and personality with flow experiences in a sample of 9- to 12-year-olds. They examined the dimensions of parental warmth and control and the personality traits that would be related to an autotelic personality: *extraversion* which includes being outgoing, self-assured, and loving challenges; *openness* that includes curiosity and imagination; and *conscientiousness* which encompasses self-control, organization, and an orientation towards achievement. In contrast, the personality trait of *neuroticism*, a tendency to experience negative states such as self-doubt, anxiety, and irritability, was expected to be negatively associated with flow. Mesurado and colleagues hypothesized that parenting would associate with flow by influencing the child's personality. Indeed, children with positive personality traits who also experienced their parents as accepting and moderately controlling reported greater flow. Conversely, children whose parents were pathologically controlling experienced more neuroticism, which in turn impeded the experience of flow. Thus, perceptions of parental control and acceptance either increased or decreased flow state depending on the child's personality. Interestingly, parental negligence directly hindered flow, without relating to personality first, but acceptance and moderate control had only indirect effects on flow.

Negative parenting, in the form of neglect or pathological control, is often indicative of dysfunction within the family, a type of childhood adversity. This raises the question of whether childhood adversity generally hinders flow experiences. On one hand, flow may protect children from the consequences of adversity. Non-clinical research shows that college students with multiple adverse experiences engaged in more creative pursuits like sports, playing music, cooking, and drawing, which were distinctive, immersive, enjoyable, transformative, and provided a sense of purpose (Thomson & Jaque, 2019). During flow, anxiety and sadness dissipate, and self-perception becomes positive and self-validating. Studies involving children and adolescents (9–18 years) indicate that those with childhood adversity reported similar flow levels as their non-adversity counterparts. However, flow alone cannot safeguard the well-being of youth with a history of adversity as these students used less effective coping strategies compared to those with lower adversity (Thomson & Jaque, 2016). Lastly, limited evidence from a qualitative study suggests that young children (7–11) may experience flow through art therapy, a potentially promising area for future research (Lee, 2015).

Other contextual factors have been hypothesized as hindering flow but remain subject to research exploration. Perry (2009b) uses the term *antiflow* to describe all experiences that make it hard for children to concentrate and enter a zone of absorption and creativity. Antiflow results from fragmented school days with short class segments that do not allow children to concentrate. Rathunde (2015) argues that the education system should encourage opportunities for children to avoid distractions, boring and repetitive work, and constant interruptions in the classroom. He identifies the Montessori method as one approach to creating conditions for children to achieve deep concentration or flow. This method provides activities that are intrinsically motivating so that students become immersed in them and pay little to no attention to their surroundings. Antiflow originates from offering unnecessary rewards for activities that are intrinsically motivating, thus preventing children from exploring their interests. Rathunde also suggests that teachers and parents should experience flow themselves to better facilitate it in their students and children. Those with flow experiences can appreciate the value of intrinsically rewarding experiences over extrinsic outcomes, such as grades. Adults who experience flow are more likely to recognize and protect children's deep concentration by providing appropriate time and space. Teachers and parents who engage in meaningful activities, discovering their potential and achieving self-actualization, can better support children's personal growth through recurrent flow experiences.

In summary, flow is a positive experience potentially linked to children's well-being and personal growth. It is associated with higher self-esteem, increased engagement, better self-control, and improved mood. Flow experiences in sports show promising outcomes, but limited evidence connects flow to increased happiness or greater accomplishments in children. Research on flow in younger children is scarce, and exploring flow in art therapy could provide valuable insights for enhancing children's well-being. Flow states in children are influenced by various factors, including personality traits, self-control, confidence, family dynamics, and school environment. Balancing children's abilities with task demands, shielding from negative emotions, and protecting from distractions facilitate flow states. Self-control and confidence, especially in sports, have strong correlations with flow experiences in children. Autotelic personalities, characterized by a willingness to embrace challenges for the sake of learning, tend to actively seek or create flow-inducing opportunities. An optimal family environment for achieving flow is characterized by parental unconditional love, warmth, support, and adaptive control. Antiflow, which hinders children's concentration and immersion in activities, can arise from fragmented school days, constant interruptions, and unnecessary extrinsic rewards for intrinsically motivating tasks. Childhood adversity does not necessarily hinder flow experiences, but flow alone cannot safeguard the well-being of youth with a history of adversity. Teachers and parents who experience flow themselves are better equipped to facilitate and protect flow experiences in children, fostering personal growth and self-actualization.

Flow: Discoverable and Teachable

Although research on flow experiences in young children remains limited, there is a widespread belief that flow is a universal human experience. The extent to which flow is discovered spontaneously or taught depends largely on how we define and measure it. Applying Csikszentmihalyi's (1990) nine criteria to identify a flow in very young children presents challenges and may constrain our understanding of their flow states and the role these states play in their well-being. Children may experience early precursors of flow that later become more consolidated and recognizable as they grow more aware of their mental states and the connections between their thoughts and emotions. At this point, seeking flow may become a deliberate pursuit, strongly linked to subjective well-being. In other words, children can recognize the benefits of flow and use it to enhance their happiness and success.

In the first vignette, little Sophia focused her attention, controlled her eye and hand movements, and gained self-confidence while discovering the new skill of flipping pages. Time passed although she did not understand the concept of time. Her mother did not intentionally teach her flow, yet Sophia discovered it on her own. Throughout her childhood and adolescence, Sophia pursued her interests in reading, writing, and art. To her parents' surprise, she pursued a science major in college but took courses in cinematography, dance, and piano for the sake of learning. Her parents did not explicitly teach flow but have unknowingly modeled flow experiences and encouraged the pursuit of intrinsically rewarding activities and the development of characteristics of an autotelic personality.

Explicitly teaching children about flow experiences may have benefits, and future research will provide more insights. But we can identify some general guidelines to help parents and teachers recognize these experiences, protect them, and help children identify their benefits. As discussed earlier, children in flow seem deeply engaged with the activity and appear as if they temporarily lost touch with their surroundings. They may forget to drink water or struggle to answer a parent's questions due to their intense concentration. The activities and experiences that allow for flow depend on the child's age. Babies extensively observe visual stimuli or touch objects and body parts while in flow, like when playing with their toes and hands or observing a shadow (Perry, 2009a). Toddlers, preschoolers, and school-age children may find flow in more hands-on activities like putting a puzzle together, drawing, cooking, or doing craft projects. These activities require concentration, challenge the child, and offer opportunities for gradual mastery. Research indicates that children and adolescents can find flow in music and sports. In these contexts, parents and teachers can foster flow experiences by creating tasks that interest the child, present achievable challenges, promote autonomy, and align with the child's personal goals (Shernoff et al., 2014). Children's own characteristics may further enhance flow experiences, but a warm and safe environment that supports self-control and exploration is crucial. Parents and teachers should encourage children to engage in activities that match their abilities with task demands and cultivate confidence in their skills. Adults may nurture positive personality traits such as extraversion, openness, and conscientiousness, which are associated with autotelic personalities and flow experiences, and minimize neuroticism by providing a supportive and secure environment. Parents and teachers can be more attentive to and respectful of their child's concentration by allowing them to complete activities without interruptions. Adults can also pinpoint instances where the children are so absorbed in an activity that they miss calls for their attention, emphasizing the enjoyment of the activity. Building this self-awareness may prompt children to seek out flow states more consciously. Finally, adults can share their own experiences with flow and discuss the rewards of discovering new things while in flow.

Flow can be experienced both in the presence of others and as a solitary state. However, as discussed in this chapter, children often view aloneness negatively. Solitary play in preschool is associated with cognitive but not social skills, and excessive solitary play during school age is linked to peer difficulties. Additionally, parents may be concerned if their children spend a significant amount of time alone. Nevertheless, parents should find reassurance in knowing that time spent alone in a flow state can be highly beneficial to their children's well-being. Therefore, parents should encourage a balance between social and solitary activities by allowing the children to engage in solitary activities that promote creativity, self-improvement, and emotional regulation but also ensure that they participate in social activities to develop social skills. Monitoring the type and quality of solitary activities is therefore important. Children should engage in constructive solitary activities, such as hobbies, homework, or interactive technology, rather than passive activities like watching TV. Parents need to be mindful of their children's social interactions. If children show a preference for solitude that is accompanied by social anxiety or peer rejection, parents need to intervene to provide support and guidance to help them navigate social situations. Parents may also foster a positive attitude towards solitude by helping children view solitude as an opportunity for growth and self-reflection, rather than associate it with loneliness or sadness. Parents may help children find solitary activities that are enjoyable and rewarding, such as those that induce a state of flow.

References

Akutsu, T. (2018). Observable flow experience in a two-year-old Japanese child's violin playing. *Music Education Research*, *20*(1), 126–140. https://doi.org/10.1080/14613808.2017.1409202

Ceci, M. W., & Kumar, V. K. (2016). A correlational study of creativity, happiness, motivation, and stress from creative pursuits. *Journal of Happiness Studies*, *17*(2), 609–626. https://doi.org/10.1007/s10902-015-9615-y

Coplan, R. J., Ooi, L. L., & Nocita, G. (2015). When one is company and two is a crowd: Why some children prefer solitude. *Child Development Perspectives*, *9*(3), 133–137. https://doi.org/10.1111/cdep.12131

Corsano, P., Grazia, V., & Molinari, L. (2019). Solitude and loneliness profiles in early adolescents: A person-centered approach. *Journal of Child and Family Studies*, *28*(12), 3374–3384. https://doi.org/10.1007/s10826-019-01518-1

Csikszentmihalyi, M. (1990). *Flow: The psychology of optimal experience*. Harper & Row.

Csikszentmihalyi, M., & Csikszentmihalyi, I. S. (Eds.). (1988). *Optimal experience: Psychological studies of flow in consciousness*. Cambridge University Press.

Csikszentmihalyi, M., & Larson, R. (2014). Validity and reliability of the experience-sampling method. In M. Csikszentmihalyi & R. Larson (Eds.), *Flow and the foundations of positive psychology* (pp. 35–54). Springer. https://doi.org/10.1007/978-94-017-9088-8_3

Custodero, L. A. (2005). Observable indicators of flow experience: A developmental perspective on musical engagement in young children from infancy to school age. *Music Education Research*, *7*(2), 185–209. https://doi.org/10.1080/14613800500169431

Daly, O., & Willoughby, T. (2020). A longitudinal person-centered examination of affinity for aloneness among children and adolescents. *Child Development*, *91*(6), 2001–2018. https://doi.org/10.1111/cdev.13411

Drane, C. F., & Barber, B. L. (2016). Who gets more out of sport? The role of value and perceived ability in flow and identity-related experiences in adolescent sport. *Applied Developmental Science*, *20*(4), 267–277. https://doi.org/10.1080/10888691.2015.1114889

Galanaki, E. (2004). Are children able to distinguish among the concepts of aloneness, loneliness, and solitude? *International Journal of Behavioral Development*, *28*(5), 435–443. https://doi.org/10.1080/01650250444000153

Galanaki, E. P. (2013). Solitude in children and adolescents: A review of the research literature. *Psychology and Education–An Interdisciplinary Journal*, *50*(3–4), 79–88. Retrieved May 3, 2023, from www.researchgate.net/profile/Laurie-Theeke-2/publication/286044814_Loneliness_in_school_age_Children_An_integrative_review_of_quantitative_studies/links/568fd5ec08aed0aed810bb31/Loneliness-in-school-age-Children-An-integrative-review-of-quantitative-studies.pdf#page=83

Hane, A. A., Cheah, C., Rubin, K. H., & Fox, N. A. (2008). The role of maternal behavior in the relation between shyness and social reticence in early childhood and social withdrawal in middle childhood. *Social Development*, *17*(4), 795–811. https://doi.org/10.1111/j.1467-9507.2008.00481.x

Hipson, W. E., Coplan, R. J., Dufour, M., Wood, K. R., & Bowker, J. C. (2021). Time alone well spent? A person-centered analysis of adolescents' solitary activities. *Social Development*, *30*(4), 1114–1130. https://doi.org/10.1111/sode.12518

Inal, Y., & Cagiltay, K. (2007). Flow experiences of children in an interactive social game environment. *British Journal of Educational Technology*, *38*(3), 455–464. https://doi.org/10.1111/j.1467-8535.2007.00709.x

Jackman, P. C., Dargue, E. J., Johnston, J. P., & Hawkins, R. M. (2020). Flow in youth sport, physical activity, and physical education: A systematic review. *Psychology of Sport and Exercise*, 101852. https://doi.org/10.1016/j.psychsport.2020.101852

Kuhnle, C., Hofer, M., & Kilian, B. (2012). Self-control as predictor of school grades, life balance, and flow in adolescents. *British Journal of Educational Psychology*, *82*(4), 533–548. https://doi.org/10.1111/j.2044-8279.2011.02042.x

Larson, R. W. (1990). The solitary side of life: An examination of the time people spent alone from childhood to old age. *Developmental Review*, *10*(2), 155–183. https://doi.org/10.1016/0273-2297(90)90008-R

Larson, R. W. (1997). The emergence of solitude as a constructive domain of experience in early adolescence. *Child Development*, *68*(1), 80–93. Retrieved May 3, 2023, from www.jstor.org/stable/1131927

Lee, S. Y. (2015). Flow indicators in art therapy: Artistic engagement of immigrant children with acculturation gaps. *Art Therapy*, *32*(3), 120–129. https://doi.org/10.1080/07421656.2015.1060836

Long, C. R., & Averill, J. R. (2003). Solitude: An exploration of benefits of being alone. *Journal for the Theory of Social Behaviour*, *33*(1), 21–44. https://doi.org/10.1111/1468-5914.00204

Mesurado, B., & de Minzi, M. C. R. (2013). Child's personality and perception of parental relationship as correlates of optimal experience. *Journal of Happiness Studies*, *14*(1), 199–214. https://doi.org/10.1007/s10902-012-9324-8

Morneau-Vaillancourt, G., Dionne, G., Brendgen, M., Vitaro, F., Feng, B., Henry, J., Forget-Dubois, N., Tremblay, R., & Boivin, M. (2019). The genetic and environmental etiology of shyness through childhood. *Behavior Genetics*, *49*(4), 376–385. https://doi.org/10.1007/s10519-019-09955-w

Ooi, L. L., Baldwin, D., Coplan, R. J., & Rose-Krasnor, L. (2018). Young children's preference for solitary play: Implications for socio-emotional and school adjustment. *British Journal of Developmental Psychology*, *36*(3), 501–507. https://doi.org/10.1111/bjdp.12236

Perry, S. (2009a, November 8). *Creative Kids learn to flow (part 2): Seven ways to teach flow*. Retrieved September 30, 2021, from www.psychologytoday.com/us/blog/creating-in-flow/200911/creative-kids-part-2-7-ways-teach-flow

Perry, S. (2009b, November 9). *Creative kids learn to flow (part 1)*. Retrieved September 30, 2021, from www.psychologytoday.com/us/blog/creating-in-flow/200911/creative-kids-learn-flow-part-1

Rathunde, K. (2015). Creating a context for flow: The importance of personal insight and experience. *NAMTA Journal*, *40*(3), 15–27. https://eric.ed.gov/?id=EJ1077078

Shernoff, D. J., Csikszentmihalyi, M., Schneider, B., & Shernoff, E. S. (2014). Student engagement in high school classrooms from the perspective of flow theory. In M. Csikszentmihalyi (Ed.), *Applications of flow in human development and education* (pp. 475–494). Springer. https://doi.org/10.1007/978-94-017-9094-9_24

Thomson, P., & Jaque, S. (2016). Achieving optimal flow in three activity-based groups regardless of early-childhood adversity. *American Journal of Play*, *8*(3), 345–361. Retrieved May 3, 2023, from https://files.eric.ed.gov/fulltext/EJ1108741.pdf

Thomson, P., & Jaque, S. V. (2019). History of childhood adversity and coping strategies: Positive flow and creative experiences. *Child Abuse & Neglect*, *90*, 185–192. https://doi.org/10.1016/j.chiabu.2018.12.019

Van Roekel, E., Scholte, R. H., Engels, R. C., Goossens, L., & Verhagen, M. (2015). Loneliness in the daily lives of adolescents: An experience sampling study examining the effects of social contexts. *The Journal of Early Adolescence*, *35*(7), 905–930. https://doi.org/10.1177/0272431614547049

Winnicott, D. W. (1958). The capacity to be alone. *The International Journal of Psychoanalysis*, *39*, 416–420.

4 Spirituality

> "One day one of my teachers at the Abbey asked me what I did on my free afternoons when I was alone. I told her I went behind my bed in an empty space which is there, and that it was easy to close myself in it with my bed curtain and that 'I thought.' 'But what do you think about?' she asked. 'I think about God, about life, about ETERNITY . . . I think!' . . . I understand now that I was making mental prayer without knowing it and that God was already instructing in secret."
>
> (Clarke, 2017, p. 74)
> Saint Therésé of Lisieux,
> around 10 years old

The rare instances of looking into the childhood of those who reached sainthood provide an insight into the spiritual life of children and raise questions about what psychological phenomena can be answered by research. The study of the lives of highly religious and spiritual individuals from different theological and philosophical traditions reveals a strong longing to connect with God at a very young age, a desire to act with piety, a need to act righteously, an overwhelming compassion for others, an enjoyment with being in nature, a higher intelligence, a love for reading, and a recognition by others that they were graced by a higher power (Clarke, 2017; Papadopoulos, 2009).

Currently, there is general acknowledgment that the capacity for spirituality is innate and universal. In the last 20 years, there has been a strong interest in the spiritual development of children and adolescents that stemmed from the recognition in the field of positive psychology that spirituality enhances the well-being of adults. Research has shown strong associations between spirituality and both positive (e.g., happiness) and negative (e.g., depression) indices of well-being in adults and adolescents. The research in younger children is less abundant, however. This chapter explores children's ability to ponder existential matters from an early age by examining theoretical perspectives as well as contemporary research on the manifestation of existential or spiritual intelligence in childhood. The chapter also examines research-supported relationships between spirituality and/or religiosity and personal happiness in children of different ages. Questions such as when children are more open to spiritual teachings, what aspect of spirituality is more

DOI: 10.4324/9780429356414-6

meaningful to children and adolescents, and how to nurture spirituality and mindfulness are also addressed.

Understanding Spirituality

As the attention to the study of spirituality increased in the last 20 years, the conceptualizations of spirituality constructs have varied. Historically, spirituality was synonymous with religion, but the two concepts are currently considered operationally different by most but not all scientists. Religiousness is seen as the relationship with an institutionalized faith tradition or organized religion and is expressed by participating in set practices, sacraments, and other rituals that support the connection with the transcendent (King & Boyatzis, 2015). A broadly accepted definition of spirituality is "the intrinsic human capacity for self-transcendence, in which the self is embedded in something greater than the self, including the sacred," and is "shaped both within and outside of religious traditions, beliefs, and practices," and drives the "search for connectedness, meaning, purpose, and contribution" (Benson et al., 2003, p. 205). The transcendent, the something bigger than the self, is identified in "Western traditions as God, Allah, HaShem, or a Higher Power, and in Eastern traditions as Brahman, manifestations of Brahman, Buddha, Dao, or ultimate truth/reality" (Koenig, 2012, p. 3). Researchers who view spirituality and religiousness as different from each other highlight that spirituality refers to an inner belief system that a person relies on for strength and comfort, whereas religiousness refers to institutional religious rituals, practices, and beliefs. The outward expression of religious worship and doctrine may or may not have a strong relationship to the transcendent and it may or may not further cultivate one's spiritual life. Religiousness can be viewed as a cognitive and/or behavioral expression of one's spirituality. For other researchers, the two concepts overlap or are synonymous because religion also includes beliefs about how to live life in relation to others and how to connect with the divine (Koenig, 2012).

In Piedmont's view (1999), spirituality, or spiritual transcendence, unlike religiousness, is a personality characteristic. It refers to the ability to separate the self from time and space and ponder life from a larger perspective, where the unity of the universe in the form of interconnections of all beings can be observed. This feeling of interconnectedness creates a sense of responsibility to others and commitment to their welfare (Piedmont, 1999). The main dimensions of spiritual transcendence are *prayer fulfillment*, a feeling of joy and contentment that results from personal encounters with a transcendent reality; *universality*, a belief in the unitive nature of life; and *connectedness*, a belief that one is part of a larger human reality that cuts across generations and groups of people. The view of spirituality as a personality trait is supported by evidence of the stability of these qualities in adolescence. Furthermore, it appears that spirituality emerges as an independent factor when related to other personality characteristics that reflect intrapersonal, interpersonal, and intellectual strengths (Kor et al., 2019).

Spirituality may also relate to existential intelligence, viewed by Gardner, the creator of the theory of multiple intelligences, as sensitivity and capacity to ponder deep questions about human existence, such as the meaning of life, why we die, how we get here, and what a person's relation to nature and others is (Gardner, 2000; Skrzypińska, 2021). Such inquiries may occur in philosophical dialogue, spiritual contemplation, or religious discourse (Hyde, 2008). The empirical evidence to validate existential intelligence as part of the theory of multiple intelligences is nonexistent. However, a related concept that has received more investigation is spiritual intelligence which reflects the mental capacity of contemplation of existential and metaphysical issues, the ability to find personal meaning and craft a life of purpose, transcendental awareness, and the ability to enter spiritual states of consciousness (e.g., meditation, prayer). Research shows that spiritual intelligence is independent of IQ but correlates with emotional intelligence (Skrzypińska, 2021).

Studies support that, in adults, there are strong correlations between spirituality and religiousness and that both relate to subjective and psychological well-being (e.g., lower depression). In a review of several adult studies where both religiousness and spirituality were considered, Koenig (2012) reported positive relationships with social support, optimism, greater self-esteem, and internal self-control. Inverse relationships were observed with depression and anxiety, suicide, psychoticism, neuroticism, and marital instability. Koenig (2012) explained that religiosity and spirituality provide resources for coping with stress, beliefs that give meaning to life and purpose, an optimistic point of view, satisfying answers to existential questions, positive appraisals of negative events, and rules about how to treat others. Spirituality and religiousness produce positive emotions, enhance love and compassion, and promote human virtues of honesty, forgiveness, gratefulness, patience, and dependability all of which promote the quality of social relationships.

Spiritual Development

Considering spirituality as a form of intelligence or personality trait implies that there would be individual differences in the level of spirituality among children as well as in their spiritual development, much like one observes individual differences in intellectual talents and behavioral styles. But, how exactly spirituality develops is not clear in the literature. While some theorists expect a stage-like development that reflects Piaget's stages of cognitive development (i.e., moving from concrete to abstract understandings of spiritual subjects), others consider spiritual development as a transactional process between children and multiple contexts. In other words, spirituality develops through the child's experiences in the family, school, and religious communities. What exactly develops is also understudied. One idea is that spiritual development is the path to developing an identity and beliefs that propel the individual to commit acts that benefit the self and others (King & Boyatzis, 2015). That is to say, spirituality develops as a dimension of self and is part of children's evolving self-concept. Examining the early manifestations of spirituality in children may shed some light on what develops and how.

In Hyde's 2008 review, a comprehensive summary of earlier studies exploring various facets of children's spirituality is provided. In one study, Heller (1988) examined 40 children from diverse religious backgrounds in middle childhood and found that they perceived God as a being who alleviated suffering and was associated with light that helped them feel positive about themselves. However, God was not seen by children as having total control over everything (i.e., God does not always cure things like cancer). Another study involving 6- to 13-year-olds discovered that children discussed God in the context of religious traditions and beliefs, but many of them were interested in supernatural concepts and the meaning of life outside of religious practices. This was true even for children with atheist or agnostic parents (Coles, 1991). Coles concluded that spirituality could extend beyond traditional religious practices and is a universal human trait, present in all individuals regardless of religious affiliation. Erricker and Erricker (1996) found that children's understanding of existential issues, such as loss and conflict, was influenced by their experiences. Some children reflected on existential questions in the context of materials and pleasures and others reflected on relationships and their importance. They suggested that grasping a child's life perspective can help better comprehend and nurture their spirituality. Hay and Nye (2006) also posited that children use religious language and ideas to make sense of their experiences, even without a religious affiliation. They found that children aged 6–11 exhibited unique spiritual expressions influenced by their personal lives, including references to the present (e.g., the experience of stillness), mystical ideas (e.g., questions about the universe), moral values (e.g., sense of goodness, or evil), and relationships with others including the transcendent.

Regarding expressions of spirituality, Champagne (2001) identified three modes of children's spirituality: sensitivity to the environment, relating to the environment, and experiencing life in time and space. Children demonstrate awareness of spirituality by attending to the here and now; expressing wonder, awe, and fascination; and by showing moral sensitivity (e.g., despair and delight reactions to evil and good). Hart (2003) identified five spiritual capacities in children that also serve as expressions of spirituality: wisdom (i.e., being open to the matters of heart and mind), wonder/awe (i.e., experiencing a deep sense of joy), relationship with one's self and the other (i.e., capacity to care about others and nature), seeing the invisible (i.e., experience aspects of the multidimensional and mysterious universe), and pondering life's ultimate questions of life. Similarly, Scott (2004) examined retrospective stories of spiritual experiences in childhood and identified the themes of death, mortality, visions, and connections beyond oneself.

In sum, the development of spirituality in children is not clearly understood; whether it follows a stage-like development or is a transactional process or a path towards forming an identity and beliefs that are oriented towards others remains a subject of future investigation. Nonetheless, the review reveals that children are interested in spiritual matters and understand spirituality in a rich but very individual way. Their understanding as well as the expression of their spirituality seem to be influenced by their own experiences. The patterns of spiritual understanding and experiences found in the literature align with Fisher's (1998) four domains of spirituality. The *personal* domain is reflected in the meaning, purpose, and values in life. The *communal* domain reflects the quality of the relationship with others, including attitudes of love, hope, and justice. The *environmental* domain deals with the relationship with the world, including feelings of awe, wonder, and unity with the physical world. The *transcendental* domain refers to the relation with a transcendent entity, which is bigger than the physical and biological world, and includes feeling adoration and having faith in this reality beyond the human level. Fisher considered that these four domains determine the child's spiritual entity.

These patterns are also observed in adolescence, which is an important period for developing spiritual beliefs. Because adolescents are capable of abstract thought, have stronger metacognitive skills, and are in search of identity formation, they are specifically open to exploring their spiritual dimension. Findings from a global survey of spiritual experiences of over 6,000 adolescents and young adults (12–25 years old) from eight countries revealed that 77% of them had a religious affiliation. The majority of the participants reported that following or being close to God or a higher power and communicating through prayer and meditation were very important life goals (Benson et al., 2012). Moreover, based on the participant's responses, the researchers recognized two types of processes that underpin spiritual development. *Psychological* processes referred to making connections with others through prosocial acts (e.g., protecting the environment as all life is interconnected), discerning meaning and purpose, discovering mindfulness (i.e., focusing on the present), and allowing beliefs to guide actions. *Engagement* processes involved connecting with God, having experiences with the transcendent, and performing religious and spiritual practices (Benson et al., 2012). It therefore seems that adolescents' experiences too fall within Fisher's four domains of spirituality. More developmental research is needed to examine the four domains of spirituality and the psychological and engagement manifestations of spirituality in younger children. Future research may also investigate individual differences in children's spirituality in response to genetic and environmental influences.

Spirituality, Religiousness, and Subjective Well-Being

The benefits of spirituality and religiousness can be found in a wide range of indices of well-being among adults, older children, and adolescents. As previously mentioned, spirituality and religiosity foster a sense of community, combat feelings of loneliness, reduce stress, enhance coping mechanisms, and offer a sense of coherence and purpose in life. These factors collectively contribute to a sense of fulfillment and promote improved physical well-being. Not surprisingly, spirituality protects from negative psychological outcomes such as depression and anxiety and contributes to happiness and life satisfaction. The benefits of spirituality and religiousness have been shown in at-risk as well as typically developing populations (King & Boyatzis, 2015). And while the results are universally positive in adults and adolescents, for younger children it seems that different aspects of spirituality relate to well-being in a more nuanced way. In addition, most studies are correlational, and they demonstrate associations between spirituality and subjective well-being variables or moderating effects of spirituality. However, some intervention studies show improvements in subjective well-being as a result of spiritual experiences, such as prayer or meditation.

The most comprehensive study about the benefits of spirituality and religiousness on well-being was conducted by Holder et al. (2010). The study relied on multiple methods and informants thus rendering the findings more reliable. Children 8–12 years of age completed questionnaires about religious practices and beliefs, spirituality, and happiness, while parents also provided assessments of happiness. More specifically, spirituality was measured by the Spiritual Well-Being Questionnaire (SWBQ, Gomez & Fisher, 2003) which assesses the four dimensions of spirituality discussed earlier: personal focuses on one's search for meaning and purpose in life; communal which focuses on relationships with others; environmental that taps on connections with nature; and transcendental that gauges the relationship with a higher power or the Divine. Religiousness was measured with the Practices and Beliefs Scale (PBS; Holder et al., 2010) which assesses practicing religion, beliefs in a higher power, the role of spirituality in coping, the extent to which one depends on religion and an overall perception of how religious or spiritual one is. Happiness was assessed by two questionnaires and the Faces Scales, where children and parents chose the face that best depicted their feelings, ranging from very happy to very unhappy. The results revealed that the domains of spirituality and the total score from the PBS were significantly and positively correlated with happiness scores (Faces Scales and questionnaires) with a few exceptions. The correlations between the transcendental domain and the self-reports of happiness were not significant and the PBS was only correlated to the Faces Scale rating provided by children. Lastly, there were no significant associations between the frequency of practicing religion and any of the four measures of happiness. Subsequent regression analyses showed that combined spirituality and religiousness accounted for 5% to 27% of the variance depending on the happiness measure that was used. However, the personal and communal domains were the only significant predictors. The environmental and transcendental domains, and the PBS did not significantly predict children's happiness. Similar results were revealed when the regression analyses were performed while accounting for the effects of demographic variables and personality. The personal and communal domains were consistently significant predictors, with each explaining a range of 4% to 5% of the variance. The contribution of PBS was either nonsignificant or small (less than 1%) and limited to one index of happiness. The environmental domain did not predict any of the happiness measures and the transcendental domain was a weak predictor of only one assessment of happiness. Lastly, neither spirituality nor religiousness predicted the happy face rating provided by the parents.

Altogether the findings suggest that aspects of spirituality and religiosity may relate differently to happiness. Children of this age who have a sense of identity, love for life, and sense of meaning in life (personal domain), as well as children who are oriented towards others and exhibit respect, trust, and forgiveness (communal domain), tend to be happier. The idea that relationships are expressions of spirituality supports the concept of "relational" spirituality in children at this age period (King & Boyatzis, 2015). Sawatzky et al. (2009) further provide evidence for a stronger link between the personal dimension of spirituality and subjective well-being by examining specific spiritual beliefs and their relationship with the quality of life among adolescents. In their study, 8,225 participants from grades 7 to 12 (average age = 15) were included. Spiritual attitudes accounted for 26% of the variance in perceived mental health and 13% of perceived physical health status. Spiritual beliefs such as, "I believe there is some real purpose for my life" were significantly associated with satisfaction in various life domains, including family, school, living environment, friends, self, and overall quality of life.

The lack of association between the environmental domain and happiness is intriguing as most children love to be outdoors. In a follow-up study, Holder and colleagues addressed this question in a sample of children (7–12 years old) and adolescents (13–19 years old) from Zambia who spend a lot of time in nature and attend church frequently. They used a measure of spirituality that primarily reflected the environmental domain. The relationship between happiness and environmental spirituality was reported in the order group only. Spirituality was also consistently correlated with self-reported life satisfaction in both age groups (Holder et al., 2016). Possibly, by fostering a deeper connection between children and nature through increased time spent outdoors and cultivating appreciation, the link between environmental transcendence and happiness might be strengthened in younger children as well.

Another insight as to how the four domains of spirituality are relevant to perceived well-being comes from Michaelson et al. (2019) who enlisted over 28,000 children ages 11 to 15 years from Canada, England, and Scotland and asked them to report their spirituality and health complaints (e.g., headaches, feeling low). The results revealed that all four domains related to health complaints, but there were also interconnections between the domains that created different pathways to health complaints. Specifically, the personal domain acted as a mediator between each one of the remaining three domains ("others," "nature," and the "transcendent") and health complaints. It appears that experiencing spirituality with others, nature, and the transcendent enhances the sense of meaning and purpose in life which in turn protects well-being at least in the form of reducing physical and mental health problems. Lastly, Schnitker et al. (2017) reported a connection between transcendent spirituality and well-being via the development of patience. Combining ideas from theology and psychology, Schnitker et al. (2017) conceptualized patience as a virtue that integrates emotion regulation and a narrative identity that views suffering as having a purpose. They proposed a path in which transcendent spirituality and religiousness predicted patience and adaptive coping which in turn predicted well-being. Using a sample of 406 adolescents (ages 13–18 years), they found a direct link between religion/spirituality, happiness, and life satisfaction as well as behavior regulation. The hypothesized indirect paths were also significant. Religious commitment and spirituality correlated with patience and cognitive reappraisal, an adaptive form of coping, which in turn significantly predicted subjective well-being.

The preceding results point out that the personal and communal domains of spirituality consistently relate to happiness in older children and that all domains connect to happiness by adolescence. In addition, the literature is just beginning to unravel the complexity of the relationships between the domains of spirituality and possible mediators that explain the benefits that we observe in subjective well-being. Two questions arise from the preceding discussion. What is the direction of the relationship between spirituality/religiousness and happiness? And what is the relative importance of spirituality versus religiousness? The cross-sectional and correlational nature of the aforementioned studies makes it impossible to decipher the direction of the relationship between spirituality and well-being. Are happy children more likely to explore spirituality, or are spiritual children more likely to report happiness? In response to this question, Kor et al. (2019) conducted a longitudinal study to investigate the contribution of spirituality to positive psychological functioning of adolescents (13–17 years old) over 14 months. The researchers used several scales to capture attitudes toward faith, devotion, practice, and transcendence. Spirituality was stable over time and correlated with subjective well-being and prosocial orientation, at all times of measurement. Moreover, adolescents who showed growth in spirituality also reported increased positive affect, and life satisfaction during the 14 months. The inverse pattern was true for those who reported decreased spirituality over time; decreased spirituality predicted lower positive affect and life satisfaction. Such findings suggest that interventions to increase spirituality are worth pursuing as they are likely to have a longitudinal effect.

Whether religiousness or spirituality is a better predictor of well-being is not clear in the literature. Unlike the American sample where religiousness did not predict happiness (Holder et al., 2016), the Zambian adolescents' religiousness, indexed by attendance to church, made a small contribution to positive affect although not to life satisfaction. Additionally, results from a sample of Iranian adolescents (mean age = 16 years), showed a correlation between religious attitudes and happiness, with religious attitudes (e.g., believing in God and practicing the religion) accounting for only 2% of the variance in happiness (Fariddanesh & Rezaei, 2019). On the other hand, a longitudinal study with Portuguese adolescents aged 15 to 19 demonstrated the higher predictive power of spirituality. While religious practice had a weak association with life satisfaction, spirituality was a strong predictor of life satisfaction both concurrently and over time. Spirituality remained stable throughout the study, with initial spirituality scores predicting life satisfaction after a year, even when controlling for initial life satisfaction levels. The study also revealed no significant changes in spirituality, religious practice, or life satisfaction during the study period (Marques et al., 2013).

Krok (2018) offers evidence that helps elucidate the relationship between religiosity and well-being by distinguishing various aspects of religiosity. Adolescents aged 15–20 who held affirmative attitudes, meaning high scores in religiosity and orthodoxy, and low scores in relativism, reported higher levels of life satisfaction. Conversely, adolescents with high scores in relativism and less centrality of religiosity in their lives experienced lower life satisfaction. Additionally, Schnitker et al. (2017) found that commitment to religious practices, such as prayer, meditation, and fasting, predicted life satisfaction and positive affect. Kim et al. (2013) explored this question in a sample of 174 Korean American adolescents, aged 11.6 to 19.2, attending Catholic schools. The results showed a positive link between life satisfaction and both religious and spiritual dimensions in this sample. Life satisfaction was predicted by daily spiritual experiences (e.g., feeling God's presence), forgiveness (e.g., having forgiven oneself and others), as well as having congregational support (e.g., people in one's congregation helping one). The current review indicates that spirituality may be a bigger predictor of well-being than religiousness. However, in cultures or communities where religiousness is emphasized, or religiousness and spirituality are not strongly distinguished the predictive value of religiousness and spirituality may not be discernible.

Mindfulness as a Spiritual Experience

Another way that children may experience spirituality, especially in school settings, is through the practice of mindfulness, which is a significant contributor to the psychological well-being of adults and children (Benson et al., 2012). Mindfulness is defined as purposefully paying attention to the present moment in an accepting and non-judgmental manner. When the mind wonders or when uninvited thoughts, feelings, or emotions cross awareness, the person gently acknowledges their mental state, without passing any judgment, and regains focus on the present (Kabat-Zinn, 2001). Mindfulness cultivates an awareness of moments in life that promote positive emotions such as gratitude and hope and supports positive thinking through journal writing or daily spiritual exercises. Mindfulness increases connectivity with others, develops a sense of awe at the realization of the vastness of the universe and the smallness of human beings, creates an altered state of consciousness, and builds on one's personal sense of purpose. All of these are spiritual experiences. Mindfulness is commonly achieved through the practice of meditation during which the person maintains stillness while focusing on one element such as breathing or imagery. Meditation is considered a secular method to approach transcendence but can be found in different theological traditions. For example, prayer provides an opportunity to engage in a meditative act. Although meditation is a solitary activity as one spends time with their own mind, it often takes place under the guidance of a coach and in the presence of other people, who often share their experiences at the end of the meditation session.

Practicing mindfulness is linked with the psychological well-being of children and adolescents particularly in intervention studies where mindfulness-based programs were implemented in school settings. Mindfulness programs typically build awareness of inner experiences like breathing as well as thoughts and emotions. Children may engage in mindful listening, seeing, tasting, smelling, and moving. Programs may also promote perspective-taking and empathy and include lessons in gratitude, kindness, and optimism. Yoga postures and walking meditations may also be included (Jackman, 2020). Examples of such programs are Mindful Schools (2014), the Inner Resilience Program (Lantieri & Goleman, 2008), and MindUp (Hawn Foundation, 2011; Cobb et al., 2016). Studies reveal benefits across several areas of development. Mindfulness improves cognitive functioning and attentional abilities in children as young as 6 years of age (Emerson et al., 2017). After 16 weeks of the Learn to Breathe program (Broderick, 2021), 11th graders showed improvements in performance-based measures of executive function (Frank et al.,

2021). A meta-analysis of 21 studies involving children from ages 3 to 12 years showed that mindfulness-based interventions reduced inattention and hyperactivity-impulsivity, as reported by teachers but not as reported by parents and children. Therefore, the benefits of the programs are more readily seen in a school setting than at home (Vekety et al., 2021).

School interventions of mindfulness also increase social-emotional awareness, decrease emotional reactivity, and assist in controlling rumination and intrusive thoughts that disrupt behavior (Cobb et al., 2016). A meta-analysis of experimental and quasi-experimental studies with anxious children (5–18 years) from multiple countries supported a significant moderate reduction in anxiety (Borquist-Conlon et al., 2019). Similar results were reported with non-clinical samples. For example, in addition to anxiety, the Learn to Breathe program reduced stress, depression, and substance abuse among 11th graders (Frank et al., 2021). After an eight-week mindfulness intervention in a group of 7- to 8-year-olds, there was a reduction in internalizing problems compared to a control group although the decline in depression was only supported by teachers' reports and not children's (Crescentini et al., 2016). A review of previous comprehensive evaluations (e.g., review papers and meta-analytic studies) of the effectiveness of mindful-based interventions in education revealed a reduction in symptoms of psychopathology (e.g., internalizing and externalizing problems) and confirmed the improvement in cognitive functioning and educational outcomes (Schutt & Felver, 2020).

The effect of mindfulness on subjective well-being, especially in young children is understudied. Some evidence suggests no change in life satisfaction of 6- to 7-year-old children throughout a four-week program that emphasized awareness of behaviors, thoughts, and emotions, related to the self, others, and the surroundings (Emerson et al., 2017). In contrast, another study demonstrated that the age-related growth in the ability to become aware of distressing mental states without judgment and reaction was accompanied by a reduction in negative affect and an increase in positive affect, during the transition from middle school to high school (Galla et al., 2020). These findings imply that perhaps the connection between mindfulness, happiness, and life satisfaction solidifies in middle childhood. The current literature provides enough data to support the general benefit of mindfulness interventions, particularly in the school setting. The current research, however, is not without limitations. Not all studies utilize control groups, and not all rely on multiple informants. Moreover, it is unknown how long-lasting the effects are. Lastly, research with young children is particularly challenging because the current measures of mindfulness are self-reports suitable for children older than 9 (Eklund et al., 2017), although attempts for age-appropriate adaptations have been made by researchers (e.g., Emerson et al., 2017).

Raising Spiritual and Mindful Children

Because the dimensions of personal and communal spirituality have a more evident connection with the subjective well-being of children, it is crucial to examine the role of the family context in spiritual development, as family relationships are the initial experiences children encounter. Fowler's theory of faith development claims that the roots of faith are in early attachment where the infant has the opportunity to experience trust in others for the first time (Fowler, 1981). Miller (2016) considers parents as "spiritual ambassadors" (p. 90) because they are the ones who introduce the child to the transcended life. The child who experiences unconditional love from the parent also experiences unconditional love from the transcendent. Miller cites evidence that children and adolescents assign to God the attributes of their parents. An unconditionally loving and reliable parent is associated with a strongly felt sense of an always-present, accepting, and loving God. In contrast, when the relationship with the parent is negative, the child views God as punitive, and uncaring. Miller believes that this correspondence between God and parents in the minds of children is the foundation of further spiritual development. The family provides a "field of love: a place to learn spirituality in daily life" (p. 137). Furthermore, Miller notes that the shared spirituality between the caregiver and the child is a major protective factor against depression. In Miller's studies, when mothers and children were similar in their spirituality, the incidence of depression in the family was cut by 80% and by 90% when spirituality was shared among three generations. For children, shared spirituality was three to seven times more protective than any medical and psychosocial factor and four times more protective than demographic factors such as higher education and socioeconomic status. Similar outcomes were reported in Asia and the Middle East across different religions (Miller, 2016). Additional research studies support Miller's findings regarding the protective influence of parental spirituality. For example, preschoolers, whose parents frequently attend religious services and engage in discussions about religious and spiritual matters, tend to have better self-control and fewer externalizing problems (Bartkowski et al., 2008). Moreover, Wu et al. (2020) demonstrated that similarity in spirituality between partners directly predicted their adolescents' life satisfaction.

Raising spirituality through religious education is advocated by several religions. Such education may begin early as even young children may question existential matters. Many religions also believe that children are open to embrace spirituality at a young age. In her memoir, *Story of a Soul*, Saint Therésé of Lisieux discusses how little children are soft as wax and therefore, virtues can be easily imprinted on them (Clarke, 2017). In Christianity, children are considered spiritual beings with open hearts and minds to receive God. In Judaism, childhood is considered the purest human form of God's Image and the time of utmost potential for goodness (Ingall, 2006). In Islam, the child has purity and needs to be set on the right path through religious education (Osman, 2005). In Hinduism, children are considered to have an innate connection to spirituality, and it is the responsibility of parents and the community to nurture that connection (Mittal & Thursby, 2004).

Regardless of religious tradition, several recommendations about raising spiritual children can be made based on the research presented earlier. Parents should strive to create a secure, supportive, and affectionate environment that reflects unconditional love and act as spiritual role models. Parents who see their children as full of goodness are more likely to be patient and forgiving with them.

Engaging in spiritual activities, such as prayer, meditation, or attending religious services, as a family strengthens spiritual bonds and creates shared spiritual experiences. Parents who provide membership to spiritual communities validate the child's self-concept or identity as a spiritual being. Parents should live out the spiritual and moral values of gratitude, kindness, respect, courage, and compassion and encourage their children to practice these values in their daily lives to develop a strong spiritual foundation. These expressed values towards others increase the meaning of life, and enhance happiness (Holder et al., 2010). Encouraging open discussions about spirituality can help children develop a deeper understanding of their spirituality and its importance in their lives. Parents should take advantage of children's existential questions such as why there is suffering, why bad things happen to good people, and what happens after death, to introduce spiritual/religious answers and instigate further conversation. Such discussions may begin in the preschool and parents should provide honest answers at the level of their child. Children who learn that asking stressful questions is taken seriously are more likely to trust the parents and engage them in such discussions again and again as they develop and even when they begin to question parental beliefs and attitudes. Children and adolescents do not have to agree with their parents, but the parents should support the spiritual journeys of their children. Lastly, encouraging human connections and experiences for self-growth instead of materialist values and behaviors promotes the child's personal and communal dimensions of their spirituality (Miller, 2016).

There is hesitancy in bringing spirituality-enhancing interventions in schools because spirituality is often connected with a practice of a particular religion or tradition. However, Miller and others argue that spirituality can be integrated into education by making spirituality part of the school culture, a culture that focuses on how one treats the other. Children may be encouraged to use language that supports love and respect for each other; for example, saying, "I love you." Other activities that drive out spirituality are connecting with nature and experiencing transitions from a state of stillness to motion. Children may collectively share transcendent experiences such as dancing, singing, reading, art, and group meditation (Miller, 2016; Young, 2020).

As noted earlier in the chapter, practicing mindfulness is a form of secular spirituality and has found its way into schools as part of an effort to enhance the academic performance and social-emotional well-being of children. The evidence that exists may encourage not only schools but also parents to intentionally nurture their children's spiritual living through mindfulness experiences. Parents may encourage children to engage in mindful listening, seeing, tasting, smelling, and moving. Incorporating yoga postures and walking meditations further enhances the practice of mindfulness. Practicing meditation at home would help children connect with themselves at a deeper level and promote a sense of autonomy and self-control. Joint activities, outside the context of practicing mindfulness, that inspire awe in nature or creation may enhance the children's connection with the environment and others. Parents may capitalize on children's plentiful love for people and animals. Taking time to appreciate natural beauty and discuss existential concerns with children would nurture the children's personal connection with the environment and the transcendent.

References

Bartkowski, J. P., Xu, X., & Levin, M. L. (2008). Religion and child development: Evidence from the early childhood longitudinal study. *Social Science Research*, *37*(1), 18–36. https://doi.org/10.1016/j.ssresearch.2007.02.001

Benson, P. L., Roehlkepartain, E. C., & Rude, S. P. (2003). Spiritual development in childhood and adolescence: Toward a field of inquiry. *Applied Developmental Science*, *7*(3), 205–213. https://doi.org/10.1207/S1532480XADS0703_12

Benson, P. L., Scales, P. C., Syvertsen, A. K., & Roehlkepartain, E. C. (2012). Is youth spiritual development a universal developmental process? An international exploration. *The Journal of Positive Psychology*, *7*(6), 453–470. https://doi.org/10.1080/17439760.2012.732102

Borquist-Conlon, D. S., Maynard, B. R., Brendel, K. E., & Farina, A. S. (2019). Mindfulness-based interventions for youth with anxiety: A systematic review and meta-analysis. *Research on Social Work Practice*, *29*(2), 195–205. https://doi.org/10.1177/1049731516684961

Broderick, P. C. (2021). *Learning to breathe: A mindfulness curriculum for adolescents to cultivate emotion regulation, attention, and performance*. New Harbinger Publications.

Champagne, E. (2001). Listening to . . . listening for . . . : A theological reflection on spirituality in early childhood. In J. Erricker, C. Ota, & C. Erricker (Eds.), *Spiritual education: Cultural religious and social differences* (pp. 76–87). Sussex Academic.

Clarke, J. (2017). *Story of a soul: The autobiography of Saint Thérèse of Lisieux*. ICS Publications. (Original work published 1996)

Cobb, E. F., McClintock, C. H., & Miller, L. J. (2016). Mindfulness and spirituality in positive youth development. In I. Ivtzan & T. Lomas (Eds.), *Mindfulness in positive psychology: The science of meditation and wellbeing* (pp. 245–264). Routledge.

Coles, R. (1991). *The spiritual life of children*. Houghton Mifflin.

Crescentini, C., Capurso, V., Furlan, S., & Fabbro, F. (2016). Mindfulness-oriented meditation for primary school children: Effects on attention and psychological well-being. *Frontiers in Psychology*, *7*, 805. https://doi.org/10.3389/fpsyg.2016.00805

Eklund, K., O'Malley, M., & Meyer, L. (2017). Gauging mindfulness in children and youth: School-based applications. *Psychology in the Schools*, *54*(1), 101–114. https://doi.org/10.1002/pits.21983

Emerson, L. M., Rowse, G., & Sills, J. (2017). Developing a mindfulness-based program for infant schools: Feasibility, acceptability, and initial effects. *Journal of Research in Childhood Education*, *31*(4), 465–477. https://doi.org/10.1080/02568543.2017.1343211

Erricker, C., & Erricker, J. (1996). Where angels fear to tread: Discovering children's spirituality. In R. Best (Ed.), *Education, spirituality, and the whole child*, (pp. 184–195). Cassell.

Fariddanesh, M., & Rezaei, A. M. (2019). Predicting the happiness of adolescents based on coping styles and religious attitudes. *Journal of Religion and Health*, *58*(2), 537–553. https://doi.org/10.1007/s10943-017-0497-7

Fisher, J. W. (1998). *Spiritual health: Its nature, and place in the school curriculum* [Unpublished doctoral dissertation, The University of Melbourne].

Fowler, J. W. (1981). *Stages of faith: The psychology of human development and the quest for meaning*. Harper One.

Frank, J. L., Broderick, P. C., Oh, Y., Mitra, J., Kohler, K., Schussler, D. L., Geier, C., Roeser, R. W., Berrena, E., Mahfouz, J., Levitan, J., & Greenberg, M. T. (2021). The effectiveness of a teacher-delivered mindfulness-based curriculum on adolescent social-emotional and executive functioning. *Mindfulness, 12*(5), 1234–1251. https://doi.org/10.1007/s12671-021-01594-9

Galla, B. M., Tsukayama, E., Park, D., Yu, A., & Duckworth, A. L. (2020). The mindful adolescent: Developmental changes in nonreactivity to inner experiences and its association with emotional well-being. *Developmental Psychology, 56*(2), 350–363. https://doi.org/10.1037/dev0000877

Gardner, H. E. (2000). *Intelligence reframed: Multiple intelligences for the 21st century*. Hachette.

Gomez, R., & Fisher, J. W. (2003). Domains of spiritual well-being and development and validation of the spiritual well-being questionnaire. *Personality and Individual Differences, 35*(8), 1975–1991. https://doi.org/10.1016/S0191-8869(03)00045-X

Hart, T. (2003). *The secret spiritual world of children*. Inner Ocean.

Hawn Foundation. (2011). *The MindUp curriculum: Grades 6–8: Brain-focused strategies for learning and living*. Scholastic Teaching Resources. https://mindup.org/mindup-program/

Hay, D., & Nye, R. (2006). *The spirit of the child*. Jessica Kingsley Publishers.

Heller, D. (1988). *The children's god*. University of Chicago Press.

Holder, M. D., Coleman, B., Krupa, T., & Krupa, E. (2016). Well-being's relation to religiosity and spirituality in children and adolescents in Zambia. *Journal of Happiness Studies, 17*(3), 1235–1253. https://doi.org/10.1007/s10902-015-9640-x

Holder, M. D., Coleman, B., & Wallace, J. M. (2010). Spirituality, religiousness, and happiness in children aged 8–12 years. *Journal of Happiness Studies, 11*(2), 131–150. https://doi.org/10.1007/s10902-008-9126-1

Hyde, B. (2008). *Children and spirituality: Searching for meaning and connectedness*. Jessica Kingsley Publishers.

Ingall, C. K. (2006). The Jewish day school in America: A new history. *Jewish Education, 74*(1), 1–33. https://doi.org/10.1080/00216244.2006.10896127

Jackman, M. M. (2020). Teaching mindfulness to children. In N. N. Singh & S. D. S. Joy (Eds.), *Mindfulness-based interventions with children and adolescents* (pp. 141–161). Routledge.

Kabat-Zinn, J. (2001). *Mindfulness meditation for everyday life*. Piatkus Books. Retrieved May 4, 2023, from http://realestateconsultingservice.com/wp-content/uploads/2018/03/97291641-Mindfulness-Meditation-for-Everyday-Life-Kabat-Zinn-Jon.pdf

Kim, S., Miles-Mason, E., Kim, C. Y., & Esquivel, G. B. (2013). Religiosity/spirituality and life satisfaction in Korean American adolescents. *Psychology of Religion and Spirituality, 5*(1), 33–40. https://doi.org/10.1037/a0030628

King, P. E., & Boyatzis, C. J. (2015). Religious and spiritual development. In M. E. Lamb & R. M. Lerner (Eds.), *Handbook of child psychology and developmental science: Socioemotional processes* (pp. 975–1021). John Wiley & Sons, Inc. https://doi.org/10.1002/9781118963418.childpsy323

Koenig, H. G. (2012). Religion, spirituality, and health: The research and clinical implications. *International Scholarly Research Notices*, *2012*, 1–33. https://doi.org/10.5402/2012/278730

Kor, A., Pirutinsky, S., Mikulincer, M., Shoshani, A., & Miller, L. (2019). A longitudinal study of spirituality, character strengths, subjective well-being, and prosociality in middle school adolescents. *Frontiers in Psychology*, *10*, 377. https://doi.org/10.3389/fpsyg.2019.00377

Krok, D. (2018). Examining the role of religion in a family setting: Religious attitudes and quality of life among parents and their adolescent children. *Journal of Family Studies*, *24*(3), 203–218. https://doi.org/10.1080/13229400.2016.1176589

Lantieri, L., & Goleman, D. P. (2008). *Building emotional intelligence: Techniques to cultivate inner strength in children*. Sounds True.

Marques, S. C., Lopez, S. J., & Mitchell, J. (2013). The role of hope, spirituality, and religious practice in adolescents' life satisfaction: Longitudinal findings. *Journal of Happiness Studies*, *14*(1), 251–261. https://doi.org/10.1007/s10902-012-9329-3

Michaelson, V., King, N., Inchley, J., Currie, D., Brooks, F., & Pickett, W. (2019). Domains of spirituality and their associations with positive mental health: A study of adolescents in Canada, England, and Scotland. *Preventive Medicine*, *125*, 12–18. https://doi.org/10.1016/j.ypmed.2019.04.018

Miller, L. (2016). *The spiritual child: The new science on parenting for health and lifelong thriving*. Macmillan.

Mindful Schools. (2014). *Mindfulness curriculum kindergarten-5th grades*. https://www.mindfulschools.org/wp/wp-content/uploads/2017/03/K5-Curriculum-2014.pdf

Mittal, S., & Thursby, G. (Eds.). (2004). *The Hindu world*. Routledge.

Osman, F. (2005). Educating the Muslim child. In M. S. Merry (Ed.), *Education and society: Philosophical essays* (pp. 81–98). Springer.

Papadopoulos, S. (2009). *Blessed Jacob Tsalikis*. Akritas.

Piedmont, R. L. (1999). Does spirituality represent the sixth factor of personality? Spiritual transcendence and the five-factor model. *Journal of Personality*, *67*(6), 985–1013. https://doi.org/10.1111/1467-6494.00080

Sawatzky, R., Gadermann, A., & Pesut, B. (2009). An investigation of the relationships between spirituality, health status and quality of life in adolescents. *Applied Research in Quality of Life*, *4*(1), 5–22. https://doi.org/10.1007/s11482-009-9065-y

Schnitker, S. A., Houltberg, B., Dyrness, W., & Redmond, N. (2017). The virtue of patience, spirituality, and suffering: Integrating lessons from positive psychology, psychology of religion, and Christian theology. *Psychology of Religion and Spirituality*, *9*(3), 264–275. https://doi.org/10.1037/rel0000099

Schutt, M. K. A., & Felver, J. C. (2020). Mindfulness in education. In *Mindfulness-based interventions with children and adolescents* (pp. 57–73). Routledge.

Scott, D. G. (2004). Retrospective spiritual narratives: Exploring recalled childhood and adolescent spiritual experiences. *International Journal of Children's Spirituality*, *9*(1), 67–79. https://doi.org/10.1080/1364436042000200834

Skrzypińska, K. (2021). Does spiritual intelligence (SI) exist? A theoretical investigation of a tool useful for finding the meaning of life. *Journal of Religion and Health*, *60*(1), 500–516. https://doi.org/10.1007/s10943-020-01005-8

Vekety, B., Logemann, H. A., & Takacs, Z. K. (2021). The effect of mindfulness-based interventions on inattentive and hyperactive–impulsive behavior in childhood:

A meta-analysis. *International Journal of Behavioral Development, 45*(2), 133–145. https://doi.org/10.1177/0165025420958192

Wu, R., Liu, Z., Guo, Q., Cai, M., & Zhou, J. (2020). Couple similarity on personality, moral identity and spirituality predict life satisfaction of spouses and their offspring. *Journal of Happiness Studies, 21*(3), 1037–1058. https://doi.org/10.1007/s10902-019-00108-8

Young, R. (2020, January 20). *Bringing secular spirituality in education*. Retrieved May 4, 2023, from www.wbur.org/hereandnow/2020/01/20/secular-spirituality-schools-education

5 Sound Body, Sound Mind

> "A sound mind in a sound body is a short but full description of a happy state in this world."
>
> John Lock (2007, p. 25)

The importance of maintaining a sound mind in a sound body for our well-being is an old idea with a timeless value but is especially relevant nowadays as childhood obesity has become a serious problem. According to the Centers for Disease Control (CDC, 2021), in the years 2017–2018, 19.3% of children and adolescents ages 2 to 19 years are classified as obese, meaning that the body mass index (BMI) is above the 95th percentile of growth based on sex and age. The rate is lower in preschoolers at 13.4% but increases significantly in middle childhood (20.3%) and continues an upward trend in adolescence (21.2%). Moreover, minority and lower socioeconomic status groups are overrepresented with higher obesity rates. The increased prevalence of obesity is largely attributed to poor nutrition and lack of physical activity.

In the field of positive psychology, the close connection between mind and body is considered one of the indicators of well-being. Physical activity not only protects from and alleviates symptoms of mental health problems but also directly associates with subjective well-being. Researchers assess physical well-being by the level of physical activity or physical fitness, health status, diet and nutrition, quality of sleep, BMI, and objective biomedical markers of health (e.g., blood pressure, cholesterol). This chapter explores the connection between physical activity, health, and being overweight with reports of happiness and life satisfaction. Being physically active is also associated with academic performance, cognitive skills, and other positive indices of well-being such as self-esteem and self-control. The chapter also reviews the literature on the connection that sleep duration and quality have with positive and negative affect. Evidence from cross-sectional and intervention studies, conducted in different parts of the world, is examined throughout the chapter, and recommendations for parents and child practitioners are made.

DOI: 10.4324/9780429356414-7

Physical Activity and Happiness

Among adults, there is a positive dose-response relationship between physical activity and happiness (Zhang & Chen, 2019). Specifically, happiness increases by 20% if one is somewhat active, by 29% if one is sufficiently active, and by 52% if one is very active. Such evidence comes from cross-sectional and non-randomized studies; hence the data are correlational. However, longitudinal studies shed some light on the direction of the relationship. According to a study, the happiness of sedentary people increases over time if they become active. Participants who were sedentary at the beginning of the study were three times more likely to be unhappy after two years if they remained sedentary, compared to those who were initially inactive but became active. Those who were active at baseline but slowed down in two years reported 1.7 times lower happiness compared to those who maintained their activity level. In addition, the magnitude of the benefits of physical activity on subjective well-being is similar to that on mental health (Zhang & Chen, 2019). Despite the positive dose-response relationship between physical activity and happiness, there seems to be a threshold effect as well, above which no additional benefits are observed. Correlational and randomized-controlled intervention studies show no difference in happiness levels between those who performed 150–300 minutes of moderate to vigorous activity per week and those who engaged in more than 300 minutes of moderate to vigorous activity. In addition, research evidence suggests that there is no optimal type or level of activity that is more beneficial to happiness. Both aerobic as well as lighter forms of exercise such as stretching equally improve perceived happiness in adults. Moreover, even a small amount of physical activity may increase levels of happiness, especially among overweight individuals who report a greater change in happiness than normal-weight adults do. Interestingly, the connection between physical activity and happiness is stronger for men than women (Zhang & Chen, 2019).

The evidence regarding the benefits of physical activity on children's and adolescents' well-being stems from correlational studies that rely on self-reports and objective measures of physical activity. Evidence also comes from intervention studies where children participated in exercise programs aimed to enhance their subjective well-being. Furthermore, research has focused primarily on older children and adolescents. Most researchers have used the recommendations from the World Health Organization (WHO, 2020) as benchmarks to study appropriate levels of physical activity. For children 5–18 years of age, WHO recommends 60 minutes of moderate, aerobic activity a day and vigorous activity that includes strength training three times a week, as well as reduced sedentary activity. These recommendations aim to keep children physically healthy because activity is critical in restoring and maintaining physical health. Overweight children and adolescents who participated in programs of moderately intense exercise of 30 to 60 minutes, three to seven days per week, experienced a total reduction in fat and visceral adiposity. For normal-weight boys and girls, fat reduction occured with longer and more vigorous workouts. Physical activity reduces blood pressure, lipids, and triglycerides, and improves aerobic fitness. Moreover, it benefits cognitive performance as it enhances concertation and memory and promotes mental health as it reduces anxiety and depression symptoms (Strong et al., 2005). Therefore, the WHO recommendations seem appropriate although not many children around the world meet them.

The benefits of physical activity cover a wide range of positive well-being indicators and are shown in older children and adolescents from different geographical regions. Data from 9- to 11-year-olds from North Ireland show that about a quarter of students experienced moderate to vigorous physical activity of 60 minutes a day, every day of the week, with more boys than girls achieving this level. Children with higher activity levels reported higher psychological well-being that included higher self-esteem and feeling more satisfied, comforted, and socially accepted and supported by peers (Breslin et al., 2012). Moljord et al. (2011) studied 1,500 adolescents (13–18 years) from Norway who rated their happiness and stress in different domains (e.g., family, school, finances). Physical activity was measured by answering the question of how frequently they engaged in physical activity that caused them to break a sweat and increased their heart rate for at least 20 minutes. Almost 70% of adolescents reported being physically active two to three times a week, 26% were active every day, while the remaining were not physically active at all. Correlational analyses revealed a positive association between physical activity and happiness for girls. For boys, physical activity was positively associated with happiness and negatively with stress. When comparing different groups of physical activity, those in the high group had significantly lower scores of stress and higher scores of happiness than the moderate and low groups did. The girls' level of stress and happiness did not vary by level of physical activity, however. Min et al. (2017) studied 370,000 students (mean age = 13) from South Korea who completed online surveys about their weight, psychological well-being, and physical activity. They reported the frequency of aerobic and muscle-strengthening activity, their global happiness, and perceived stress. More boys participated in more vigorous activity than girls. That is, 19.2% of boys did physical activity more than five times a week whereas only 5.8% of girls did so. In all weight statuses (underweight, typical, overweight), those who participated in physical activity at least once a week reported higher happiness and a lower frequency of stress. Moreover, one day increase of 20 minutes of vigorous physical activity or strengthening exercises increased the odds of happiness and decreased the odds of stress. García-Hermoso et al. (2020) found that 8- to 12-year-olds from Chile, who were active more than 2 hours per day, had higher life satisfaction and positive affect than less active children. In addition, life satisfaction and positive affect were higher among those who exercised six or more times a week compared to those who exercised three or fewer times a week.

Altogether, the preceding findings show that physical activity relates to more happiness, life satisfaction, positive affect, and lower stress. The findings also imply a dose-response relationship between physical activity and subjective well-being, similar to adults. The association between physical activity and subjective well-being is also supported by intervention studies, either randomized controlled trials or quasi-experimental ones. In a meta-analytic review of such studies,

Rodriguez-Ayllon et al. (2019) discovered a small but significant overall effect of physical activity on the mental health and psychological well-being of children and adolescents, aged 6–18 years. The indices of mental health included anxiety and depression and the indices for psychological well-being included happiness, positive affect, and self-esteem. However, when the analyses were performed separately for adolescents and children, the effect was only significant for adolescents, possibly because of the small number of intervention studies involving younger children. On that note, such intervention studies are non-existent for preschoolers.

Moreover, studies relying on objective measures of physical activity generally support the aforementioned findings. For example, Costigan et al. (2019) asked 8th graders from Australia to wear an actigraphy accelerometer for a week and report their positive and negative emotions. There were no significant correlations between low and moderate physical activity and well-being but there was a positive link between rigorous physical activity and positive affect, up to a point. Similarly, negative affectivity declined with high-intensity physical activity up to a point after which it began to increase. The researchers estimated that the turning point is somewhere between 31 and 44 minutes of high-intensity activity. In a longitudinal study, van Woudenberg et al. (2020) examined accelerometer data from 1,500 adolescents (ages 8–17 years) from the Netherlands for three years. The authors reported a weak correlation between average physical activity and average happiness; for every 1,000 steps, the level of happiness increased by 0.20 on a scale of 1–100. The number of steps on one day did not predict happiness the day after and similarly, happiness on any given day did not predict the number of steps on the subsequent day. However, the number of steps in each hour predicted happiness during the following hour, and happiness in the previous hour predicted the number of steps in the following hour. These findings show the bidirectionality of happiness and physical activity, but the reciprocal effects are rather short-term.

Opposite results are shown when considering sedentary behaviors. García-Hermoso et al. (2020) discovered that children with more than 2 hours of screen time a day reported higher negative affect (i.e., irritated, embittered, sad) compared to those with less than 2 hours of screen time per day. Moreover, those who had 2 hours of screen time a day for more than four days a week reported an increased negative affect compared to those who had this amount of screen time less than twice a week. The differences in positive affect and life satisfaction based on the level of screen time were not significant. Similarly in a sample of 6- to 8-year-olds from Finland, Ikävalko et al. (2018) found that boys with more sedentary behaviors, including screen time, had higher internalizing and externalizing symptoms than boys with lower sedentary behaviors. Boys with general sedentary behaviors had a four times increased risk for low psychological well-being. Boys with 2 hours of screen-based sedentary behaviors per day had a two-time higher risk for low psychological well-being. Girls had higher sedentary behaviors than boys, but their psychological well-being did not vary by the level of sedentary behaviors. Because the ratings were provided by the parents, gender differences may be explained by whether parents tolerate sedentary behaviors more for girls than boys. A review of studies to determine the association between physical activity, sedentary behaviors, and indices of psychosocial well-being of preschoolers (17 months to 5 years) were rather inconclusive for both physical activity and sedentary behaviors. There was evidence, however, of a dose-response relationship between sedentary behaviors and aggression, attention problems, and decreased classroom engagement (Hinkley et al., 2014). Active play, on the other hand, improved preschoolers' attentional processes and self-regulation (Becker et al., 2013). Lastly, the meta-analysis of Rodriguez-Ayllon et al. (2019) revealed a positive association between sedentary behaviors and depression and a negative association between sedentary behavior and satisfaction with life and happiness in older children and adolescents.

Lastly, researchers have attempted to explain how physical activity relates to subjective well-being by examining possible mediators. Kleszczewska et al. (2018) explored the relationship of physical activity to general life satisfaction by surveying more than 4,000 Polish adolescents while considering factors such as affluence and family relationships. Physical activity and affluence, measured by material possessions, such as having your own room, predicted almost 3% of the variance in life satisfaction. Adding quality of family relationships did not change the percentage of physical activity explained. The researchers also tested a mediation model to explain the effect of physical activity via self-esteem. Indeed, physical activity increased self-esteem which in turn increased life satisfaction. Moreover, the effect was stronger when the family affluence decreased. Physical activity is a much more important predictive factor in children from less affluent families. Additionally, children may be more likely to engage in physical activity if they feel confident about their sports ability or are raised in families where sports are encouraged. Holder et al. (2009) found that sports ability and the importance of sports to parents explained 7–16% of the variance in happiness of 8–12-year-olds. Physical activity may also affect well-being because it promotes cardiorespiratory fitness. Marques et al. (2017) found that cardiorespiratory fitness related to health measures, happiness, and life satisfaction in adolescence and according to Eddolls et al. (2018), cardiorespiratory fitness acted like a partial mediator in the path linking physical activity and perceived quality of life.

In conclusion, 20% to 25% of older children and adolescents meet the WHO criteria of having moderate to vigorous activity a day, and more boys than girls do so. This level of activity is associated with improving body composition, cognitive performance, and mental health (anxiety, depression). However, mental health is supported by all kinds of activities from stretching to muscle conditioning, dancing, and aerobics. The research presented here indicates that moderate to vigorous activity is associated with reduced stress, and increased happiness, life satisfaction, and positive affect. There is also evidence that even 20 minutes of vigorous activity may increase feelings of happiness and that there is a dose-response relationship but after 31–44 minutes of high-intensity physical activity there is a turning point after which the positive affect declines and the negative affect inclines. Sedentary behaviors on the other hand increase negative affect and internalizing and externalizing symptoms and decrease life satisfaction and positive affectivity. The relationship between sedentary behaviors and subjective well-being is more pronounced in boys, although more research is needed in this area. Intervention studies as well as studies relying on objective measures of physical activity support a modest but significant association between activity and happiness. This association is more consistent with boys and older children and adolescents. Evidence in the preschool period is scarce but sedentary behaviors of preschoolers are related to increased externalizing behaviors and attention problems, while active play supports self-regulation. These findings are generally in agreement with the ones found in adults. Some research has sought to explain the relationship between physical activity and well-being by examining possible mediators such as self-esteem, family affluence, and cardiorespiratory fitness. These factors appear to influence the impact of physical activity on well-being, with self-esteem and cardiorespiratory fitness acting as partial mediators, and affluence as a moderator.

Physical Activity and Academic Performance

In addition to improving overall health, physical activity causes changes in the brain that result in better academic performance and behavioral regulation. Research from neuroscience reveals that exercise brings about neurogenesis in the hippocampus which is involved in memory and learning. It also affects the production of neurotransmitters, such as dopamine which improves learning, and serotonin which affects the regulation of mood and behavior. Exercise also increases the production of the brain-derived neurotrophic factor, a protein that acts as a buffer towards stress, and reduces inflammation that affects cognitive processes, especially the ability to memorize. Furthermore, the cerebellum, the center for motor skills, agility, and coordination, is connected with the prefrontal cortex which is involved in the regulation of attention and working memory. Therefore, the brain provides the connection between movement and learning (Blaydes, 2008; Ratey, 2008).

This evidence has bolstered claims about the benefits of physical education in schools and several cases with exceptional results reached the popular media. One well-known case is the physical education program in Naperville, Illinois, where students experience mandatory physical activity every day. Specifically, the program known as the Learning Readiness Physical Education (LRPE) entails three days of intense cardiovascular workouts lasting about 30 minutes each and two days of other activities like swimming, rock climbing, and team-building exercises.

The primary objective of these activities is to engage students and help them discover forms of physical movement they might enjoy pursuing into adulthood. The school district gained national recognition when its students ranked 1st in science and 6th in math in global assessments. Other schools that adopted this physical education program showed improvement in academic performance and school-related behavior regulation, such as increased attendance and fewer suspension days (Zientarski, 2016). Further experiments showed that physical activity before literacy and math classes raised the students' reading and math levels compared to students who had physical activity after these classes. These interventions were designed specifically for students who needed help with these subjects. Brain imaging confirmed that the brain was much more active after exercise and before the test compared to a sitting brain before the test (Hillman et al., 2009).

More comprehensive research evidence for the effects of physical activity on the brain and academic performance is provided by de Greef et al.'s meta-analytic study (2018). The authors identified 31 intervention studies aiming to improve the executive functions (inhibition, working memory, attention) and academic performance of 6- to 12-year-olds. Intense physical activity had a small to moderate effect on inhibition, selective attention, and spelling but not on working memory, math, and reading. However, long-term physical activity was related to all cognitive functions and had a positive effect on math and overall academic performance. A previous meta-analysis of studies focusing on elementary school-age children supported a positive effect of physical education on math and reading (Fedewa & Ahn, 2011). However, the effect of physical activity on executive function and language was weaker in the preschool years (Carson et al., 2016). Lastly, another meta-analysis supports a much stronger connection between physical activity and a larger range of cognitive abilities (speed of processing, inhibition, cognitive flexibility, attention, working memory) as well as language skills in studies that employed adolescents and young adults (Haverkamp et al., 2020). Overall, this evidence is in line with the brain changes that are affected by physical activity and supports the importance of regular physical education in schools. The findings also imply that the effect of physical activity on cognition and academic skills becomes more pronounced as children get older.

Health and Happiness

Given the positive link between physical activity and happiness and the relationship between physical activity and health outcomes (Strong et al., 2005) one would expect that subjective and objective measures of health would also correlate with indices of positive functioning and subjective well-being. It is speculated that the relationship between happiness and health is truly bidirectional. As health causes happiness, happiness may also cause the perception of a healthy status and even foster physical health (Mahon et al., 2005). Seligman (2002) expected that only severe and chronic health problems could cause unhappiness and that the subjective belief that one is healthy is enough to bring about happiness. Research has explored the relationship between health and happiness from different angles including the influence of global perception of health, diet, nutrition, overweight, and obesity.

Atienza-González et al. (2020) analyzed the relationships between self-reported life satisfaction, and self-rated health in Spanish adolescents (12 and 17 years old). Same-day perceived health was positively correlated with life satisfaction and negatively associated with anxiety and depression. Age and gender seemed to somewhat moderate these relationships. The relationship between life satisfaction and perceived health in everyday activities was stronger in younger than older adolescents, and girls reported lower perceived health than boys did. Mahon et al. (2005) explored similar questions in a US sample of early adolescents (12–14 years) who reported current physical health, mental wellness, and clinical health (i.e., illnesses and health concerns). Participants also completed a well-being scale that contained items for overall perceived happiness. All three health variables correlated positively with happiness for boys. For girls, only physical health and wellness were associated with happiness. These findings suggest that gender may moderate the effect, but more research is needed in the future to confirm it.

Other researchers examined the relationship between health and subjective well-being by considering the child's excessive weight. Overweight and obesity are determined by the BMI index which does not show the percentage of fat in the body but correlates highly with direct measures of fat such as densitometry and skinfold thickness (CDC, 2021). Overweight and obesity increase the risk for diabetes, heart disease, and cancer. This begs the question of whether overweight and obese children are unhappy. There is evidence for a direct link between BMI and depression among adolescents from the UK, an indirect link between BMI and physical quality of life, as it was mediated by cardiorespiratory fitness (measured by an actigraph), and an indirect link between BMI and psychological well-being, as it was mediated by depression (Eddolls et al., 2018). Breslin et al. (2012) did not find an effect of type of weight (thin, average weight, overweight, obese) on psychological well-being that included factors such as resilience, self-esteem, and satisfaction. Their sample included primary school children aged 9–11 years from North Ireland. The only effect that weight had was that overweight and obese children reported more risk avoidance than average-weight students. Girls were more likely to be in the overweight category, but gender did not interact with the weight category to affect psychological well-being. Based on a review of several studies, Flodmark (2005) revealed that overweight children and adolescents reported lower overall self-competence, and specifically in the subscales of athletic competence and physical appearance. Parents' and children's reports showed a positive emotional and school functioning of overweight children but lower physical and social functioning. Moreover, in some samples the difference in self-esteem between overweight and normal-weight children was small. Flodmark concluded that overweight children were happy when they received social support from their parents.

Based on a qualitative analysis of interviews of sixteen 10–12-year-old children from Sweden, who were classified as overweight, Mériaux et al. (2010) found that overweight children connected their negative well-being to insufficient sleeping, poor physical activity, and a feeling of being victimized. Being happy meant feeling able, to have support from others and a sense of community. These children were aware of their body image and what a healthy style might be but spent a lot of sedentary time and ate a lot of junk food. Parents therefore may not only provide emotional support but also encourage a more active lifestyle and healthier diet. However, how parents perceive their children's overweight may interfere with their ability to provide the right amount and type of support. Syrad et al. (2014) addressed parental perceptions by extensively interviewing parents who were informed that their child (4–5 years and 10–11 years) was overweight and at health risk. Parents tended to dismiss the evaluation, with 57% of them failing to recognize that their child looked overweight. They embraced broad definitions of healthy by emphasizing the child's emotional and physical health, their overt happiness, and their lifestyle in terms of diet and physical activity. They attributed the overweight to genetic factors and expressed a cultural acceptance of being overweight. Such attitudes may bolster the children's self-esteem as shown in the research described earlier but interfere with necessary changes in diet and activity to reduce the risk of disease down the road.

In fact, there is ample evidence to support the connections between dietary behaviors and subjective well-being. In a sample of 11–19 Iranian girls, it was found that positive predictors of happiness included low BMI, the consumption of fruits and vegetables, regular exercise, reduced exposure to second-hand smoking, and leisure time (Fararouei et al., 2013). A similar connection was found in South Korea in a sample of adolescents (12–18 years). Happy students were less likely to smoke or drink. There was also a positive association between fruit consumption and happiness but only in girls. For boys, physical activity was a significant predictor of happiness (Kye et al., 2016). Additionally, Hong and Peltzer (2017) investigated how dietary intake was related to the psychological well-being of over 65,000 students (average age = 15) from Korea. Dietary behaviors included the consumption of soft drinks, highly caffeinated drinks, sweetened drinks, fast food, fruits, vegetables, and milk. About a quarter of the participants perceived themselves as very healthy. Regression analyses accounting for demographic variables showed that consuming fruits and vegetables, having breakfast every day, and drinking milk positively predicted happiness and was negatively associated with depression and perceived stress. In contrast, the consumption of caffeine, and soft and sweet drinks were negative predictors of happiness and positive predictors of depression and stress.

The literature shows associations between perceived health and life satisfaction and self-reported global happiness. The evidence of the association of overweight and obesity to happiness is not straightforward, and it is likely mediated by other physical and psychosocial factors. There is an obvious lack of studies examining these relationships in younger children and experimental designs. While there is evidence that perceived health is related to happiness just as Seligman suggested, longitudinal studies are needed to confirm the direction of this relationship. Moreover, the long-term effect of the relationship between health and later happiness has not been examined. Böckerman et al. (2017) somewhat addressed the issue by exploring whether biometric indices of well-being in childhood predicted happiness in adulthood. The authors considered measures such as height, body fat, pulse, systolic blood pressure, diastolic blood pressure, triglycerides, and creatinine and controlled for several demographic variables. Only pulse and triglycerides were significant predictors of adult happiness. Specifically, an increase of one standard deviation in these predictors was associated with an increase of about .05 in adult happiness (scale 1–5). The effect of triglycerides persisted even after controlling for demographic variables, physical activity, and dietary choices. The effect was robust for women and younger adults. In general, the authors concluded that biomarkers of health were not very good predictors of happiness in the long run.

Lastly, undernutrition or overnutrition is associated with difficulties in becoming successful in school. Undernourished children experience hunger and often homelessness and other traumatic events. At school, they receive low scores in main academic areas and often exhibit behavior problems such as hyperactivity. The effects are seen in childhood and adolescence by which time many have stayed a grade behind. Overweight children do not necessarily present academic problems, but such difficulties are often a secondary marker of how they are doing in school. When socioeconomic status and behavior difficulties are controlled, overweight children do not fall behind normal-weight children in academic achievement tests. Nonetheless, some research showed that women who were overweight as children had achieved academic attainment and earned less income than their normal-weight peers (Pyle et al., 2009).

In conclusion, research examining the connection between health and happiness has found associations between perceived health, life satisfaction, and global happiness, while the connection between overweight, obesity, and happiness is less straightforward and likely mediated by other factors. Dietary behaviors also play a role in subjective well-being, with fruit and vegetable consumption, regular exercise, and low BMI positively predicting happiness. Both undernutrition and overnutrition can be associated with difficulties in school, but overweight children do not necessarily experience academic problems once socioeconomic status and behavior difficulties are accounted for. The literature highlights the need for more research on these relationships in younger children and experimental designs, as well as the need for longitudinal studies to confirm the direction of the association between health and happiness.

Sleep Into Happiness

The relationship between sleep deprivation and negative outcomes for well-being is very well established. Beginning in the preschool period, children with sleep difficulties develop externalizing behavior problems in adolescence (Quach et al., 2018). A meta-analysis of 86 studies involving 5- to 12-year-olds showed strong associations between sleep duration and a range of cognitive (executive function, memory, attention, multi-tasking) and externalizing problems (Astill et al., 2012). Sleep deprivation in the same age range was related to decreased health quality, reflected in health complaints like headaches, backache, dizziness, and abdominal pain (Paiva et al., 2015). Furthermore, short sleep duration was associated with negative mood in adolescence. Short and Louca (2015) reported an increase in negative mood after three days of sleep deprivation, which was induced at a sleep laboratory. The participants experienced increased depression, anger, anxiety, confusion, fatigue, and lower vigor. Interestingly, the effect was stronger for girls. A meta-analysis of 74 studies revealed a 55% increase in mood deficits overall. Specifically, short sleep duration increased the likelihood to experience anger by 83%, depression by 62%, negative affect by 60%, and anxiety by 41% (Short et al., 2020).

Research also demonstrates a link between sleep and happiness. A Korean study provided correlational evidence for a positive link between happiness and sleep duration even after accounting for academic grades (Lee et al., 2013). Additionally, Fuligni and Hardway (2006) showed that shorter steep duration predicted lower happiness the following day in 14–15-year-olds, over two weeks. Otsuka et al. (2020) found a dose-response relationship between happiness and sleep problems in a large data set of over 60,000 students from Japan (ages 12–18 years). After controlling for demographic variables, lifestyle choices such as drinking, and mental health, they found that among those with the lowest happiness score (0–2 out of 10), 40% reported insomnia, 49.5% short sleep duration, and 62% poor quality of sleep. In contrast, among those with the highest scores of happiness, the prevalence of insomnia was 13.5%, short sleep duration was 24%, and poor quality of sleep was 24%.

Furthermore, Shen et al. (2018) confirmed the relationship between sleep duration and happiness but also examined the role of sleep quality in a sample of over 7,000 students (grades 7–12) from Australia. Poor sleep quality was measured by addressing common sleep problems, like having a late sleep onset, waking up feeling tired, waking up during the night, and having a sleep disorder (e.g., snoring, restless leg syndrome). Almost 62% of adolescents reported sleeping 8 or more hours and 76% reported being happy in general. Sleep duration was positively correlated with overall happiness and negatively associated with negative affect, as expected. The association of sleep duration with happiness was statistically stronger than the association with negative affect. Low sleep quality correlated with lower happiness and higher negative affect. Unlike sleep duration, the association between sleep quality and negative affect was stronger than the association with happiness. These differential effects suggest interventions should address both duration and quality of sleep. A strong association between happiness and sleep duration has been found across geographic regions, therefore it is a rather robust finding (Short et al., 2020). Perhaps lack of sleep weakens the pathways between the prefrontal cortex and the limbic system thus influencing emotion regulation.

Lastly, there is a lack of research on sleep and happiness among young children, but Hale et al. (2011) showed that parents who use language-based bedtime routines such as reading books, storytelling, and singing had preschoolers who slept more at night, had fewer behavior problems, and had better physical health. This was the case regardless of the child (e.g., low birth weight), parent (e.g., education), and family (e.g., number of children) characteristics. It seems that language-based routines set the path for longer sleep during the night which then may lead to other positive outcomes. Longitudinal evidence could shed light on this interesting question. Lastly, there is evidence of the benefit of napping in middle childhood. Liu et al. (2019) explored the relationship between napping and the well-being of 4th to 6th graders from China. The researchers found positive associations between napping duration (30–60 minutes) and napping frequency (five to seven times a week) with happiness measured by the Oxford Happiness Questionnaire. Children who napped five to seven times a week and slept for more than 60 minutes reported an increase of .24 units in happiness compared to non-nappers (scale of happiness 1–6). In addition, the benefits of napping extended to improved academic performance, grit, and self-control and lower internalizing and externalizing problems. These are interesting findings although cultural norms may not support establishing nap routines in children of this age range elsewhere.

In conclusion, adequate sleep duration, better quality of sleep, and fewer sleep problems predict global perceptions of happiness. On the other hand, poor sleep quality and short sleep duration are strongly correlated with negative affect. Napping may be a promising positive factor in enhancing happiness in children. More research is needed to understand the benefits of sleep for happiness, especially in younger children.

Raising Physically Active and Healthy Children

Following the WHO recommendations for physical activity is a good starting point to improve overall physical health. Parents should encourage their children to spend at least 60 minutes of moderate to vigorous aerobic activity daily, such as running, swimming, dancing, or playing sports, and incorporate strength training exercises at least three times a week. Interventions that increase cardiovascular health promote perceptions of well-being as well. Research shows that any form of activity may improve subjective happiness in children and adolescents. Parents should be cautious about encouraging prolonged vigorous activity as it can generate a negative effect. There may be a turning point where the positive affect declines and the negative affect increases after 31–44 minutes of high-intensity physical activity. Balancing the intensity and duration of physical activity to optimize well-being is important. For children who are inactive starting with 20 minutes of exercise would be enough to create a state of feeling good. In contrast, sedentary behaviors and specifically excessive screen time increase negative affect and decrease life satisfaction. Strong et al. (2005) recommend that as children get older, activities should shift from focusing on the development of motor skills to activities that enhance health and cardiovascular and muscular fitness. For preschoolers, the emphasis should be primarily on motor coordination. Encouraging active play improves their attentional processes and self-regulation. School-age children advance their motor skills and can apply them to a variety of organized sports and other athletic activities. The physical activities of adolescents are more structured (Strong et al., 2005). Parents may help their child to discover physical activities that they enjoy and can pursue into adulthood. Whenever possible, parents may arrange for their children to engage in physical activity before tackling homework or studying. Research shows that exercise can improve cognitive functioning and help students better retain information during academic tasks. However, even active leisure time is beneficial (Holder et al., 2009). Leisure activities that are chosen by children are more likely to be enjoyable because they support the child's autonomy and self-confidence.

Parents may support the children's activities by encouraging involvement in sports and expressing their confidence in their children's ability to improve in their sports. Griffin (1998) encourages every parent to enroll their child in some organized sport when they are very young so that children can associate physical activity with having social fun and connecting with others. After age 11, when sports become more competitive children may choose to continue or decide that they prefer other activities. Those who go on enjoy long-term friendships with their teammates and see sports as an area where they feel competent (Griffin, 1998). Parents should teach their children about the numerous benefits of exercise, including improved brain function, better academic performance, enhanced mood, and overall well-being. This knowledge can motivate them to maintain an active lifestyle. Parents can set a positive example by engaging in regular physical activity themselves or make exercise a family affair by engaging in physical activities together, such as family bike rides, hikes, or participating in local sports teams.

The research review here gives another reason to parents to encourage the consumption of healthy foods and the creation of healthy eating habits as both have been associated with increased happiness. Interventions should target educating parents and children about nutrition, increasing physical activity, and teaching behavioral strategies to curb caloric intake. One program that educates children about different foods is the Traffic Light Diet developed by Epstein et al. (1984). Foods are color-coded based on their density of calories and nutritional value. Vegetables and fruit, for example, are green foods, yellow foods include lean meats, seeds, and nuts, and examples of red foods are cookies and cakes. Behavioral interventions include self-monitoring (e.g., keeping a diary of food intake), stimulus control (e.g., avoiding environmental triggers for overeating), eating management (e.g., restricting the places where eating takes place), and operant conditioning (e.g., provide rewards for changing eating habits and creating new ones; Pyle et al., 2009). While the causes of obesity among children extend beyond health style and diet to sociocultural factors (see Robinson et al., 2012 for a review) parents can too be educated about healthy diets and be trained to apply the aforementioned behavioral techniques to promote healthy eating in their children. Adapting a more authoritative feeding style is related to normal BMI among preschoolers and school-age children whereas an indulgent or uninvolved feeding style is related to a higher risk for obesity (Shloim et al., 2015). Research suggests that overweight children who receive social support from their parents are more likely to be happy.

Lastly, parents may establish consistent sleep routines. Good quality and adequate duration of sleep contribute to happiness and positive affect in children. Encouraging a consistent sleep schedule and establishing calming bedtime routines, such as reading or storytelling, promote better sleep quality. Excessive screen time, especially close to bedtime, can negatively impact sleep quality and duration. Because sleep disturbances relate to subjective well-being, parents should identify any sleep problems their children might be experiencing, such as insomnia or sleep disorders, and work together with healthcare professionals to address these issues.

References

Astill, R. G., Van der Heijden, K. B., Van IJzendoorn, M. H., & Van Someren, E. J. (2012). Sleep, cognition, and behavioral problems in school-age children: A century of research meta-analyzed. *Psychological Bulletin, 138*(6), 1109. https://doi.org/10.1037/a0028204

Atienza-González, F. L., Martínez, N., & Silva, C. (2020). Life satisfaction and self-rated health in adolescents: The relationships between them and the role of gender and age. *The Spanish Journal of Psychology, 23*. https://doi.org/10.1017/sjp.2020.10

Becker, D. R., McClelland, M. M., Loprinzi, P., & Trost, S. G. (2013). Physical activity, self-regulation, and early academic achievement in preschool children. *Early Education and Development*, *25*(1), 56–70. https://doi.org/10.1080/10409289.2013.780505

Blaydes, J. (2008). Does exercise make you smarter? *Active and Healthy Magazine*, *19*(3–4). Retrieved May 5, 2012, from https://shop.achper.org.au/sb_cache/blog/id/122/f/Does%20Exercise%20Make%20You%20Smarter%20by%20Jean%20Blaydes.pdf

Böckerman, P., Bryson, A., Viinikainen, J., Hakulinen, C., Hintsanen, M., Pehkonen, J., Viikari, J., & Raitakari, O. (2017). The biometric antecedents to happiness. *PloS One*, *12*(9), e0184887. https://doi.org/10.1371/journal.pone.0184887

Breslin, G., Gossrau-Breen, D., McCay, N., Gilmore, G., MacDonald, L., & Hanna, D. (2012). Physical activity, gender, weight status, and wellbeing in 9- to 11-year-old children: A cross-sectional survey. *Journal of Physical Activity and Health*, *9*(3), 394–401. https://doi.org/10.1123/jpah.9.3.394

Carson, V., Hunter, S., Kuzik, N., Wiebe, S. A., Spence, J. C., Friedman, A., Tremblay, M. S., Slater, L., & Hinkley, T. (2016). Systematic review of physical activity and cognitive development in early childhood. *Journal of Science and Medicine in Sport*, *19*(7), 573–578. https://doi.org/10.1016/j.jsams.2015.07.011

Centers for Disease Control and Prevention (CDC). (2021, April). *Prevalence of childhood obesity*. Retrieved May 5, 2023, from www.cdc.gov/obesity/data/childhood.html

Costigan, S. A., Lubans, D. R., Lonsdale, C., Sanders, T., & Del Pozo Cruz, B. (2019). Associations between physical activity intensity and well-being in adolescents. *Preventive Medicine*, *125*, 55–61. https://doi.org/10.1016/j.ypmed.2019.05.009

de Greeff, J. W., Bosker, R. J., Oosterlaan, J., Visscher, C., & Hartman, E. (2018). Effects of physical activity on executive functions, attention, and academic performance in preadolescent children: A meta-analysis. *Journal of Science and Medicine in Sport*, *21*(5), 501–507. https://doi.org/10.1016/j.jsams.2017.09.595

Eddolls, W. T., McNarry, M. A., Lester, L., Winn, C. O., Stratton, G., & Mackintosh, K. A. (2018). The association between physical activity, fitness, and body mass index on mental well-being and quality of life in adolescents. *Quality of Life Research*, *27*(9), 2313–2320. https://doi.org/10.1007/s11136-018-1915-3

Epstein, L. H., Wing, R. R., Koeske, R., & Valoski, A. (1984). Effects of diet plus exercise on weight change in parents and children. *Journal of Consulting and Clinical Psychology*, *52*(3), 429. https://doi.org/10.1037/0022-006X.52.3.429

Fararouei, M., Brown, I. J., Toori, M. A., Haghighi, R. E., & Jafari, J. (2013). Happiness and health behavior in Iranian adolescent girls. *Journal of Adolescence*, *36*(6), 1187–1192. https://doi.org/10.1016/j.adolescence.2013.09.006

Fedewa, A. L., & Ahn, S. (2011). The effects of physical activity and physical fitness on children's achievement and cognitive outcomes: A meta-analysis. *Research Quarterly for Exercise and Sport*, *82*(3), 521–535. https://doi.org/10.1080/02701367.2011.10599785

Flodmark, C. E. (2005). The happy obese child. *International Journal of Obesity*, *29*(2), 31–33. https://doi.org/10.1038/sj.ijo.0803060

Fuligni, A. J., & Hardway, C. (2006). Daily variation in adolescents' sleep, activities, and psychological well-being. *Journal of Research on Adolescence*, *16*(3), 353–378. https://doi.org/10.1111/j.1532-7795.2006.00498.x

García-Hermoso, A., Hormazábal-Aguayo, I., Fernández-Vergara, O., Olivares, P. R., & Oriol-Granado, X. (2020). Physical activity, screen time and subjective well-being among children. *International Journal of Clinical and Health Psychology*, *20*(2), 126–134. https://doi.org/10.1016/j.ijchp.2020.03.001

Griffin, R. S. (1998). *Sports in the lives of children and adolescents: Success on the field and in life*. Greenwood Publishing Group.

Hale, L., Berger, L. M., LeBourgeois, M. K., & Brooks-Gunn, J. (2011). A longitudinal study of preschoolers' language-based bedtime routines, sleep duration, and well-being. *Journal of Family Psychology*, *25*(3), 423. https://doi.org/10.1037/a0023564

Haverkamp, B. F., Wiersma, R., Vertessen, K., van Ewijk, H., Oosterlaan, J., & Hartman, E. (2020). Effects of physical activity interventions on cognitive outcomes and academic performance in adolescents and young adults: A meta-analysis. *Journal of Sports Sciences*, *38*(23), 2637–2660. https://doi.org/10.1080/02640414.2020.1794763

Hillman, C. H., Pontifex, M. B., Raine, L. B., Castelli, D. M., Hall, E. E., & Kramer, A. F. (2009). The effect of acute treadmill walking on cognitive control and academic achievement in preadolescent children. *Neuroscience*, *159*(3), 1044–1054. https://doi.org/10.1016/j.neuroscience.2009.01.057

Hinkley, T., Teychenne, M., Downing, K. L., Ball, K., Salmon, J., & Hesketh, K. D. (2014). Early childhood physical activity, sedentary behaviors, and psychosocial well-being: A systematic review. *Preventive Medicine*, *62*, 182–192. https://doi.org/10.1016/j.ypmed.2014.02.007

Holder, M. D., Coleman, B., & Sehn, Z. L. (2009). The contribution of active and passive leisure to children's well-being. *Journal of Health Psychology*, *14*(3), 378–386. https://doi.org/10.1177/1359105308101676

Hong, S. A., & Peltzer, K. (2017). Dietary behaviour, psychological well-being, and mental distress among adolescents in Korea. *Child and Adolescent Psychiatry and Mental Health*, *11*(1). https://doi.org/10.1186/s13034-017-0194-z

Ikävalko, T., Lehto, S., Lintu, N., Väistö, J., Eloranta, A. M., Haapala, E. A., Vierola, A., Myllykangas, R., Tuomilehto, H., Brage, S., Pahkala, R., Närhi, M., & Lakka, T. A. (2018). Health-related correlates of psychological well-being among girls and boys 6–8 years of age: The Physical Activity and Nutrition in children study. *Journal of Paediatrics and Child Health*, *54*(5), 506–509. https://doi.org/10.1111/jpc.13891

Kleszczewska, D., Dzielska, A., Salonna, F., & Mazur, J. (2018). The association between physical activity and general life satisfaction in lower secondary school students: The role of individual and family factors. *Community Mental Health Journal*, *54*(8), 1245–1252. https://doi.org/10.1007/s10597-018-0309-x

Kye, S. Y., Kwon, J. H., & Park, K. (2016). Happiness and health behaviors in South Korean adolescents: A cross-sectional study. *Epidemiology and Health*, *38*. https://doi.org/10.4178/epih.e2016022

Lee, J., Kang, J., Rhie, S., & Chae, K. Y. (2013). Impact of sleep duration on emotional status in adolescents. *Journal of the Korean Child Neurology Society*, *21*(3), 100–110. Retrieved May 8, 2023, from www.koreamed.org/SearchBasic.php?RID=1961824

Liu, J., Feng, R., Ji, X., Cui, N., Raine, A., & Mednick, S. C. (2019). Midday napping in children: Associations between nap frequency and duration across cognitive, positive psychological well-being, behavioral, and metabolic health outcomes. *Sleep*, *42*(9). https://doi.org/10.1093/sleep/zsz126

Locke, J. (2007). *Some thoughts concerning education: (Including of the conduct of the understanding)*. Courier Corporation.

Mahon, N. E., Yarcheski, A., & Yarcheski, T. J. (2005). Happiness as related to gender and health in early adolescents. *Clinical Nursing Research*, *14*(2), 175–190. https://doi.org/10.1177/1054773804271936

Marques, A., Mota, J., Gaspar, T., & de Matos, M. G. (2017). Associations between self-reported fitness and self-rated health, life satisfaction, and health-related quality of life among adolescents. *Journal of Exercise Science & Fitness*, *15*(1), 8–11. https://doi.org/10.1016/j.jesf.2017.03.001

Mériaux, B. G., Berg, M., & Hellström, A. L. (2010). Everyday experiences of life, body, and well-being in children with overweight. *Scandinavian Journal of Caring Sciences*, *24*(1), 14–23. https://doi.org/10.1111/j.1471-6712.2008.00678.x

Min, J. H., Lee, E. Y., Spence, J. C., & Jeon, J. Y. (2017). Physical activity, weight status, and psychological well-being among a large national sample of South Korean adolescents. *Mental Health and Physical Activity*, *12*, 44–49. https://doi.org/10.1016/j.mhpa.2017.02.004

Moljord, I. E. O., Eriksen, L., Moksnes, U. K., & Espnes, G. A. (2011). Stress and happiness among adolescents with varying frequency of physical activity. *Perceptual and Motor Skills*, *113*(2), 631–646. https://doi.org/10.2466/02.06.10.13.PMS.113.5.631-646

Otsuka, Y., Kaneita, Y., Itani, O., Jike, M., Osaki, Y., Higuchi, S., Kanda, H., Kinjo, A., Kuwabara, Y., & Yoshimoto, H. (2020). The relationship between subjective happiness and sleep problems in Japanese adolescents. *Sleep medicine*, *69*, 120–126. https://doi.org/10.1016/j.sleep.2020.01.008

Paiva, T., Gaspar, T., & Matos, M. G. (2015). Sleep deprivation in adolescents: Correlations with health complaints and health-related quality of life. *Sleep Medicine*, *16*(4), 521–527. https://doi.org/10.1016/j.sleep.2014.10.010

Pyle, S. A., Hyder, M. L., Haddock, C. K., & Poston, W. C. (2009). Nutrition: The foundation of health, happiness, and academic success. In R. Gilman, E. S. Huebner, & M. Furlong (Eds.), *Handbook of positive psychology in* schools (pp. 441–450). Routledge. https://doi.org/10.4324/9780203884089

Quach, J. L., Nguyen, C. D., Williams, K. E., & Sciberras, E. (2018). Bidirectional associations between child sleep problems and internalizing and externalizing difficulties from preschool to early adolescence. *JAMA Pediatrics*, *172*(2). https://doi.org/10.1001/jamapediatrics.2017.4363

Ratey, J. J. (2008). *Spark: The revolutionary new science of exercise and the brain*. Hachette.

Robinson, S., Yardy, K., & Carter, V. (2012). A narrative literature review of the development of obesity in infancy and childhood. *Journal of Child Health Care*, *16*(4), 339–354. https://doi.org/10.1177/1367493512443908

Rodriguez-Ayllon, M., Cadenas-Sánchez, C., Estévez-López, F., Muñoz, N. E., Mora-Gonzalez, J., Migueles, J. H., Molina-García, P., Henriksson, H., Mena-Molina, A., Martínez-Vizcaíno, V., Catena, A., Löf, M., Erickson, K. I., Lubans, D. R., Ortega, F. B., & Esteban-Cornejo, I. (2019). Role of physical activity and sedentary behavior in the mental health of preschoolers, children, and adolescents: A systematic review and meta-analysis. *Sports Medicine*, *49*(9), 1383–1410. https://doi.org/10.1007/s40279-019-01099-5

Seligman, M. E. P. (2002). *Authentic happiness: Using the new positive psychology to realize your potential for lasting fulfillment*. Free Press.

Shen, L., van Schie, J., Ditchburn, G., Brook, L., & Bei, B. (2018). Positive and negative emotions: Differential associations with sleep duration and quality in adolescents. *Journal of Youth and Adolescence*, *47*, 2584–2595. https://doi.org/10.1007/s10964-018-0899-1

Shloim, N., Edelson, L. R., Martin, N., & Hetherington, M. M. (2015). Parenting styles, feeding styles, feeding practices, and weight status in 4–12-year-old children: A systematic review of the literature. *Frontiers in Psychology*, *6*, 1849. https://doi.org/10.3389/fpsyg.2015.01849

Short, M. A., Booth, S. A., Omar, O., Ostlundh, L., & Arora, T. (2020). The relationship between sleep duration and mood in adolescents: A systematic review and meta-analysis. *Sleep Medicine Reviews*, *52*, 101311. https://doi.org/10.1016/j.smrv.2020.101311

Short, M. A., & Louca, M. (2015). Sleep deprivation leads to mood deficits in healthy adolescents. *Sleep Medicine*, *16*(8), 987–993. https://doi.org/10.1016/j.sleep.2015.03.007

Strong, W. B., Malina, R. M., Blimkie, C. J., Daniels, S. R., Dishman, R. K., Gutin, B., Hergenroeder, A. C., Must, A., Nixon, P. A., Pivarnik, J. M., Rowland, T., Trost, S., & Trudeau, F. (2005). Evidence-based physical activity for school-age youth. *The Journal of Pediatrics*, *146*(6), 732–737. https://doi.org/10.1016/j.jpeds.2005.01.055

Syrad, H., Falconer, C., Cooke, L., Saxena, S., Kessel, A. S., Viner, R., Kinra, S., Wardle, J., & Croker, H. (2014). 'Health and happiness are more important than weight': A qualitative investigation of the views of parents receiving written feedback on their child's weight as part of the National Child Measurement Programme. *Journal of Human Nutrition and Dietetics*, *28*(1), 47–55. https://doi.org/10.1111/jhn.12217

van Woudenberg, T. J., Bevelander, K. E., Burk, W. J., & Buijzen, M. (2020). The reciprocal effects of physical activity and happiness in adolescents. *International Journal of Behavioral Nutrition and Physical Activity*, *17*(1), 1–10. https://doi.org/10.1186/s12966-020-01058-8

World Health Organization (WHO). (2020, November). *Physical activity*. Retrieved May 5, 2023, from www.who.int/news-room/fact-sheets/detail/physical-activity

Zhang, Z., & Chen, W. (2019). A systematic review of the relationship between physical activity and happiness. *Journal of Happiness Studies*, *20*(4), 1305–1322. https://doi.org/10.1007/s10902-018-9976-0

Zientarski, P. (2016). The school study sparking major change. *Physical & Health Education Journal*, *81*(4), 1. Retrieved May 5, 2023, from www.proquest.com/openview/5c1756245d726378944e2435a002ea3a/1?pq-origsite=gscholar&cbl=42913

Part 2

The Science of Success

6 The Power of Thinking Right

> Hey,
> Just following up based on our convo today.
> 1. You rock. (need I say more?)
> 2. You still rock. Colleges are gonna be chomping at the bit to get you on campus.
> 3. You rock(?) I'm glad we had a chance to connect today. I really hope that you'll reach out when you need nudges in the right direction (or at least my best attempt at finding the right direction).
> 4. You rock! There. That should do it.
> Let me know if there's anything I forgot.
> Mr. X
>
> (a teacher's email to a high school senior)

You rock! You are deserving! You are wonderful! These are all positive affirmations that aim to boost self-esteem and provide comfort, especially during challenging and stressful times such as when applying to colleges. Children welcome them, and adults feel good when they give them. But what is the effect of such person-oriented affirmations on the child's theory about their own ability and most importantly their success? Carol Dweck, the author of *Mindset: The New Psychology of Success*, argues that children who hear comments that validate or threaten their ability, come to believe that ability is fixed instead of something that grows. In turn, this mindset can hinder future success. In contrast, comments that focus on what one can do to achieve success allow children to overcome obstacles in their way. According to Dweck (2008), the way adults respond to children's successes and failures encourages two different mindsets: growth and fixed. Cultivating an ability requires effort and dedication to the goal regardless of setbacks. Angela Duckworth (2016) proposes that grit, a combination of perseverance and committed interest in long-term goals, is what it takes to become successful. This chapter is dedicated to exploring the concepts of growth and fixed mindset, their relationship with grit, and the evidence that links mindsets and grit with successful outcomes in school and broader psychological well-being. The development of a growth mindset is discussed along with other motivational findings to reconcile positive affirmations with the theory of mindsets. A review of guidelines for fostering a growth mindset

DOI: 10.4324/9780429356414-9

is also provided. Altogether, it appears that growth mindsets develop in environments where growth mindsets are lived in, experienced, modeled, discussed, and taught by adults whom children trust.

Growth and Fixed Mindsets

The key to success in school, relationships, parenting, and work, according to Dweck (2008), is the person's view of their own intelligence. While intelligence is influenced by genetics, it is not determined entirely by genes and therefore it can change, grow, and improve. Those who subscribe to the view that ability is malleable hold a growth mindset whereas those who believe that ability is static and unchangeable hold a fixed mindset. The fixed mindset stands in the way of development, change, and ultimately success. Dweck is quick to point out that believing that ability is changeable does not necessarily apply to everything, or that everything should be changeable. People may hold a growth mindset in one area and not another, or they may not act consistently with a growth mindset within one area. Nonetheless, Dweck (2008) draws several distinctions between the two mindsets that extend beyond believing that ability is malleable or not. People with a growth mindset believe that effort improves ability and that learning from mistakes is important for success. They accept feedback from others even when it is unflattering and utilize it to improve. They accept that failures are part of success even though they are hurtful, and they are not afraid to take on new challenges and learn new things. In fact, they actively seek out opportunities to stretch their minds and grow. They approach difficulties with patience and persistence because they understand that building new skills takes time. They are not phased when others succeed but rather use other people's successes for inspiration. They understand that others' successes say nothing about what they can achieve. Having a growth mindset means that learning is a journey, that has bumps on the way, but it is greatly enjoyed. This attitude provides confidence that anything can be conquered to some extent and that the sky's the limit. In school, those with a growth mindset have strong metacognitive skills and a firm attitude that achievement requires a clear focus, an all-out effort, and a wide repertoire of effective strategies (Dweck, 2008).

People with fixed mindsets allow their abilities to define them. Thinking that ability is permanent, the need to work hard at something threatens their identity. As a result, they devalue effort, idolize effortless accomplishment, seek validation of their abilities, and stay away from challenges that would jeopardize their self-concept. Consequently, they are often inaccurate about their level of skill or tend to distort their abilities by augmenting positive outcomes and downplaying negative ones. They also devalue feedback from others especially when it is negative and feel threatened by other people's successes. Their focus is on small achievable goals that are easy to get instead of bigger goals that require long-term commitments and sustained effort. Outcomes such as grades are evidence of how smart they are, and they may resort to cheating in order to preserve their self-image. In school, students use ineffective strategies for learning, such as memorizing, instead of trying to understand. The purpose of learning is to get correct answers and receive good grades, not learning itself. Success is the outcome, and the outcome defines who they are. When they are successful, they feel better than other people, and this sense of superiority feeds their self-esteem. In the face of painful failures, their fixed mindset deprives them of effective strategies to cope and consequently, they are prone to experiencing helplessness (Dweck, 2008).

The conceptual differences between the growth and the fixed mindset are supported by neurocognitive research. In people with a fixed mindset, the brain shows activity when they receive feedback about their ability. The brain does not respond when the feedback is about how to learn better (Dweck, 2008). Electrophysiological findings support that children with a growth mindset, similar to adults, pay attention to errors when they perform cognitive tasks. For example, Schroder et al. (2017) measured event-related potentials (ERP) in school-age children while they performed a go/no-go, reaction time task. They found that children with a growth mindset demonstrated an increased amplitude of Pe or error positivity, which is linked to allocating attention. Moreover, their accuracy increased after they committed errors. These results reveal the neural mechanisms of recovering from failure, a main characteristic of a growth mindset.

Dweck and colleagues conducted several studies to demonstrate how inducing a growth or fixed mindset in students may in fact change the child's orientation towards success. In a correlational study, Heyman and Dweck (1998) found that 8-year-old children who endorsed the idea that ability is stable explained academic difficulties in terms of lack of ability and believed that people possibly cannot learn certain things. Hong et al. (1999) in an experimental design showed that undergraduate students regardless of how confident they were, attributed failure to lack of effort if they held a belief that ability is malleable and were more likely to take corrective actions to recover from setbacks. Mueller and Dweck (1998), in a series of six studies involving 5th graders, showed that when children's ability was emphasized, children tended to attribute their poor performance to low ability and showed lowered task persistence. Kamins and Dweck (1999) showed that 5- and 6-year-old children modified their responses based on the kind of feedback they received while role-playing scenarios. For example, in one scenario, children pretended to build a block tower that was crooked and looked like a mess. Then they were given either person-oriented criticism (e.g., "I am disappointed in you," p. 838) or process-oriented feedback (e.g., "Maybe you can think of another way to do it," p. 838), or feedback that focused on the outcome (e.g., "That's not the right way to do it, because the blocks are not straightened up and are still messy," p. 938). The researchers then measured the children's affect, persistence, and beliefs about themselves. Children made more negative self-assessments and reported more negative affect and lower persistence when they received feedback that criticized the person. Lastly, Zhao et al. (2017b) demonstrated the negative consequences of having the reputation of being smart in a group of preschoolers (3–5 years of age). Before starting a guessing card game, the researchers told the children either "I know teachers and kids in your class and they told me you are a smart kid" (smart reputation condition, p. 3) or they were told, "I know teachers and kids in your class and they told me you are a clean kid" (irrelevant reputation condition, p. 3), or no reputational information. When the children were left alone in the lab, they had the chance to look at a card that would advance the game. The children in the smart reputation condition were more likely to cheat than the children in the other two conditions. The findings show that attempts to preserve the stability of ability may lead to cheating and they are consistent with the distinction between the growth and the fixed mindset. In a related study, Zhao et al. (2017a) more directly examined the effects of feedback on cheating among 3–5-year-olds. This time they told children "You are so smart" (ability condition, p. 1865) or "You did very well this time" (performance condition, p. 1865), or nothing at all (control condition) before they left children alone with the opportunity to peek at the hidden card. In agreement with the previous findings, children in the ability condition cheated more than children in the other two conditions.

In sum, Dweck (2008) proposes that the key to success in academics, and beyond, depends on a child's view of their intelligence, which can be categorized into a growth mindset (believing that ability is malleable) and a fixed mindset (believing that ability is static). Children with a growth mindset tend to be more open to learning from mistakes, accepting feedback, focusing on learning for the sake of learning, and embracing challenges, while those with a fixed mindset avoid challenges, discount the significance of effort, focus on performance goals, and feel threatened by others' success. Neurocognitive research and experimental studies support the distinction between the two mindsets, revealing how they affect behavior, self-perceptions, and responses to failures and successes.

Origins of the Growth Mindset

A mindset about ability likely begins to develop at an early age. Smiley and Dweck (1994) showed that 4- and 5-year-olds may hold a learning or performance orientation based on whether they embraced or shied away from a challenging task. Those with low confidence and a performance orientation experienced helplessness while trying to solve a difficult puzzle. Those with high confidence and a performance orientation used effective strategies but expressed more concerns about their performance. Their mastery of the puzzle was not as strong as that of the students with a learning orientation, who additionally expressed positive affect during the task.

Where do these beliefs about performance and learning come from? Socialization agents such as parents and teachers must play an important role while communicating their beliefs about ability. However, studies show zero to little correlation between the children's mindsets and the mindsets of parents and teachers. Moreover, this lack of association is not a matter of measurement error (Haimovitz & Dweck, 2017). Other studies showed that parents have the capacity to adapt to one or the other mindset and can change their behavior accordingly while supervising their child during a cognitive task. For example, Moorman and Pomerantz (2010) demonstrated that mothers, who were induced to have a fixed mindset, were more likely to tell their children the right answer, disregarding the importance of learning, took more control, and expressed more frustration than mothers who were induced to have a growth mindset.

Haimovitz and Dweck (2017) reveal that the type of feedback parents and teachers give in response to the children's successes and failures is crucial in shaping a growth or fixed mind regardless. When children share a successful outcome adults may respond with praise directed to the child or the process that led to the successful outcome. Children who receive person-praise such as "You are so bright" attribute their success to ability and are likely to develop a fixed mindset. When they later encounter difficulties, they assume that they cannot do well. In experimental studies, children who received person-praise did worse on a subsequent challenging task. Alternatively, adults may praise the actions or steps that led to the success by saying something like "Your idea of using flash cards paid off." This type of process-praise gives the message that success is an outcome of what the child can do, not what the child has already possessed. Process-praise emphasizes the children's skills that are under their control instead of something fixed that they can do nothing about. Studies show that children who received process-praise after a successful outcome were more persistent and enthusiastic when they tackled a more challenging task afterward. Similarly, when children face setbacks, adults may respond with comments that either target the person or the process. In research, children endorsed a fixed mindset when they received criticism that focused on them (e.g., "I am disappointed with how you did"). However, when they were given a positive message that addressed their strategies, persistence, and what they learned in the process, children adopted a growth mindset and were more motivated to pursue academic tasks despite their difficulty. These results were shown in children from 5 and 6 years of age to college years. When undergraduate students were told that they received a low grade on their assignment because they have not mastered the topic *yet*, they were more likely to show a growth mindset than when they were told the same phrase without the word yet. Simple words can make a difference in activating the right mindset for success (Haimovitz & Dweck, 2017).

Haimovitz and Dweck (2017) found that oftentimes parents and teachers with a growth mindset do not necessarily respond to children's successes or failures in ways that would enhance a growth mindset. For example, parents and teachers with a growth mindset do not always provide process-praise. To explain why adults with a growth mindset do not respond to children's successes and failures in a congruent way, Haimovitz and Dweck (2017) speculate that adults' theories of motivation get in the way, sometimes. Parents and teachers may consider that children need more positive affirmation or a quick boost. There is evidence, for example, that parents are likely to give person-praise if they perceive that the child has low self-esteem. Perhaps it is really rewarding to the parents when they call their children smart or bright. It is a tendency to claim credit for good things that happen. Future research could address how the differences in intelligence mindsets and motivational theories contribute to the origins of children's mindsets, and the conditions under which they align to better promote a mindset for success.

From a developmental perspective, how children's self-concepts develop over time may be an important factor to consider in the development of mindsets. In preschool, self-concepts hold more descriptions of what the child likes or does instead of psychological traits or labels of who one is. At this age, children's self-concepts reflect very closely their parents' descriptions. Parents often call their little children "smart, beautiful, and great" to boost their self-esteem. When children start school, they begin to compare themselves with others and experience a drop in their self-esteem as they realize that others may be more beautiful, smarter, and greater. Gradually, children consolidate their behaviors, activities, and preferences in more stable characteristics around age 8. It seems that the time between preschool to early middle childhood is the critical time to intentionally support a growth mindset not only about ability but any other skill and personality trait. Socialization happens not only inside the classroom but also in the broader school community and culture. Children receive messages about performance versus learning from morning messages, posters on the walls, school meetings, and most importantly the school's pedagogical approach. According to Haimovitz and Dweck (2017), there are currently 150 schools in the United States that promote a culture of growth mindset inside and outside the classroom. In these schools, students are trained to focus on learning by checking their understanding, noticing how learning is built up over time, and how achieving learning goals is not an all-or-none process. These schools celebrate learning instead of performance outcomes and educate families and community stakeholders to actively practice a growth mindset.

In summary, mindsets about ability begin to develop early in childhood, with socialization agents such as parents and teachers playing a crucial role in shaping these beliefs. Feedback given by parents and teachers can either encourage a growth mindset (emphasizing learning and improvement) or a fixed mindset (emphasizing innate ability). Process-praise, which focuses on actions or strategies leading to success, promotes a growth mindset, while person-praise, which focuses on a child's inherent traits, fosters a fixed mindset. However, the correlation between the mindsets of parents, teachers, and children is not always strong, as parents and teachers with a growth mindset may not always provide congruent responses. Adult responses to children's successes and failures are also influenced by their theories of how to best motivate children. Attempts to foster a growth mindset may start in early childhood by immersing children in a culture that values learning and improvement at home and school.

Impact of Growth Mindset on Academic Achievement

Dweck and colleagues as well as independent researchers established that children may hold different views about their intelligence and that these theories when primed affect children's motivation, task persistence, self-defeating beliefs, and inevitably their academic performance. Blackwell et al. (2007) revealed evidence for the role of mindsets in long-term achievement, looked for mediators that would explain such a role, and showed that teaching children that learning is incremental affected academic performance. This evidence was provided in a series of two studies that followed children at the beginning of junior high for a couple of years. Having an incremental theory of intelligence was correlated with beliefs that effort matters, lower helpless characterizations, the use of more effective strategies, and having more learning than performance goals. While students' scores in math did not differ at the beginning of the study, those students with a growth mindset had higher scores than students with a fixed mindset two years later. Two mediational paths were also identified. A belief in incremental ability helped students set learning goals that increased the use of positive strategies and led to higher math scores. Also, a belief in incremental ability increased effort which led to lower helplessness and then to higher math scores. In the second study, 7th graders were taught about incremental ability in a series of eight sessions while the control group read about the nature of memory. The students in the intervention group showed a better understanding of incremental ability and more of them endorsed the theory of incremental ability than the control group. Most importantly, the intervention group did not experience the anticipated decrease in grades, a trend that Dweck explained is typical during school transitions. In contrast, the control group showed an expected decline in grades.

In the years that followed, several intervention studies were conducted across the country and the world, motivated by the need to support underperforming students who are at risk of dropping out. In fact, 20% of the students in the US do not complete high school on time (Yeager et al., 2019) and 5% drop out entirely (Hanson, 2021). Dropping out of high school places them at risk for homelessness, poverty, violence, and poor health. As growth mindset interventions gained traction in schools, a closer examination of the studies supporting their impact became necessary. Furthermore, emerging evidence revealed that the actual effects of these interventions might be minimal or even non-existent.

Li and Bates (2019) attempted to replicate Dweck's findings with 9– to 13-year-old Chinese children but did not find consistent evidence that the growth mindset induced resilient responses to failure or that it improved educational outcomes. In their first study, the activation of the growth mindset enhanced children's performance on a task. However, they did not demonstrate all the other learning and motivational attributions that were associated with the growth mindset (e.g., learning goals, effort, openness, and enthusiasm for a challenge). In additional studies, Li and Bates (2019) included a control group and a more difficult task but failed to replicate the effect of the growth mindset. Furthermore, the growth mindset was not related to student's GPA at the beginning or during the semester even when the researchers controlled for cognitive ability. Cognitive ability was the only predictor of GPA and did not interact with the growth mindset to affect GPA, hence not supporting the idea that a growth mindset builds ability. Similar results were obtained when the researchers examined specific subjects like math, English, and Chinese. Lastly, the growth mindset did not predict any change in GPA over time.

Because Dweck and colleagues emphasized the protective nature of a growth mindset during transitions, Li and Bates (2020) tested these assumptions in another series of studies involving undergraduate students as they were transitioning and adjusting to college in the UK. First, they examined the association between having a growth mindset and grades. They used Dweck's (1999) assessment for theories of intelligence that consists of eight items, four of which assess the incremental view of intelligence (e.g., "No matter who you are, you can significantly change your intelligence level") and another four assessing the fixed view of intelligence (e.g., "You have a certain amount of intelligence, and you can't really do much to change it). Interestingly, the association between growth mindset and grades of the past semesters was in the opposite direction although not significant. The results did not change when sex and age were accounted for in the analyses. Moreover, the researchers found that having high self-esteem significantly predicted GPA. Additionally, the researchers studied the progression of the students' grades over four years and again did not find any positive associations. According to Li and Bates (2019, 2020), these results reveal that a growth mindset is not related to intelligence and therefore the claim that the growth mindset can change intelligence simply cannot stand. Moreover, the growth mindset did not have any enduring effect on academic performance.

As the criticism for the theory of growth mindset increased, researchers conducted meta-analytic analyses of correlational and intervention studies to determine the actual size of the effect that the growth mindset has on academic performance. Sisk and colleagues (2018) reported two such analyses. First, they focused on 273 studies that simply examined the association between a growth mindset and academic achievement but also considered potential moderator variables. They explored the possibility that the effect varied by developmental age (primary school, middle school, and high school) and by academic risk status, socioeconomic status, and type of measure of academic performance. Overall, the average correlation of various population effects between growth mindset and academic achievement was .10. In 6% of the studies, the effect indicated that a growth mindset was associated with lower academic achievement, 58% did not reveal a significant effect size, and 37% actually supported a positive association of a magnitude of .19. None of the moderators was significant except the measure of academic achievement when laboratory-based measures were included (e.g., tests administered by the researchers). In that case, the correlation was .11.

In the second meta-analytic study, the authors reviewed the 29 intervention studies in which the goal was to enhance the students' belief that ability could be improved with effort. The researchers analyzed the difference in academic outcome between the intervention and the control group post-intervention and considered similar moderators as earlier, including additionally the type and timing of intervention. Twelve percent of the effect sizes were statistically significant, and clearly showed the impact of the intervention. The child's age did not moderate the effect, but the socioeconomic and risk status did. Children and adolescents who were from low socioeconomic status and higher risk for academic failure benefited from the intervention, but other groups did not. Overall, the significant effects were between the intervention and the control group, because in the studies where a fixed mindset intervention was included the difference in the performance between the growth and the fixed mindset was not significant. In studies that showed the effect, students' academic scores were improved when the intervention required students to reflect upon the malleability of their ability. The length of the intervention and the time that passed between intervention and the assessment of academic outcomes were nonsignificant moderators. Lastly, the only index of academic performance that showed improvement was the GPA; no improvement was observed in standardized scores. Overall, Sisk et al. (2018) concluded that the effect, when significant, tended to be small or borderline and benefited specific students. They also raised the concern that a growth mindset intervention might even harm students who are confident in their abilities.

On the other hand, Dweck and Yeager spearheaded a national longitudinal study, known as the National Study of Learning Mindsets (NSLM) or the students' Perspectives about the Transition to High School (PATHS), which involved several schools from all over the country that had agreed to implement a growth mindset intervention to their students. The purpose of this study was three-fold: examine the protective effect of a growth mindset on academic performance and behaviors such as taking challenging courses; reveal whether the effect was uniform across diverse student populations; and identify the conditions under which the intervention was most or least effective. The intervention took place in two 25-minute, online sessions, 20 days apart. Each session included five parts: reading information about the neuroplasticity of the brain, reading stories about people who changed their behaviors, reading stories of youth applying the growth mindset when dealing with negative situations, reading information about how the growth mindset works, and creating personal stories about applications of the growth mindset that could benefit other youth. To avoid any potential bias, the researchers contracted an independent research company to randomly select the schools and analyze the data. In 2019, they published their first results from 65 schools. In less than 1 hour, this online intervention reduced the frequency of the fixed mindset among low-achieving 9th graders and resulted in higher GPAs. The net gain in GPA was estimated to be .10 grade points while these students also experienced a 5% reduction in poor performance. Similar findings were reported in the subjects of mathematics and science. The effect was greater in already high-achieving schools that had wholeheartedly integrated a growth mindset into their culture, ranging from .18 to .25 grade points. In addition, both high- and low-achieving 9th graders who were in the growth mindset condition chose more advanced math courses in 10th grade (Yeager et al., 2019).

Lastly, Yeager and Dweck (2020) in a subsequent publication attempted to reconcile the somewhat contradictory findings and the small effect of the growth mindset interventions. They remind the scientific community that the mindset theory is a theory about recovering from setbacks, and not one to explain all that contributes to academic achievement. They point out that the effect of the growth mindset intervention is evident in representative and independent studies often conducted in other countries, and that the lack of effect was demonstrated in studies with Chinese students. They raise the possibility that the Chinese culture already emphasizes hard work and effort and therefore the intervention does not further enhance academic performance. However, they note that among Chinese students the correlation between the fixed mindset and fear of failure is pretty strong. They agree that the effect of the growth mindset is heterogeneous across students and contexts, and advocate that the improvements reported in Yeager et al. (2019) should not be discounted as minimal. When these results are applied to all US students who are at risk for academic failure, several thousand of them may be protected. Lastly, they agree that interventions delivered by teachers are not effective and propose direct-to-student training that is available from their website (www.perts.net) while future research should address how teachers' professional development may support the growth mindset interventions in schools.

In summary, the growth mindset theory has significant implications for academic achievement but the findings regarding its efficacy are conflicting. Dweck and colleagues have shown that children's beliefs about intelligence can influence their motivation, persistence, and academic performance. Blackwell et al.'s (2007) study demonstrated that teaching children about incremental learning positively affected their academic performance over time. However, other research found minimal or non-existent effects of growth mindset interventions on academic performance, with Li and Bates (2019) unable to replicate the findings of Dweck's research. Meta-analytic analyses, such as Sisk et al. (2018), show a small effect size when growth mindset interventions significantly impact academic performance, predominantly benefiting students from low socioeconomic backgrounds or those at higher risk of academic failure. The National Study of Learning Mindsets, led by Dweck and Yeager, demonstrated the positive impact of growth mindset interventions on GPA and course choices in 9th-grade students. Yeager and Dweck (2020) emphasize that the growth mindset theory is primarily about recovering from setbacks rather than explaining overall academic achievement. They acknowledge that the effect is heterogeneous across different student populations and contexts and suggest that direct-to-student training should be prioritized over teacher-led interventions. Future research should focus on understanding these nuances and optimizing interventions for specific groups.

Impact of Growth Mindset on Mental Health

According to Dweck (2008), the theory of growth mindset also applies to any ability, talent, or personality trait. Those who believe that personal characteristics are changeable are less likely to let negative labels define them or prejudice affect them. They understand that a stereotype is another person's view, and it should not affect them. They carefully choose whose opinion matters and thrive in a group where the growth mindset is protected. Furthermore, believing that personal qualities can change is expected to reduce psychological stress that is often manifested in mental health problems of anxiety and depression. A growth mindset should also promote greater agency in coping with problems that cause stress. For example, in a randomized study involving 12–15-year-old adolescents at high risk for anxiety and depression, Schleider and Weisz (2018) showed that a one-time growth mindset intervention had several positive effects. Adolescents in the intervention group experienced a faster improvement in primary coping (i.e., the agency in coping by influencing the environment) and a greater decline in anxiety and depression over nine months. In addition, significantly fewer youth who experienced the intervention were above the clinical cut-off for anxiety and depression than those in the control group.

In a meta-analytic report involving 72 studies, Burnette and colleagues (2020) examined the association between growth mindset, mental health, active coping, and the value placed on seeking treatment. They also considered several moderators that would affect the strength of these associations, including the age of the participants and the time of assessment (immediate versus longitudinal). The findings confirmed a positive correlation with active coping and treatment value and a negative correlation with psychological stress. The link with psychological stress was stronger for order samples and in studies where data were based on self-reports instead of manipulations of the mindset. Also, the association was stronger in cross-sectional than in longitudinal studies, implying that the effect fades away with time. Lastly, how psychological stress was defined did not affect the relationship, suggesting a broad effect of a growth mindset on mental health.

Lastly, Perkins et al. (2021) expanded the literature by testing the effectiveness of a psychological, growth-mindset intervention beyond anxiety and depression to include personality, self-acceptance, self-compassion, and self-esteem. Participants were 80 older adolescents (16–18) who were randomly assigned to the intervention or control group. About 40% of the intervention group were less likely to aspire to a fixed personality theory and reported greater self-acceptance and compassion, although fewer of them did so four and eight weeks after the intervention. Less than 10% of the control group reported any improvement and about 20% of them actually reported a decline in their personality flexibility at the eight-week follow-up. Therefore, the gain seems to be short-term, but without intervention, matters may worsen. When comparing the two groups at four weeks, the intervention group reported higher self-compassion, self-esteem, and lower depression and anxiety. At the eight-week follow-up, the differences in self-esteem, anxiety, and depression persisted, although moderate, and the difference in self-compassion became insignificant. Even though the sample was small, the findings are promising because they indicate that these positive interventions are feasible in school settings. Alto gether, the evidence points out that the size of the effect that the growth mindset has on mental health is twice as high as the effect it has on academic performance. The findings highlight the need to consider the theory of growth mindset, especially the mindset about the malleability of emotions, in clinical settings.

Grit and Its Relation to Growth Mindset and Well-Being

People with a growth mindset emphasize effort over ability or talent. As shown earlier, this helps achieve better grades and improve mental health. However, this cognitive frame of mind may not be enough to achieve goals that are long-term and require greater motivation and dedication. Angela Duckworth proposed that the personality trait of grit is needed to reach bigger and distant goals. She defined grit as the combination of perseverance and passion for long-term goals (Duckworth et al., 2007) and developed an eight-item grit scale that reflects sustained effort (e.g., I finish whatever I begin) and interest in the goal (e.g., negatively worded: "New ideas and projects sometimes distract me from previous ones"; Duckworth & Quinn, 2009). In a series of studies, Duckworth and her colleagues demonstrated that grit is what distinguished those who achieved higher goals, such as winning the Spelling Bee and completing the training at the United States Military Academy in West Point. Spelling Bee competitors who scored one standard deviation above average on the grit scale were 38% more likely to advance in the competition. Moreover, cadets scoring one standard deviation above the average were 90% more likely to complete the training. The researchers also demonstrated that grit increased with age and that it predicted GPA in adolescence and future educational attainment.

Research has examined the association that grit has with personality traits and growth mindsets in predicting academic outcomes. According to Duckworth and Quinn (2009), grit is related to conscientiousness which refers to being efficient, organized, and task-oriented, but it makes independent contributions to academic achievement. However, others found a significant overlap between grit and conscientiousness to the point that grit made null contributions to performance. A meta-analytic study showed grit to have weak associations with performance and retention and a very strong correlation with conscientiousness. When controlling for conscientiousness, only the perseverance aspect of grit maintained its predictive value for academic achievement. The sustained interest did not have any utility (Credé et al., 2017). Similarly, a study from Finland demonstrated a direct and strong association between the perseverance aspect of grit and academic achievement in 8th graders as well as their engagement a year later, while controlling for conscientiousness, previous academic outcomes, and demographic variables (Tang et al., 2019).

The advantages of grit seem to be primarily focused on the perseverance aspect. It is possible that maintaining interest in a goal over an extended period or having a strong passion for achieving a goal are influenced by other factors, such as beliefs about potential rewards and confidence in one's abilities. Dale et al. (2018) discovered that grit contributed to task persistence when participants were aware of a reward and believed they could achieve it. Some studies indicate that the connection between grit and academic achievement is mediated by self-efficacy. Usher et al. (2019) conducted research with elementary and middle school students who evaluated their self-efficacy and grit. Teachers provided assessments of competence and motivation, while schools supplied achievement records. The researchers identified a robust correlation between grit and self-efficacy. Self-efficacy was associated with all outcomes, while grit exhibited modest to weak correlations with achievement variables. Additionally, self-efficacy either partially or fully mediated the relationship between grit and outcomes, whereas the opposite was not true; grit did not mediate the connection between self-efficacy and achievement.

In an effort to further clarify the construct of grit and its benefits, researchers studied the connection between growth mindset and grit. Brain imaging supports that grit activates connections in the region that monitors rewards whereas the growth mindset is related to regions that are activated with error tracking (Myers et al., 2016; Wang et al., 2018). Duckworth (2016) proposed that a growth mindset would lead to the development of grit because the belief that ability and personality are malleable promotes confidence in the fruits of hard work, and therefore encourages the pursuit of long-term and bigger goals. Park et al. (2020) explored this relationship but also the possibility that grit supports a growth mindset. They argued that in the process of working hard to achieve goals, the person may realize that personal qualities and abilities can be changed for the better. Park et al. (2020) recruited 1,667 8th graders from several schools across the US and assessed their grit and growth mindset four times, six months apart from each other. Both constructs showed strong stability over time. The cross-lagged paths from grit to growth mindset and from growth mindset to grit were significant, meaning that one predicted the other's development over two years. Moreover, the predictive validity of grit for a growth mindset was twice as strong, supporting the initial rationale of the researchers that competence and confidence may engender the idea that personal attributes are changeable. Other research also points in that direction. Tang et al. (2019) found that grit did not mediate the relationship between growth and mindset and academic outcomes in a sample of 6th to 9th graders from Finland.

Lastly, there is emerging evidence that highlights the positive associations of grit with subjective well-being. Jiang et al. (2020) hypothesized that applying grit would promote feelings of autonomy, competence, and relatedness, all of which are considered main psychological needs, according to the self-determination theory (Ryan & Deci, 2000). Thus, grit was expected to correlate with measures of subjective well-being. In a sample of 15-year-old adolescents, Jiang et al. showed that grit was indeed related to life satisfaction, positive affect, and negative affect. However, the relationship was also mediated by the extent to which their psychological needs were satisfied. Moreover, the effects were significant even after the researchers controlled for conscientiousness. More nuanced findings from another study indicated that satisfying the need for autonomy mediated the relationship between grit and decreased depression while satisfying the need for competence mediated the relationship between grit and greater life satisfaction, at least among young adults (Jin & Kim, 2017).

In conclusion, grit is an essential personality trait that encompasses perseverance and passion for long-term goals. While there is debate over the degree of its association with conscientiousness, perseverance remains an important aspect of grit. Grit has been found to be a predictor of academic achievement and has connections with a growth mindset. However, recent studies have shown that grit could have an even stronger impact on the development of a growth mindset, as competence and confidence may influence one's beliefs about personal attributes being changeable. Furthermore, research has shown that grit is positively associated with subjective well-being, with connections to autonomy, competence, and relatedness, which are considered key psychological needs in the self-determination theory. Consequently, grit is a valuable quality to foster in children, as it can contribute to better academic outcomes, personal growth, and overall well-being.

What About Positive Affirmations?

Carol Dweck's theory of growth mindset contrasts with a culture of boosting children's self-esteem by lavishing them with praise, despite the children's level of effort or commitment to learning. Dweck expected that person-centered praise results in a fixed mindset and that children with a fixed mindset would develop fragile self-esteem. In her research, children who were induced to adopt a fixed mindset made helpless comments during a challenging task (Dweck, 2008). However, as noted earlier, the meta-analysis by Sisk et al. (2018) revealed no differences in outcomes between those with growth and fixed mindset and even suggested that a growth mindset intervention may be harmful to those who are confident in their abilities. In addition, research suggests that students (6–8 grades) with objectively measured high ability (e.g., IQ) were no more representative in the growth or fixed mindset even though they held stronger beliefs about their ability and performance. Furthermore, they were no different from typical students in terms of motivation and self-regulation (Mofield & Parker Peters, 2018). This leaves room for the possibility that fixed mindset students with great confidence in their abilities can be very successful in school.

Influenced by positive psychology, there is currently a popular trend of practicing positive affirmations as a way to enhance one's self-esteem, regardless of their mindset. Under what circumstances then might self-esteem help in coping with challenging academic times by increasing confidence and providing the motivation to persist? Is it possible that praise and positive affirmation such as the one that started this chapter activate a growth mindset in students who value learning and work hard to achieve their goals? Or are praise and positive affirmations part of a motivational system that affects the ability to persist—in other words may also relate to the development of grit? The answers to these questions are subject to future investigation, but there is evidence to support the effectiveness of positive affirmations.

Proponents of positive affirmations argue that this practice helps people to view negative and challenging events as less threatening and open up to the idea that they are instead valuable opportunities to grow (Falk et al., 2015). Positive affirmations may also change the way people think about themselves (Emanuel et al., 2018), and therefore create feelings of hope and optimism, both of which are linked with improved academic performance (see Chapter 2). In fact, some research showed that hope explained more variance in the academic achievement of high schoolers than a growth mindset did (Dixson, 2020). Practicing self-affirmations in writing has indeed resulted in an improvement in GPA among college students (Layous, 2017). Similar results were also reported with young adolescents as they transitioned to middle school (Binning et al., 2021). In a longitudinal study, a group of 6th graders experienced an intervention for affirming self-integrity and were compared with a control group for three years. The affirmed group was asked to choose three personal values and write down why they were important to them (e.g., athletic ability, independence, politics, relationships with friends). They experienced several affirmation sessions during the length of the study. The researchers also assessed GPA and the level of psychological threat in the academic environment. The psychological threat was a composite score of several indices: school belonging, test anxiety, academic stress, and social evaluations from others (e.g., biases). The researchers found a difference of .29 in GPA favoring the affirmed group, during the third year when the students were in 8th grade. There was also a connection between the psychological threat and GPA. In the control group, the GPA declined by .15 grade points for every standard deviation increase in psychological threat. However, in the affirmed group there was no association indicating that affirmations at the very least neutralized the effect of psychological threat.

Current research on academic emotions and their effect on academic performance provides at least some insight as to whether positive affirmations have a place in academic settings. Putwain et al. (2022) proposed that academic emotions affect academic buoyancy, which in turn affects performance. Academic emotions can be positive or negative and they are experienced in the classroom, in the school corridors, in conversations with teachers or classmates, and while doing homework at home. Academic buoyancy is the ability to adapt to daily academic challenges such as lower motivation, poor grades, negative comparisons with others, receiving negative feedback, and pressure from exams, school projects, and college applications. Putwain et al. (2022) demonstrated a reciprocal relationship between academic emotions and performance in primary school students (average age = 9) as one supported the other over time. Moreover, academic buoyancy moderated the relationship between academic emotions (e.g., anxiety) and test scores. Perhaps, positive affirmations fit into this model by reducing either negative academic emotions at times of distress or directly impacting academic buoyancy that would then affect academic performance. Further research is needed to investigate these ideas.

In conclusion, Carol Dweck's theory of growth mindset has contributed significantly to the understanding of how beliefs about intelligence and abilities can impact motivation and achievement. However, recent research has questioned the generalizability of the theory and suggested that there may not be a clear-cut difference in outcomes between students with growth and fixed mindsets. In some cases, a fixed mindset may even be beneficial, particularly for students who are confident in their abilities. The current trend of positive affirmations, inspired by positive psychology, has shown promise in enhancing self-esteem and academic performance. Evidence suggests that positive affirmations can reduce negative emotions, increase hope and optimism, and improve academic buoyancy, which in turn supports better performance in academic settings. While positive affirmations may not directly activate a growth mindset, they can create an environment in which students feel more confident and motivated to face challenges, thus supporting persistence and learning. Future research should continue to explore the complex relationship between mindset, self-esteem, positive affirmations, academic emotions, and academic performance. This will help educators and researchers develop more effective strategies for supporting student success and well-being in academic settings.

Raising the Power of Thinking Right

Notwithstanding the role of positive affirmations, a growth mindset fosters a sense of agency that in turn makes children more resilient. The beliefs about the nature of ability (changeable versus static) and orientation towards learning (mastery versus performance) are nurtured in families and schools. As discussed earlier, however, even parents who have a growth mindset do not always respond to their children in ways that promote a growth mindset. For example, according to their beliefs about what motivates their children, parents may use praise that fits a fixed mindset. Some parents and teachers may even project a false growth mindset, meaning that they deny their own fixed mindset and falsely claim that they have a growth mindset (Dweck, 2015). Therefore, parents need to be mindful of their own mindsets and how they communicate with their children. Teaching a growth mindset starts with parents and teachers learning how to use the right language in their feedback on children's successes and failures. Despite the conflicting results from cross-sectional and intervention studies, there is evidence from a naturalistic, longitudinal study that the process begins very early and may have long-term effects on children's academic performance. Gunderson et al. (2018) found that observed process-praise during the first three years of life predicted a growth mindset in 2nd and 3rd grade and better academic achievement in 4th grade. The same results held even after controlling for socioeconomic status, gender, and grades in 2nd grade. The ripe time to introduce a growth mindset, therefore, is in early childhood.

Dweck (2015) points out that feedback about children's learning goals is just as important as messages about the nature of their abilities. Parents and teachers, for example, should replace "Great effort! You tried your best" with "The point isn't to get it all right away. The point is to grow your understanding. What can you try next?" (Dweck, 2015, p. 1). Dweck (2008) prompts parents to treat their children as geniuses, giving them the message that they can learn anything that others have managed to learn if they put in the time and effort. Parents can also be powerful models of using a growth mindset when they face challenges, successes, and failures. Parents may discuss how working hard paid off, how failure is just another step that brings success, and that learning new things is exciting and interesting. Children may watch their parents or join them in taking on a new hobby or skill that they know nothing about. Parents need to be sensitive to children's attributions about failures that associate with a fixed mindset and be mindful of the kind of feedback their children receive from their teachers. Conflicting messages can be confusing to children and may be undermining their confidence. Parents should provide encouragement and support while avoiding labeling their children as good or bad at something. Parents who shame their children, compare them with others, blame them for causing disappointment, induce guilt, and withdraw affection have children with fixed mindsets who suffer academically (Gao et al., 2020).

Despite its heterogeneity, the effect of a growth mindset on academic achievement is a desirable goal in many schools, especially for low-achieving students. Unfortunately, the current research shows that teacher-delivered interventions of growth mindset are not very effective and suggests that teachers' professional development should address this matter. Indeed, although teachers acknowledge that children should have a growth mindset and that teaching a growth mindset is among the teachers' responsibilities, only one-third of teachers have the confidence that they can teach a growth mindset (Nestor, 2017). Moreover, while teachers consider the development of a growth mindset important, they do not necessarily have it at the top of their priorities list. In one qualitative study, teachers reported that forming positive relationships within the school community and following a developmentally appropriate philosophy were their top priorities. Their third priority was to foster a sense of agency in students' learning (Boylan et al., 2018). This goal is the closest to the idea of a growth mindset but not explicitly the same.

Dweck and colleagues have also suggested that changes in the school culture are needed for interventions to be successful. Thomas et al. (2019) discovered that children were more open to accepting messages for a growth mindset if they perceived a sense of justice, care, and trust in their school environment. Therefore, teachers would be more effective if they first established trusting relationships with their students. In addition, teachers may explore ways of integrating ideas of the growth mindset in their teaching instead of implementing a specific training program. An example of such integration is provided by Clark et al. (2018, May/June) who used literature to promote a growth mindset. Books such as *After the Fall: How Humpty Dumpty Got Back Up Again* by Dan Santat (Roaring Brook) and *Stuck* by Oliver Jeffers (Philomel) are excellent ways to discuss the character's attitudes and thinking processes that reveal a growth mindset. For example, perseverance is revealed by asking children what strategies the person used to succeed. Questions about ways and strategies that solve a problem reveal that abilities are traits that are not static. Questions about what children would do if they were in the shoes of the story character encourage students to adopt another's perspective and mindset.

In conclusion, fostering a growth mindset in children may have a significant impact on their resilience and academic performance. Parents and teachers play a crucial role in nurturing beliefs about the nature of ability and learning orientation. Parents and teachers need to be mindful of their own mindsets and the language they use when providing feedback to children. Early childhood presents a prime opportunity to instill a growth mindset, and the right kind of feedback can contribute to long-term effects on academic performance. To promote a growth mindset, parents and teachers must focus on learning goals and model growth mindset behaviors in their own lives. Providing encouragement and support; avoiding labeling children; and having open conversations about effort, failure, and learning can contribute to the development of a growth mindset. Although teacher-delivered growth mindset interventions have shown mixed results, professional development and changes in school culture can enhance their effectiveness. Establishing trust and positive relationships within the school community, as well as prioritizing the fostering of agency in student learning, can create a more conducive environment for nurturing a growth mindset. As research continues to explore the complex relationships between growth mindset, self-esteem, academic emotions, and academic performance, educators and researchers can develop more effective strategies for supporting student success and well-being. Altogether, it appears that growth mindsets develop in environments where growth mindsets are lived in, experienced, modeled, discussed, and taught by adults who children trust.

References

Binning, K. R., Cook, J. E., Purdie-Greenaway, V., Garcia, J., Apfel, N., & Sherman, D. K. (2021). Securing self-integrity over time: Self-affirmation disrupts a negative cycle between psychological threat and academic performance. *Journal of Social Issues*, *77*(3), 801–823. https://doi.org/10.1111/josi.12461

Blackwell, L. S., Trzesniewski, K. H., & Dweck, C. S. (2007). Implicit theories of intelligence predict achievement across an adolescent transition: A longitudinal study and an intervention. *Child Development*, *78*(1), 246–263. https://doi.org/10.1111/j.1467-8624.2007.00995.x

Boylan, F., Barblett, L., & Knaus, M. (2018). Early childhood teachers' perspectives of growth mindset: Developing agency in children. *Australasian Journal of Early Childhood*, *43*(3), 16–24. https://doi.org/10.23965/AJEC.43.3.02

Burnette, J. L., Knouse, L. E., Vavra, D. T., O'Boyle, E., & Brooks, M. A. (2020). Growth mindsets and psychological distress: A meta-analysis. *Clinical Psychology Review*, *77*, 101816. https://doi.org/10.1016/j.cpr.2020.101816

Clark, S. R., Enriquez, G., & Calce, J. D. (2018). Inspiring agency: Teaching a growth mindset through children's literature. *Literacy Today*, *35*(6), 28–29.

Credé, M., Tynan, M. C., & Harms, P. D. (2017). Much ado about grit: A meta-analytic synthesis of the grit literature. *Journal of Personality and Social Psychology*, *113*(3), 492 511. https://doi.org/10.1037/pspp0000102

Dale, G., Sampers, D., Loo, S., & Green, C. S. (2018). Individual differences in exploration and persistence: Grit and beliefs about ability and reward. *PloS One*, *13*(9), e0203131. https://doi.org/10.1371/journal.pone.0203131

Dixson, D. D. (2020). How hope measures up: Hope predicts school variables beyond growth mindset and school belonging. *Current Psychology*, 1–13. https://doi.org/10.1007/s12144-020-00975-y

Duckworth, A. (2016). *Grit: The power of passion and perseverance* (Vol. 234). Scribner.

Duckworth, A. L., Peterson, C., Matthews, M. D., & Kelly, D. R. (2007). Grit: Perseverance and passion for long-term goals. *Journal of Personality and Social Psychology*, *92*(6), 1087–1101. https://doi.org/10.1037/0022-3514.92.6.1087

Duckworth, A. L., & Quinn, P. D. (2009). Development and validation of the Short Grit Scale (GRIT–S). *Journal of Personality Assessment*, *91*(2), 166–174. https://doi.org/10.1080/00223890802634290

Dweck, C. (1999). *Self-theories: Their role in motivation, personality, and development*. Psychology Press.

Dweck, C. (2015, September). Growth mindset, revisited: Commentary. *Education Week*, *35*(5), 20–24. Retrieved May 20, 2023, from www.studentachievement.org/wp-content/uploads/Carol-Dweck-Revisits-the-Growth-Mindset.pdf

Dweck, C. S. (2008). *Mindset: The new psychology of success*. Random House Digital, Inc.

Emanuel, A. S., Howell, J. L., Taber, J. M., Ferrer, R. A., Klein, W. M., & Harris, P. R. (2018). Spontaneous self-affirmation is associated with psychological well-being: Evidence from a US national adult survey sample. *Journal of Health Psychology*, *23*(1), 95–102. https://doi.org/10.1177/1359105316643595

Falk, E. B., O'Donnell, M. B., Cascio, C. N., Tinney, F., Kang, Y., Lieberman, M. D., Taylor, S. E., An, L., Resnicow, K., & Strecher, V. J. (2015). Self-affirmation alters the brain's response to health messages and subsequent behavior change. *Proceedings of the National Academy of Sciences*, *112*(7), 1977–1982. https://doi.org/10.1073/pnas.1500247112

Gao, X., Liu, C., Guo, X., Liu, J., Qi, B., & Luo, L. (2020). Relationship between parental psychological control and children's academic achievement in China: The role of children's failure mindsets. *Children and Youth Services Review*, *119*, 105627. https://doi.org/10.1016/j.childyouth.2020.105627

Gunderson, E. A., Sorhagen, N. S., Gripshover, S. J., Dweck, C. S., Goldin-Meadow, S., & Levine, S. C. (2018). Parent praise to toddlers predicts fourth-grade academic achievement via children's incremental mindsets. *Developmental Psychology*, *54*(3), 397–409. https://doi.org/10.1037/dev0000444

Haimovitz, K., & Dweck, C. S. (2017). The origins of children's growth and fixed mindsets: New research and a new proposal. *Child Development*, *88*(6), 1849–1859. https://doi.org/10.1111/cdev.12955

Hanson, M. (2021, September 13). *High school drop-out rate*. Retrieved October 5, 2021, from https://educationdata.org/high-school-dropout-rate

Heyman, G. D., & Dweck, C. S. (1998). Children's thinking about traits: Implications for judgments of the self and others. *Child Development*, *69*(2), 391–403. https://doi.org/10.1111/j.1467-8624.1998.tb06197.x

Hong, Y.-Y., Chiu, C.-Y., Dweck, C. S., Lin, D. M.-S., & Wan, W. (1999). Implicit theories, attributions, and coping: A meaning system approach. *Journal of Personality and Social Psychology*, *77*(3), 588–599. https://doi.org/10.1037/0022-3514.77.3.588

Jiang, W., Jiang, J., Du, X., Gu, D., Sun, Y., & Zhang, Y. (2020). Striving and happiness: Between-and within-person-level associations among grit, needs satisfaction and subjective well-being. *The Journal of Positive Psychology*, *15*(4), 543–555. https://doi.org/10.1080/17439760.2019.1639796

Jin, B., & Kim, J. (2017). Grit, basic needs satisfaction, and subjective well-being. *Journal of Individual Differences*, *38*(1), 29–35. https://doi.org/10.1027/1614-0001/a000219

Kamins, M. L., & Dweck, C. S. (1999). Person versus process praise and criticism: Implications for contingent self-worth and coping. *Developmental Psychology*, *35*(3), 835–847. https://doi.org/10.1037/0012-1649.35.3.835

Layous, K., Davis, E. M., Garcia, J., Purdie-Vaughns, V., Cook, J. E., & Cohen, G. L. (2017). Feeling left out but affirmed: Protecting against the negative effects of low belonging in college. *Journal of Experimental Social Psychology*, *69*, 227–231. https://doi.org/10.1016/j.jesp.2016.09.008

Li, Y., & Bates, T. C. (2019). You can't change your basic ability, but you work at things, and that's how we get hard things done: Testing the role of growth mindset on response to setbacks, educational attainment, and cognitive ability. *Journal of Experimental Psychology: General*, *148*(9), 1640–1655. http://dx.doi.org/10.1037/xge0000669

Li, Y., & Bates, T. C. (2020). Testing the association of growth mindset and grades across a challenging transition: Is growth mindset associated with grades? *Intelligence*, *81*, 101471. https://doi.org/10.1016/j.intell.2020.101471

Mofield, E. L., & Parker Peters, M. (2018). Mindset misconception? Comparing mindsets, perfectionism, and attitudes of achievement in gifted, advanced, and typical students. *Gifted Child Quarterly*, *62*(4), 327–349. https://doi.org/10.1177/0016986218758440

Moorman, E. A., & Pomerantz, E. M. (2010). Ability mindsets influence the quality of mothers' involvement in children's learning: An experimental investigation. *Developmental Psychology*, *46*(5), 1354–1362. https://doi.org/10.1037/a0020376

Mueller, C. M., & Dweck, C. S. (1998). Praise for intelligence can undermine children's motivation and performance. *Journal of Personality and Social Psychology*, *75*(1), 33–52. https://doi.org/10.1037/0022-3514.75.1.33

Myers, C. A., Wang, C., Black, J. M., Bugescu, N., & Hoeft, F. (2016). The matter of motivation: Striatal resting-state connectivity is dissociable between grit and growth mindset. *Social Cognitive and Affective Neuroscience*, *11*(10), 1521–1527. https://doi.org/10.1093/scan/nsw065

Nestor, A. L. (2017). *Investigating mindset theories: The implications for classroom instruction and professional development* [Doctoral dissertation, University of Pittsburgh]. http://d-scholarship.pitt.edu/32709/1/Nestor%20ETD%20Final%20%20with%20SD%20edits%20Aug%202017.pdf

Park, D., Tsukayama, E., Yu, A., & Duckworth, A. L. (2020). The development of grit and growth mindset during adolescence. *Journal of Experimental Child Psychology*, *198*, 104889. https://doi.org/10.1016/j.jecp.2020.104889

Perkins, A. M., Bowers, G., Cassidy, J., Meiser-Stedman, R., & Pass, L. (2021). An enhanced psychological mindset intervention to promote adolescent wellbeing within educational settings: A feasibility randomized controlled trial. *Journal of Clinical Psychology*, *77*(4), 946–967. https://doi.org/10.1002/jclp.23104

Putwain, D. W., Wood, P., & Pekrun, R. (2022). Achievement emotions and academic achievement: Reciprocal relations and the moderating influence of academic buoyancy. *Journal of Educational Psychology*, *114*(1), 108–126. https://doi.org/10.1037/edu0000637

Ryan, R. M., & Deci, E. L. (2000). Self-determination theory and the facilitation of intrinsic motivation, social development, and well-being. *American Psychologist*, *55*(1), 68–78. https://doi.org/10.1037/0003-066X.55.1.68

Schleider, J., & Weisz, J. (2018). A single-session growth mindset intervention for adolescent anxiety and depression: 9-month outcomes of a randomized trial. *Journal of Child Psychology and Psychiatry*, *59*(2), 160–170. https://doi.org/10.1111/jcpp.12811

Schroder, H. S., Fisher, M. E., Lin, Y., Lo, S. L., Danovitch, J. H., & Moser, J. S. (2017). Neural evidence for enhanced attention to mistakes among school-aged children with a growth mindset. *Developmental Cognitive Neuroscience*, *24*, 42–50. https://doi.org/10.1016/j.dcn.2017.01.004

Sisk, V. F., Burgoyne, A. P., Sun, J., Butler, J. L., & Macnamara, B. N. (2018). To what extent and under which circumstances are growth mindsets important to academic achievement? Two meta-analyses. *Psychological Science*, *29*(4), 549–571. https://doi.org/10.1177/0956797617739704

Smiley, P. A., & Dweck, C. S. (1994). Individual differences in achievement goals among young children. *Child Development*, *65*(6), 1723–1743. https://doi.org/10.1111/j.1467-8624.1994.tb00845.x

Tang, X., Wang, M. T., Guo, J., & Salmela-Aro, K. (2019). Building grit: The longitudinal pathways between mindset, commitment, grit, and academic outcomes. *Journal of Youth and Adolescence*, *48*(5), 850–863. https://doi.org/10.1007/s10964-019-00998-0

Thomas, K. J., Moreira de Cunha, J., Americo de Souza, D., & Santo, J. (2019). Fairness, trust, and school climate as foundational to growth mindset: A study among Brazilian children and adolescents. *Educational Psychology*, *39*(4), 510–529. https://doi.org/10.1080/01443410.2018.1549726

Usher, E. L., Li, C. R., Butz, A. R., & Rojas, J. P. (2019). Perseverant grit and self-efficacy: Are both essential for children's academic success? *Journal of Educational Psychology*, *111*(5), 877–902. https://doi.org/10.1037/edu0000324

Wang, S., Dai, J., Li, J., Wang, X., Chen, T., Yang, X., He, M., & Gong, Q. (2018). Neuroanatomical correlates of grit: Growth mindset mediates the association between gray matter structure and trait grit in late adolescence. *Human Brain Mapping*, *39*(4), 1688–1699. https://doi.org/10.1002/hbm.23944

Yeager, D. S., & Dweck, C. S. (2020). What can be learned from growth mindset controversies? *American Psychologist*, *75*(9), 1269–1284. https://doi.org/10.1037/amp0000794

Yeager, D. S., Hanselman, P., Walton, G. M., Murray, J. S., Crosnoe, R., Muller, C., Tipton, E., Schneider, B., Hulleman, C. S., Hinojosa, C. P., Paunesku, D., Romero, C., Flint, K., Roberts, A., Trott, J., Iachan, R., Buontempo, J., Yang, S. M., Carvalho, C. M., & Dweck, C. S. (2019). A national experiment reveals where a growth mindset improves achievement. *Nature*, *573*(7774), 364–369. https://doi.org/10.1038/s41586-019-1466-y

Zhao, L., Heyman, G. D., Chen, L., & Lee, K. (2017a). Praising young children for being smart promotes cheating. *Psychological Science*, *28*(12), 1868–1870. https://doi.org/10.1177/0956797617721529

Zhao, L., Heyman, G. D., Chen, L., & Lee, K. (2017b). Telling young children, they have a reputation for being smart promotes cheating. *Developmental Science*, *21*(3), e12585. https://doi.org/10.1111/desc.12585

7 Self-Control

> While still in high school, Jeannette Walls bravely resolved to leave her impoverished family home in Welsh and set her sights on New York to pursue a college education. The goal of escaping from extreme poverty, food insecurity, and parental neglect was not a small feat. Jeannette bought a pink piggy bank, affectionately named Oz, where she and her siblings would put every single penny they earned from chores toward their "escape fund." A decision was made that her older sister would leave first and the rest would follow. Despite a heartbreaking setback when Jeannette discovered Oz shattered and their hard-earned saving gone, staying committed to the goal and resisting impulses to spend the money elsewhere paid off.
>
> Walls (2005)

Deciding between an immediate, small-value prize and a remote, bigger-value reward depends greatly but not exclusively on the child's ability to manage impulses and resist temptation. Self-control is a regulatory process that is intertwined with the control of emotion, behavior, and cognition. When the child is called to resist temptation and postpone the action of reaching for a desired food or toy several things happen. The child must regulate the intensity of the desire to have the reward (emotion regulation) and choose behaviors and thoughts (cognitive control) that support this decision both mentally and outwardly (behavioral expression of regulation). Self-control, also referred to in the literature as impulse control, effortful control, and inhibitory control, is often discussed as part of a broader theory of self-regulation, whose development is central to school readiness and therefore, academic achievement, and psychological well-being of children (Liew, 2012). There are several theoretical approaches to understanding self-regulation, and the literature is not only voluminous but also changing to reflect the improved neurobehavioral understanding of regulatory processes. This chapter offers an understanding of self-control as a reflexive, fast, and stimulus-dependent system that has its origins in temperament. This type of control is different from cognitive control which has origins in executive function although the two are intertwined. The chapter traces the development of self-control and highlights its importance in achieving personal goals and protecting well-being in childhood and adolescence. It includes the review of studies that have utilized the delay of gratification task,

DOI: 10.4324/9780429356414-10

assessments of self-control, and performance on inhibitory motoric tasks to demonstrate long-lasting connections between self-control and academic and social outcomes in childhood and beyond. The chapter discusses the unique role of self-control in predicting academic outcomes in comparison to IQ and explains the difficulties some adolescents have with impulse control. It concludes with general recommendations that enhance self-control in children of all ages.

Self-Control in Self-Regulation Theory

Self-regulation incorporates psychological processes through which people control their own thoughts, emotions, and behaviors. According to Kopp's model of the development of self-regulation in childhood, the processes begin with the infants' increasing ability for neurophysiological modulation (Kopp, 1982). The infant relies on innate mechanisms that shield the baby from too much stimulation and arousal (e.g., gaze away, sucking). Such modulation becomes gradually more under the voluntary and intentional control of infants by the end of the first year. Twelve-month-old children become aware of the caregiver's demands for control and begin to use these external signals to resist impulses and wait for things to happen. Caregivers provide support or co-regulation throughout the first year and beyond. For example, children accept distractions from the caregiver while waiting for dinner to get ready. Impulse control is evident by 2 years of age when toddlers rely on language as well as the caregiver to inhibit behaviors according to rules. For example, a child points to the hot stove while murmuring "No, no, no, hot!" Kopp (1982) speculates that regulatory processes gradually become under the control of the child sometime in the third year, as is evident by their ability to inhibit impulses and initiate and terminate behaviors without the external reminder of the caregiver or other adult. When these abilities broaden in scope, children can adapt flexibly in response to changing environmental demands and true self-regulation emerges. The transition from impulse or inhibitory control to self-regulation happens when the children monitor their responses to external expectations, identify the desired responses, internalize external expectations that lead to favorable responses, and eventually come to balance expectations with their personal desires and goals. In this model, the transition from other- to self-regulation is central to the development of regulatory capacity (Bronson & Bronson, 2001). In summary, impulse control is a fundamental aspect of Kopp's model of self-regulation, serving as an essential building block in a child's journey toward developing true self-regulation.

Blair et al. (2010) also propose a theory of self-regulation in which impulse control is a built-in mechanism that contributes to adaptation as well as self-development. They define self-regulation as "the processes by which the individual actively maintains set points or levels of emotional and cognitive arousal that promote positive adaptation and that lead to the development of a positive sense of efficacy, agency, and self-worth" (p. 65). Blair et al. propose a dichotomy to regulatory systems, supported by different biological processes. One is a low-effort, almost automatic approach-withdrawal system that resides in the subcortical brain.

The other entails a slower and more purposeful cognitive control that is based on the cortical brain. The first system influences and is influenced by higher cognitive control but is closer to the concept of impulse control, seen in Kopp's model as well as in theories of temperament that entail dimensions of emotionality and approach or withdrawal tendencies.

Liew (2012) also makes a similar distinction to Blair et al. (2010) by identifying temperament-based control as effortful control and cognitive control as executive function. Effortful control is "voluntary control over approach (activation) or withdrawal (inhibition) of behavioral tendencies via attentional (shifting and focusing) and inhibitory control mechanisms" (p. 106). Cognitive control is "the ability to engage in deliberate, goal-directed thought and action via inhibitory control, attention shifting or cognitive flexibility, and working memory processes" (p. 106). Liew (2012) notes that these constructs share the same regulatory processes of inhibitory and attentional control but remain distinct as they make independent contributions to children's academic achievement. Moreover, effortful control resembles a trait characteristic because it shows stability over time whereas executive functions respond to interventions and training.

Denham et al. (2012), like others, consider two factors in their model that are behaviorally and neurally separable although both implicate the prefrontal cortex. They call the first factor the "cool executive control" and the second the "hot executive control." The cool system develops more slowly and tends to be affect-free, whereas the hot system is more reflexive, acts fast, and is stimulus dependent. Neurologically, the prefrontal cortex is activated when higher-order cognitive functions such as memory and attention are employed during cognitive control. The hot system, however, in addition to activating the prefrontal cortex, also engages the limbic system. The anterior cingular cortex is believed to function as the bridge between the prefrontal cortex and the limbic system. The developing child who starts preschool needs to deploy all of these processes to successfully adapt to the demands of the classroom setting. The cool system allows children to shift and sustain attention when called upon while managing distractions that come from competing and often emotionally arousing actions. The hot system allows them to control emotional arousal and shift motivation where is needed. For example, the child who is eager to get the red marker from his friend to complete his picture, patiently waits for their turn, while focusing on their own coloring within the lines and carrying a conversation about how beautiful their painting will turn out to be. The child exerts both cognitive and impulse control and acts in accordance with internalized behavior rules of "wait for your turn" and "be nice to your friends."

Hofmann and colleagues (2012) also discuss impulse control but refer to it as self-control. In their view, self-regulation is broadly referred to as any "goal-directed behavior" and has three components: endorsed or internalized standards for behavior, motivation to act by those standards as closely as possible, and the capacity to do so despite tempting alternatives. Self-control is considered a subset of self-regulatory processes, "those that aim to override unwanted, prepotent impulses or urges" (p. 174), so essentially the term refers to impulse control and is similar to effortful control if one considers its dispositional origin. Hofmann and colleagues propose that cognitive control is involved in all three components of self-regulation but mostly subserves the capacity component. Cognitive control supports either direct (e.g., don't eat the marshmallow) or indirect inhibition (e.g., do something else), and both are involved in impulse control.

In the literature, the terms impulse control, inhibitory control, effortful control, and self-control are used interchangeably. This type of control is also seen as a trait or dispositional control because it is influenced by the genetic constitution of the child. The evidence points out that control of impulses resides in the subcortical areas although it branches to the prefrontal cortex where cognitive control or executive functions are implicated. It is expected that impulse control improves with age because the prefrontal cortex matures and executive functions (discussed in Chapter 8) support better decision-making and planning. The following sections trace the role of impulse control in psychological well-being and mostly on the capacity to succeed in school and beyond. The reviewed research that follows covers studies that have focused on resistance to temptation as an indication of impulse control as well as its long-term effects in predicting academic and employment outcomes throughout the lifespan (Mischel, 2011; Watts et al., 2018). Some researchers have particularly investigated impulse control in adolescence to explain the increased risk-taking that occurs during this period (Steinberg, 2010). Yet, others take a more general view of impulse control to understand the achievement of distant but more valuable goals, a key to success (Duckworth & Gross, 2014). In all studies, self-control is assessed by reports of children's control (i.e., impulsivity, persistence, completion of the task, effortful control) as well as behavioral tasks in which children must suppress a motoric response in favor of another (motoric inhibition).

Resisting Temptation: The Case for the Two Marshmallows

In his interview to *Monitor on Psychology*, the premier magazine of the American Psychological Association, Walter Mischel revealed the inspiration for the now famous marshmallow test. Mischel observed the significant change in his children's ability to control impulses and extend the time of waiting for favorable things, like dessert, to happen. Between the ages of 2 and 5, children become more patient and show self-control in many situations. Mischel set out to investigate resistance to temptation and the outcomes it is associated with in adulthood (Winerman, 2014). He devised the task where children were offered two pairs of treats like snacks and small toys. Children could have the immediate treat (e.g., one cookie) or choose to wait for 15 minutes alone in the laboratory to receive the higher value treat (e.g., two cookies). The pairs of treats were designed based on the children's preferences. All children had the opportunity to play with some attractive toys at the end of the session regardless of their decision to wait or not. The most widely known version of this task that made it to the popular media is the choice between one and two marshmallows. This ability to delay gratification or resist immediate temptation to receive a better reward reflects the ability to control impulses. Michel proposes that it is an outcome of affective and cognitive processes working together, an idea reminiscent of the integration of the cortical (cool system) and limbic (hot system) processes that were discussed earlier in the chapter. Several studies conducted by Mischel and colleagues (1989) revealed individual differences in the ability to delay gratification. Children delayed longer as they got older, and when the value of the deferred reward was much higher than the value of the immediate reward (e.g., one candy, versus two candies, versus a whole bag of candies). In contrast, children waited less when the postponement time for the bigger reward increased. Mischel also demonstrated that the choice to delay was associated with personal characteristics such as higher intelligence, a sense of social responsibility, and academic aspirations (Mischel et al., 1989).

To better understand these effects, Mischel and colleagues (1989) designed studies to explore the role of attention in the choice to wait. For example, they let children see both rewards at the same time, or made one visible and the other invisible. When children could see the immediate reward, they were more likely to go for it than when the immediate reward was hidden. Children also waited less when they were asked to think about the delayed reward, but delayed longer when they were told to think about something else that made them happy. More successful children devised their own distraction strategies while waiting such as playing with their hands, covering their eyes, and singing. These results clearly showed that the preschoolers' ability to distract themselves explained their choice to wait. In situations where the hot system overpowered the cool system, however, resistance to temptation failed.

Mischel further studied the long-term effects of this early ability to wait and whether individual differences mattered in the long run. As adolescents, children who waited longer at age 4, were rated by their parents higher than their peers in academic and social domains. Parents also rated their children higher in resisting temptation, ability to concentrate, and cope with stress. Children who waited longer also had higher SAT scores when they applied to college. In follow-up studies, Mischel and colleagues (1989) explored how early individual differences would predict differential outcomes. They expected that in conditions where no strategies for successful delay were offered and the children had to rely on their own (i.e., reveal individual differences), the outcomes would be more pronounced in the group that chose to wait. Indeed, the children who waited in this condition were rated by their parents as more competent, brighter, goal-oriented, and resourceful when dealing with stressful events in adolescence. Moreover, those adolescents had higher SAT scores in math and reading. These differential outcomes in adolescence were not predicted when the rewards were hidden during the preschool delay of gratification task. In this condition, the wait time did not reflect the self-control strategy and therefore lost its predictive value (Mischel et al., 1989). Most importantly, Mischel and colleagues (2011) were able to follow a subset of these preschoolers for over 40 years and made connections between early delay of gratification and later psychological and socioeconomic outcomes. Those who waited longer as children became adults with higher educational attainment (e.g., more likely to attend and graduate from college), higher incomes, better self-worth, and better health (e.g., less likely to be overweight, less drug use) (Mischel et al., 2011) and higher cognitive control (Casey et al., 2011).

Mischel acknowledges that the causal links between early resistance to temptation in light of a better reward/goal and positive outcomes are not clear (Mischel et al., 1989). "Self-imposed delay" (p. 244) may be socialized in the family and linked to other skills that may explain the association with positive parental views and objective achievement scores. The early studies demonstrate that self-distraction (e.g., looking away from the temptation) and cognitive reframing or reappraisal (e.g., I do not like marshmallows that much or the marshmallow looks like a cloud) support delay of gratification, whereas thinking about how appealing the delayed reward is undermines self-control. Mischel et al. (2011) suggest that preschoolers who waited relied on specific inhibitory control mechanisms that they continued to use throughout their lives, hence the longitudinal associations with positive adult outcomes. They propose that this early form of "willpower" supports a certain way of processing information, such as keeping only relevant information in working memory while suppressing unhelpful information, as well as a selection of behavioral responses (e.g., keeping hands off the desired object).

Most of Mischel and his colleagues' studies were conducted in the 1960s. Therefore, one may ask about the relevance of these findings nowadays when due to technological advancements children and adults become more accustomed to receiving instant gratification. Carlson et al. (2018) addressed this question by first asking adults what their beliefs are about their children's self-control and delay of gratification and second by comparing three cohorts of children who experienced the marshmallow test in the 1960s, 1980s, and 2000s. They found that adults believed that children would have waited less in the marshmallow test than children 50 years ago had done and reported the effect to be more prominent among Hispanic individuals. Moreover, participants, who were parents, believed that when they were 4 years old, they would have waited longer than their children would wait nowadays. However, these expectations were not supported when the authors compared the three cohorts. In fact, they found a significant linear trend showing an increase in the delay of gratification. Each cohort waited about one minute longer than the previous. The results held even when the researchers controlled for age, gender, and geographical location of the samples. Additional comparisons showed that the portion of children who waited for 10 minutes increased while the portion of children who waited for 30 seconds decreased. Another interesting comparison was that the 5-year-old children in the 1980s cohort delayed as long as the 3.5-year-old children from the 2000s cohort did. Carlson et al. (2018) explained that this observed overall improvement in the ability to delay gratification is likely due to enhanced cognitive control, alligning with a general increase in IQ scores that has been noted over the last century.

However, despite the extensive research linking delay of gratification with long-term positive outcomes, researchers have questioned the strength of these relationships, the extent to which the findings are heterogeneous (i.e., the effect varies when specific factors are considered), and whether the results may be explained by other factors. For example, the positive association between delay of gratification and later academic achievement may be accounted for by academic competence in the preschool period or characteristics of the home environment. Watts et al. (2018)

used existing data from the National Institute of Child Health and Development study (NICHD Early Child Care Research Network, 2002) to conceptually replicate Mischel's findings. They identified children who were able to wait for 7 minutes at the age of 54 months. Because more children hit this benchmark among families whose mothers had college degrees than those who did not, the researchers performed separate analyses for the two groups. The analyses with children whose mothers did not, have a degree revealed a significant association between minutes waited for, and academic achievement in 1st grade, but the association was not as strong as reported in Mischel's studies. Furthermore, this association became weaker when child and family factors were controlled for and were nonsignificant when concurrent cognitive abilities were accounted for. The same pattern of results was revealed when early delay of gratification was associated with academic outcomes at age 15. In addition, the researchers failed to show any connections between the delay of gratification and behavior problems at either grade 1 or age 15. The associations were either weaker or nonsignificant for children whose mothers had college degrees. However, adolescents who experienced an academic boost waited for at least 20 seconds at 54 months. This conflicts with Michel's speculation that cognitive control and strategies played a role. Watts and colleagues argued that it is unlikely that these cognitive skills were activated in 20 seconds. The researchers suggested that it was rather a pure impulse control that explained the delay and that most academic outcomes were explained by concurrent cognitive skills such as intelligence or other unobserved variables.

In conclusion, Mischel's marshmallow test has significantly contributed to the understanding of self-control as indicated by the ability to control impulses and delay gratification. This ability is influenced by many factors including age, the value of the deferred reward, and attentional processes. Moreover, children who could wait longer in their early years showed better academic and social outcomes, and these effects could be linked to the development of inhibitory control mechanisms. However, some researchers question the strength of these relationships and suggest that the positive outcomes may be accounted for by other factors such as academic competence in preschool years or home environment characteristics. Despite these debates, Mischel's marshmallow test remains a landmark study in the field of developmental psychology. Further research is necessary to explore the nuances of the relationships between these early abilities and their long-term outcomes.

Trait-Like Self-Control and Long-Term Outcomes

The idea that pure impulse control, independent of higher cognitive control, predicts academic outcomes is consistent with the view of control as a trait whose strength varies among children. Researchers have mostly focused on the concept of effortful control to denote dispositional or trait-like self-control. In temperament research, effortful control, mostly rated by parents, assesses the young child's ability to "pay attention, persist on tasks and suppress inappropriate behaviors" (Daly et al., 2015). Researchers have explored the effect of effortful control on psychological well-being, including academic outcomes. For example, in a meta-analytic study, de Ridder et al. (2012) examined how trait self-control related to several domains of behavior outcomes such as interpersonal functioning, school achievement, eating, and weight-related behaviors. They defined self-control as "people's capacity to override or change their inner responses, to inhibit undesired behavioral tendencies, and to facilitate desired-behavior tendencies" (p. 79). They reported medium to strong effects of self-control on academic outcomes, prosocial behaviors, and well-being. Moreover, the effect of self-control was stronger among adolescents than young adults. Gender did not moderate the effect for desired outcomes; in other words, the strength of the association of self-control and behaviors was the same in boys and girls. However, the effect of self-control on unwanted behaviors was stronger in male participants, perhaps because boys have a propensity to engage in more aggressive impulsive behaviors.

Daly et al. (2015) explored the long-term effects of childhood effortful control on work-related outcomes by following two cohorts pulled from the British National Child Development Study. In their first study, they investigated how self-control at age 10 predicted the probability of unemployment (ages 21, 26, 30, 34, 38, and 42), and the total number of months of unemployment when the cohort participants were ages 16 to 38. At age 10, self-control was related to intelligence and socioeconomic status. Moreover, boys had significantly lower self-control than girls did. Consequently, the researchers controlled for these variables in the analyses. Across the six time points, one standard deviation in self-control at age 10 decreased the probability of unemployment by 1.3 percentage points, on average. This was double the effect that childhood intelligence had. Lower self-control was associated with a greater total number of unemployed months. From ages 16 to 38, participants with low self-control experienced about 60% more unemployment time than those with high self-control. In their second study, the researchers recruited another cohort where they assessed self-control at ages 7 and 11 and unemployment outcomes in adulthood up to age 50. Controlling for gender, intelligence, and socioeconomic status, childhood self-control reduced the probability of unemployment by 2.6% at age 23, 1.2% at age 33, 0.9% at age 42, and 0.8% at age 50. Across study time points, one standard deviation in self-control decreased the unemployment probability by 1.4 percentage points. Similarly to the previous cohort, participants with low self-control experienced about 60% more unemployment time than those with high self-control. Notably, these results were unaffected when researchers controlled for mental health problems that related to poor self-control (e.g., conduct disorder).

Allan et al. (2014) conducted a meta-analysis of 74 studies and over 14,000 preschoolers (average age 55 months) to determine the effect size of the correlation between effortful control and academic skills. They argued that effortful control is not different from inhibitory control as both refer to "the ability to inhibit prepotent thoughts or actions flexibly, often in favor of a subdominant action, typically in goal-directed behavior" (p. 2368) and therefore, included studies that focused on inhibitory control. Furthermore, they made the distinction between "hot" tasks that required children to regulate some emotion such as the case of delay of gratification tasks, and "cool" tasks that required children to follow instructions in an emotionally neutral task, such as touching their head when they heard the word toes. The researchers expected that cool tasks and teachers' reports of inhibitory control would be better predictors of academic skills. Allan et al. (2014) found a significant, modest, and positive effect of effortful/inhibitory control on academic skills regardless of the children's age. The effect was stronger in the cool than hot tasks.

In another meta-analytic review, Robson et al. (2020) sought to identify the concurrent effect of self-control on academic, social, and health outcomes in the preschool period as well as the long-term effect on these outcomes in adolescence and adulthood. They defined control as "the ability to inhibit dominant impulses to modify thought, feeling and behavior" (p. 325) and therefore this term is close to conceptions of impulse control, inhibitory control, and self-control discussed in this chapter. The researchers included studies that assessed self-control via a delay of gratification task and motor impulse tasks (e.g., the child touches their head when is called to touch toes), as well as parent and teacher ratings of impulsivity and persistence on difficult tasks. Because the degree of convergence of these measures was relatively low, the researchers used the method of assessment in the studies as a moderator that could potentially affect the strength of the relationship between self-control and outcomes. Additional moderator variables included age and gender because of previous evidence that the effect was more pronounced in younger children and boys. Based on cross-sectional studies, self-control was positively associated with academic performance while gender and age did not have a significant moderating effect. The results from longitudinal studies in the meta-analysis also showed that self-control in the preschool years (age 4) was associated with overall academic outcomes in the early (age 8) and later school years (age 12). These associations were stronger when they were based on task assessments and teachers' ratings compared to parents' ratings. Similar results were reported when the researchers examined the specific subjects of math literacy and vocabulary. In general, the strength of the relationship did not vary by gender, but the association between self-control and math was stronger in younger children and the association between self-control and vocabulary was stronger in older children.

Moreover, self-control was positively associated with intelligence and school engagement in the early school years and early self-control predicted educational attainment as well as unemployment in adulthood. Children with self-control regardless of their age and gender had better social skills, and preschool self-control predicted social competence during school years and adulthood. Preschoolers with high self-control were less likely to be victimized as they started formal schooling and those who continued to have high self-control at that time were less likely to be rejected by their peers in later school years. The same pattern was revealed for externalizing and internalizing problems as well as depression. Interestingly, childhood self-control negatively predicted depression, anxiety, and suicidal thoughts in adulthood. Regarding physical health, self-control in childhood and adolescence predicted body mass index, alcohol use, substance abuse and cigarette smoking, and physical illness in adulthood. Robson et al. (2020) findings highlight the far-reaching and wide-reaching effects of early self-control control and pinpoint the importance of interventions in the early years that support self-control.

Despite the diversity in definitions and measurements of the ability to control impulses in favor of more desired responses, several trends can be observed in the literature. In tasks where impulsive emotion must be controlled such as in delay of gratification tasks, there is a clear association between time of delaying and academic skills. However, the association is stronger in tasks that require impulsive control of movement. Moreover, pure impulse control (without deployment of cognitive processes) in preschool provides an academic boost in adolescence. Evidence from ratings and behavioral tasks demonstrates that the relationship of control with academic and social outcomes begins in the preschool period and stretches into adolescence. Better dispositional control of impulses in early childhood protects adults' physical and mental health problems. Impulse control in the form of effortful control in middle childhood decreases the likelihood of unemployment and reduces the unemployment period in adulthood. Even though girls have better self-control than boys, the strength of the association with academic outcomes does not differ by gender. Impulse control is related to intelligence, but both make individual contributions to developmental outcomes.

Self-Control and Grit

The findings from the meta-analytic studies discussed earlier clearly show that the ability to "inhibit dominant impulses to modify thought, feeling and behavior" (Robson et al., 2020, p. 325) is critical not only for school success but also success in multiple domains of adult life. Duckworth et al. (2014) provide a framework to understand how such control is related to achieving goals that are long-term, personally meaningful, and passion driven. Duckworth considers self-control as the "voluntary regulation of attentional, emotional, and behavioral impulses" (p. 200) while the individual chooses between tempting short-term goals and more enduring ones. Duckworth views this ability to resist impulses for immediate gratification as key to school success and proposes a hierarchical organization of goals to explain how self-control is related to grit, which too is associated with academic achievement and attainment (see Chapter 6). In this hierarchical goal framework, there are superordinate goals that relate to several lower-lever goals, which are linked to actions that include attention, emotion, and behavior. Self-control takes place when the individual resolves a conflict between two "impulse actions" that are linked to goals of short-term value and goals of steadfast value. These higher-value goals align with passion in a specific domain. For example, a student who is determined to become a fashion designer (superordinate and psychologically distant goal) chooses actions that serve lower goals leading to acceptance to a top design school in the country. For instance, the student buys a high-quality book about fashion design instead of a ticket to a concert or spends every Friday night designing instead of binging on TV series. The self-control of impulses is seen as willpower that improves with age because the prefrontal cortex that supports it also develops. It is a skill that Duckworth believes can be strengthened with training; in contrast, grit improves with increasing motivation (Duckworth & Gross, 2014).

Duckworth and Gross (2014) propose that self-control is highly correlated with grit but not perfectly. Some may be very good at handling temptations but do not have the perseverance to pursue long-term goals. And gritty individuals may be high achievers in one domain but show poor self-control of impulses in other domains. Moreover, Duckworth and Gross (2014) argue that self-control is more related to daily success while grit is associated with momentous achievements in one's life. In a school setting, self-control successes include: paying attention in class, double-checking work, tuning into what the teacher is saying, finishing homework on time, giving others a chance to talk during discussions, not watching TV at the same time as doing homework, and asking for help if needed. (p. 201) Examples of self-control failures include: "asking for help without trying first, mocking a teacher, doing something irrelevant to what is going on in class, cutting class, and fooling around instead of completing work" (p. 201). Exercising self-control successfully supports students' study in the classroom and at home and should associate with positive outcomes. Duckworth and colleagues (2012) demonstrated the differential predictive value of self-control and IQ in relation to academic achievement. Measures of self-control in 4th grade predicted longitudinal changes in report card grades from 8th and 9th grade whereas IQ scores in 4th grade predicted longitudinal changes in standardized test scores from 5th to 9th grade. In a follow-up study, Duckworth et al. (2012) replicated that self-control, measured by an impulsivity scale, was associated with GPA while IQ was associated with standardized test scores. Additionally, they demonstrated that the link between self-control and grades was mediated by completing homework and not getting into trouble. These findings imply that self-control may be more relevant to academic achievement in the classroom whereas IQ may support performance on tests that are unrelated to classroom learning.

Returning to the vignette that started this chapter, it is almost certain that Jeannette Walls and her siblings resisted using their money to buy extra food or sweet treats they rarely tasted, or better clothes to fit in with their peers. Building the escape fund was a more important goal that would lead to the ultimate goal of freedom and a chance to a better life. In the literature, it is unclear how children come to develop higher-order goals and identify the steps to reach them despite challenges. Goal setting is an important process that relates to academic achievement and subjective happiness (Street et al., 2004). Additionally, what motivates children may influence how they set the hierarchy of their goals. Depressed 10- to 12-year-old children tend to choose conditional goals, meaning that they believe that happiness is only reached through the achievement of one specific lower-level goal (Street et al., 2004). For example, they may think that they can only be happy if they make straight "As" in all their courses. Future research should explore how children direct their self-control towards maladaptive goals and misguided notions of happiness and achievement.

Self-Control and Risk-Taking in Adolescence

The period of adolescence is known as a time of increased risk-taking such as alcohol and drug abuse, deviant behavior, careless driving, and unprotected sex, all of which threaten the psychological well-being of adolescents and specifically their ability to meet academic challenges. Studies demonstrate an increase in risk-taking from preadolescence to adolescence and a decline thereafter. Steinberg (2010) proposed a dual systems model to understand the processes that happen during adolescence that explain why they are more prone to risk-taking. He expects that around puberty, the brain's reward system, and specifically its connection with the limbic system, is changed by increased dopaminergic activity. As a result, he hypothesized that adolescents seek out more thrilling and sensational activities. At the same time, the synaptic pruning and further myelination that take place during this time, allow for more efficient information processing in the prefrontal cortex, where rational decisions and planning are made. In fact, impulsivity appears to decline from age 7 to young adulthood. As a result, Steinberg hypothesized that adolescents should be able to better control their inclination for sensation or reward seeking. Is, however, the eventual decline in risk behavior an outcome of these neurobiological changes that increase sensitivity to reward and improve impulse control? In a group of 10- to 30-year-olds, Steinberg found a linear effect of age on impulsivity as it was measured by self-reports and performance on experimental inhibitory tasks (e.g., go/no go tasks). Reward seeking, however, followed a curvilinear path, showing an increase during the first half of adolescence and then a steady decline from age 16. These findings imply that adolescents with low impulse control and high tendency for reward-seeking are at heightened risk for engaging in behaviors that threaten their health and ability to succeed. The combination of low impulse and heightened sensitivity to reward seems to occur in middle adolescence (14–16 years).

Some evidence from neuroimaging supports the existence of dual systems. van Duijvenvoorde et al. (2016) studied changes in intrinsic functional connectivity in networks involved in cognitive (cortical) control and affective/motivational processes (subcortical, limbic system) in 269 participants ranging in age from 8 to 25 years. They found an age-related increase in connectivity between the dorsolateral prefrontal cortex (cortical) involved in cognitive control and the thalamus and striatum (subcortical) that are implicated in affective/motivational processes. They also found a decrease in connectivity with cortical and motor centers, thereby supporting increased cognitive control and decreased impulsive behavior over time. The emotional processing center in the prefrontal cortex and the reward evaluation centers appeared to be somewhat independent although the researchers showed an age-related increase in connectivity in some reward-related centers.

Additional support for the function and development of the two systems is provided by a comprehensive review. Shulman et al. (2016) reviewed studies that included both psychological and neurobiological assessments of reward sensitivity, sensation seeking, cognitive control, and self-regulation. They confirmed that sensitivity to rewards peaks in mid-adolescence and that sensation-seeking and reward sensitivity are heightened in adolescents, who experience puberty earlier, particularly boys. Self-reports support that impulse control continues to improve from childhood to adolescence and adulthood with 18–19-year-olds still reporting higher impulsivity compared to young adults in their 20s. Inhibitory cognitive tasks reveal that adolescents perform as well as adults implying that regulatory processes are in place; however, they fall behind when the task becomes more challenging (e.g., Tower of London that requires greater strategic planning). Adolescents may show adult-level control at age 15, but control is more often susceptible to contextual factors. While this research agrees with the dual systems theory, Shulman et al. (2016) noted that the evidence for heightened risk-taking during adolescence as an outcome of increased reward-seeking and still developing cognitive control is still in its infancy. The existing evidence implies that the two systems make independent contributions to explaining risk-taking behaviors in adolescence such as drug use and sexual activity, even after controlling for age and gender. There are very few neuroimaging studies that examine brain functional connectivity during risk-taking tasks, such as simulating speedy driving, and the results are promising. For example, there is evidence for higher activation of the reward processing centers and lower activation in the cognitive control system while participants engage in simulated risk-taking. Moreover, there is evidence that during risk-taking, the activation of the prefrontal cortex increases as age and the riskiness of the behavior also increase.

In summary, during adolescence, self-control becomes challenging for some adolescents. Although impulsivity declines with improved cognitive control, reward-seeking is heightened in middle adolescence. As a result, adolescents may engage in risk-taking which can negatively impact psychological well-being and academic success. Evidence from neuroimaging studies supports the existence of the dual systems, but research shows that each makes independent contributions to explaining risk-taking behaviors in adolescence. Further neuroimaging studies examining brain functional connectivity during risk-taking tasks could provide valuable insights into the underlying neural mechanisms of adolescent risk-taking behavior.

Raising Self-Controlled, Non-Impulsive Children

The literature review here has focused on studies that conceptualized self-control as impulse control, effortful control, and inhibitory control. The underlining idea that connects these concepts is children's ability to suppress an unwanted behavior, emotion, or thought in favor of a more desirable response. It is considered as part of the child's constitution; hence some children are born with better control than others. Its growth is tied to brain maturation and the development of cognitive control, particularly attentional processes (see Chapter 8). Because the roots of self-control can be found in temperament, the goodness of fit between the child's temperament and parenting is crucial in the development of self-control. Children vary in their emotional reactivity, the intensity of emotion, and effortful control. Given the far-reaching effects of preschool self-control on academic, emotional, social, and health outcomes, interventions should focus on early childhood. Infants and toddlers, and especially those with impulsive tendencies, benefit from parenting that structures their environment, provides lots of warnings, rewards controlled behaviors, and supports being patient and thoughtful. In the preschool period and beyond, parents may explicitly teach strategies for better control. Based on the evidence presented here, parents may encourage distraction strategies (e.g., looking away from the temptation) or cognitive reappraisal of the desired stimulus to prolong delay of gratification (e.g., I do not like marshmallows that much or the marshmallow looks like a cloud). When teaching children to delay gratification, parents should use rewards that are appropriate for their children's age and interests, as this can help increase their motivation to wait. Praising and rewarding children when they display self-control reinforces the importance of delaying gratification and fosters a sense of accomplishment. Creating the right motivational environment also supports impulse control. Research shows that evoking positive emotions by recalling positive memories increases the ability to delay gratification in 3- to 5-year-olds. In contrast, recalling negative experiences hampers the ability to wait. Positive emotions may elevate feelings of competence and success. However, not all emotions are helpful. Shimoni et al. (2016) showed that in 8-year-olds, evoking pride did not support the choice of the delayed but a more valued award. Parents need to be patient and consistent as children's self-control abilities develop gradually, and each child may progress at a different pace. Parental interventions also need to be balanced with guidance that promotes a sense of agency and autonomy. Mischel argued that children need to develop self-control so they can make choices (Winerman, 2014) and pursue their own goals (Duckworth et al., 2014). Self-control allows children to optimize their opportunities and direct their skills and motivation towards goals of their own choosing.

Children learn about giving in or withstanding impulses by observing others, therefore parents who wish their children to learn self-control should model responsible decision-making, planning, and delaying gratification. Watching the parent working towards an important personal goal, sacrificing small pleasures and indulgences to finally achieve the ultimate goal gives the message that long-term goals are worth pursuing. Parents may encourage their children to set goals and identify the steps to reach them. For example, a 4-year-old may work towards collecting tokens to receive a bigger award. A 10-year-old child may set a goal to win the classroom reading competition by reading every night for 30 minutes and denying the pleasure of playing video games. Families may also create their own goals such as a family vacation for which weekly take-outs are suspended for a certain period to save money for the vacation. These techniques may be applied in the classroom as well. For example, students may work throughout the year towards individual learning projects by following specific steps leading to the final project. One specific concern in the classroom may be the gender gap in self-control that favors girls in the preschool period. Research shows that this gap may be behind the more advanced language skills in girls (Daly & Corcoran, 2019), therefore addressing self-control in preschool and being mindful of the gender difference is of great importance.

Because self-control becomes challenging for some adolescents with high impulsivity, parents should openly communicate about the consequences of engaging in risky behaviors. Parents may help their children understand the potential long-term consequences of their actions and discuss strategies for making healthier decisions. Parents need to promote healthy outlets for sensation-seeking like sports that satisfy the need for new experiences without putting well-being at risk. Setting clear expectations regarding acceptable behavior and consequences for crossing boundaries helps structure the environment for adolescents with a tendency for risk-taking. Lastly, parents and teachers may encourage adolescents to practice mindfulness techniques, problem-solving, and planning strategies to strengthen their cognitive control abilities that in turn support self-control.

References

Allan, N. P., Hume, L. E., Allan, D. M., Farrington, A. L., & Lonigan, C. J. (2014). Relations between inhibitory control and the development of academic skills in preschool and kindergarten: A meta-analysis. *Developmental Psychology*, *50*(10), 2368–2379. https://doi.org/10.1037/a0037493

Blair, C., Calkins, S., & Kopp, L. (2010). Self-regulation as the interface of emotional and cognitive development: Implications for education and academic achievement. In R. H. Hoyle (Ed.), *Handbook of personality and self-regulation* (pp. 64–90). Wiley Blackwell. https://doi.org/10.1002/9781444318111.ch4

Bronson, M. B., & Bronson, M. (2001). *Self-regulation in early childhood: Nature and nurture*. Guilford press.

Carlson, S. M., Shoda, Y., Ayduk, O., Aber, L., Schaefer, C., Sethi, A., Wilson, N., Peake, P. K., & Mischel, W. (2018). Cohort effects in children's delay of gratification. *Developmental Psychology*, *54*(8), 1395–1407. https://doi.org/10.1037/dev0000533

Casey, B. J., Somerville, L. H., Gotlib, I. H., Ayduk, O., Franklin, N. T., Askren, M. K., Jonides, J., Berman, M. G., Wilson, N. L., Teslovich, T., Glover, G., Zayas, V., Mischel, W., & Shoda, Y. (2011). Behavioral and neural correlates of delay of gratification 40 years later. *Proceedings of the National Academy of Sciences of the United States of America*, *108*, 14998–15003. http://dx.doi.org/10.1073/pnas.1108561108

Daly, M., & Corcoran, R. P. (2019). Kindergarten self-control mediates the gender reading achievement gap: A population-based cohort study. *Journal of Research in Personality*, *83*, 103881. https://doi.org/10.1016/j.jrp.2019.103881

Daly, M., Delaney, L., Egan, M., & Baumeister, R. F. (2015). Childhood self-control and unemployment throughout the life span: Evidence from two British cohort studies. *Psychological Science*, *26*(6), 709–723. https://doi.org/10.1177/0956797615569001

Denham, S. A., Warren-Khot, H. K., Bassett, H. H., Wyatt, T., & Perna, A. (2012). Factor structure of self-regulation in preschoolers: Testing models of a field-based assessment for predicting early school readiness. *Journal of Experimental Child Psychology*, *111*(3), 386–404. https://doi.org/10.1016/j.jecp.2011.10.002

de Ridder, D. T., Lensvelt-Mulders, G., Finkenauer, C., Stok, F. M., & Baumeister, R. F. (2012). Taking stock of self-control: A meta-analysis of how trait self-control relates to a wide range of behaviors. *Personality and Social Psychology Review*, *16*(1), 76–99. https://doi.org/10.1177/1088868311418749

Duckworth, A., & Gross, J. J. (2014). Self-control and grit: Related but separable determinants of success. *Current Directions in Psychological Science*, *23*(5), 319–325. https://doi.org/10.1177/0963721414541462

Duckworth, A. L., Gendler, T. S., & Gross, J. J. (2014). Self-control in school-age children. *Educational Psychologist*, *49*(3), 199–217. https://doi.org/10.1080/00461520.2014.926225

Duckworth, A. L., Quinn, P. D., & Tsukayama, E. (2012). What no child left behind leaves behind: The roles of IQ and self-control in predicting standardized achievement test scores and report card grades. *Journal of Educational Psychology*, *104*(2), 439–451. https://doi.org/10.1037/a0026280

Hofmann, W., Schmeichel, B. J., & Baddeley, A. D. (2012). Executive functions and self-regulation. *Trends in Cognitive Sciences*, *16*(3), 174–180. https://doi.org/10.1016/j.tics.2012.01.006

Kopp, C. B. (1982). Antecedents of self-regulation: A developmental perspective. *Developmental Psychology*, *18*(2), 199. https://doi.org/10.1037/0012-1649.18.2.199

Liew, J. (2012). Effortful control, executive functions, and education: Bringing self-regulatory and social-emotional competencies to the table. *Child Development Perspectives*, *6*(2), 105–111. https://doi.org/10.1111/j.1750-8606.2011.00196.x

Mischel, W., Ayduk, O., Berman, M. G., Casey, B. J., Gotlib, I. H., Jonides, J., Kross, E., Teslovich, T., Wilson, N. L., Zayas, V., & Shoda, Y. (2011). 'Willpower over the life span: Decomposing self-regulation. *Social Cognitive and Affective Neuroscience*, *6*(2), 252–256. https://doi.org/10.1093/scan/nsq081

Mischel, W., Shoda, Y., & Rodriguez, M. I. (1989). Delay of gratification in children. *Science*, *244*(4907), 933–938. https://doi.org/10.1126/science.2658056

NICHD Early Child Care Research Network. (2002). Early childcare and children's development prior to school entry: Results from the NICHD Study of Early Child Care. *American Educational Research Journal*, *39*, 133–164. www.jstor.org/stable/3202474

Robson, D. A., Allen, M. S., & Howard, S. J. (2020). Self-regulation in childhood as a predictor of future outcomes: A meta-analytic review. *Psychological Bulletin*, *146*(4), 324–354. https://doi.org/10.1037/bul0000227

Shimoni, E., Asbe, M., Eyal, T., & Berger, A. (2016). Too proud to regulate: The differential effect of pride versus joy on children's ability to delay gratification. *Journal of Experimental Child Psychology*, *141*, 275–282. https://doi.org/10.1016/j.jecp.2015.07.017

Shulman, E. P., Smith, A. R., Silva, K., Icenogle, G., Duell, N., Chein, J., & Steinberg, L. (2016). The dual systems model: Review, reappraisal, and reaffirmation. *Developmental Cognitive Neuroscience*, *17*, 103–117. https://doi.org/10.1016/j.dcn.2015.12.010

Steinberg, L. (2010). A dual systems model of adolescent risk-taking. *Developmental Psychobiology: The Journal of the International Society for Developmental Psychobiology*, *52*(3), 216–224. https://doi.org/10.1002/dev.20445

Street, H., Nathan, P., Durkin, K., Morling, J., Dzahari, M. A., Carson, J., & Durkin, E. (2004). Understanding the relationships between well-being, goal setting, and depression in children. *Australian & New Zealand Journal of Psychiatry*, *38*(3), 155–161. https://doi.org/10.1080/j.1440-1614.2004.01317.x

van Duijvenvoorde, A. C., Achterberg, M., Braams, B. R., Peters, S., & Crone, E. A. (2016). Testing a dual-systems model of adolescent brain development using resting-state connectivity analyses. *Neuroimage*, *124*, 409–420. https://doi.org/10.1016/j.neuroimage.2015.04.069

Walls, J. (2005). *The glass castle: A memoir*. Scribner.

Watts, T. W., Duncan, G. J., & Quan, H. (2018). Revisiting the marshmallow test: A conceptual replication investigating links between early delay of gratification and later outcomes. *Psychological Science*, *29*(7), 1159–1177. https://doi.org/10.1177/0956797618761661
Winerman, L. (2014). Acing the marshmallow test. *Monitor on Psychology*, *45*(11). Retrieved May 7, 2023, from www.apa.org/monitor/2014/12/marshmallow-test

8 Cognitive Control

> "What story are you going to tell us tonight, Daddy?" Sophia and Demetra asked in unison as they tacked themselves in their beds. Storytelling has become a bedtime routine for these three. Dad would rather tell tales from his favorite childhood books, often mixing characters from different stories to the girls' delight. Commercial characters occasionally made an unexpected and comical entrance into the tale. Tarzan met the Swiss Robinsons and Geico's lizard encountered Crusoe. Only Odysseus' adventures remained intact to ensure that the girls had an unadulterated understanding of their cultural inheritance.

According to Adele Diamond (2016), a neurocognitive scientist, this father did more than put his daughters to bed. In the absence of any book illustrations, the girls had to pay close attention to the story and remember all pieces of information about the characters and their actions in order to understand the plot, and even predict the next steps. Storytelling is one of the ways to sharpen children's executive functions. Executive functions include the cognitive abilities of working memory, inhibition, attention, and cognitive flexibility which are important for behavioral regulation and academic success. Research indicates that stress, poverty, trauma, and family dysfunction have negative effects on the development of executive functioning and academic performance. The chapter traces the development of executive functions and their biological underpinning before it discusses the relationship that executive functions have with academic achievement and mental health. The chapter also reviews the threats to executive functions and offers ideas for family and school interventions.

Executive Functions: Origins, Development, and Assessment

Executive function refers to a cluster of cognitive abilities that are involved in processing information in a way that allows the individual to make and execute plans and decisions about thoughts, feelings, and behaviors in order to achieve personal goals. The main executive functions that have been studied are attention shifting, working memory, and inhibition. These functions are presumed to be different from each other, as they can be assessed by different behavioral tasks,

DOI: 10.4324/9780429356414-11

but they are also correlated with each other (Miyake et al., 2000). However, there are questions in the literature about the actual number of executive functions. In preschool, for example, these three functions are not always distinguished while in some studies they emerge as a single unified functor. Furthermore, researchers have recently questioned whether these factors are unitary or consist of multiple other functions. For example, inhibition involves ignoring irrelevant information, suppressing interference from information that is currently processed in the working memory, and inhibiting prepotent responses in preference for more appropriate ones. Researchers also have identified additional executive functions such as planning, cognitive flexibility (often overlapping with attention shifting), and speed of processing information (Morra et al., 2018). With growing research on executive function, researchers caution about the inconsistencies that exist in the literature. Morra and colleagues (2018) point out "that similar constructs are called by different names, different constructs receive the same name, and similar tasks are used to index different constructs or at least constructs called by different names" (p. 249). For example, attention shifting is not the same as flexibility which allows the child to flexibly adapt to changing conditions than simply changing the focus of attention.

Executive functions emerge in infancy and are seen in infants' efforts to solve problems such as how to pull a toy out of a container or in playing games such as pat-a-cake. They develop in the preschool period and subserve children's increasing ability to engage in self-regulatory and intentional behaviors (e.g., delay of gratification, task persistence). They are also considered the mechanisms that underlie the development of reasoning and theory of mind in preschoolers (i.e., an awareness of their and others' minds). In the school-age period, these skills are considered to drive academic performance as well as social cognition (e.g., understanding multiple perspectives) and general social-emotional development. Executive functions in adolescence may protect children from engaging in high-risk behaviors and peer pressure. Performance on simple working memory tasks is evident in late infancy and appears to improve from preschool to adolescence in a rather linear fashion, as the complexity of memory tasks also increases. The ability to supersede an immediate desired response improves more in preschool while the inhibition of action later improves more in the school-age period. Thus, the developmental trajectory of inhibitory control is somewhat multifaceted as it continues to develop into middle childhood with early qualitative and later quantitative changes. Lastly, the ability to shift attention between tasks follows a prolonged path as it continues to strenghten into adolescence (Karbach & Unger, 2014).

The improvement in executive function with age relates to increased activity and development in the prefrontal cortex. Baum et al. (2017) demonstrated an age-related increase in the segregation of network modules that are densely interconnected nodes processing specialized information, such as the frontoparietal, somatomotor, and visual modules. This increased modular segregation was more prominent in childhood and adolescence and was associated with increased executive function. In addition, the development of structural segregations mediated the age-related improvement in executive function. Furthermore, the brain analysis revealed the development of the edge connections between the hubs, which are the shorter paths of communications, indicating an improvement in global efficiency. This improvement was too associated with executive function and mediated the relationship with the age-related change in executive function. Altogether, as children grow, these critical modules become more segregated but also more efficient in communicating with each other, and these changes explain the positive relationship between increased age and improved executive function. Along the same lines, Cui et al. (2020) demonstrated in a sample of 8- to 23-year-olds that the energy needed to activate the frontoparietal system decreased with age, suggesting a more efficient executive functioning with age. Scans revealed that white matter networks, which are the fatty fiber tracts that connect regions in the frontal and parietal cortex, matured during adolescence. In addition, studies using event-related potential (ERP) show specific ERP components to be markers of executive functions that change as children develop from childhood to adolescence. Furthermore, these ERP components follow different developmental trajectories in cases of atypical development of the executive function, as is the case with Attention Deficit and Hyperactivity Disorder (ADHD; Downes et al., 2017). Thus, these findings further support the segregation of cortical structures and executive functions. More to the point, Fiske and Holmboe (2019) reviewed fMRI studies to match developmental changes in working memory, inhibition, and cognitive flexibility (i.e., shifting between cognitive tasks) with changes in the brain. They found that brain networks subserving these functions are active and functional in the first year of life, and change over time both structurally (e.g., cortical thickness, volume, and white matter in the prefrontal cortex) and in terms of connectivity with other regions. In addition, they become more specialized with age. These findings indicate that executive function is more unified in the early years and becomes more specialized in subcomponents in school-age children and adolescents (Karbach & Unger, 2014).

Research suggests that the first months after birth might constitute a sensitive period for the development of executive functions. Specifically, social interactions are considered experiences that are expected to stimulate the attentional systems and shape the infants' expectations about their ability to control their environment. Changes in the prefrontal context coincide with the development of the attachment system that is implicated in the development of early capacity for self-regulation. Younger children are also more responsive to training of executive functions indicating that preschool years may be part of the sensitive period for the development of executive functions. Given that executive functions consist of distinct components, there may be different sensitive periods for their optimal development (Thompson & Steinbeis, 2020).

Executive functions are typically assessed through behavioral tasks. In preschool, sustained attention is usually measured by asking children to copy increasingly more complex designs or identify duplicates of target drawings in a series of drawings. Attention shifting is observed when children are asked to sort cards by one dimension and then shift to sorting them by another criterion. Working memory is assessed when children are asked to recall images or digits in the same or reverse order. Inhibitory control is seen when children are asked to perform motoric acts that are either congruent or incongruent with a verbal command (e.g., a child touches their knee when the command is to touch their head). School-age children and adolescents can test their executive functions by completing computer tasks. Inhibition, for example, is tested when the participant pushes the key that identifies a target image from very similar images that aim to confuse the participant. Working memory computer tasks may assess recall for spatial and verbal information. Attention shifting may be measured by some more complex variation of a Stroop task. Executive function tasks are linked to academic achievement (Lipsey et al., 2017) and may be used for clinical assessment (Kramer et al., 2013).

In conclusion, executive function is a crucial set of cognitive abilities that emerge in infancy and continue to develop throughout childhood and adolescence. These abilities include attention shifting, working memory, inhibition, and other recently identified functions such as planning and cognitive flexibility. Although there are inconsistencies in the literature regarding the number and differentiation of these functions, it is widely accepted that they play an essential role in children's cognitive, social, and emotional development. The developmental trajectory of executive functions is closely tied to changes in the prefrontal cortex, which becomes more specialized with age. Increased segregation of network modules and improved global efficiency in the brain contribute to age-related improvements in executive function. Research also suggests that early years might constitute a sensitive period for executive function development, with social interactions playing a critical role in shaping these abilities.

Executive Functions and Academic Success

The manifestation of cognitive processes in overt behavior is seen in applied settings such as school where children must employ executive functions to behave in an organized manner while listening to the teacher. Research has linked improvements in executive function with improved academic performance and deficits in executive function with learning difficulties and mental health problems. Most evidence comes from extensive reviews and meta-analytic studies that cover the period of preschool to young adulthood. Examining the associations between executive functions, academic success, and mental health is complex as it is difficult to establish causality or directionality in these relationships. However, researchers have employed longitudinal designs in which the temporal relationship of the variables may provide the closest evidence for directionality. Furthermore, academic skills at one age may predict academic skills later, and therefore the stability in academic skill or ability over time may confound the predictive role of executive functions. The individual timeline for the development of each executive function also perplexes the understanding of the role of executive functions in academic success and well-being.

Beginning with a focus on the early years, evidence from a meta-analytic study revealed that the tasks assessing inhibitory control and sustained attention at the end of pre-K were stronger predictors of academic achievement (oral comprehension, vocabulary, quantitative concepts) at the end of kindergarten. Moreover, the gains in performance in these executive tasks during this period were correlated with gains in academic performance (Lipsey et al., 2017). Because previous research has linked fine motor skills with academic skills such as math, reading, and spelling, Khng and Ng (2021) attempted to separate the effects of executive and fine motor skills (FMS) using a sample of over 1,200 children from 60 different kindergarten classrooms. They assessed the three main executive functions (working memory, inhibition, and attention switching) using nine behavioral tasks which were combined to create one general measure of performance on executive functions. While controlling for non-verbal intelligence, time spent in kindergarten, and the family's socioeconomic status (SES), they found an interaction effect of executive and fine motor skills on math, and spelling, and a main effect of executive functions on spelling. There were no effects on reading. The analysis of interactions revealed that the relationship between executive functions and math was significant only for children with very high fine motor skills. In other words, executive functions contribute more to math in children with high than poor fine motor skills. For spelling, the relationship with the executive function was significant for children with poor fine motor skills. The contribution of fine motor skills to spelling was only significant for children with poor executive functions. Spelling may involve high demands on executive function. These findings show the intimate connection between executive and motor skills and invite the question of whether improving fine motor skills can support a positive connection between executive function and academic skills in the preschool period.

As children transition to elementary school, researchers sought to reveal the continuing effect of executive functions. In longitudinal investigations, it is important to control for the effect of prior academic skills that are specific (e.g., math scores) as well as general (e.g., standardized test scores). For example, math scores predict not only future math but also future reading scores. While controlling for these variables as well as SES, Morgan et al. (2019) found that working memory, cognitive flexibility, and inhibitory control of over 8,000 kindergarteners predicted reading, math, and science scores in 2nd grade. The stronger predictor was inhibitory control as it predicted reading, math, and science as well as externalizing and internalizing problems in the classroom in grade 2. Working memory and cognitive flexibility only predicted academic performance.

Magalhães et al. (2020) sought to determine the unique contributions of each executive function, with a focus on cognitive flexibility in students from grades 2, 4, and 6, due to its relationship with memory and inhibition. The researchers employed performance tasks to evaluate executive functions and subject tests to measure academic performance. In grade 2, cognitive flexibility did not significantly contribute to literacy beyond the effects of intelligence and inhibitory control. For math in grade 2, intelligence, attention, and inhibitory control were the predictors, while cognitive flexibility did not make a notable impact. In grade 4, intelligence, inhibitory control, and working memory were predictors for literacy, with cognitive flexibility adding some additional variance. For math in grade 4, intelligence, inhibitory control, working memory, and planning were the predictors, with cognitive flexibility also being a significant contributor. In grade 6, intelligence, inhibitory control, and working memory predicted literacy outcomes, with cognitive flexibility accounting for an additional 4% variance. Lastly, intelligence, inhibitory control, and working memory were significant predictors for math in grade 6, with cognitive flexibility contributing a unique 6% variance. These findings indicate that the influence of executive functions, particularly cognitive flexibility, increases with age and becomes more critical for complex tasks in higher grades. Cognitive flexibility starts to differentiate after age 10, and its contribution to academic outcomes grows accordingly. The study highlights that cognitive flexibility is essential for both math and literacy performance.

Evidence for the trajectory of the relationship between executive functions and academic performance from kindergarten to 6th grade comes from a meta-analysis conducted by Spiegel et al. (2021). The analysis revealed that the relationship between executive function and academic skills was weaker than previously reported because they controlled for the effect of the intercorrelations between the individual components of executive function. However, all components of executive function remained uniquely predictive of all academic outcomes, suggesting that specific components of executive function are also important for reading, math, and oral language. The relations between the components of executive function and academic achievement were generally small. The analysis also showed moderate correlations between working memory and reading, math, and literacy in both early and late elementary school. However, the relationship between inhibitory control and shifting varied in early and late elementary school, depending on the academic skill. Inhibitory control was more strongly associated with academic achievement in early elementary school than in late elementary school, although the relationship between inhibitory control and math was not significantly different across the two periods. While the size of the correlations between shifting and academic achievement was generally greater in early than in late elementary school, this difference was only statistically significant for math achievement. The findings suggest that the unique relations between specific executive function components and academic achievement vary across development and possibly the demands of specific academic tasks, and more research is needed to understand these patterns further.

In summary, the relationship between executive functions and academic performance has been extensively studied, and evidence suggests that improvements in executive functions are linked to better academic performance, while deficits in executive functions are linked to learning difficulties and mental health problems. Studies focusing on preschoolers have found that inhibitory control and sustained attention tasks are strong predictors of academic achievement a year after and gains in executive function performance during this period are correlated with gains in academic performance. Fine motor skills have been found to interact with executive functions in predicting math and spelling outcomes in kindergarten-aged children, with executive functions contributing more to math in children with high fine motor skills and to spelling in children with poor fine motor skills. Longitudinal studies have also found that inhibitory control, working memory, and cognitive flexibility continue to play a role in academic performance during elementary school years. More research is needed to understand the complex relationship between executive functions and academic achievement, especially with respect to the unique contributions of specific executive function components across different ages and academic domains.

Executive Function and Mental Health

Because executive functions are involved in purposeful behavior, deficits in them are often characteristics of mental health problems. The link between executive function and psychopathology is either general or specific. In severe disorders like schizophrenia, the impairments in executive functions are severe and broad (Bloemen et al., 2018). Children who perform low on executive function behavioral tasks report general symptoms in psychopathology instead of specific internalizing or externalizing disorders (Caspi et al., 2013). In a large-scale study with adolescents, Bloemen et al. (2018) confirmed the link between widespread executive function impairment and general psychopathology but also some specific associations. Impairments in visuospatial working memory, sustained attention, feedback responsiveness, and cognitive flexibility were related to Autism Spectrum Disorder (ASD) and ADHD. In addition, marked deficits in working memory and psychomotor control were associated with ADHD. The only executive function that predicted internalizing disorders was cognitive inflexibility. White et al. (2017) examined the association between attention vigilance, inhibition, flexibility, and working memory with overall psychopathology and specific internalizing and externalizing symptoms (e.g., fear and anxiety) in 8- to 21-year-old participants. General executive function was correlated with general psychopathology, anxiety, and psychosis but not with externalizing symptoms and fear. When examining specific domains of executive function, there were correlations between all components and anxiety and psychosis. Moreover, the associations were stronger for younger children. Lastly, having higher executive function was more protective of mental health in female than male participants.

It is unknown if deficits precede developing psychopathology or if they are consequences or simple correlates of psychopathology. It is entirely possible that trait characteristics related to psychopathology may affect the development of executive function. For example, preschoolers with trait-like anxiety performed worse in working memory and attention-shifting tasks (Visu-Petra et al., 2014). Castagna et al. (2019) considered how anxiety may impact the effect on executive function among children who have ADHD and found that those with anxiety had worse attention shifting and working memory. This was true for children who were diagnosed with ADHD and were more inattentive than hyperactive. In addition, third factors may explain both the developing psychopathology as well as deficits in executive function. Zelazo (2020) reports evidence from twin studies that genetic influences on general executive function are correlated with genetic influences on the general psychopathology factor. In addition, risks to executive function are also risk factors for psychopathology. Childhood adversities influence the development of executive function and the prefrontal cortex through heightened physiological responses to stress. Zelazo (2020) believes that executive function disruption causes behavior and developmental problems in social, emotional, and academic functioning and proposes that the link between high stress and high psychopathology is mediated by low executive function. Consequently, Zelazo argues that interventions to track executive functions should take place in preschool, when great development in the prefrontal cortex takes place, and during developmental transitions (e.g., into adolescence).

Altogether the evidence suggests that deficits in generalized and specific executive functions are considered risk factors for emotional, behavioral, and psychotic disorders (Snyder et al., 2015). Executive functions have transdiagnostic effects and play a central role in specific disorders of ADHD, ASD, and internalizing symptomatology. Executive functions may be also affected by psychopathology or act as mediators to explain how risk factors, such as adversity, lead to psychopathology. More research is needed in this area, especially regarding the effect of interventions that aim to improve executive functions. Current evidence suggests that such training may improve performance on executive tasks but does not improve psychopathological symptoms (Snyder et al., 2015).

Threats to Executive Function

Exposure to adversities such as childhood maltreatment, parental mental illness, domestic violence, and poverty increase the level of stress in the child's life and may interfere with the development of executive functions. For example, it is shown that harsh parenting predicts poorer behavior inhibition in early (Treat et al., 2019) and middle (Halse et al., 2019) childhood and early exposure to trauma interferes with the development of cognitive inhibitory control (van der Kolk, 2017). Furthermore, retrospective research with adults points out that exposure to childhood adversity matters in executive functioning. Unpredictable harsh and stressful early environment is associated with impaired inhibition (Mittal et al., 2015) and diminished performance in working memory tasks by demanding more cognitive sources (Philip et al., 2016). Similar results by Mark et al. (2018) show the link between history of abuse and poor working memory, based on EEG metrics.

In a recent review of 36 studies, Lund et al. (2020) examined the association between a range of adverse childhood experiences and difficulties in executive functions. Maltreatment that included all forms of abuse and neglect as well as exposure to domestic violence correlated with general executive function deficit. Specific associations with attention, working memory, inhibitory control, and cognitive flexibility were also significant although the results were not always consistent. Some evidence suggested that children who experienced multiple forms of abuse and neglect did worse in the areas of verbal working memory, problem-solving, and planning compared to children who experienced only neglect. Another study showed that children exposed to familial trauma performed worse on tasks of working memory, inhibitory control, attention, and speed of processing than children who were not exposed to familial trauma. Focusing further on the effect of neglect on executive function, the authors reviewed studies that compared children who were institutionalized prior to adoption with non-institutionalized children and reported heightened deficits in all executive functions. Moreover, children who remained in institutions compared to those given for adoption or placed in foster care had more pronounced deficits in overall executive function. Therefore, the more severe or extensive the form of maltreatment is, the greater and broader the deficits are (Lund et al., 2020). Although there are direct links between maltreatment and cognitive impairment some studies suggest that the relationship is mediated by psychopathology. However, not all children develop psychopathology in response to adversity (Su et al., 2019).

Maternal depression, another childhood adverse experience, was related to lower executive function in infancy and preschool years, and maternal depression in early childhood predicted poor executive function in elementary school. Moreover, these associations were mediated by decreased maternal sensitivity and warmth. These results were true for inhibitory control, attention, and verbal memory. Interestingly, maternal mental illness in preschool was unrelated to non-verbal memory and visual-spatial problem-solving in adolescence. Limited evidence suggests that family member addiction too relates to poor executive function after controlling for maternal depression and demographic characteristics. Witnessing domestic violence is usually included as a variable among cumulative maltreatment but its unique contribution to executive function has not been studied. Lastly, no studies have examined the contribution of a family member's incarceration (Lund et al., 2020). In conclusion, the general negative association between maltreatment and executive functions is well established although the connections between specific adverse childhood experiences and specific executive functions need further investigation. Moreover, the timing of the adversity and its impact on executive functions on the developing child is not clear but it seems that exposure to adversity in the early years is more consequential.

Poverty is considered a major risk factor and its negative and lasting effect on all domains of child development, including cognitive, has been well studied. Researchers often use the family's income-to-needs ratio (family income/federal level of poverty for a family of four) to estimate the resources available to children. The parents' education is also often used as an index of the social and financial status of a family. Hackman et al. (2015) explored the relationship between SES and working memory and planning as well as the trajectory of this relationship from early childhood to grade 5 using participants from the National Institute of Child Health and Development Study of Early Child Care. Early assessment of income predicted working memory at 54 months and planning in grade 1. Maternal education predicted working memory in grade 1 and planning in grade 3. Moreover, the differences in performance in executive function were stable as the socioeconomic differences remained stable. There was also a significant decrease in planning ability and a declining trend for working memory when the family income-to-needs decreased. These results held when the researchers accounted for race and ethnicity, gender, maternal depression, presence of a father figure at home, and maternal verbal ability. Mediation models revealed that early childhood home enrichment and maternal sensitivity were significant full mediators between income-to-needs and executive functions, explaining 38% of the variance in working memory and 65% of the variance in planning ability. Therefore, similarly to the effect of other childhood adverse experiences discussed by Lund et al. (2020), the absence of parental care and low maternal sensitivity are important mediators that may protect or jeopardize the development of the executive function.

Haft and Hoeft (2017) argued that the effect of poverty on executive functions would be different in children raised in countries with more disadvantaged contexts compared to low-income children in Western, high-income countries. By reviewing several studies, the authors concluded that the mediators between poverty and executive function are indeed different. In low-income children who are raised in affluent countries, parental responsiveness and sensitivity mediate the relationship, as stated earlier. Parenting and specifically being able to promote autonomy and guide children, as well as the parent's ability to support goal-directed behavior and planning seem to be significant protective buffers for executive functions. Furthermore, studies also show that the level of enrichment in the home environment is also a mediator in poor children living in high-income countries. Having books, computers, and toys that cognitively stimulate the child can protect them from the effects of low socio-economic status. However, in low-income countries, the parent's ability to promote executive function may be more restricted as parents face more stressors, such as infectious diseases, and environmental toxins. Children in poor countries also have limited access to print. Instead, research shows that in these contexts, the most significant mediator between poverty and deficits in executive function is stunting. Children whose growth is restricted, as an outcome of poverty, experience poor executive function.

Interestingly, Haft and Hoeft (2017) found evidence that the children who spent their unsupervised time on the streets maintained their executive functions. Presumably, learning to survive on the streets forces children to practice independent problem-solving. Not all children are affected by poverty in the same way, and this is probably due to the individual temperament and response to stress, both of which are biologically based. Of course, such variables interact with familiar and other contextual factors adding more complexity to understanding the web of interactions between variables that determine the development of the executive function.

The bottom line is that childhood adversities and poverty expose children to heightened and prolonged stress which in turn changes the biochemistry and structure of the brain. The chronic stimulation of the Hypothalamic-Pituitary-Adrenal Axis (HPA) axis in response to protracted stress results in low tolerance for stress, and exaggerated response. The HPA axis is connected to the prefrontal cortex and the system becomes dysregulated after chronic exposure to stress. The child has difficulty assessing the level of threat and coping appropriately. Engaging in goal-directed behavior that depends on the development of executive function is a challenge for children exposed to chronic stress. The volume of gray matter in areas dedicated to emotional regulation becomes smaller in children with a history of trauma (Wagner et al., 2016). Maltreatment changes the reactivity of the neural structures responding to stress and alters the functionality of brain regions involved in executive function and regulation. Maltreatment affects the speed of processing, attention, memory, and ability to learn, leading to small size hippocampus (Lund et al., 2020). Moreover, children who experience harsh corporal punishment have a smaller volume of the prefrontal cortex (Tomoda et al., 2009).

Preschoolers with high cortisol levels have parents who report high parenting stress and lower executive function composite score of inhibitory control and cognitive flexibility (Wagner et al., 2016). DePasquale et al. (2021) further explored the role of cortisol and specifically hair cortisol in understanding the relationship between stress and executive function in a sample of 13- to 18-year-old children. Hair cortisol is a biomarker of cumulative activity in the HPA axis. Indeed, there was a correlation between the total number of stressful events and higher hair cortisol concentration. There was a negative association between lifetime exposure to stress and lower composite executive function scores. Hair cortisol was a significant mediator in younger children, but it did not correlate with executive function in older children. Therefore, the risk for neurotoxins effect on brain development is higher in younger children but as children get older there may also be a stress inoculation effect. Age appears to be a moderator in the hair cortisol and executive function relationship.

In conclusion, exposure to childhood adversity negatively impacts children's executive functions by increasing their stress levels and interfering with their brain development. Exposure to prolonged stress alters the biochemistry and structure of a child's brain, leading to dysregulation of the HPA axis and impairing executive functions. The negative effects of stress on executive function may be higher in younger children, while older children may experience a stress inoculation effect. Poverty is a major risk factor that can have lasting effects on children's ability to succeed, with parental care, maternal sensitivity, and home enrichment being significant mediators between low socio-economic status and executive function in affluent countries, while stunting is a significant mediator in low-income countries. The relationship between specific adversities and executive functions needs further investigation, as well as understanding the role of the timing of adversity on the developing child.

Enhancing Executive Function

Given the importance of executive functions in academic performance and achievement, researchers have created intervention programs to enhance executive functions in school settings, specifically targeted for poor children and children with ADHD and brain injuries. Some of these interventions are specific to executive functions and others aim to improve self-regulation skills such as taking turns and paying attention to instructions. Ursache et al. (2012) reviewed studies that utilized three interventions for self-regulation to observe their effect on the executive functions of preschoolers attending Head Start Preschools. The Head Start Research-Based Developmentally Informed (REDI) is an intervention that includes literacy and language instruction as well as social-emotional skills. The Chicago School Readiness Project (CSRP) focuses on emotional and behavioral self-regulation by improving teachers' ability to control their own emotions and behaviors. The Tools of the Mind curriculum specifically promotes behaviors that depend on executive functions like taking others' perspectives and monitoring own and others' behaviors. REDI improved executive function in a sorting task and in turn mediated the effects on literacy outcomes. Creating an emotionally positive and relaxing environment by supporting teachers' management skills also improved executive function as shown by less student impulsivity and greater sustained attention, after one year of implementation. The Tools of the Mind program improved performance on tasks that assessed working memory, inhibitory control, and attention-shifting abilities after two years of implementation. Interestingly, Tools did not directly improve academic performance, but executive function did. Blair and Raver (2015) also applied the Tools of the Mind training in 29 high-poverty area schools and showed improvement in executive function and self-regulation when the training was implemented in kindergarten. Along the same lines, Jones, Bailey, et al. (2014; Jones, Kargman, et al., 2014) designed a similar school-based intervention tailored for children from K to 3rd grade. The program called Social, Emotional, and Cognitive Understanding and Regulation in Education (SECURE) was designed to improve executive function and self-regulation as well as literacy in low-income children. The intervention included structural changes in the school routines to provide a well-regulated environment, and weekly lessons focusing on attention, listening, and behavior regulation. The program that was implemented with more than 4,000 students increased students' attention skills and decreased impulsivity in the classroom. These results highlight the importance of providing a consistently structured environment to support children's ability to use language to plan, monitor, and self-reflect. Consequently, children learn to apply executive function skills to regulate their social and learning behaviors.

Interventions that focus on specific executive functions indicate that they are effective in improving performance in tasks that assess these specific abilities. Cognitive flexibility or attention-shifting is improved in preschoolers by asking them to switch between two or three tasks. For example, children decide whether a picture on a screen is a flower or not and then decide whether its color is red or not. Working memory is improved when children practice remembering whether a specific stimulus was presented at an earlier trial as well as by recalling a list of items (i.e., working memory capacity). Interestingly, improvements in attention shifting transfer to similar (near transfer) but also structurally different tasks of inhibition and working memory (far transfer) although the transfer was limited in adolescents. Improvements in working memory also transfer to other cognitive abilities, but only to those who experienced great as opposed to moderate improvement. These outcomes apply to both verbal and visuospatial working memory. Regarding inhibitory control, explicit training programs are scarce, but inhibition is generally improved by training programs aiming to improve attention and complex working memory tasks, for preschoolers. Children with known impairment in executive function such as ADHD benefit more from targeted interventions. School-age children improved their inhibition and working memory by practicing attention-switching tasks (Karbach & Unger, 2014).

Researchers have also examined the effect of mindfulness, physical activity, and cognitive behavioral interventions on the executive functions of young children. Mindfulness is expected to improve sustained attention by asking children to notice when the mind wanders and practice refocusing. A 12-week mindfulness-based curriculum that consisted of 20–30 sessions each week improved empathy, compassion, and school grades but the effect on executive function was only trending (Flook et al., 2015). Programs that increase the physical activity of children and adolescents enhance mostly the composite scores of executive functions although there is some evidence that non-verbal memory is specifically improved (Wassenaar et al., 2020). Randomized controlled trials indicate that 30 minutes of activity of moderate intensity, three times a week, improves attention and inhibition, particularly for those who have ADHD or are overweight (Suarez-Manzano et al., 2018). Children with ADHD additionally benefit from cognitive behavioral therapy and computer-aided programs specifically targeting selective attention and working memory. Meta-analytic evidence shows that the effect of cognitive training on attention is small but significant and somewhat larger than the effect on memory. The effects were generally stronger at the end of the intervention than later after the training ended. Similar results were obtained for children with various brain injuries caused by infections, tumors, or trauma (Karch et al., 2013).

While research shows that executive function skills develop as children mature and can be improved by formal and structured intervention programs, parents and teachers can support executive functions by engaging them in developmentally appropriate activities but also simple, playful interactions. The Center for the Developing Child has published a guide with resourceful suggestions that support the skills of paying attention adaptively, processing and recalling information, and self-regulating thoughts and impulsive responses. In infancy, hiding and rhythmic games, and simple conversations allow babies to practice skills of inhibition, memory, and concentration. Older toddlers additionally benefit from active games that require them to imitate (e.g., Follow the Leader) or to explicitly practice inhibition (e.g., Freeze Dance). Preschoolers may practice storytelling, play matching games, and engage in imaginative play. These opportunities strengthen their ability to engage in planful actions. As children transition to grade school, they improve their ability to follow instructions by playing card or board games. Playing with other children without adult supervision offers the opportunity to self-regulate independently of adult presence. Quiet activities like making puzzles, solving brain teasers, and spying games also allow children to practice executive skills on their own. In middle childhood, children may expand their previous activities to include learning music, singing, dancing, and playing sports. Self-monitoring of executive functions and metacognitive skills begin to develop at this time as children become more introspective and self-reflective. In adolescence, these skills expand while children begin to set their own goals such as getting a driver's license, completing college applications, or saving money for their first car. Parents may facilitate the planning process by allowing adolescents to choose goals that are meaningful to them and encourage them to think about the role of distractions and interruptions. Discussing the causes of successes and failures builds awareness of how cognitive skills and effort are combined to achieve goals. Adolescents may enjoy activities such as computer games, logic games, yoga, meditation, school plays, sports, and music that contribute to the development of executive functions. Ultimately, executive functions do not develop in a vacuum but are embedded in the interactions and contexts in which children participate.

Executive functions are necessary abilities that children develop through specific training programs, unstructured and structured school activities, recreational engagement such as hobbies, unsupervised time, and opportunities for independent thinking and action. Parental warmth and support provide a significant buffer even at the face of adversity. Chronic stress and maltreatment are the major threats to the healthy development of executive functions. Children in low-SES families may benefit from interventions that improve parental sensitivity and enrich the home environment. In turn, executive functions support children's overall well-being and most specifically their academic performance. While the research on this area is abundant, the relationship between executive functions and academic achievement needs further research to establish connections between individual or global executive functions and specific academic skills as children grow. Such evidence would allow the development of diagnostic tools and interventions at the right developmental time. For example, perhaps improving working memory in preschoolers would forecast strong math and language skills, especially in children from low-SES families.

In closing, intervention programs targeted at improving executive functions and self-regulation skills in school settings have proven to be effective, particularly for children from low-income backgrounds, children with ADHD, and those with brain injuries. Various approaches such as mindfulness, physical activity, and cognitive behavioral interventions have shown the potential in enhancing executive functions in children. Importantly, improvements in specific executive functions like attention-shifting, working memory, and inhibitory control can transfer to other cognitive abilities, albeit with some limitations. Structured and unstructured school activities, recreational hobbies, and opportunities for independent thinking contribute to the development of executive functions. Further research is necessary to establish connections between individual or global executive functions and specific academic skills as children grow, which could enable the development of diagnostic tools and interventions at the appropriate developmental stages.

References

Baum, G. L., Ciric, R., Roalf, D. R., Betzel, R. F., Moore, T. M., Shinohara, R. T., Kahn, A. E., Vandekar, S. N., Rupert, P. E., Quarmley, M., Cook, P. A., Elliott, M. A., Ruparel, K., Gur, R. E., Gur, R. C., Bassett, D. S., & Satterthwaite, T. D. (2017). Modular segregation of structural brain networks supports the development of executive function in youth. *Current Biology*, *27*(11), 1561–1572. https://doi.org/10.1016/j.cub.2017.04.051

Blair, C., & Raver, C. C. (2015). School readiness and self-regulation: A developmental psychobiological approach. *Annual Review of Psychology*, *66*, 711–731. https://doi.org/10.1146/annurev-psych-010814-015221

Bloemen, A. J. P., Oldehinkel, A. J., Laceulle, O. M., Ormel, J., Rommelse, N. N. J., & Hartman, C. A. (2018). The association between executive functioning and psychopathology: General or specific? *Psychological Medicine*, *48*(11), 1787–1794. https://doi.org/10.1017/S0033291717003269

Caspi, A., Houts, R. M., Belsky, D. W., Goldman-Mellor, S. J., Harrington, H., Israel, S., Meier, M. H., Ramrakha, S., Shalev, I., Poulton, R., & Moffitt, T. E. (2013). The p-factor: One general psychopathology factor in the structure of psychiatric disorders? *Clinical Psychological Science*, *2*, 119–137. https://doi.org/10.1177/2167702613497473

Castagna, P. J., Calamia, M., Roye, S., Greening, S. G., & Davis, T. E. (2019). The effects of childhood inattention and anxiety on executive functioning: Inhibition, updating, and shifting. *ADHD Attention Deficit and Hyperactivity Disorders*, *11*(4), 423–432. https://doi.org/10.1007/s12402-019-00306-7

Cui, Z., Stiso, J., Baum, G. L., Kim, J. Z., Roalf, D. R., Betzel, R. F., Gu, S., Lu, Z., Xia, C. H., He, X., Ciric, R., Oathes, D. J., Moore, T. M., Shinohara, R. T., Ruparel, K., Davatzikos, C., Pasqualetti, F., Gur, R. E., Gur, R. C., & Satterthwaite, T. D. (2020). Optimization of energy state transition trajectory supports the development of executive function during youth. *Elife*, *9*. https://doi.org/10.7554/eLife.53060

DePasquale, C. E., Tyrell, F. A., Kalstabakken, A. W., Labella, M. H., Thibodeau, E. L., Masten, A. S., & Barnes, A. J. (2021). Lifetime stressors, hair cortisol, and executive function: Age-related associations in childhood. *Developmental Psychobiology*, *63*(5), 1043–1052. https://doi.org/10.1002/dev.22076

Diamond, A. (2016, November 17). *How do children develop executive functions?* [Video]. YouTube. www.youtube.com/watch?v=pRB6gzgFa2s

Downes, M., Bathelt, J. O. E., & De Haan, M. (2017). Event-related potential measures of executive functioning from preschool to adolescence. *Developmental Medicine & Child Neurology*, *59*(6), 581–590. https://doi.org/10.1111/dmcn.13395

Fiske, A., & Holmboe, K. (2019). Neural substrates of early executive function development. *Developmental Review*, *52*, 42–62. https://doi.org/10.1016/j.dr.2019.100866

Flook, L., Goldberg, S. B., Pinger, L., & Davidson, R. J. (2015). Promoting prosocial behavior and self-regulatory skills in preschool children through a mindfulness-based kindness curriculum. *Developmental Psychology*, *51*(1), 44–51. https://doi.org/10.1037/a0038256

Hackman, D. A., Gallop, R., Evans, G. W., & Farah, M. J. (2015). Socioeconomic status and executive function: Developmental trajectories and mediation. *Developmental Science*, *18*(5), 686–702. https://doi.org/10.1111/desc.12246

Haft, S. L., & Hoeft, F. (2017). Poverty's impact on children's executive functions: Global considerations. *New Directions for Child and Adolescent Development*, *2017*(158), 69–79. https://doi.org/10.1002/cad.20220

Halse, M., Steinsbekk, S., Hammar, Å., Belsky, J., & Wichstrøm, L. (2019). Parental predictors of children's executive functioning from ages 6 to 10. *British Journal of Developmental Psychology*. https://doi.org/10.1111/bjdp.12282

Jones, S. M., Bailey, R., & Jacob, R. (2014). Social-emotional learning is essential to classroom management. *Phi Delta Kappan*, *96*(2), 19–24.

Jones, S. M., Kargman, M., Kargman, M., & Bailey, R. (2014). Preliminary impacts of SECURE PreK on child-and classroom-level outcomes. *Society for Research on Educational Effectiveness*. Retrieved May 11, 2023, from https://files.eric.ed.gov/fulltext/ED562750.pdf

Karbach, J., & Unger, K. (2014). Executive control training from middle childhood to adolescence. *Frontiers in Psychology*, *5*, 390. https://doi.org/10.3389/fpsyg.2014.00390

Karch, D., Albers, L., Renner, G., Lichtenauer, N., & von Kries, R. (2013). The efficacy of cognitive training programs in children and adolescents: A meta-analysis. *Deutsches Ärzteblatt International*, *110*(39), 643. https://doi.org/10.3238/arztebl.2013.0643

Khng, K. H., & Ng, E. L. (2021). Fine motor and executive functioning skills predict math and spelling skills at the start of kindergarten: A compensatory account. *Journal for the Study of Education and Development*, *44*(3), 675–718. https://doi.org/10.1080/02103702.2021.1897232

Kramer, J. H., Mungas, D., Possin, K. L., Rankin, K. P., Boxer, A. L., Rosen, H. J., Bostrom, A., Sinha, L., Berhel, A., & Widmeyer, M. (2013). NIH EXAMINER: Conceptualization and development of an executive function battery. *Journal of the International Neuropsychological Society*, *20*(1), 11–19. https://doi.org/10.1017/s1355617713001094

Lipsey, M. W., Nesbitt, K. T., Farran, D. C., Dong, N., Fuhs, M. W., & Wilson, S. J. (2017). Learning-related cognitive self-regulation measures for prekindergarten children: A comparative evaluation of the educational relevance of selected measures. *Journal of Educational Psychology*, *109*(8), 1084. https://doi.org/10.1037/edu0000203

Lund, J. I., Toombs, E., Radford, A., Boles, K., & Mushquash, C. (2020). Adverse childhood experiences and executive function difficulties in children: A systematic review. *Child Abuse & Neglect*, *106*, 104485. https://doi.org/10.1016/j.chiabu.2020.104485

Magalhães, S., Carneiro, L., Limpo, T., & Filipe, M. (2020). Executive functions predict literacy and mathematics achievements: The unique contribution of cognitive flexibility in grades 2, 4, and 6. *Child Neuropsychology*, *26*(7), 934–952. https://doi.org/10.1080/09297049.2020.1740188

Mark, C. A., Poltavski, D. V., Petros, T., & King, A. (2019). Differential executive functioning in young adulthood as a function of experienced child abuse. *International Journal of Psychophysiology*, *135*, 126–135. https://doi.org/10.1016/j.ijpsycho.2018.12.004

Mittal, C., Griskevicius, V., Simpson, J. A., Sung, S., & Young, E. S. (2015). Cognitive adaptations to stressful environments: When childhood adversity enhances adult executive function. *Journal of Personality and Social Psychology*, *109*(4), 604–621. http://dx.doi.org/10.1037/pspi0000028

Miyake, A., Friedman, N. P., Emerson, M. J., Witzki, A. H., Howerter, A., & Wager, T. D. (2000). The unity and diversity of executive functions and their contributions to complex "frontal lobe" tasks: A latent variable analysis. *Cognitive Psychology*, *41*, 49–100. https://doi.org/10.1006/cogp.1999.0734

Morgan, P. L., Farkas, G., Hillemeier, M. M., Pun, W. H., & Maczuga, S. (2019). Kindergarten children's executive functions predict their second-grade academic achievement and behavior. *Child Development*, *90*(5), 1802–1816. https://doi.org/10.1111/cdev.13095

Morra, S., Panesi, S., Traverso, L., & Usai, M. C. (2018). Which tasks measure what? Reflections on executive function development and a commentary on Podjarny, Kamawar, and Andrews (2017). *Journal of Experimental Child Psychology*, *167*, 246–258. https://doi.org/10.1016/j.jecp.2017.11.004

Philip, N. S., Sweet, L. H., Tyrka, A. R., Carpenter, S. L., Albright, S. E., Price, L. H., & Carpenter, L. L. (2016). Exposure to childhood trauma is associated with altered n-back activation and performance in healthy adults: Implications for a commonly used working memory task. *Brain Imaging and Behavior*, *10*(1), 124–135. https://doi.org/10.1007/s11682-015-9373-9

Snyder, H. R., Miyake, A., & Hankin, B. L. (2015). Advancing understanding of executive function impairments and psychopathology: Bridging the gap between clinical and cognitive approaches. *Frontiers in Psychology*, *6*, 328. https://doi.org/10.3389/fpsyg.2015.00328

Spiegel, J. A., Goodrich, J. M., Morris, B. M., Osborne, C. M., & Lonigan, C. J. (2021). Relations between executive functions and academic outcomes in elementary school children: A meta-analysis. *Psychological Bulletin*, *147*(4), 329. https://doi.org/10.1037/bul0000322

Su, Y., D'Arcy, C., Yuan, S., & Meng, X. (2019). How does childhood maltreatment influence ensuing cognitive functioning among people with the exposure of childhood maltreatment? A systematic review of prospective cohort studies. *Journal of Affective Disorders*, *252*, 278–293. https://doi.org/10.1016/j.jad.2019.04.026

Suarez-Manzano, S., Ruiz-Ariza, A., De La Torre-Cruz, M., & Martínez-López, E. J. (2018). Acute and chronic effect of physical activity on cognition and behaviour in young people with ADHD: A systematic review of intervention studies. *Research in Developmental Disabilities*, *77*, 12–23. https://doi.org/10.1016/j.ridd.2018.03.015

Thompson, A., & Steinbeis, N. (2020). Sensitive periods in executive function development. *Current Opinion in Behavioral Sciences*, *36*, 98–105. https://doi.org/10.1016/j.cobeha.2020.08.001

Tomoda, A., Suzuki, H., Rabi, K., Sheu, Y. S., Polcari, A., & Teicher, M. H. (2009). Reduced prefrontal cortical gray matter volume in young adults exposed to harsh corporal punishment. *Neuroimage*, *47*. https://doi.org/10.1016/j.neuroimage.2009.03.005

Treat, A. E., Sheffield-Morris, A., Williamson, A. C., & Hays-Grudo, J. (2019). Adverse childhood experiences and young children's social and emotional development: The role of maternal depression, self-efficacy, and social support. *Early Child Development and Care*, 1–15. https://doi.org/10.1080/03004430.2019.1578220

Ursache, A., Blair, C., & Raver, C. C. (2012). The promotion of self-regulation as a means of enhancing school readiness and early achievement in children at risk for school failure. *Child Development Perspectives*, *6*(2), 122–128. https://doi.org/10.1111/j.1750-8606.2011.00209.x

van der Kolk, B. A. (2017). Developmental trauma disorder: Toward a rational diagnosis for children with complex trauma histories. *Psychiatric Annals*, *35*(5), 401–408. https://doi.org/10.3928/00485713-20050501-06

Visu-Petra, L., Stanciu, O., Benga, O., Miclea, M., & Cheie, L. (2014). Longitudinal and concurrent links between memory span, anxiety symptoms, and subsequent executive functioning in young children. *Frontiers in Psychology*, *5*, 443. https://doi.org/10.3389/fpsyg.2014.00443

Wagner, S. L., Cepeda, I., Krieger, D., Maggi, S., D'Angiulli, A., Weinberg, J., & Grunau, R. E. (2016). Higher cortisol is associated with poorer executive functioning in preschool children: The role of parenting stress, parent coping and quality of daycare. *Child Neuropsychology*, *22*(7), 853–869. https://doi.org/10.1080/09297049.2015.1080232

Wassenaar, T. M., Williamson, W., Johansen-Berg, H., Dawes, H., Roberts, N., Foster, C., & Sexton, C. E. (2020). A critical evaluation of systematic reviews assessing the effect of chronic physical activity on academic achievement, cognition and the brain in children and adolescents: A systematic review. *International Journal of Behavioral Nutrition and Physical Activity*, *17*, 1–18. https://doi.org/10.1186/s12966-020-00959-y

White, L. K., Moore, T. M., Calkins, M. E., Wolf, D. H., Satterthwaite, T. D., Leibenluft, E., Pine, D. S., Gur, R. C., & Gur, R. E. (2017). An evaluation of the specificity of executive function impairment in developmental psychopathology. *Journal of the American Academy of Child & Adolescent Psychiatry*, *56*(11), 975–982. https://doi.org/10.1016/j.jaac.2017.08.016

Zelazo, P. D. (2020). Executive function and psychopathology: A neurodevelopmental perspective. *Annual Review of Clinical Psychology*, *16*, 431–454. https://doi.org/10.1146/annurev-clinpsy-072319-024242

Part 3

The Individual and the Context

9 Individual Differences Matter

> In her memoir, The Glass Castle, Jeannette Walls (2005) recounts numerous adversities from her childhood including neglect, parental mental health illnesses, food insecurity, poverty, unsafe and unsanitary living conditions, environmental hazards, lack of health care, and inconsistent schooling. She and her family travel so much that her definition of home is a place where they had the time to unpack. Despite the challenges, young Jeannette is bright, hardworking, persistent, hopeful, ingenious, and industrious. She manages to leave behind her dilapidated house in Welch, West Virginia, to go to New York City where she attends college, begins her career as a journalist, and later becomes a best-selling author. What triggered Jeannette's success against all odds?

Psychologists who study individual differences or variations in traits and abilities among children do so to account for different outcomes in development. Such differences have been studied in the fields of personality and intelligence. Variability in intelligence has been assessed with IQ tests that tap into general information processing. Childhood personality differences are seen as innate predispositions to react in certain ways to environmental influences that then evolve into certain traits and abilities. While the environment certainly interacts with genetically inherent predispositions for personality and intellect to determine outcomes, studies have revealed high genetic influences in IQ scores and certain personality traits (e.g., extroversion) with heritability estimates that range from .70 to. 80 for intelligence (Bouchard, 2013) and from .40 to .50 for some personality traits among adults (Power & Pluess, 2015). Because of the genetic influence, individual differences in personality and intelligence are seen in infancy and persist in adulthood. Both personality and IQ have been linked with academic achievement, educational attainment, and subjective well-being in children. This chapter explores how individual differences in personality traits and IQ support children's ability to become happy and successful. It begins with an exploration of the links between childhood and adult personality by associating main temperament characteristics with the Big Five Factors of personality. The chapter reviews how personality traits predict childhood outcomes and foretell success in adulthood. The role of intelligence in school success and adult outcomes is also explored. Lastly, the chapter offers a discussion of how to enhance traits in children that are mostly linked with success.

DOI: 10.4324/9780429356414-13

Temperament and Its Links to Personality in Adults

Researchers use the term temperament to describe how infants and young children differ from one another in reactivity, attention, adaptability, activity, affectivity, and regulation. Thomas and Chess' theory of temperament, also known as a clinical model (Al-Hendawi, 2013), is often used in research and practice to describe patterns of behaviors or responses in infancy and the preschool period. Thomas and Chess (1977) have identified nine temperamental dimensions: activity level (i.e., the level of physical and mental energy), rhythmicity (i.e., regularity of biological rhythms), approach-withdrawal (i.e., the tendency to embrace or reject new stimuli at initial encounter), adaptability (i.e., degree of adjustment to new experiences), quality of mood (i.e., a tendency to experience more positive or negative emotions), the threshold of responsiveness (i.e., level of stimulation that is taken in before a behavioral response), intensity of response (i.e., the energy level of a behavioral reaction), distractibility (i.e., ability to shift attention to complete goals such as waiting), and attention span (i.e., focusing attention on a stimulus).

More contemporary perspectives have taken a narrower approach to studying temperament. For example, Kagan (1997) focused on behavioral inhibition or shyness. He thought of temperament as how reactive the brain becomes in response to new stimuli. An infant who becomes highly reactive as shown by general tension in the body, increased heart rate, and activation of the left hemisphere, is likely to show fearful responses as a toddler and shyness as a preschooler. In contrast, an infant with low reactivity and heart rate, and activation of the right hemisphere becomes a fearless toddler and an uninhibited preschooler. Because of its narrow scope, Kagan's model leaves out regulatory mechanisms like attention, which contribute to individual differences (Shiner & Masten, 2008). Rothbart's and Bates' (2006) model is another contemporary approach that is widely used in research and has influenced research on temperament in the last two decades (Fernández-Vilar & Carranza, 2013). Rothbart and Bates identified three dimensions of temperament. Surgency refers to the extent to which the child embraces positively and energetically the environmental stimulation. Negative affectivity refers to the extent to which the child experiences negative emotions such as fear, anger, and social anxiety. Effortful control taps into the child's ability to control attentional processes and inhibit undesirable responses.

Despite the differences in scope, these theorists agree that temperament is shaped by the environment. For example, Kagan found that with time, most children who were extremely inhibited or uninhibited moved toward the middle, becoming neither too shy nor too sociable. Thomas and Chess expected that temperamental characteristics would change based on the goodness of fit between parenting and the child's characteristics. For example, a child with a tendency to withdraw from new experiences may eventually become more approaching if parents provide the right support. Rothbart expects that in addition to experiences, maturation also influences how temperamental characteristics may develop. For example, with the development of the prefrontal lobe, attentional and regulatory mechanisms also develop.

In addition to the developmental changes that occur, research shows that temperamental dimensions and adult personality traits share a lot in common. According to Shiner and Masten (2008), researchers avoid using the term personality about children, who are still developing, because personality traits are seen as being stable across situations and time. Nonetheless, they argue that the basic personality structure that is observed in children and adolescents corresponds with the predominant personality model that is used to study individual differences in adults. This is the Big Five Factor model that includes the personality traits of *extroversion* (e.g., being active, assertive, and sociable), *neuroticism* (e.g., being emotionally unstable, experiencing anxiety and depression), *agreeableness* (e.g., being compassionate, friendly, and warm towards others), *conscientiousness* (e.g., being efficient, organized, and task-oriented), and *openness* (e.g., being curious and creative). It seems that these adult traits share a lot in common with temperamental dimensions. Surgency and extroversion reflect positive emotions, high energy, and sociability. Negative emotionality and neuroticism both tap into stress reactivity, experiencing more negative emotions, and having difficulty regulating them. Effortful control and conscientiousness reflect self-regulation, behavioral organization, and persistence. In a longitudinal investigation, Shiner and Masten (2008) found meaningful links between these temperamental traits in middle childhood and their corresponding personality traits at age 30. Additionally, they demonstrated links between adult agreeableness and being cooperative, considerate, and generous as a child. Openness was the only trait with weaker connections to childhood, but it was reflected as an eagerness to engage in creative and intellectual explorations. Research suggests that temperament in early and middle childhood predicts one-third of the personality in late adolescence and emerging adulthood (Deal et al., 2005). These connections between childhood and adulthood highlight personality stability which in turn implies a powerful and far-reaching influence of personality on personal happiness and success. The associations between personality and academic outcomes in childhood and adolescence are examined next.

Personality, Academic Achievement, and Academic Adjustment

Children in the classroom bring with them not only their cognitive abilities and skills but also behaviors, habits, and specific characteristics that define them. These abilities, behaviors, skills, and traits influence how children adjust in the school setting and perform academic tasks. Research has examined a broad range of temperamental characteristics and their relationship to academic adjustment and achievement. For children to be successful there must be a goodness of fit between the child's temperament and the school environment (Thomas & Chess, 1977). One of the temperamental characteristics that emerges as a significant predictor of academic success is effortful control. Effortful control allows children to control attentional processes and inhibit undesirable responses. In a review paper that followed several longitudinal studies, including the one by the National Institute of Child Health and Human Development (NICHD Early Child Care Research Network, 2003), Fernández-Vilar and Carranza (2013) found that effortful control consistently predicted academic performance and competence, as rated by teachers and standardized tests. Based on the NICHD study, effortful control in infancy predicted school performance and competence from preschool to 6th grade. Specifically, at the primary school level, attentional characteristics predicted math and reading scores. Other longitudinal studies extended these findings to adolescence. In another review of studies that included children from pre-kindergarten to 12th grade, it was revealed that children with the right balance of attention span, activity level, and distractibility were better able to focus on tasks and perform better academically. While these traits allow children to concentrate and complete classwork, thus predicting academic performance, they did not associate with math achievement at all. Further, the correlations between achievement and attention span, activity level, and distractibility were higher for younger children regardless of whether achievement was measured by teacher ratings or standardized tests. The findings suggest that the correlations become weaker in adolescence when children engage in independent behaviors like study habits that become more predictive of achievement (Al-Hendawi, 2013). Effortful control also has a significant positive correlation with school adjustment and is related to both internalizing and externalizing problems. Other studies have shown that the relationship between effortful control and problems is mediated by other factors. For example, anger and satisfaction with the school climate mediate effortful control and externalizing problems in preadolescence. Therefore, the risk that low effortful control poses can be offset if the child perceives the school culture as positive and supportive (Fernández-Vilar & Carranza, 2013).

Another temperamental characteristic that emerges as a strong predictor in the aforementioned reviews was negative emotionality. Negative emotionality is negatively correlated with school adjustment and positively with internalizing and externalizing problems (Al-Hendawi, 2013; Fernández-Vilar & Carranza, 2013). Compared to effortful control, negative emotionality has the strongest correlation with adjustment. Children who experience strong negative emotions are likely to engage in inappropriate classroom behavior and have difficulty regulating their emotions and following instructions. The demands of the classroom can be overwhelming to them. Negative emotionality therefore may interfere with children's success in school. Indeed, the tendency to experience fear and frustration predicts low academic scores and behavior problems in children and preadolescents. In contrast, students who are rated by their mothers as more adaptable and with positive emotionality are viewed by their teachers as better students. In general, temperamental characteristics related to self-regulation were associated with better school adjustment. Adaptability in turn relates to math and reading scores although to a lesser degree. Children who process social information more effectively and can empathize with others are also friendlier and have better relationships with others. These findings have been observed in multiple cultural contexts such as in Spanish and Chinese school settings. However, children with extremely high extroversion/surgency scores, in other words, students with high positive energy and sociability, tend to also have low self-control in the classroom which often leads to academic troubles (Fernández-Vilar & Carranza, 2013).

Scrimin et al. (2019) provided physiological and behavioral evidence that further unravels the connection between temperament and academic performance by examining the relationship between cardiac parasympathetic activity in response to stress and cognitive functioning in early adolescence (9th to 7th graders). In their methodology, they induced academic stress by presenting a video in which a student experienced a panic attack during a test and ended up failing it, while their classmates were able to concentrate on the exam and complete it. The researchers then measured heart rate variability (HRV) during and after the video (recovery phase). A decrease in HRV when faced with a stressor enables cognitive functioning and an increase in HRV during recovery allows the child to stay on task. Children with high basal cardiac regal tone have better self-regulation and can recoup from upsetting situations by recovering their heart rate. The researchers also assessed temperament and utilized school grade records. Indeed, students who experienced a decrease in HRV while watching the upsetting video had higher academic scores. Children with an inhibited temperament (i.e., they scored low in activity and sociability and higher in negative emotionality and shyness) had lower academic scores, presumably because they experience more negative emotions that they have trouble regulating, especially when faced with academic failure. Moreover, the researchers found an interaction between temperament and HRV. Students with inhibited temperament who increased their HRV during the recovery phase, signaling good regulation, had better scores than those who did not regulate well during recovery. This interaction was not present among outgoing children. Therefore, while inhibited temperament may associate with negative academic outcomes, the physiology of the child may be protective. Inhibited children who learn how to cope with their negative emotions are more successful in school, based on the evidence provided by Scrimin and colleagues (2019).

Further research has examined whether temperament functions as a mediator between academic outcomes and other factors that predict it like school readiness. For example, Valiente et al. (2021) considered the role of temperament in explaining the relationship between school preparedness and academic achievement. They measured readiness in literacy and numeracy when children were 5 years old by asking parents to complete relevant assessments. Three years later, the researchers assessed effortful control and shyness by utilizing teacher reports. At that time, the researchers also assessed achievement in math and reading. As expected, school readiness in kindergarten was predictive of academic scores at age 8. Consistent with previous research, effortful control was positively correlated with math and literary scores while shyness had a negative correlation with both. Moreover, the interaction between effortful control and school readiness was significant, as expected. Specifically, the relationship between school readiness and reading scores was high when effortful control was high. The interaction was also significant for shyness and school readiness. Children with low shyness and high school readiness scored higher in reading at age 8. Again, these findings highlight that shyness, a form of negative emotionality, is not a desirable trait in the school setting. Inhibited children may hesitate to ask teachers for help or clarification and may become easily embarrassed.

Other research has focused on explaining the correlations between temperamental characteristics and academic outcomes by identifying possible mediators. For example, Dollar et al. (2018) attempted to explain the link between temperament and academic achievement by using children's social skills as the mediator. They argued that negative emotional reactivity (i.e., an expression of negative emotionality) interferes with the children's ability to develop social skills and their ability to develop and maintain quality relationships with peers. Children with poor social skills then face more academic challenges. In contrast, positive emotionality promotes social skills and academic competence. The authors found that 2-year-olds who rated high on the dimension of negative reactivity and more specifically a tendency to become angry easily had lower social skills at age 7. In turn, social skills at age 7 predicted academic competence at ages 7 and 10. Children's characteristics may also evoke responses from the environment that affect academic performance. According to Viljaranta (2015), children's characteristics may elicit how teachers control the students' behavior by engaging in either psychological or behavioral control. Psychological control reflects the teacher's expression of disappointment and guilt to influence students. Behavioral control refers to teachers' attempts to directly control behavior through consequences. In 1st grade, the negative relationships between low task orientation (high activity level, low persistence, and high distractibility) and math and between high negative emotionality and math were mediated by behavioral control for both boys and girls. Furthermore, the negative relationship between negative emotionality and math performance was mediated by psychological control but only for girls. The fact that psychological control had a harmful effect on girls only indicates that such attempts diminish the girls' perception about their math ability which may already be lower than that of boys. Thus, it appears that behavioral control is protective for children who have low effortful control and high negative emotionality. Psychological control is not helpful for girls with high negative emotionality. Lastly, children's positive mood elicited more affection from the teachers and lower behavioral and psychological control but had no association with math and reading scores.

In sum, various temperamental characteristics significantly influence a child's academic success and adjustment in a school setting. Effortful control, perhaps a precursor to conscientiousness, consistently emerges as a major predictor of academic performance, competence, and school adjustment. It positively correlates with academic success and is related to both internalizing and externalizing problems. However, the risks associated with low effortful control can be mitigated by a supportive and positive school environment. Negative emotionality, perhaps a precursor to neuroticism, is another strong predictor negatively correlating with school adjustment and positively with internalizing and externalizing problems. Children who experience strong negative emotions may struggle with appropriate classroom behavior, emotional regulation, and following instructions, ultimately affecting their academic success. The physiological response of a child to stress, such as heart rate variability (HRV), can also impact academic performance. Inhibited children who can regulate their negative emotions more effectively tend to perform better in school. Temperament can also act as a mediator between academic outcomes and other factors, like school readiness. For example, effortful control and shyness can interact with school readiness to affect academic scores. Additionally, social skills and teacher behavior can serve as mediators in the relationship between temperament and academic achievement.

Other researchers have applied the Big Five Factor model to predict academic outcomes either via behavioral tasks or self-reports. For example, Poorthuis et al. (2014) developed behavioral measures to assess the personality traits of conscientiousness and agreeableness during the transition to secondary school (mean of 12.2 years). In addition to finding correlations between behavioral tasks and self-reports, the researchers also found that behavioral conscientiousness predicted academic achievement (grades and standardized scores) and social acceptance (how much they were liked by their peers) even after controlling for self-reported conscientiousness and past achievement. Behavioral agreeableness also predicted academic adjustment (Poorthuis et al., 2014). In a meta-analytic study that focused on adult measures of the Big Five in primary school children, all five personality traits correlated with academic performance. Conscientiousness and openness had the strongest correlations with academic performance (.50 and .43 respectively) which are equal in magnitude to the correlation between intelligence and academic performance. Agreeableness, extroversion, and emotional stability/neuroticism had significant correlations with academic achievement but were of smaller size (Poropat, 2014). Similarly, Tetzner et al. (2020) found that conscientiousness, openness, agreeableness, and extroversion correlated positively with academic achievement while neuroticism was negatively associated with achievement in a sample of 6th and 9th graders. They also reported that conscientiousness was more highly correlated with grades than with scores from standardized tests. Moreover, the associations persisted even after the researchers controlled for academic ability except for openness. The relationship between openness and academic outcomes weakened when the cognitive ability was controlled, suggesting that cognitive ability and openness may intersect. Lastly, all associations, except for openness, decreased in strength from 6th to 9th grade.

In addition to academic performance, personality traits are also predictive of school adjustment and overall well-being in school. Perret et al. (2019) operationalized academic adjustment as earning good grades and demonstrating habits that promote academic achievement such as being motivated, paying attention, and working independently. They also operationalized school well-being as feeling connected with the school, having a love for learning, having educational goals, and being efficient when pursuing academic tasks. In a sample of 9- to 13-year-olds, the authors found that children's personality explained 18% of the variance in academic adjustment when it was measured by mothers, and 12% when measured by the children. Based on mothers' data, conscientiousness and openness were positively related to academic adjustment while extroversion was negatively correlated with academic adjustment. Based on children's data, only conscientiousness was correlated with academic achievement. Regarding subjective well-being at school, personality explained almost 11% of the variance when the informants were the mothers and 31% when the informants were the children. Based on the mothers' data, only conscientiousness was positively correlated with well-being but based on children's data, agreeableness and openness in addition to conscientiousness were correlated with subjective well-being. Lastly, a nonlinear relationship between agreeableness and subjective well-being was found. Children with low agreeableness reported low subjective well-being but children with moderate or high levels of agreeableness did not differ much in their self-reported well-being at school. The results show that while agreeableness may contribute to gratifying relationships with peers, too much of it may be linked to hypersensitivity when coping with interpersonal difficulties. Similarly, a nonlinear pattern was revealed for extroversion. Children with high and low scores in extroversion reported lower well-being at school. It, therefore, seems that the optimal level of extroversion for school well-being is at the intermediate level.

Conscientiousness emerges as the personality trait that consistently predicts both grades, adjustment, and overall well-being at school. According to Perret et al. (2019), too much extroversion may interfere with paying attention and working independently. Shiner and Masten (2012) too reported a negative correlation between extroversion and rule-abiding behaviors at school at age 10. Extroversion predicts grades in 6th and 9th grades, according to Tetzner et al. (2020). Neuroticism has a negative association with academic scores (Poropat, 2014; Tetzner et al., 2020) and social adaptation at school (Shiner & Masten, 2012). The relationships that agreeableness and openness have with academic scores are not always consistent in the literature. Agreeableness, however, is positively related to school adjustment (Perret et al., 2019; Shiner & Masten, 2012). Several factors may moderate the associations between personality and success. The results may be influenced by how variables are measured and by who provides the information about the child's personality. Correlations between reports by parents and children are modest during primary school age but converge in a secondary school as children become more aware of their own traits. In addition, the associations between main personality traits and success become weaker from 6th to 9th grade (Tetzner et al., 2020). This pattern is consistent with the trend found by Al-Hendawi (2013), according to which, the correlations between traits that resemble effortful control and achievement were higher for younger children than adolescents, regardless of whether achievement was measured by teacher ratings or standardized tests. This declining association with age may be explained by the nature of the educational context because as children move into secondary education, they encounter stricter and higher demands that may not allow opportunities for personality influences to emerge. Lastly, evidence shows that the associations between personality and academic outcomes may vary depending on the academic status of the child. Researchers have indeed identified differences in the personality-achievement associations among high- and low-achievement students. Openness and conscientiousness are important for high achievers. On the other hand, agreeableness is associated with academic achievement among low achievers (Tetzner et al., 2020). These patterns suggest nonlinear relationships between personality traits and academic success.

Childhood Personality Predicting Success in Adulthood

Despite some variation in the findings, personality traits are strongly associated with school success, beyond what academic ability predicts. But how powerful is the effect of childhood personality in determining adult success? Moreover, inspired by the story of Jeanette Walls, can childhood personality predict success even in the face of adversity? In a longitudinal study, Shiner and Masten (2012) assessed the Big Five in childhood at age 10 to predict competence and resilience at two-time points in adulthood. They assessed adaptive functioning at 20 years of age or emerging adulthood, and then again at 30 years of age or young adulthood. They focused on academic attainment, social competence (i.e., close friendships, quality of social life), and behavioral conduct (i.e., rule-abiding versus rule-breaking) as indicators of successful functioning in children and emerging adulthood. In young adulthood, they focused on three additional domains: work, romantic relationships, and parenting. In addition, the researchers assessed adversity by counting stressful life events that occurred from birth to emerging adulthood, like exposure to marital conflict, divorce, and illness of a family member. Childhood personality characteristics were correlated with success variables in early and young adulthood. Conscientiousness notably predicted educational attainment and rule-abiding behavior at both time periods. Agreeableness correlated with all outcomes except romantic competence. Academic attainment in emerging adulthood was predicted by all personality traits except extroversion and by childhood academic achievement, rule-abiding behavior, and social competence. Furthermore, the researchers examined in regression analyses whether personality traits and their interaction with adversity predicted competence in emerging and young adulthood, after considering the effect of childhood competence. Academic success in adulthood was predicted by significant childhood academic achievement, conscientiousness, and agreeableness. As expected, adversity was a negative predictor. This research shows the powerful and extensive effect of middle childhood personality on adult success.

The researchers then compared the personality characteristics of participants based on their ability to demonstrate competence in the face of adversity. They identified the *competence* group that showed adequate competence in the face of low adversity, the *resilient* group that demonstrated adequate competence in the face of high adversity, and the *maladaptive* group that developed low competence in response to high adversity. Interestingly, the three groups did not differ in terms of extroversion. The competent and resilient groups did not differ from one another but in emerging and young adulthood both groups reported higher scores in conscientiousness, agreeableness, openness, and lower scores in neuroticism than the maladaptive group. In emerging adulthood, the trait of conscientiousness differentiated the three groups with the competent group having the highest level followed by the resilient group and then the maladaptive group. In childhood, the competent and resilient groups had achieved the typical range of these personality characteristics, whereas the maladaptive group displayed more negative personality traits like neuroticism and low conscientiousness. Furthermore, the adults who switched from the maladaptive group to one of the competent groups from emerging to young adulthood had a history of higher conscientiousness in childhood than those who remained in the maladaptive group. Participants who switched from the resilient to the maladaptive group had one standard deviation higher scores in neuroticism as children. These results reveal the protective role of childhood conscientiousness and reveal neuroticism as a risk factor.

Another longitudinal study corroborated the long-term consequences of behaviors that demonstrate conscientiousness in the school setting. Spengler and colleagues (2015) examined how, at age 12, being an attentive, studious, responsible, optimistic student who abided by rules could foretell the educational and professional goals achieved 40 years later. After considering the effects of parental socioeconomic status (SES) and IQ scores, the researchers found that teacher-rated studiousness directly predicted educational attainment. Moreover, occupational success was directly predicted by both ratings of studiousness and responsibility (i.e., being achievement-minded and completing assignments on time). In addition, a substantial part of this relationship was mediated by educational attainment. In middle childhood, students who demonstrate characteristics of conscientiousness by working hard and completing academic assignments tend to achieve higher educational goals which in turn improve their career outcomes in adulthood. Lastly, in a longitudinal study of over 1,000 participants, researchers found that childhood personality traits of agreeableness, conscientiousness, and extroversion predicted health after 40 years, in middle adulthood. These links were mediated by educational attainment, healthy eating habits, and physical activity. Specifically, agreeableness and conscientiousness predicted higher educational attainment which in turn predicted lower rates of smoking and healthier eating habits which in turn predicted better health. In addition, extroverted children were more likely to engage in physical activity which in turn predicted better health (Hampson et al., 2007).

In conclusion, childhood personality traits have long-lasting effects on adult success and resilience, even in the face of adversity. Specifically, conscientiousness and agreeableness are powerful predictors of academic attainment, behavior conduct, and social competence. Adversity, while a negative predictor, can be mitigated by the presence of positive personality traits like high conscientiousness and low neuroticism. Longitudinal studies further emphasize the importance of conscientiousness-related behaviors, such as studiousness and responsibility, in predicting educational attainment and occupational success throughout life. Moreover, childhood personality traits like agreeableness, conscientiousness, and extroversion can influence health in middle adulthood. Overall, the impact of childhood personality on adult success is profound and far-reaching. By understanding and fostering positive personality traits in children, it is possible to help them develop resilience, achieve academic and professional success, and maintain better health throughout their lives.

Personality, Happiness, and Life Satisfaction

Personality traits predispose individuals to experience emotions in terms of valence and intensity. Extroversion influences positive affect, whereas neuroticism influences negative affect. The correlations that these two traits have with subjective well-being are strong when standard scales are used with adults. For example, the correlation between extroversion and positive affect is .44 and the correlation between neuroticism and negative affect is .54. The correlation between agreeableness and happiness is .30, and between conscientiousness and life satisfaction is .40. According to temperament theories, these correlations do not stem from choices about how to live life, but they are direct lines. Moreover, the correlations between personality and happiness are higher than the correlations that demographic characteristics and life events have with happiness (Lucas & Diener, 2009). Holder and Coleman (2008) revealed similar results in children. Fourth and 6th graders who were rated by their parents as socially outgoing and positively energetic were perceived as being happier. In contrast, children who are perceived as neurotic were also perceived as being less happy. In another study by Holder, temperamental traits of sociability, emotionality, and activity made unique contributions to all measures of happiness (self and other ratings) and in total contributed up to 29% of the variance in happiness (Holder & Klassen, 2010). Similar results were reported in adolescence. Fogle et al. (2002) found a significant positive correlation between extroversion and life satisfaction among early adolescents. On the other hand, increased neuroticism was associated with decreased perceptions of life satisfaction. Moreover, neuroticism had a stronger relationship with life satisfaction than extroversion. Research from Sweden confirms that adolescents who worry tend to be pessimistic and show fear and doubt, and report lower life satisfaction, increased negative affectivity, and decreased positive affectivity. In contrast, adolescents who seek novelty by being curious, somewhat impulsive, disorderly, and enthusiastic reported higher levels of subjective well-being (Garcia & Moradi, 2012). In late adolescence, extroversion and neuroticism appear to have direct links to happiness while controlling for demographic characteristics. Specifically, extroversion accounted for one-quarter of the variance in happiness (Cheng & Furnham, 2002). Fogle and colleagues (2002) additionally explored possible mediators that explain the divergent associations between extroversion and neuroticism with life satisfaction. They found that outgoing and assertive adolescents perceived themselves as more efficacious in social interactions, which in turn increased their life satisfaction. Through self-efficacy, extroversion had a stronger association with life satisfaction. Social self-efficacy also mediated the relationship between neuroticism and life satisfaction. Neuroticism reduces confidence in social situations and results in lower life satisfaction. Thus, traits under the general cluster of neuroticism and extroversion predict perceived happiness and life satisfaction in children and adolescents.

Being Smart. Is It Enough to Succeed?

Intelligence is a constitutional factor with individual variations that are influenced by heredity. Adoption and twin studies demonstrate that half of the variability in intelligence scores in children is accounted for by their inherited genetic makeup (Bouchard, 2013). Since the inception of the first intelligence test, measuring cognitive ability and predicting academic success has been the subject of much research. Psychometric tests, like IQ tests, are widely used to identify students who may be gifted or face struggles at school. The most common IQ tests include the Wechsler Intelligence Scale for Children-V (WISC-V; ages 6 to 16) and the Stanford-Binet Intelligence Scales (5th Edition, ages 2 to adulthood). Both tests include verbal and nonverbal tasks and provide a score of general intelligence, also known as factor g, as well as scores for specific mental abilities such as general knowledge, quantitative reasoning, verbal reasoning, visual-spatial reasoning, working memory, and processing speed. Children may perform in some subtests better than others, but the factor g determines how well the child does across the board. Even though critics of IQ testing claim that these scores do not capture all that is needed to be successful, research shows an undeniable connection between IQ scores and academic performance in math, science, and language (Calvin et al., 2010). Currently, there are several meta-analytic studies that highlight the extent to which general intelligence and specific mental abilities influence academic performance. In addition to establishing the effect size, researchers have also attempted to demonstrate whether the effect changes with moderators such as age (i.e., is the correlation stronger in younger or older children?), and academic domain (i.e., reading versus math scores), or with increased variability in the mental abilities of the individual child.

Roth et al. (2015) conducted a meta-analysis based on 240 samples of students in primary and secondary education. They investigated the size of the population correlation between factor g and GPA, regardless of the subject domain, grade, country of study origin, or year of publication. Additionally, they examined the role of moderating variables such as type of intelligence test (verbal versus nonverbal), academic domain (math and science, languages, social sciences, fine art and music, sports) grade level (elementary school, middle school, high school), and gender. Results revealed a population correlation of .54, with the observed correlation at .44. This is considered a large-size correlation. Moderator analyses showed that the population correlation was higher when mixed or verbal IQ tests were compared to nonverbal tests. It is implied that mixed IQ tests may be better because they provide a more comprehensive measure of intelligence. Regarding subject domains, the higher correlation was with math and sciences followed by languages, social sciences, fine art and music, and lastly, sports. Gender did not change the size of the effect as it was identical in both groups, but age did. The high school subgroup had the strongest population correlation between factor g and school grades (.58), followed by middle school (.54) and elementary school (.45). The increase in the population correlation from elementary to high school is interesting. It likely reflects the increasing importance of intelligence in education as students master more complex content in their courses. Developmentally this also reflects the increasing ability for abstract reasoning, improved speed of processing, and developing executive functions. Peng et al. (2019) too conducted a meta-analysis and focused on measures of fluid intelligence, which is the ability to apply reasoning in solving novel problems without having any prior knowledge. It is assessed by tasks that can be verbal or non-verbal and tasks that require inductive (i.e., generalizing) and deductive reasoning (i.e., making inferences). The meta-analysis was based on 793 samples from as early as possible to 2017. The size of the correlation between fluid intelligence and reading scores was .38 and .41 for fluid intelligence and mathematics (i.e., word problems).

The findings from meta-analytic studies support a high correlation between IQ scores and academic performance that seems to increase during childhood and adolescence. Furthermore, the relationship is stronger for math, science, and reading scores. When IQ scores are used for diagnostic purposes and creating educational plans for students it is important to know how valid the specific factors are in predicting academic achievement, especially for students who show increased subtest variability. Freberg et al. (2008) tested the validity of IQ scores in predicting academic outcomes in a sample of 6–13-year-old students who indeed showed a discrepancy between factor scores (i.e., verbal comprehension, perceptual organization, freedom from distractibility, and speed of processing). Despite the variability, the global intelligence score predicted 44% and 48% of the variance in reading and math scores, respectively. There is agreement that the clinical utility of intra-individual variation was not supported by research.

Zaboski et al. (2018) provided more evidence about the association between specific subtest scores and academic scores in comparison to the association that general intelligence has with academic scores. They found that comprehensive knowledge explained 20% of the variance in basic reading skills, fluid intelligence predicted 15% of the variance in basic mathematic skills and 10% in mathematical reasoning, and auditory processing predicted 10% of the variance in reading. Visual processing did not relate to any academic skill. However, factor g correlated much higher with basic reading (.74), reading comprehension (. 76), basic math (.72), and mathematical reasoning (.32) while the average effect size for factor g was .54. Further analyses showed significant increases with age in the relationships between factor g and basic reading and reading comprehension scores. Looking at the specific factors, only general knowledge comprehension and its relationship with basic reading increased with age. Fluid reasoning was more important for basic mathematical skills and mathematical reasoning over time. Overall, factor g was a stronger predictor of all academic outcomes because it reflects the information processing that is required for comprehension and mathematical reasoning, thus validating the use of the overall score of intelligence for diagnosing academic or learning difficulties.

The potential influence of intelligence reaches far beyond academic performance during school years. Intelligence is considered a key factor in predicting socioeconomic success in adults. In fact, meta-analytic evidence suggests that IQ scores in childhood and adolescence correlate with both occupational status and income (.41 and .22, respectively). Intelligence influences outcomes directly by performing better at the job or indirectly by contributing to educational attainment (Strenze, 2007). Becker and colleagues (2019) used data from a German longitudinal study to further investigate the relative effect that 7th-grade intelligence had 12 years later. They also considered the possible effect of parents' occupation and income. Adulthood outcomes included occupational status, income, and education.

Childhood intelligence was highly associated with all three adult outcomes with correlations like the ones found in previous studies. These relationships were mediated by years of education. Lastly, intelligence in 7th grade was a stronger predictor than parental socioeconomic status.

To conclude, intelligence is a critical factor in predicting academic performance and long-term success. Heredity plays a significant role in determining individual variations in intelligence, with studies showing that genetic makeup accounts for about half of the variability in children's intelligence scores. Meta-analytic studies consistently demonstrate a strong correlation between IQ scores and academic performance, especially in math, science, and reading. This correlation increases during childhood and adolescence, reflecting the growing importance of intelligence in education and the development of abstract reasoning, processing speed, and executive functions. In addition, the general intelligence factor (factor g) is a stronger predictor of academic outcomes than specific subtest scores, validating the use of overall intelligence scores for diagnosing academic or learning difficulties. Intelligence also has a long-term impact on socioeconomic success in adulthood, with childhood and adolescent IQ scores correlating with occupational status, income, and educational attainment. Understanding and fostering cognitive abilities in children can have a positive impact on their educational and professional outcomes throughout their lives.

What Can Parents and Teachers Do?

As stated at the beginning of the chapter, core personality characteristics and intelligence are highly influenced by heredity and tend to show high stability. Furthermore, personality and intelligence have strong associations with subjective well-being and academic success in childhood and adolescence as well as professional status in adulthood. Despite the strong genetic influence, the interactions with the environment are powerful in nurturing traits that support success. For example, conscientiousness is seen as an outcome of transactions between the individual and changing socioeconomic and family processes. Conger et al. (2021) propose that SES (education and income of parents) and parenting predict conscientiousness during adolescence and that conscientiousness from this period predicts educational attainment, income, and conscientiousness in adulthood. They explain that high SES parents invest more time and effort in parenting and exhibit more warmth and support, stimulate more learning, and generally promote skills important for success. Their parenting is low in hostility and consistent in discipline. Moreover, these parents make material investments like providing a safe neighborhood, good housing, good schools, health care, computers, and books. Consistent with previous research, Conger et al. (2021) found that adolescent conscientiousness predicted education and income nine years later which in turn predicted conscientiousness in adulthood. The researchers then found that second-generation conscientiousness, education, and income contributed to the third generation's conscientiousness. In addition, there were correlations in education between the parents and children which also predicted the conscientiousness of the third generation. First-generation parenting predicted the investments that second-generation parents did which then predicted conscientiousness. These findings show that heredity (i.e., high stability in the trait), as well as social influences, play a role in sustaining these intergenerational effects that in turn enhance success within families. It seems that success is bred in families with these characteristics and that there is a cumulative advantage.

To identify ways to promote conscientiousness in children, it is worth first examining the precursors to conscientiousness. According to Eisenberg et al. (2014), the roots of conscientiousness can be found in self-regulation, internalization of norms and standards, and academic motivation. Regulatory skills include inhibitory and attentional control as well as planning. These skills are essentially executive functions. Internalization of rules begins when children demonstrate compliance to rules without being reminded by adults as well as by generalization of rules across settings. For example, a preschooler who has internalized the rule of washing hands before eating a meal does so without being told by an adult. Additionally, the child remembers to wash their hands not only at home but also at school, the grandparents' home, or the restaurant. Academically motivated children have a positive learning attitude and engage in school activities. These three sets of skills contribute to the development of self-control (e.g., avoiding temptations), responsibility (e.g., doing homework), industriousness (e.g., working hard toward goals despite setbacks, being busy), and orderliness (e.g., staying organized). Parents and teachers who engage in behaviors that support executive functions (see Chapter 8) and the development of self-control (see Chapter 7) and grit (see Chapter 6) also promote conscientiousness.

As discussed earlier in this chapter, children with negative emotionality have difficulties in doing well at school both in terms of academic scores and adjustment (Dollar et al., 2018; Viljaranta, 2015). However, those who have strong social skills and those who have teachers who rely on behavioral control are at an advantage (Dollar et al., 2018; Viljaranta, 2015). Therefore, parents and teachers are encouraged to control children's behavior by focusing on consequences rather than emotionally manipulating the child. Positive and consistent discipline is important to support self-regulation in children. Furthermore, parents and teachers may actively practice social-emotional learning that aims to help children understand and manage their emotions, become aware of others' needs and act with compassion and care, create positive relationships, and engage in responsible decision-making (Mahoney et al., 2021). In a school setting where all children develop social and emotional competencies, peers support positive personality traits in others. For example, children with high effortful control engage more in the classroom when their peers have low or moderate negative emotional expressivity. Therefore, peers with low negative emotional expressivity contribute to a less distracting school climate while they also model positive learning behaviors such as listening to the teacher, paying attention to instructions, staying on task, and asking task-oriented questions (Johns et al., 2019). Social and emotional learning teaches skills that children need to nurture their positive personality traits and compensate for their weaknesses. Supporting emotional regulation helps children who experience negative emotionality. Nurturing positive social behaviors and relationships encourages children to be extroverted and agreeable. The social-emotional competencies that children develop may have a lasting effect on school performance and adjustment as well as educational attainment and college or career preparedness (Mahoney et al., 2021).

Regarding intelligence, despite its strong effect on academic performance, it is not the only factor that predicts success. As discussed in previous chapters, the beliefs that students have about ability and effort as well as executive functions are highly associated with academic achievement. Studies show that when IQ is controlled, these other factors explain unique variance in academic performance. For example, self-perceived ability predicts academic achievement three years later while controlling for cognitive ability measured by IQ scores (Chamorro-Premuzic et al., 2010). Furthermore, the studies on intelligence ignore that intelligence may be a multi-structural construct. According to Gardner (2011), there are multiple intelligences, only two of which, the logico-mathematical and verbal intelligence, are tapped by IQ tests. The remaining abilities, musical, spatial, bodily-kinesthetic, interpersonal, intrapersonal, and naturalistic, are largely understudied regarding their role in academic success and general subjective well-being. Similarly, Sternberg (2018) considered intelligence to be a set of interrelated components that allow one to be successful in life. In addition to analytical intelligence that reflects general information processing, Sternberg considered creative (e.g., finding novel solutions to problems) and practical intelligence (e.g., adapting to environmental demands) as important factors for success. Therefore, there are other ways to understand intelligence and how it predicts success that need to be investigated in future research.

In conclusion, personality traits such as conscientiousness and low negative emotionality as well as intelligence have a strong effect on academic achievement and adjustment in childhood and adolescence and predict success in adulthood. Personality and intelligence are highly influenced by genetics, but interventions that target the development of social and emotional competencies and executive functions support success and well-being.

References

Al-Hendawi, M. (2013). Temperament, school adjustment, and academic achievement: Existing research and future directions. *Educational Review*, *65*(2), 177–205. https://doi.org/10.1080/00131911.2011.648371

Becker, M., Baumert, J., Tetzner, J., Maaz, K., & Köller, O. (2019). Childhood intelligence, family background, and gender as drivers of socioeconomic success: The mediating role of education. *Developmental Psychology*, *55*(10), 2231. https://doi.org/10.1037/dev0000766

Bouchard, T. J. (2013). The Wilson effect: The increase in heritability of IQ with age. *Twin Research and Human Genetics*, *16*(5), 923–930. https://doi.org/10.1017/thg.2013.54

Calvin, C. M., Fernandes, C., Smith, P., Visscher, P. M., & Deary, I. J. (2010). Sex, intelligence, and educational achievement in a national cohort of over 175,000 11-year-old schoolchildren in England. *Intelligence*, *38*(4), 424–432. https://doi.org/10.1016/j.intell.2010.04.005

Chamorro-Premuzic, T., Harlaar, N., Greven, C. U., & Plomin, R. (2010). More than just IQ: A longitudinal examination of self-perceived abilities as predictors of academic performance in a large sample of UK twins. *Intelligence*, *38*(4), 385–392. https://doi.org/10.1016/j.intell.2010.05.002

Cheng, H., & Furnham, A. (2002). Personality, peer relations, and self-confidence as predictors of happiness and loneliness. *Journal of Adolescence*, *25*(3), 327–339. https://doi.org/10.1006/jado.2002.0475

Conger, R. D., Martin, M. J., & Masarik, A. S. (2021). Dynamic associations among socioeconomic status (SES), parenting investments, and conscientiousness across time and generations. *Developmental Psychology*, *57*(2), 147. https://doi.org/10.1037/dev0000463

Deal, J. E., Halverson, C. F., Jr., Havill, V., & Martin, R. P. (2005). Temperament factors as longitudinal predictors of young adult personality. *Merrill-Palmer Quarterly*, *51*(3), 315–334. https://doi.org/10.1353/mpq.2005.0015

Dollar, J. M., Perry, N. B., Calkins, S. D., Keane, S. P., & Shanahan, L. (2018). Temperamental anger and positive reactivity and the development of social skills: Implications for academic competence during preadolescence. *Early Education and Development*, *29*(5), 747–761. https://doi.org/10.1080/10409289.2017.1409606

Eisenberg, N., Duckworth, A. L., Spinrad, T. L., & Valiente, C. (2014). Conscientiousness: Origins in childhood? *Developmental Psychology*, *50*(5), 1331. https://doi.org/10.1037/a0030977

Fernández-Vilar, M. A., & Carranza, J. A. (2013). Temperament in the school context: A historical review. *European Journal of Psychology of Education*, *28*, 923–944. https://doi.org/10.1007/s10212-012-0147-0

Fogle, L. M., Scott Huebner, E., & Laughlin, J. E. (2002). The relationship between temperament and life satisfaction in early adolescence: Cognitive and behavioral mediation models. *Journal of Happiness Studies*, *3*, 373–392. https://doi.org/10.1023/A:1021883830847

Freberg, M. E., Vandiver, B. J., Watkins, M. W., & Canivez, G. L. (2008). Significant factor score variability and the validity of the WISC-III full scale IQ in predicting later academic achievement. *Applied Neuropsychology*, *15*(2), 131–139. https://doi.org/10.1080/09084280802084010

Garcia, D., & Moradi, S. (2012). Adolescents' temperament and character: A longitudinal study on happiness. *Journal of Happiness Studies*, *13*, 931–946. https://doi.org/10.1007/s10902-011-9300-8

Gardner, H. E. (2011). *Frames of mind: The theory of multiple intelligences*. Basic Books.

Hampson, S. E., Goldberg, L. R., Vogt, T. M., & Dubanoski, J. P. (2007). Mechanisms by which childhood personality traits influence adult health status: Educational attainment and healthy behaviors. *Health Psychology*, *26*(1), 121–125. https://doi.org/10.1037/0278-6133.26.1.121

Holder, M. D., & Coleman, B. (2008). The contribution of temperament, popularity, and physical appearance to children's happiness. *Journal of Happiness Studies*, *9*, 279–302. https://doi.org/10.1007/s10902-007-9052-7

Holder, M. D., & Klassen, A. (2010). Temperament and happiness in children. *Journal of Happiness Studies*, *11*, 419–439. https://doi.org/10.1007/s10902-009-9149-2

Johns, S. K., Valiente, C., Eisenberg, N., Spinrad, T. L., Hernández, M. M., Southworth, J., Berger, R. H., Thompson, M. S., Silva, K. M., & Pina, A. A. (2019). Prediction of children's early academic adjustment from their temperament: The moderating role of peer temperament. *Journal of Educational Psychology*, *111*(3), 542–555. https://doi.org/10.1037/edu0000288

Kagan, J. (1997). Temperament and the reactions to unfamiliarity. *Child Development, 68*(1), 139–143. https://doi.org/10.1111/j.1467-8624.1997.tb01931.x

Lucas, R., & Diener, E. (2009). Personality and subjective well-being. In E. Diener (Ed.), *The science of well-being. The collected works of Ed Diener* (pp. 75–102). Springer.

Mahoney, J. L., Weissberg, R. P., Greenberg, M. T., Dusenbury, L., Jagers, R. J., Niemi, K., Schlinger, M., Schlund, J., Shriver, T. P., VanAusdal, K., & Yoder, N. (2021). Systemic social and emotional learning: Promoting educational success for all preschool to high school students. *American Psychologist, 76*(7), 1128–1142. https://doi.org/10.1037/amp0000701

NICHD Early Child Care Research Network. (2003). Do children's attention processes mediate the link between family predictors and school readiness? *Developmental Psychology, 39*(3), 581–593. https://doi.org/10.1037/0012-1649.39.3.581

Peng, P., Wang, T., Wang, C., & Lin, X. (2019). A meta-analysis on the relation between fluid intelligence and reading/mathematics: Effects of tasks, age, and social economics status. *Psychological Bulletin, 145*(2), 189. https://doi.org/10.1037/bul0000182

Perret, P., Ayad, M., Dauvier, B., & Congard, A. (2019). Self-and parent-rated measures of personality are related to different dimensions of school adjustment. *Learning and Individual Differences, 70*, 182–189. https://doi.org/10.1016/j.lindif.2019.02.007

Poorthuis, A. M., Thomaes, S., Denissen, J. J., van Aken, M. A., & de Castro, B. O. (2014). Personality in action. *European Journal of Psychological Assessment, 30*(3). https://doi.org/10.1027/1015-5759/a000186

Poropat, A. E. (2014). A meta-analysis of adult-rated child personality and academic performance in primary education. *British Journal of Educational Psychology, 84*(2), 239–252. https://doi.org/10.1111/bjep.12019

Power, R. A., & Pluess, M. (2015). Heritability estimates of the Big Five personality traits based on common genetic variants. *Translational Psychiatry, 5*(7). https://doi.org/10.1038/tp.2015.96

Roth, B., Becker, N., Romeyke, S., Schäfer, S., Domnick, F., & Spinath, F. M. (2015). Intelligence and school grades: A meta-analysis. *Intelligence, 53*, 118–137. https://doi.org/10.1016/j.intell.2015.09.002

Rothbart, M. K., & Bates, J. E. (2006). Temperament. In W. Damon, R. Lerner, & N. Eisenberg (Eds.), *Handbook of child psychology: Social, emotional, and personality development* (Vol. 3, 6th ed., pp. 99–106). Wiley.

Scrimin, S., Moscardino, U., Finos, L., & Mason, L. (2019). Effects of psychophysiological reactivity to a school-related stressor and temperament on early adolescents' academic performance. *The Journal of Early Adolescence, 39*(6), 904–931. https://doi.org/10.1177/0272431618797008

Shiner, R. L., & Masten, A. S. (2008). Personality in childhood: A bridge from early temperament to adult outcomes. *International Journal of Developmental Science, 2*(1–2), 158–175. https://doi.org/10.3233/DEV-2008–21210

Shiner, R. L., & Masten, A. S. (2012). Childhood personality as a harbinger of competence and resilience in adulthood. *Development and Psychopathology, 24*(2), 507–528. https://doi.org/10.1017/S0954579412000120

Spengler, M., Brunner, M., Damian, R. I., Lüdtke, O., Martin, R., & Roberts, B. W. (2015). Student characteristics and behaviors at age 12 predict occupational success 40 years later over and above childhood IQ and parental socioeconomic status. *Developmental Psychology, 51*(9), 1329. https://doi.org/10.1037/dev0000025

Sternberg, R. J. (2018). The triarchic theory of successful intelligence. In D. P. Flanagan & E. M. McDonough (Eds.), *Contemporary intellectual assessment: Theories, tests, and issues* (pp. 174–194). The Guilford Press.

Strenze, T. (2007). Intelligence and socioeconomic success: A metanalytic review of longitudinal research. *Intelligence*, *35*, 401–426. http://dx.doi.org/10.1016/j.intell.2006.09.004

Tetzner, J., Becker, M., & Brandt, N. D. (2020). Personality-achievement associations in adolescence—examining associations across grade levels and learning environments. *Journal of Personality*, *88*(2), 356–372. https://doi.org/10.1111/jopy.12495

Thomas, A., & Chess, S. (1977). *Temperament and development*. Brunner/Mazel.

Valiente, C., Doane, L. D., Clifford, S., Grimm, K. J., & Lemery-Chalfant, K. (2021). School readiness and achievement in early elementary school: Moderation by students' temperament. *Journal of Applied Developmental Psychology*, *74*, 101265. https://doi.org/10.1016/j.appdev.2021.101265

Viljaranta, J., Aunola, K., Mullola, S., Virkkala, J., Hirvonen, R., Pakarinen, E., & Nurmi, J. E. (2015). Children's temperament and academic skill development during first grade: Teachers' interaction styles as mediators. *Child Development*, *86*(4), 1191–1209. https://doi.org/10.1111/cdev.12379

Walls, J. (2005). *The glass castle: A memoir*. Scribner.

Zaboski, B. A., II, Kranzler, J. H., & Gage, N. A. (2018). Meta-analysis of the relationship between academic achievement and broad abilities of the Cattell-Horn-Carroll theory. *Journal of School Psychology*, *71*, 42–56. https://doi.org/10.1016/j.jsp.2018.10.001

10 Character Matters

"I have a dream that my four little children will one day live in a nation where they will not be judged by the color of their skin but by the content of their character."

Martin Luther King Jr.

"Character cannot be developed in ease and quiet. Only through experience of trial and suffering can the soul be strengthened, ambition inspired, and success achieved."

Helen Keller

"Courage is the most important of all the virtues because without courage, you can't practice any other virtue consistently."

Maya Angelou

Martin Luther King Jr. (1963) pleads that character is the substance of the human being to be judged. Helen Keller (1957) speculates that character is developed through adversity and implies that character is critical for success. Maya Angelou (2011) considers courage as the highest character characteristic or virtue above all others. These different perspectives on character are reflected in current research in the field of positive psychology. A virtuous life is considered a happy and successful life. The chapter describes the contemporary understanding of character from a psychological perspective. It takes the position that character is different from personality traits that are highly influenced by genetics. Character strengths consist of positive qualities that capture the person's core values and support a flourishing life. Character is an outcome of the moral and socioemotional development of children and relies heavily on parenting, education, and life experiences. Being able to solve moral dilemmas and being able to form healthy relationships with others are related to a set of values like fairness that children acquire. Other character strengths, such as perseverance, allow children to succeed. The chapter traces the early character strengths in childhood in expressions of sharing and acts of kindness. It discusses the Values in Action (VIA) strengths and reviews their links to happiness, life satisfaction, risky behaviors, and academic success throughout childhood and adolescence. The chapter also discusses the effectiveness of character education programs and

DOI: 10.4324/9780429356414-14

concludes with suggestions for parents and teachers to support the development of character strengths.

What Is Character?

According to Peterson and Seligman (2004), character is a set of skills and abilities that are learned, taught, and practiced. They are reflected in thoughts, feelings, and behaviors and have practical value in that they allow one to live a virtuous or good life. Some view character as adherence to certain values that are influenced by culture and historical times. Lickona and Davidson (2005) make a distinction between moral and performance character, but each complements the other. Moral character consists of virtues like kindness and fairness that enable the child to make ethical decisions and build positive relationships with others. Performance character consists of virtues such as perseverance and teamwork that enable the child to succeed. In their complementary relationship, the moral character supports children in ethically applying their performance character, and the performance character allows the child to act on moral principles (Lickona & Davidson, 2005).

Peterson and Seligman (2004) have identified six sets of character strengths that include *wisdom and knowledge* (e.g., ingenuity, curiosity, open-mindedness, and love for learning), *courage* (e.g., bravery, persistence, integrity, and zest), *humanity* (e.g., love, kindness, and social intelligence), *justice* (e.g., social responsibility, fairness, and leadership), *temperance* (e.g., forgiveness, humility, prudence, and self-regulation), and *transcendence* (e.g., appreciation of beauty and excellence, gratitude, hope, humor, and spirituality). Furthermore, Peterson and Seligman (2004) created a behavioral assessment of these strengths, known as the Values in Action (VIA) inventory, and hailed it against the pathological model of the Diagnostic and Statistical Manual of Mental Disorders (DSM). Peterson and Seligman (2004) emphasized that character strengths help people reach their potential and live a fulfilling life, an antithesis to the clinical model that emphasizes psychopathology. Research with adults indeed supports the association between character strengths and resilience, effective coping with loss, and academic success (Ruch & Stahlmann, 2019). There are currently adaptations of the VIA assessment for adults, youth, school-age children, and preschoolers. In addition, character strengths are now integrated into counseling to highlight the potential to flourish and can be found in educational programs in schools that aim to build character in their students.

The capacity for many character strengths appears very early. For example, anecdotal evidence suggests that even 2-year-old children show kindness and may express concerns about what is fair and just even though their understanding of fairness and justice is restricted by egocentric thinking and limited knowledge and life experiences. Preschoolers begin to show cooperation in collaborative play and teamwork in dramatic play. Preschoolers also begin to show the ability to inhibit impulse and delay gratification. In middle school, children demonstrate curiosity, zest, emotional intelligence, gratitude, grit, and hope. It is expected that some character strengths such as open-mindedness, forgiveness, and spirituality do not fully develop until adolescence.

Park and Peterson (2006) conducted the only investigation that shed light on character strengths that children possess as they map onto the 24 VIA character strengths. They asked 680 parents of young children ages 3 to 9 to provide open-ended descriptions of their children and then coded these descriptions based on the VIA strengths. For example, a description of "loves to look at paintings" was coded as *appreciation of beauty*, and "always looks at the bright sight" was coded as *hope* (Park & Peterson, 2006, p. 330). The results showed that love, curiosity, kindness, creativity, and humor were the most frequently reported character strengths. However, qualities that may require more maturation such as open-mindedness, gratitude, forgiveness, modesty, and authenticity were the least mentioned. Nonetheless, the researchers were able to identify all VIA character strengths in the parent descriptions with 54% of the character descriptions occurring twice. Future longitudinal research may examine the development of character strengths over time to reveal the most optimal times for nurturing these strengths in children and adolescents.

How Does Character Develop?

Currently, the approach to defining character is to consider it as a collection of desired qualities or virtues that primarily stem from philosophical and religious traditions. Critics, however, argue that this approach lacks a coherent conceptual framework. One perspective is that moral agency should be the focus of character development and that character is part of a self-system where virtues do not exist independent from actions within contexts (e.g., family, peer group, school; National Academies of Sciences, Engineering, and Medicine, 2017). Developmental research supports that character development is an outcome of multiple factors including cognitive maturation, a sense of personal autonomy, belonging to a group (e.g., family, peers), and emotional experiences. With cognitive maturation, children become capable of reasoning about the perspective of others when they encounter moral dilemmas. With a developing sense of identity and agency, children can understand free decisions and choices and begin to develop a sense of reciprocity and collaboration with others. Belonging to a group allows children to consider moral decisions in light of compliance with authority or empathy. Emotional experiences where children associate events with positive (e.g., rewarding) or negative affect (e.g., shaming) influence how brain structures are wired and hence how ethical expressions of character manifest in context (Arthur et al., 2014). There is evidence that human infants are born with moral intuition about how to evaluate events without having to resort to reasoning and that indeed the emotional brain is activated in these situations. A series of experiments using puppets demonstrated that infants preferred a puppet that was helpful over another puppet that was mean, illustrating that they had a rudimentary sense of right and wrong. Additionally, infants also preferred the puppet that delivered punishment to a thief puppet that stole a ball and ran away. Furthermore, individuals with childhood brain injury in the emotion-related structures experience deficits in moral development. Therefore, emotional processing seems to have a causal relationship with moral development (Van de Vondervoort & Hamlin, 2016).

From the perspective of positive psychology, character development expands beyond moral virtues. Understanding the contexts in which these qualities develop is also important. Attachment may be the developmental context where character strengths of hope, zest, and self-regulation initially emerge. These qualities are critical for children's subjective well-being and academic success. Sensitive and responsive parenting creates the foundations of a secure attachment that has long-term influences on all domains of development. Kerns et al. (2022) explored the relationship between secure attachment and character strengths in early adolescence (10–14 years). They hypothesized that because a secure attachment is a basis for social competence and regulation, securely attached children would possess more character strengths related to interpersonal relationships, such as teamwork, fairness, and forgiveness, and greater temperance strengths, such as honesty and prudence. In addition, the researchers explored the relationship between attachment security and transcendence (e.g., spirituality) and intellectual strengths (e.g., love of learning). Based on adolescents' self-reports forgiveness and teamwork were strongly positively associated with all factors that indicated a secure attachment. Bravery, fairness, humor, kindness, and social intelligence were positively related to several of these indicators as well, while leadership and perspective had no significant correlations with security. Therefore, their first prediction was supported. Regarding temperance strengths, they found that prudence positively correlated with all secure attachment indicators while the remaining temperance strengths related to at least some of the indicators. Intellectual strengths were not related to attachment security, but spirituality was. Moreover, when the researchers accounted for demographic characteristics, child's IQ, and child's temperament, security of attachment still accounted for at least 10% of the variance in many of the character strengths. This evidence suggests that secure children are more likely to demonstrate forgiveness, fairness, kindness, persistence, honesty, and thoughtfulness; employ humor, and seek spirituality. This research calls for replication of these findings and invites further exploration of the association that insecurity has with character development.

Liu and Wang (2021) somewhat expanded this research by additionally exploring the role of parental warmth and peer attachment on character strengths in a Chinese sample of 11–17- year-old adolescents. They found that parental emotional warmth directly and indirectly (via parental attachment and peer attachment) related to character strength, which was the sum of the VIA scores. However, they also found that parental attachment contributed to adolescents' character strengths via the mediation of parental emotional warmth and peer attachment. Furthermore, peer attachment had a direct effect on the overall character strengths score. Therefore, these findings highlight the importance of positive and warm relationships in the development of character. Building on this research, Thomas et al. (2022) investigated how relationships with peers and teachers related to character strengths in a sample of 4th and 5th graders from Brazil, over one academic year. Students assessed their bravery, fairness, hope, self-regulation, social responsibility, prosocial leadership, and teamwork via self-reports The relationships with teachers and other students predicted character strengths at the beginning of the year as well as the increase in strengths that occurred during the year. The connection between the higher quality of relationships and a larger increase in character strengths was stronger among boys.

To summarize, developmental research supports that character development results from multiple factors, including cognitive maturation, personal autonomy, group belonging, and emotional experiences. Emotional processing appears to have a causal relationship with moral development, as illustrated by experiments with infants and the impact of childhood brain injury on moral development (Van de Vondervoort & Hamlin, 2016). In the context of positive psychology, character development extends beyond moral virtues and considers the contexts in which these qualities develop, such as attachment. Secure attachment has been linked to the development of character strengths related to interpersonal relationships, temperance, and spirituality, but not intellectual strengths (Kerns et al., 2022). Research has also highlighted the importance of positive and warm relationships in character development, with parental emotional warmth, parental attachment, and peer attachment all contributing to character strengths in adolescents (Liu & Wang, 2021). Furthermore, the quality of relationships with peers and teachers has been found to predict character strengths in younger students (Thomas et al., 2022).

Character Strengths and Subjective Well-Being

Positive psychologists have demonstrated that character strengths contribute to one's subjective well-being. However, there is limited research connecting character strengths with happiness and success in youth. Park and Peterson (2006), who, as mentioned earlier, provided the most complete account of character strengths in childhood, also connected them with parental descriptions of happiness. After coding graded levels of happiness, ranging from 1 to 7 (average = 2.89), they correlated happiness with the frequency of character strengths. The character strengths that were significantly correlated with happiness were love, hope, and zest. Although gratitude has strong correlations with happiness in older children, adolescents, and adults (see Chapter 2), the association was not significant in this sample of 3- to 9-year-olds. Reports of gratitude as a character strength were rare in children younger than 7, therefore the positive correlation between gratitude and happiness emerged only in children older than 7.

Research that has examined behaviors that describe character strengths has also been linked with happiness. For example, the behavior of sharing is an expression of the strength of *kindness*. Aknin et al. (2012) provided experimental evidence that very young children show happiness when they can share something that belongs to them. In a series of several phases, the experimenters created opportunities for toddlers to experience different levels of positive emotions. Toddlers first met a puppet, then they were offered yummy treats and then watched the experimenter offering treats to the puppet. The toddlers were asked to offer a found treat to the puppet, (non-costly) sharing as the experimenter had done earlier. Lastly, toddlers were asked to offer one of their treats to the puppet (costly sharing). Happiness was rated on a 7-point scale by research assistants throughout all five stages by watching the emotional expressions of the toddlers. Toddlers were happier when they directly gave treats to the puppet. They also exhibited greater happiness when giving treats to the puppet than when receiving treats for themselves. In addition, toddlers appeared the happiest in the costly-sharing condition than in the non-costly condition. These results were held when the researchers controlled for the enthusiasm that children had for the puppet. Therefore, the children's happiness was unrelated to their enthusiasm for the puppet.

Aknin and colleagues (2015) later replicated these findings in a larger, slightly older sample from the small island of Vanuatu. The children (ages 2 to 5) first went through the same phases as described earlier only now the researchers used candy as the treat. The sessions were videotaped, and facial expressions were coded to rate the children's happiness. Children appeared significantly happier during the giving conditions than when they received the candy for themselves. Lastly, their happiness was greater during the costly giving than in the non-costly giving phase. The researchers highlight that children from an isolated island receive more emotional rewards from acting generously than for their own benefit just like children raised in Western industrialized societies do, therefore the findings suggest that generous giving leading to emotional rewards may be universal. The findings further imply that it is worth exploring the common character strengths across cultures in future research, regardless of whether humans across the world raise children to act prosocially or humans have simply evolved to find prosocial behaviors emotionally rewarding, beginning in toddlerhood.

The connection between character strengths and life satisfaction would directly support Seligman's speculation that practicing these values would enhance the belief in living a fulfilling and contented life. Blanca et al. (2018) tested this prediction by measuring the relationship between the 24 character strengths and life satisfaction in 457 adolescents aged 11–14 years. All but forgiveness, religiousness, creativity, appreciation for beauty and excellence, curiosity, and modesty were positively correlated with life satisfaction. Love, hope, authenticity, and persistence had the strongest correlations with life satisfaction. The most significant predictors of life satisfaction for boys were love and hope, explaining 17% of the variance in life satisfaction. The stronger predictors for girls were love, hope, and authenticity, accounting for 26% of the variance. For both boys and girls, life satisfaction increased by .30 for each point increase in love and by .14 for each point increase in hope. For every point increase in authenticity, the life satisfaction in girls increased by .16. Blanca et al. (2018) speculate that the gender difference in authenticity predicting life satisfaction may be due to the earlier maturation in girls and therefore their earlier ability for self-reflection. Nonetheless, love and hope emerge as the most important strengths that contribute to life satisfaction.

For older children, additional predictors of subjective well-being emerge. In a sample of 15–18-year-olds, Toner et al. (2012) investigated the connections between the VIA character strengths, perceived happiness, and overall well-being that tapped into general satisfaction with standards of living, achievement, relationships, health, and feelings of security. They found positive associations between temperance, vitality, and transcendence with overall well-being, accounting for 40% of the variance. However, they reported that increased levels of curiosity were related to lower happiness. Temperance, vitality, and transcendence, except curiosity, were also predictive of happiness explaining more than 50% of the variance.

Lastly, the connection between life satisfaction, happiness, and character strengths has been demonstrated in college students. Evidence suggests that taking a course on how to apply the VIA character strengths to improve community and individual well-being has in fact increased assessments of happiness and decreased negative affect and loneliness in college students over an academic semester (Smith et al., 2021). In addition, Lounsbury et al. (2009) reported that all 24 character strengths were positively correlated with general life satisfaction. The median of the correlations was .38 which was higher than the one reported in adults. Zest, love, hope, and self-regulation had the strongest correlations with life satisfaction while modesty had the smallest. These variables along with self-regulation and judgment were the best predictors of life satisfaction, accounting for 32% of the variance. These results confirm the importance of temperance and vitality and extend the findings by Toner et al. (2012).

Character strengths are also believed to protect children's well-being by empowering children to avoid risky behaviors. Research shows that certain character strengths such as spirituality and hope are positively related to life satisfaction and negatively related to behavioral and emotional problems, depression, and violence (see Chapters 2 and 4) although this research did not conceptualize spirituality and hope as character strengths. Kabakci (2019) explored how the 24 character strengths would associate with lower levels of alcohol use, tobacco use, antisocial behaviors, suicide tendency, poor eating habits, and overall rating of risky behaviors in a sample of high school students. Most associations between character strengths and outcomes were significant. Further regression analyses revealed that the best protective factors for alcohol use were temperance and spirituality, explaining 9% of the variance. Temperance, perspective, appreciation for beauty and excellence, zest, industry, and curiosity accounted for 19% of the total variance in tobacco use. As curiosity and perspective scores increased, the scores for tobacco use also increased. For antisocial behaviors, temperance, appreciation for beauty and excellence, honesty, and curiosity accounted for 35% of the total variance, with curiosity increasing the scores of antisocial behaviors. For suicide tendency, the best negative predictors in order of importance were hope, zest, prudence, spirituality, love of learning, and love, accounting for over 40% of the variance. Interestingly, love for learning and spirituality had positive associations with suicide tendencies, indicating perhaps that exploring harmful ideas and misconstruing spirituality are risk factors in adolescence. Eating habits were best predicted by self-control, then fairness, and then by humor (12% of the variance). With increased self-control and fairness, poor habits decreased but increased humor was associated with increased poor eating habits. The character strengths of love, appreciation for beauty and excellence, temperance, and bravery best predicted school drop-out in that order of importance (12% of the variance). Notably, as bravery increased, the likelihood of school drop-out also increased. Lastly, general risky behaviors were predicted by temperance, appreciation of beauty and excellence, hope, perspective, and honesty and accounted for 28% of the total variance in risky behaviors. All strengths played a protective role except perspective which was associated with increased scores of risky behaviors. Overall, Kabakci reported that two-thirds of the character strengths were predictive of various risky behaviors. Temperance has been the best predictor of alcohol and tobacco use, antisocial behaviors, and total risky behaviors. In addition, the findings also highlight how some strengths such as curiosity, perspective, bravery, and love of learning may encourage engagement in risky behaviors, at least in adolescence, and invite further exploration of how perhaps having much of one of these character strengths is not adaptive.

In conclusion, the research, although generally limited, suggests that character strengths can be found in very young children and contribute to children's happiness and life satisfaction. The expression of character strengths, such as kindness through sharing, is linked to happiness in young children, suggesting that prosocial behaviors may have an emotionally rewarding effect from an early age. It is important to note that some character strengths may contribute differently to well-being depending on the age group. For example, gratitude has a stronger correlation with happiness in older children, adolescents, and adults compared to younger children. Additionally, some character strengths, such as curiosity, perspective, bravery, and love of learning, may encourage engagement in risky behaviors, especially during adolescence, highlighting the need for further exploration of these strengths' adaptive aspects. Character strengths are also believed to protect children's well-being by empowering them to avoid risky behaviors. For example, temperance is the best predictor of alcohol and tobacco use, antisocial behaviors, and total risky behaviors. Love, hope, and zest are found to be strongly correlated with happiness and life satisfaction across different age groups. This trend continues into later phases of adulthood as Kaufman (2015) too reported that the best predictors of well-being were hope, gratitude, and love in a sample of 18- to 71-year-olds. These strengths which are also known as "strengths of the heart" (Park & Peterson, 2006, p. 324) fall into *humanity* and *transcendence* clusters and reflect the importance of relationships in children's well-being. Self-regulation, a *temperance* strength, also emerges as a character strength that is significant for subjective well-being from middle childhood to emerging adulthood. It is encouraging that researchers use the 24 character strengths thus allowing for consistency in methodology. However, it is not always clear how the 24 strengths fall neatly into the main six virtues identified by Peterson and Seligman. More research is needed to address this gap in the literature or confirm whether it is best to examine the individual character strengths rather than the clusters (e.g., temperance).

Character Development and Academic Outcomes

In his book, *How Children Succeed: Grit, Curiosity, and the Hidden Power of Character*, Paul Tough (2012) popularized the importance of character strengths in academic success, as evidenced by high school graduation, college enrollment, and finally college graduation. He often references the contrast between two school districts, the affluent Riverdale and one Knowledge is Power Program (KIPP) in New York City because both apply the same character curriculum to support the success of their students. This curriculum specifically targets the development of *grit*, *self-control*, *zest*, *social intelligence*, *gratitude*, *optimism*, and *curiosity*. Research has examined the individual connections between some of these traits with well-being and academic success. For example, it has been shown that grit and self-control predict academic performance (see Chapter 7). However, new research has emerged that has examined all 24 character strengths and their association with academic achievement and adjustment in individual studies.

Using a group of 10- to 14-year-olds, Weber et al. (2016) correlated the VIA character strengths with school-related affect, positive school functioning (i.e., motivation to learn, interest, and engagement in class), and school achievement. Results showed that all character strengths except humility were positively correlated with positive affect towards school and explained 60% of the variance. Notably, the strongest correlations were with zest, perseverance, love of learning, social intelligence, perspective, hope, teamwork, and gratitude. Character strengths accounted for 40.50% of the variance in predicting negative affect, with teamwork, hope, self-regulation, and love having the strongest negative correlations with negative affect. The character strengths also accounted for 24.4% of the variance in positive school functioning, with the strongest relationships being perseverance, zest, love of learning, perspective, hope, prudence, and social intelligence. Lastly, 29.7% of the variance in overall school achievement was explained by all character strengths. The strongest correlations were observed with perspective, leadership, love of learning, perseverance, hope, social intelligence, prudence, and humor. In addition, the researchers tested the hypothesis that certain character traits that predict increased school positive affect would lead to improved school functioning which in turn would increase academic performance. The results supported this pathway that began with the character strengths of zest, perseverance, love of learning, and social intelligence. Although the researchers did not investigate all character strengths that were initially correlated with positive affect, their idea that certain traits can foster positive emotions which in turn determine school success is worth further exploring.

Like Weber et al. (2016) who found indirect paths from character strengths to school achievement, Wagner and Ruch (2015) attempted to demonstrate the character strengths that would indirectly associate with school achievement by first encouraging appropriate classroom behaviors. Using two different age groups, primary (mean age = 11.6 years) and secondary school students (mean age = 14.4 years), they found that perseverance, prudence, self-regulation, and hope were the only character strengths that had a significant indirect effect in both samples. In addition, hope maintained its direct effect on achievement, which is consistent with previous research (see Chapter 2). It appears that perseverance, hope, prudence, and self-regulation encourage students to engage in classroom-appropriate behaviors such as following rules and meeting expectations.

These strengths also seem to be among those that are important for college success. Lounsbury et al. (2009) found that the strengths of persistence, self-regulation, judgment, prudence, and love of learning had the strongest correlations with grade point average among college students. This research invites the question of how far-reaching the effect of character strengths on success is. Simpkins et al. (2020) tracked the work habits of 1st graders for six years and predicted academic outcomes and educational attainment at age 26. The work habits they studied included "follows classroom procedures," "works well independently," "works neatly and carefully," "uses time wisely," "completes work promptly," and "keeps material organized" (p. 2224). These work habits reflect the character strength of self-regulation from the VIA inventory. The researchers found that 1st graders who had strong work habits in 1st grade compared to their peers did so in 6th grade as well, indicating stability in character strengths. In addition, all children experienced growth in their work habits during this time and this growth predicted academic outcomes in high school. Students received higher grades, took more advanced courses, and were enrolled in more selective colleges. Work habits did not directly predict educational attainment at age 26 but did so indirectly via academic success in high school. Longitudinal studies could further explore the long-term effects of the character strengths that appear to be strongly associated with academic success.

Because character strengths are nurtured at home and school, future research should also consider cultural influences on parental and teacher views about which character strengths are important for academic success. Research suggests that parents consider paying attention, understanding quickly, being curious, having a good memory, and being happy, enthusiastic, self-confident, and responsible as key child characteristics that lead to success. On the other hand, parents view being shy, sensitive, emotional, intense, impulsive, and distractible as negative characteristics (Feng et al., 2020). The positive characteristics that parents identify reflect intellectual ability and the strengths of zest and self-regulation. The negative qualities reflect low self-regulation. Furthermore, research suggests that how parents weigh factors of academic success varies by country. For example, Feng et al. (2020) reported that parents from Spain value character the most while US parents value intellectual ability instead.

In conclusion, research has consistently shown that character strengths such as zest, perseverance, love of learning, social intelligence, hope, teamwork, and self-regulation are directly or indirectly associated with various aspects of academic success, including positive affect toward school, school functioning, and academic outcomes. These strengths partially overlap with the qualities identified in the character curriculum applied by the KIPP programs, which include grit, self-control, zest, social intelligence, gratitude, optimism, and curiosity. Longitudinal studies can further explore the long-term effects of character strengths on academic success, while future research should consider cultural influences in parental and teacher views about which character strengths are essential for academic success. It is crucial to investigate the effectiveness of character programs, such as KIPP's program, in enhancing character strengths and success outcomes in children. By understanding and fostering these character strengths, parents and educators can better support students' overall well-being and academic success.

Character Development Interventions

Character strength interventions offer an effective approach to enhancing children's happiness and success. The studies discussed next focus on improving either the character strengths themselves or the behavioral outcomes associated with these strengths. Some of the interventions focus entirely on moral character development, others on performance character strengths, and others on strengths that build resilience and social-emotional learning (SEL).

Meta-analytic evidence supports the benefits of character education programs. Jeynes (2019) conducted a meta-analysis based on 52 US and international studies (from the 1970s to 2014, with 81% of studies occurring in the 2000s) that specifically focused on character development, morals, and virtue education. The outcomes included grades, standardized test scores, and other academic outcomes such as dropping out or staying behind a grade. Behavioral outcomes included love, integrity, self-discipline, and compassion. The analysis revealed a relationship with all outcomes from kindergarten to college years of a magnitude of .31 (range 2.37 to .08). For US studies only, the effect size of US character education on achievement was .26 and the effect size of character education on behavior was .37. The effects were higher in high school students. Interestingly, the effect was not significant in middle and elementary school but was in the right direction. These effects were significant regardless of the measure of achievement that was used in the studies, race, and SES. The effect on behavioral outcomes suggests that programs designed for moral and virtue education may increase certain character values as well as improve academic success.

As noted earlier, KIPP adopted a character development program to enhance the academic outcomes of low-income students who typically attend these schools. KIPP's character education program aims to explicitly teach the values for success and as such, students are graded in terms of seven character strengths in their grade report: *grit* (e.g., student persists after failure), *self-control* (e.g., the student pays attention in presence of distractions; student does not lose temper), *zest* (e.g., the student participates enthusiastically), *social intelligence* (e.g., the student is able to solve conflicts with others), *gratitude* (e.g., the student is aware of things that people do for them), *optimism* (e.g., the student is motivated to combat failure), and *curiosity* (e.g., a student asks questions). These core strengths are modeled by teachers, are subjects of academic assignments, and are openly discussed in the classroom. Additionally, student demonstrations of good character are recognized and praised by teachers and administrators. In other words, students receive strong messages about identifying and applying these character strengths. Since the implementation of this character program, KIPP students have surpassed students from similar backgrounds in terms of school graduation, college enrollment, and college graduation rates. These rates are also higher than the national average. However, critics pinpoint that this character curriculum might have increased the students' knowledge of the seven core character strengths but did not improve them. In other words, when compared to a control group they were not different in how persistent, zestful, or regulated they were. Moreover, the KIPP students were not different in rates of problematic and risky behaviors (Steinberg, 2014). Steinberg proposes that other programs such as mindfulness programs may be more effective in improving certain strengths such as self-regulation. Moreover, he suggests that cognitive-behavioral approaches, as well as social-emotional learning (SEL) programs, are probably likely to be more effective.

Related evidence is provided by a meta-analysis conducted by Brown et al. (2022) who cast a broader net to capture all types of interventions aiming to develop character strengths, ranging from interventions for moral values, moral reasoning, prosocial behaviors, and social-emotional studies. Notably, all studies included a control group for comparisons. The outcomes studied were diverse, encompassing interpersonal competencies, character knowledge, social-moral cognition, academic outcomes, and risky behaviors. The review identified 214 studies with over 300,000 participants from diverse racial and ethnic backgrounds, with an average age of 11 years (range: 5–18). The analysis revealed a small yet significant overall effect of .24, with an estimated range of effects between .22 to .64. The negative sign indicates that in some contexts, these interventions might not have been beneficial. Further analyses showed that shorter programs and those involving a tutor were more effective. Among the programs tested at least four times in the literature, the most effective were I Can Problem Solve, Kohlberg's moral development (Kohlberg, 1994), and Strong Kids. Specifically, I Can Problem Solve is an SEL program lasting three weeks, targeting students from PreK to grade 5, with both classroom and family components. Students learn to recognize problems and develop strategies to solve them by generating solutions independently and evaluating them with a coach's help (Shure & Spivack, 1988). Strong Kids is another SEL program consisting of ten lessons for children ranging from preschool to teenage years, promoting self-awareness, self-management, social awareness, relationship skills, and decision-making (Brown et al., 2022).

These reviews of character intervention programs, focusing on either moral development or broader social and emotional learning, indicate a moderate yet significant impact on subjective well-being. Although there may be debates about the place of character education in schools, particularly regarding moral character, the evidence suggests that it is a valuable endeavor. The 2005 comprehensive analysis, "What Works in Character Education" (WWCE), pinpointed crucial elements of successful interventions, regardless of their specific aims. These key features include prioritization, which emphasizes character development as an essential aspect of the program; fostering positive student-teacher relationships to teach interpersonal skills; intrinsic motivation, encouraging children to use their inner drive for morally positive actions; adult and older student modeling of character strengths; and empowering students to take initiative and assume leadership roles (National Academies of Sciences, Engineering, and Medicine, 2017).

Nurturing Character Strengths at Home and School

Given the effectiveness of character development programs in improving character strengths and subjective well-being, it is important to consider strategies that parents and teachers can utilize to nurture the qualities that support living a flourishing life. Parents may adopt what is called a strength-based parenting style in which they purposefully recognize their children's positive capacities and qualities and nurture them to their fullest potential (Waters, 2017). For young children, strength-based parenting may focus on helping them to figure out their passions and interests during play. For example, parents may pinpoint the level of enthusiasm and energy their children show when involved in art projects, thus identifying creativity as a strength. For older children, parents may encourage settings, relationships, and activities that match their children's strongest qualities. For example, parents may support their adolescent who shows the strength of love by encouraging volunteering and community engagement. Strength-related parenting is associated with children's subjective well-being. For example, Jach et al. (2018) found that when adolescents use their strengths with support from their parents, they report higher life satisfaction and positive affect and lower negative affect. Additionally, adolescents with a growth mindset are more likely to apply their strengths when their parents identify the strengths for them and encourage them to use them. Strength-based parenting appears to be effective not only in encouraging children to use their strengths but also in promoting self-efficacy and effective coping strategies (Waters, 2015). Children who benefit from higher levels of strength-based parenting experience reduced stress and employ coping strategies tailored to their strengths, such as using humor in interpersonal relationships (Waters, 2015). Therefore, strength-based parenting is particularly important when children face adversity. Allen et al. (2022) explored whether adolescents (11–18 years of age), who experienced strength-based parenting also experienced stress-related growth during the COVID-19 pandemic due to employing effective coping strategies, like positive reappraisal and emotional processing (i.e., taking the time to understand feelings). The researchers considered cognitive growth, such as learning to deal with life uncertainties as well as social growth, such as reaching out to help others. Strength-based parenting had a moderate to strong correlation with emotional processing, positive reappraisal, a sense of belonging in school, and stress-related growth. Moreover, the coping strategies were significant mediators, thus supporting the researchers' prediction.

This research is exciting as it reveals paths between parenting that aim to support character development and positive psychological outcomes for children. Evidence that strength-based parenting associates with school belongingness also implies that this parenting supports academic outcomes as well. There is still a lot to explore in future research. The current measure of strength-based parenting is a self-report that assesses general perceptions of parenting that supports strengths.

For example, adolescents are asked to rate whether parents give them opportunities to practice their strengths. There is no clear connection between the VIA character strengths and what children and adolescents consider as their strengths. This is a limitation that should be addressed. Furthermore, while strength-based parenting is associated with effective coping, the connection between character strengths and coping strategies has not been investigated. Lastly, it would be useful to design and investigate the effectiveness of specific parenting strategies that exemplify strength-based parenting.

Parents may also foster positive peer relationships which, as discussed earlier, have been linked to an increase in character strengths of bravery, fairness, hope, self-regulation, leadership, and teamwork (Thomas et al., 2022). Friendly peer relationships create a safe environment for children to express their values and personal qualities. Furthermore, a school environment that teaches children how to understand and handle emotions in themselves and others contributes to character growth. Thomas et al. (2022) found that in schools where social and emotional learning is integrated into the curriculum, children report growth in interpersonal character strengths with children from low socioeconomic status showing the greater benefit. Therefore, teachers in addition to maintaining warm relationships with the students, are encouraged to engage in SEL training so that they know how to foster peer relationships as well to help students manifest their positive qualities and values.

Lottman et al. (2017) developed a model that incorporates mindfulness as a way to enhance positive qualities in preschool children by guiding teachers through four stages. First, teachers learn to be mindful of their own thoughts, particularly when their minds wander, so they can refocus their attention on the classroom and the children's behavior. Teachers also become familiar with the 24 VIA character strengths and learn to identify them in various activities, movies, songs, and books. In the second stage, teachers learn to recognize strengths in children and provide them with descriptions of these strengths. For instance, they might highlight a child's gentle handling of a baby doll and their expression of love. In the third stage, teachers actively nurture children's strengths by providing opportunities for them to display their positive qualities, using suitable language to describe mental states (e.g., "you are becoming really good at fairness"), and emphasizing that these qualities can be developed through practice. Finally, the program encourages teachers to share their knowledge of recognizing and nurturing strengths with parents. While there is no evidence yet that this program effectively improves character strengths, it offers valuable insights into how teachers and parents can approach teaching these qualities to children from a young age.

Using literature as a means to instill character strengths in children is a compelling approach, as it offers opportunities for them to relate to and understand these strengths. Edgington (2002) suggests four ways to teach values through literature: 1. Values inculcation occurs when teachers introduce a book that showcases a predetermined set of values, encouraging children to identify and discuss their significance in their lives. For instance, the book *Voices of Alamo* exemplifies values such as courage, perseverance, loyalty, and responsibility. 2. Values clarification prompts students to reflect on their preferred values by responding to open-ended questions. They might be asked to assume the protagonist's role, make choices, and reflect on their feelings, actions, and potential conflicts with societal values. 3. Values analysis requires students to examine the values involved in a specific decision made in the book, systematically exploring the decision-making process and contemplating better alternatives. 4. Moral reasoning involves students reasoning about their own decisions regarding a moral dilemma in the story, exploring the perspectives of the characters, their values, and their relationship with societal values. For young children, even fairy tales can teach character strengths. For example, while reading *Cinderella*, parents may ask children to identify good and bad characters and explain their behaviors in relation to values. Additionally, a common approach to reflecting on stories is to ask, "What went well?" This technique helps children recognize positive qualities and can be applied to their own experiences, used by both parents and teachers (O'Sullivan, 2004).

In summary, character development programs are effective in improving character strengths and positive psychological outcomes. It is important to explore strategies for parents and teachers to foster qualities that support a flourishing life for children. Strength-based parenting, which emphasizes recognizing and nurturing children's positive capacities, can lead to higher life satisfaction and effective coping strategies. Additionally, promoting positive peer relationships and incorporating social-emotional learning in schools can help children develop interpersonal character strengths. Furthermore, using literature as a tool to teach values provides opportunities for children to relate to and understand character strengths in various contexts. Teachers and parents can engage in multiple approaches, such as values inculcation, values clarification, values analysis, and moral reasoning, to help children analyze and reflect on their values and moral decisions. Fostering strength-based parenting and integrating these strategies into educational settings can support the growth of character strengths and contribute to the well-being of children.

References

Aknin, L. B., Broesch, T., Hamlin, J. K., & Van de Vondervoort, J. W. (2015). Prosocial behavior leads to happiness in a small-scale rural society. *Journal of Experimental Psychology: General*, *144*(4), 788. https://doi.org/10.1037/xge0000082

Aknin, L. B., Hamlin, J. K., & Dunn, E. W. (2012). Giving leads to happiness in young children. *PLoS One*, *7*(6), e39211. https://doi.org/10.1371/journal.pone.0039211

Allen, K. A., Waters, L., Arslan, G., & Prentice, M. (2022). Strength-based parenting and stress-related growth in adolescents: Exploring the role of positive reappraisal, school belonging, and emotional processing during the pandemic. *Journal of Adolescence*, *94*(2), 176–190. https://doi.org/10.1002/jad.12016

Angelou, M. (2011, January 17). *Maya Angelou on courage* [Video]. YouTube. www.youtube.com/watch?v=xWTXkVPhEXU

Arthur, J., Powell, S., & Lin, H. C. (2014). Foundations of character: Methodological aspects of a study of character development in three-to six-year-old children with a focus on sharing behaviors. *European Early Childhood Education Research Journal*, *22*(1), 105–122. https://doi.org/10.1080/1350293X.2012.707413

Blanca, M. J., Ferragut, M., Ortiz-Tallo, M., & Bendayan, R. (2018). Life satisfaction and character strengths in Spanish early adolescents. *Journal of Happiness Studies, 19*, 1247–1260. https://doi.org/10.1007/s10902-017-9865-y

Brown, M., McGrath, R. E., Bier, M. C., Johnson, K., & Berkowitz, M. W. (2022). A comprehensive meta-analysis of character education programs. *Journal of Moral Education*. https://doi.org/10.1080/03057240.2022.2060196

Edgington, W. D. (2002). To promote character education, use literature for children and adolescents. *The Social Studies, 93*(3), 113–116. https://doi.org/10.1080/00377990209599893

Feng, X., Harkness, S., Super, C. M., Welles, B., Bermudez, M. R., Bonichini, S., Moscardino, U., & Zylicz, P. O. (2020). Parents' concepts of the successful school child in seven Western cultures. *New Directions for Child and Adolescent Development, 2020*(170), 143–170.

Jach, H., Sun, J., Loton, D., Chin, T. C., & Waters, L. (2018). Strengths and subjective wellbeing in adolescence: Strength-based parenting and the moderating effect of mindset. *Journal of Happiness Studies, 19*(2), 567–586. https://doi.org/10.1007/s10902-016-9841-y

Jeynes, W. H. (2019). A meta-analysis on the relationship between character education and student achievement and behavioral outcomes. *Education and Urban Society, 51*(1), 33–71. https://doi.org/10.1177/0013124517747681

Kabakci, O. F. (2019). Prediction of risky behaviors in adolescents: Effect of character strengths and being virtuous. *European Journal of Educational Research, 8*(2), 501–513. https://doi.org/10.12973/eu-jer.8.2.501

Kaufman, S. B. (2015, August 2). Which character strengths are most predictive of well-being? *Scientific American*. https://blogs.scientificamerican.com/beautiful-minds/which-character-strengths-are-most-predictive-of-well-being/

Keller, H. (1957). *The open door*. Doubleday.

Kerns, K. A., Obeldobel, C. A., Kochendorfer, L. B., & Gastelle, M. (2022). Attachment security and character strengths in early adolescence. *Journal of Child and Family Studies*. https://doi.org/10.1007/s10826-022-02230-3

King, M. L., Jr. (1963, August 28). *I have a dream speech* [Video]. YouTube. www.youtube.com/watch?v=smEqnnklfYs

Kohlberg, L. (1994). *Moral development: Kohlberg's original study of moral development* (No. 3). Taylor & Francis.

Lickona, T., & Davidson, M. (2005). *Smart & good high schools: Integrating excellence and ethics for success in school, work, and beyond*. Center for the 4th and 5th Rs/Character Education Partnership.

Liu, Q., & Wang, Z. (2021). Associations between parental emotional warmth, parental attachment, peer attachment, and adolescents' character strengths. *Children and Youth Services Review, 120*, 105765. https://doi.org/10.1016/j.childyouth.2020.105765

Lottman, T. J., Zawaly, S., & Niemiec, R. (2017). Well-being and well-doing: Bringing mindfulness and character strengths to the early childhood classroom and home. In C. Proctor (Ed.), *Positive psychology interventions in practice* (pp. 83–105). Springer International Publishing.

Lounsbury, J. W., Fisher, L. A., Levy, J. J., & Welsh, D. P. (2009). An investigation of character strengths in relation to the academic success of college students. *Individual Differences Research, 7*(1), 52–69. Retrieved May 12, 2023, from www.realizingaptitudes.org/wp-content/uploads/2016/07/An-investigation-of-character-strengths-in-relation-to-the-academic-success-of-college-students.pdf

National Academies of Sciences, Engineering, and Medicine. (2017). *Approaches to the development of character: Proceedings of a workshop*. National Academies Press.

O'Sullivan, S. (2004). Books to live by: Using children's literature for character education. *The Reading Teacher*, *57*(7), 640–645. www.jstor.org/stable/20205410

Park, N., & Peterson, C. (2006). Character strengths and happiness among young children: Content analysis of parental descriptions. *Journal of Happiness Studies*, *7*(3), 323–341. https://doi.org/10.1007/s10902-005-3648-6

Peterson, C., & Seligman, M. E. (2004). *Character strengths and virtues: A handbook and classification* (Vol. 1). Oxford University Press.

Ruch, W., & Stahlmann, A. G. (2019). 15 years after Peterson and Seligman (2004): A brief narrative review of the research on the 12 criteria for character strengths–the forgotten treasure of the VIA classification. In M. Brohm-Badry, C. Peifer, J. M. Greve, & B. Berend (Eds.), *Zusammen wachsen–Förderung der positiv-psychologischen Entwicklung von Individuen, Organisationen und Gesellschaft* (pp. 142–172). Pabst Science Publishers.

Shure, M. B., & Spivack, G. (1988). Interpersonal cognitive problem-solving. In R. H. Price, E. L. Cowen, R. P. Lorion, & J. Ramos-McKay (Eds.), *Fourteen ounces of prevention: A casebook for practitioners* (pp. 69–82). American Psychological Association. https://doi.org/10.1037/10064-006

Simpkins, S. D., Tulagan, N., Lee, G., Ma, T. L., Zarrett, N., & Vandell, D. L. (2020). Children's developing work habits from middle childhood to early adolescence: Cascading effects for academic outcomes in adolescence and adulthood. *Developmental Psychology*, *56*(12), 2281. https://doi.org/10.1037/dev0001113

Smith, B. W., Ford, C. G., Erickson, K., & Guzman, A. (2021). The effects of a character strength-focused positive psychology course on undergraduate happiness and well-being. *Journal of Happiness Studies*, *22*, 343–362. https://doi.org/10.1007/s10902-020-00233-9

Steinberg, L. D. (2014). *Age of opportunity: Lessons from the new science of adolescence*. Houghton Mifflin Harcourt.

Thomas, K. J., da Cunha, J., & Santo, J. B. (2022). Changes in character virtues are driven by classroom relationships: A longitudinal study of elementary school children. *School Mental Health*. https://doi.org/10.1007/s12310-022-09511-8

Toner, E., Haslam, N., Robinson, J., & Williams, P. (2012). Character strengths and well-being in adolescence: Structure and correlates of the values in action inventory of strengths for children. *Personality and Individual Differences*, *52*(5), 637–642.

Tough, P. (2012). *How children succeed: Grit, curiosity, and the hidden power of character*. Houghton Mifflin Harcourt.

Van de Vondervoort, J. W., & Hamlin, J. K. (2016). Evidence for intuitive morality: Preverbal infants make sociomoral evaluations. *Child Development Perspectives*, *10*(3), 143–148. https://doi.org/10.1111/cdep.12175

Wagner, L., & Ruch, W. (2015). Good character at school: Positive classroom behavior mediates the link between character strengths and school achievement. *Frontiers in Psychology*, *6*, 610. https://doi.org/10.3389/fpsyg.2015.00610

Waters, L. (2015). The relationship between strength-based parenting with children's stress levels and strength-based coping approaches. *Psychology*, *6*(6), 689–699. https://doi.org/10.4236/psych.2015.66067

Waters, L. (2017). *The strength switch: How the new science of strength-based parenting can help your child and your teen to flourish*. Penguin.

Weber, M., Wagner, L., & Ruch, W. (2016). Positive feelings at school: On the relationships between students' character strengths, school-related affect, and school functioning. *Journal of Happiness Studies*, *17*(1), 341–355. https://doi.org/10.1007/s10902-014-9597-1

11 Consumerism, Materialism, and Digital Media

It is mid-October in New England and as the colors of the leaves change, shops and sellers begin their preparations for the big holiday that is coming in two months. Gemma, 7 years old, and her 4-year-old sister, Jaya, are excited to look through the mail for catalogs with gift ideas. When their parents ask them what they want for Christmas they are not quite sure. With limited TV time and therefore limited exposure to commercials, the catalogs become the main source of what toys exist out there. They peruse the pages seriously and put stars next to the things they like. They then begin their campaign to convince their parents to buy them the selected and now irresistible toys.

Luca is in 10th grade and busy with doing homework and planning the spirit week at his high school. He is in his room, sitting at his desk, but he is not alone. On the computer screen, he facetimes Enzo, while they both work on different assignments, just so they are not alone. Occasionally, they consult with each other. Luca assists Enzo in math, and Enzo helps Luca with his biology homework. However, they are not the only people present at the scene. Messages and notifications pop up on their phones. Luca coordinates with other class officers for spirit week, "Did Anna finish the class poster?" and Enzo keeps them both updated with the latest postings on Snapchat and Instagram. Luca's mother walks by his bedroom and wonders if Luca's immersion in media is any good for him.

Children are socialized to become consumers from a young age. Through exposure to advertisements at home, school, or via digital media, children acquire desires and needs and seek ways to fulfill them. They make requests to parents or direct purchases given an opportunity. Children may also influence the family's buying decisions. Displaying behaviors and attitudes that lead to the consumption of goods reflects the construct of consumerism whose development is tied to other age-related changes that occur with growth. With the acquisition of goods, children begin to recognize the value of having materials in one's life. How they think and feel about buying, owning, and displaying goods is referred to as materialism. This chapter reviews the development of consumerism and materialism in children and adolescents, explores the research that links consumerism and materialism with well-being and offers suggestions to protect well-being. Because children are also consumers of digital media and are immersed in technology at a young age, the

DOI: 10.4324/9780429356414-15

chapter provides a review of current uses and misuses of digital media, the positive and negative outcomes on well-being, conceptual frameworks to better understand the connection of digital media use and well-being, and recommendations to promote the adaptive use of digital media.

Child as a Consumer

This process of consumer socialization entails the development of consumer behaviors and skills. Consumerism begins with children experiencing needs and desires and their attempts to fulfill them through influencing adults or acting on their own. Children learn to consider choices among products and evaluate them before they make purchase decisions. These consumer behaviors are taught by family and peers who are considered "interpersonal" consumer socialization agents. However, "environmental" agents such as schools, media, and retail stores also contribute to consumer socialization. Marketers specifically view children as a primary market because they have their own money to spend or as a future market. After all, children develop loyalty to a certain brand or fashion style. Additionally, children are viewed as influencers because they affect a wide range of family decisions regarding materials (e.g., cereal brands, foods, family cars) and experiences (e.g., vacations, restaurants). In families with economic stability and power, parents allow children to offer input and negotiate when they make financial decisions, thereby creating market-savvy consumers (Lenka, 2015).

The process of becoming a consumer, however, is tied to the child's developmental level. Therefore, different consumer behaviors are observed at different developmental periods. In infancy and childhood, children begin to exhibit desires and wants. Babies show clear preferences for tastes, smells, and toys with catching sounds and lights. Once they can sit up on a shopping cart, they attend to things around them, and at 2 years, they are capable of recognizing items on the shelf and asking for them (e.g., Elmo on a cereal box). According to research, 40% of Dutch parents reported that their 2-year-olds were able to recognize an advertised product at a store. This percentage increased to 60% among 3-year-olds, and 84% among 4-year-olds. As children move into the preschool period, they not only ask their parents for things they want, often by nagging, but they also negotiate for them. The things that preschoolers ask to buy make negotiations challenging. Children are known for their magical beliefs and their difficulty in separating reality from appearance. They are often attracted to flashy objects without considering the detail and quality. Research, for example, suggests that preschoolers prefer a low-quality doll with a red sequined heart on the dress to a high-quality doll with a more realistically looking face. Preschoolers are still developing their ability to resist temptation and wait for longer-term rewards, making conflicts with parents unavoidable. In fact, 41% of parents of 2-year-olds, 59% of 3-year-olds, and 70% of 5-year-olds report disagreements in stores when they deny a desired toy to their children. The conflicts decline between 5 and 6, mostly because children develop better negotiating skills and can convince their parents to make the purchases they desire. In early elementary school (ages 6–8), children are likely to be drawn to more fast-paced entertainment, with more complex plots as is also reflected in their imaginative play. They think more logically than preschoolers, but a good number of them still believe that the actors have the professions in their televised lives and that the families in TV programs are real families. Children are still not able to evaluate advertised products and therefore, take information in commercials at face value. Most importantly, children make their first purchase, usually at a supermarket and in the presence of the parent. However, by age 8, almost half of children in the US make an independent purchase. In the late elementary years (8–12), children finally become more critical consumers because they can evaluate and compare products and related information. Their preferences change as they leave behind the childhood fantastical characters and seek out products related to real-life heroes and celebrities, and products with social function, such as music and sports equipment. Additionally, they become more sensitive to their peers' thoughts, opinions, judgments, and evaluations, and what is cool and what is in. Children at this age like to collect and demonstrate increased loyalty to brands. At the same time, their influence on household purchases increases (Valkenburg & Cantor, 2001). In the adolescent years, children may freely engage in online and in-person shopping, and this may be the time when they develop an identity regarding the level of materialism they embrace and integrate with their personalities.

According to Sweeting et al. (2012), studies show higher consumerism among boys than girls and among lower than higher SES adolescents. It is presumed that more disadvantaged children and adolescents consider consumer involvement to feel secure about themselves and think more of the present than long-term planning. In contrast, advantaged children do not consider having certain things prestigious because they can easily afford them. Regarding age trends, the literature is less consistent. It appears that consumerism increases from middle childhood to early adolescence, but it is unclear if the path continues upward in late adolescence.

Effects of Consumerism

Substantial evidence indicates that consumerism is negatively associated with overall life satisfaction in adults. Research reviewed by Sweeting et al. (2012) suggests that consumerism can lead to increased possessiveness, decreased generosity, and heightened envy, which in turn diminish personal happiness and satisfaction. Among young adults, those who aspire to achieve financial success over anything else tend to experience lower psychological adjustment and greater psychopathology, as assessed through self-report measures and structured psychiatric interviews (Sweeting et al., 2012). Studies examining the effects of consumerism on children's well-being have primarily focused on children over the age of 8 because after this age they can critically evaluate advertisements and the quality of products. The only exception is the study by Gasiorowska et al. (2016) who conducted a series of experimental studies investigating the influence of money on the behavior of 4- to 6-year-olds from Poland. The presence of money was expected to affect whether children exhibited market-oriented behaviors, such as increased effort and competitiveness, or communal behaviors, characterized by prosocial actions. In all studies, children were asked to handle either real money or something irrelevant such as papers or buttons. Afterward, the children were asked to complete a challenging task. Because money is a strong symbol of consumerism it was expected that the presence of money would increase persistence and effort and decrease behaviors that are oriented towards others. The results supported the researchers' expectations. In the money conditions, children persisted longer on a maze task and worked harder on a developmentally difficult puzzle without asking for assistance. Moreover, in the money condition, children were less likely to be helpful when asked to assist the experimenter carry some crayons and were less likely to share with others the prizes they won during the experiment. Although these experiments do not demonstrate the relationship that consumerism has on well-being, they reveal that the presence of money may impede relationship-building and the experience of gratitude, both of which are linked to happiness and life satisfaction.

In studies with older children, researchers have often used self-report measures and sometimes conflated consumerism and materialism. Children's well-being has been measured in terms of self-esteem, happiness, life satisfaction, disappointment, depression, anxiety, and health issues. Juliet Schor's, 2004 book *Born to Buy* remains one of the most comprehensive analyses of consumerism in American children. Schor explored how advertisements across various media influence consumer attitudes, which may lead to decreased self-esteem, increased depression, anxiety, and psychosomatic problems. Schor focused on how advertisements in a variety of media change consumerism attitudes which in turn may lead to decreased self-esteem, and increased depression, anxiety, and psychosomatic problems (e.g., stomach aches, boredom). She also speculated that consumerism beliefs would make children view their parents less favorably which in turn would also contribute to lower well-being. She studied these connections in a sample of 5th and 6th graders coming from either low- or high-income families. To measure consumer involvement, she created a scale that assessed brand awareness, dissatisfaction with material possessions, and consumer orientation. Schor found that media use led to consumer involvement and then to psychosomatic symptoms, depression, anxiety, and low self-esteem, confirming her prediction. The findings also supported the path of media use leading to increased consumer involvement, then to increased negative attitudes towards the parents, then to more unfavorable well-being outcomes. The effects in the reverse order were not significant. In other words, the well-being variables did not predict more fights with the parents or high consumer involvement. The effects of consumer dissatisfaction were stronger than the effects of brand awareness and consumer orientation, highlighting the likely effects of materialism.

Using an updated version of Schor's measure of consumer involvement, Sweeting et al. (2012) expanded the effects of consumerism on self-esteem and psychological distress in a Scottish sample of 12- to 14-year-old adolescents. The researchers additionally identified a list of sought-after items, such as the latest smartphones, and investigated how owning these possessions related to various aspects of consumerism. On average, students reported owning 6.8 items from this list, with the number of these items correlating with brand awareness, consumer dissatisfaction, and consumer orientation. Interestingly, the total number of possessions did not relate to life satisfaction. However, when examining ownership of the most high-end items on the list, researchers found a negative correlation with satisfaction and a positive correlation with brand awareness. Male participants generally had more premium possessions, higher brand awareness, dissatisfaction, and consumer orientation compared to female participants. Additionally, owning more items was associated with lower self-esteem for girls, while increased brand awareness among boys seemed to protect against low self-esteem. For both genders, higher consumer dissatisfaction correlated with lower self-esteem. Older children exhibited the highest brand awareness and dissatisfaction. Family income did not correlate with the total number of desirable items but positively correlated with the number of premium items, brand awareness, and consumer orientation. Notably, most students displayed a strong consumer orientation, aspiring to acquire even more items despite already owning numerous desirable possessions.

These results suggest that different aspects of consumerism appear to correlate differently with various aspects of well-being. Moreover, these relationships also differ depending on demographic variables. Continuing the work of Schor (2004), Buijzen and Valkenburg (2003) demonstrated possible mediators between consumerism and well-being in a group of Dutch 8–12-year-olds. They reported that exposure to advertising increased children's requests for purchases which in turn caused disappointment and decreased life satisfaction regarding their personal lives and their environment. Furthermore, Lapierre (2016) demonstrated that children's requests for purchases were influenced by children's emotional regulation of positive emotions. Based on parental reports, 6- to 9-year-old children who get excited with advertised products and have a hard time regulating their excitement are more likely to persist with purchase requests and then struggle with their parents' refusal. Based on the findings by Buijzen and Valkenburg (2003), these easily excitable children would likely experience lower life satisfaction in relation to consumerism. Manolis and Roberts (2012) examined how time constraints or time affluence could function as a moderator in the relationship between consumerism and self-esteem. They found that heightened compulsive buying was related to lower self-evaluations among high school students and that moderate time affluence, as inappropriate but not excessive free time, lessened the negative effects of compulsive buying. In the reverse, people with too little or too much free time fared worse regarding subjective well-being because of compulsive buying.

In conclusion, substantial evidence suggests that consumerism is negatively associated with overall life satisfaction and well-being in children. In studies with children and young adults, consumerism has been linked to lower self-esteem, increased depression, anxiety, and psychosomatic problems, as well as negative attitudes toward parents. The effects of consumerism on well-being vary depending on demographic variables and aspects of consumerism being investigated. Research has revealed that exposure to advertising can affect children's well-being by increasing purchase requests, leading to disappointment and decreased life satisfaction. Emotional regulation and time affluence have been identified as factors that can moderate the relationship between consumerism and well-being. Moderate time affluence can lessen the negative effects of compulsive buying, while both too little and too much free time can exacerbate these negative effects.

Materialist Children

There are two approaches to understanding materialism (Nairn et al., 2007). One sees materialism as a personality trait characterized by envy, lack of generosity, and possessiveness, with highly materialistic individuals tending to be socially anxious and self-conscious. The other approach views materialism as a value system where people prioritize possessions and consumer goods to achieve success and happiness. The latter is more flexible because personal values may change with life experiences and circumstances. These perspectives can overlap and therefore are hard to distinguish. Researchers studying child materialism often use the Youth Materialism Scale (YMS) and Material Values Scale (MVS) for children over 8 years old, which focus on materialism as a value system for achieving happiness and success.

Research on age trends of materialism in childhood is limited. Although very young children express strong desires for possessions, they lack the introspection to view materials as a means to achieve personal goals. Richins (2017) theorizes that after age 8, children start associating possessions with self-empowerment. As they navigate daily activities, they rely on their own skills, abilities, and possessions. For instance, popular brand items might make it easier for a child to make friends. Consequently, children integrate valued possessions with their self-concept, identity, and approach to relationships. Richins (2017) suggests that middle childhood is a crucial developmental period for materialism to become an internalized value system. Existing research indicates that children start associating material possessions with well-being as early as 1st grade. In a study conducted by Chan (2006), children aged 6 to 12 from Hong Kong were asked to illustrate two scenarios: one depicting a child with lots of expensive toys, and another with a child possessing fewer toys. The participants were then asked to identify the happier child, the one who felt better, and the child they would prefer to emulate. The children's responses included face and toy drawings. Participants on average depicted five toys for the child with many possessions, primarily gaming items like PlayStations, as well as many happy faces. In contrast, one-third of the children left a blank space for the child with a few toys. When children drew faces, most of them were sad and of those who included toys, none depicted gaming items. During the interview, most children stated that the child with many expensive toys would be happier, would have more friends, and would feel better about themselves than the child with fewer possessions. Lastly, more than half of the children wished to be like the child with many toys. A small number of participants declared that both children would be happy, explaining that the child without the toys could feel happiness by spending time with friends or reading books. These findings suggest that children in middle childhood attach emotional states and social meaning to valuable possessions.

Chaplin and John (2007) showed an age-related increase in materialism among children from 8 to 13 years old, followed by a decrease up to age 18. They assessed materialism by counting the number of possessions children included in their happiness posters (e.g., money, skateboarding, camping). The researchers also examined the relationship between materialism and self-esteem, finding an inverse age-related pattern compared to materialism, with self-esteem decreasing from middle childhood to early adolescence. In addition, the researchers found a connection between self-esteem and materialism, with self-esteem mediating the relationship between age and materialism. They also demonstrated that boosting self-esteem could reduce materialism. These findings indicate that materialism may intensify as children navigate significant developmental milestones, like transitions to middle school during which time self-esteem declines. Furthermore, the results imply that individual differences in materialism could be expected, as self-esteem varies among individuals. Children and adolescents with consistently higher self-esteem and self-efficacy may consistently report lower levels of materialism as a means to achieve happiness and success. Future research could investigate these patterns using a longitudinal approach. Some evidence suggests that materialism in pursuit of success follows a U-shaped trajectory from ages 16 to 85, with the lowest level around the mid-50s, while materialism for happiness remains steady throughout this period (Jaspers & Pieters, 2016).

Materialism and Well-Being

Current evidence supports a robust negative relationship between materialism and life satisfaction in young adults (Christopher et al., 2007). Specifically, materialist college students often engage in defensive coping strategies to protect their image by making excuses or blasting others to elevate themselves. These defensive tactics in turn lead to decreased satisfaction. Furthermore, when materialism declines, life satisfaction and overall mental health are reportedly higher among young adults (Kasser et al., 2014). Evidence from children in the UK supports the negative link between materialism and life satisfaction in middle childhood (Nairn et al., 2007). Similarly, in a US sample of 14- to 19-year-olds, materialism was negatively correlated with life satisfaction (Froh et al., 2011). In another study, only materialism as a means to achieve happiness had a negative correlation with life satisfaction among adolescents from Hungary. In contrast, higher materialism that enhances success was positively associated with life satisfaction (Piko, 2006). This research is interesting and deserves more attention in the future.

The nature of the relationship between materialism and life satisfaction is correlational, and at best bi-directional, as a third factor may explain their association. Opree et al. (2012) tested this possibility by following a Dutch sample of children ages 8–11 years for one year. The researchers failed to show that materialism at the beginning of the year predicted lower life satisfaction later. Instead, they discovered that children who had low life satisfaction increased their materialism as a coping mechanism. The researchers also examined whether exposure to advertisements could induce materialism and then lower life satisfaction. This was indeed true in their findings. When considering adolescents who tended to watch TV shows with heavy advertising, materialism predicted lower satisfaction one year after. Advertising is therefore an important moderator variable that influences how strong the connection between materialism and life satisfaction is.

Another attempt to explore the causal connection between materialism and life satisfaction was done by Kasser et al. (2014) using a sample of 10- to 17-year-olds. The researchers applied an intervention to demonstrate that when materialism declines, life satisfaction and other indices of well-being improve. The intervention was a three-session program aimed at improving financial literacy and habits among the participants. The first session covered topics such as needs versus wants, healthy money habits, sharing, saving, and spending habits. The second session focused on how consumer culture and advertising influence financial actions, emphasizing the importance of a values-based financial system for decision-making. The third session focused on creating a concrete, values-based plan for future financial behavior, with additional time spent discussing optimal allowance systems for adolescents. Adolescents and their parents were asked to complete related homework during all sessions and continue to have money conversations throughout the study period. The intervention was effective in reducing materialism in the intervention group. Interestingly, the control group and the intervention group did not differ in life satisfaction although there was a non-significant upward trend in life satisfaction in the intervention group. The researchers also examined changes in self-esteem and anxiety. Anxiety was not affected by the intervention, but self-esteem was. Specifically, adolescents who had highly materialistic values and received the intervention reported an increase in their self-esteem. In contrast, those who had high materialistic values, but did not receive the intervention, reported a decrease in their self-esteem.

Materialism is associated with additional negative outcomes as well. Among 11- to 19-year-olds from the UK, materialism was predicted by emotional and behavioral problems such as feeling unhappy and losing self-control, lower goal-directedness in life (e.g., less ambitious about pursuing future goals), and high interparental conflict. These variables explained 11% of the variance in materialism conflict (Flouri, 2004). Materialism is also associated with lower GPA and higher reported envy (Froh et al., 2011). Lastly, materialism in early adolescence was related to lower prosocial behaviors in a Chinese sample of 6th graders who were followed for a year. During this time, as materialism increased, prosocial acts toward friends and strangers declined, signifying materialism as the precursor to prosocial behaviors (Yang et al., 2018).

In sum, existing evidence demonstrates a negative relationship between materialism and life satisfaction in young adults and children. Materialist individuals often engage in defensive coping strategies, resulting in decreased satisfaction. However, the relationship between materialism and life satisfaction is largely correlational or bi-directional, with self-esteem and exposure to advertising potentially playing key roles in this association. Interventions aimed at improving financial literacy and habits have shown success in reducing materialism and, in some cases, boosting self-esteem. Materialism has also been linked to negative outcomes such as emotional and behavioral problems, lower goal-directedness, interparental conflict, lower academic performance, higher envy, and reduced prosocial behaviors.

The current literature about the relationship between materialism and well-being in children and adolescents is limited and less systematically studied. A meta-analysis revealed that in adults, the effect size of the relationship between materialism and well-being (i.e., life satisfaction, positive affect, negative affect, depression, anxiety, and other mental health problems) is .15 (Dittmar et al., 2014). The effect size of the relationship in children and adolescents is currently unknown. Therefore, there is still a lot of research that needs to be done in order to understand the role of materialism in children's well-being.

Balancing Consumerism, Materialism, and Subjective Well-Being

Understanding the factors that influence consumerism and materialism in childhood and adolescence is essential for creating interventions and strategies to promote psychological well-being and healthy value systems. Research has shown that parenting characteristics are associated with both consumerism and materialism. Rose et al. (2003) attempted to identify different parenting styles in individualistic and collectivist societies and show how these may relate to consumer socialization. In individualistic countries where the individual is emphasized, parenting aims to develop independent children. Consequently, the authoritative (high in control and nurturing), authoritarian (high in control and low in nurturing), and permissive (least restrictive) parenting styles were found primarily among such societies. In collectivist societies, parents foster dependence in the child and so they tend to be highly nurturing but also highly restrictive, hence they come across as protective. The researchers found that authoritative, permissive, and protective parents allowed their children to influence family purchase-related decisions more so than authoritarian parents did. Permissive and protective parents encouraged more co-shopping with parents for different reasons. In individualistic societies, permissive parents are more indulgent and give in to children's requests. In collectivist societies, protective parents allow co-shopping as a means to nurture interdependence. Parenting styles also impact children's exposure to advertisements, with authoritarian, authoritative, and protective parents exercising more control over TV viewing (Rose et al., 2003). Although the direct link between parenting styles and materialism is not well-established, evidence suggests that a lack of parental involvement may lead to increased materialism in adolescents (Flouri, 2004).

How parents resolve conflicts resulting from disputes over purchases is also essential to consider. Studies by Schor (2004) and Nairn (2007) in the US and UK, respectively, revealed that children exposed to commercials develop desires that they express to their parents, leading to conflicts. These conflicts can result in negative attitudes towards parents, which in turn contribute to lower self-esteem and other adverse psychological outcomes. Adopting features of the authoritative style seems to be optimal for all parents, regardless of the cultural centrality of the individual or the group. A meta-analysis of 88 studies revealed that the level of parental restrictiveness related to fewer negative outcomes, such as child consumption, problem behavior, and psychopathology, and to greater positive outcomes, such as healthy consumption (e.g., fruits), self-esteem, and consume-related skills (e.g., understanding commercials). Furthermore, restrictiveness that was accompanied by explanations and child input was mostly beneficial for adolescents (Mikeska et al., 2017). As mentioned previously, parents who consistently engage in conversations with their teenagers about the impact of consumer culture and advertising on financial decisions, as well as the importance of cultivating healthy money habits, can reduce materialism and enhance their children's self-esteem (Kasser et al., 2014).

To further empower children to become savvy consumers and less materialistic, parents can begin this socialization process at an earlier age. Young children need support to understand the intention and veracity of advertisements. Therefore, parents should encourage their children to question the claims of advertisers and reveal persuasive strategies. For example, children can become aware of the fact that they are more likely to request products endorsed by someone they know and admire. Teaching children of all ages to evaluate advertisements and products critically will help them make better-informed decisions about their wants and needs. Children who work to earn money are more thoughtful about how they spend their money. Therefore, parents should encourage their children to do paid jobs around the house and elsewhere when it is age appropriate. Parents may also model responsible spending habits by exhibiting responsible financial practices, such as budgeting, saving, and prioritizing needs over wants. Parents may model healthy financial decisions regardless of the amount spent, whether the purchase is a book or a new laptop. Studying the features, the long-term use of the purchase, and performing a cost-benefit analysis are some ideas parents may want to model and explicitly teach. Parents who are sensitive to the environmental footprint that consumerism leaves behind may also want to raise awareness of issues related to fast fashion and recycling. Enabling children to engage in efforts where consumed objects can be donated, recycled, or trashed in a landmine may allow children to experience the consequences of consumerism and materialism. Parents may encourage the use of material processions and experiences that facilitate close relationships with others which is a main source of subjective happiness (see Chapter 1). They may also encourage children to express gratitude and engage in prosocial behaviors like charity and volunteerism to help them experience meaningful connections with others. A recent study showed that adolescents who kept a gratitude journal for two weeks also experienced a drop in materialism and an increase in giving (Chaplin et al., 2019).

Consumption of Media: Uses and Misuses

Among adults, the consumption of contemporary digital media serves various purposes. Media offer opportunities for learning and seeking employment. Media also provide opportunities for socialization. Social media, with a 45% global penetration rate and 98% among developed nations, encompass various platforms such as Snapchat, TikTok, LinkedIn, Facebook, Twitter, and Reddit. Individuals also seek out media for entertainment like digital games and audio-visual recordings. Not all people consume media equally around the globe. Geographical differences exist in digital media usage, with a 95% prevalence in Northern America and Northern Europe compared to 12% in Middle Africa (Stavropoulos et al., 2021). Children and adolescents become consumers of digital media and use media for instrumental, socialization, and entertainment purposes just as adults do.

According to a recent survey by the Pew Research Center (Auxier et al., 2020), parents report that the most common digital medium their children engage with is the television. Moreover, 60% of parents say that their child started using a smartphone before the age of 5, and half of them say that their child started using the smartphone before the age of 2. Among those children who own a smartphone, 51% of the parents say that they got it between the ages of 9 and 11. Less educated parents are more likely to say that their child owns a phone. The most common reason why children own a phone is to be able to contact their parents. About 13% of children younger than 11 use social media, according to the parents, even though children younger than 13 are not allowed to join media. The majority of these children use TikTok and Snapchat (Auxier et al., 2020). According to Chassiakos et al. (2016), parents also report that young children watch YouTube or Netflix, and smaller proportions watch educational programs and play early-learning applications. Studies show that patterns and rates of social media use among older children and adolescents have continued to grow over the past decade, aided in part by the recent rise in mobile phone use among children and teenagers. According to a survey, approximately 95% of US teenagers own a smartphone and 45% say that they use the Internet constantly (Schaeffer, 2019). Teenagers report that they use their phones to connect with others (84%), learn new things (83%), and pass the time (90%). Approximately 72% of teenagers in the survey reported checking for messages or notifications immediately upon waking up. The study also showed that 56% of teenagers feel lonely, upset, or anxious without their phones, with girls more likely than boys to experience these emotions. Teenagers hold varying opinions on whether they use their phones excessively. Around 54% of teens are concerned that they spend an excessive amount of time on their phones, and out of those who feel they spend too much time on their phones, roughly 53% have taken measures to reduce their cellphone usage (Schaeffer, 2019).

Another survey by the Pew Research Center of American teenagers, aged 13 to 17, found that TikTok is now one of the top social media platforms for teens, with 67% of teens using it and 16% using it almost constantly. YouTube is the most used platform, with 95% of teens using it, followed by TikTok, Instagram, and Snapchat. The use of Facebook has declined significantly among teens. The survey also found that Black and Hispanic teens are more likely to use TikTok, Instagram, Twitter, and WhatsApp compared to White teens. Additionally, 35% of teens say they use at least one of the top five online platforms almost constantly (Vogels et al., 2022). Lastly, adolescents do not typically dedicate themselves to just one medium. It is common for adolescents to engage in more than one form of media at the same time (e.g., watching TV and being on the phone), a practice referred to as media multitasking. Data from more than a decade ago revealed that 8- to 12-year-old girls spent an average of 6.90 hours a day on total media with an average multitasking score of 1.4 devices (Pea et al., 2012). In another study, adolescents reported consuming a lot of media, with an average total of 149 hours per week (median: 128 hours per week) and a multitasking index of 3 (Cain et al., 2016).

There is no doubt that the lives of children and adolescents are immersed in technology from a young age. Children consume a variety of digital media and advertisers use media platforms to market products and influence their wants and needs. As noted earlier, children aged 8 years and younger have limited ability to understand the persuasive intent of advertising. From ages 8 to 11, children can start recognizing advertising with parental assistance, but they still lack abstract thinking skills. Teenagers aged 12 and older can identify ads and their intent to change behavior. However, recognizing persuasive intent does not guarantee resistance to marketing (Radesky, 2020). Advertisers collect data from the profiles and activities of children and use this information to make their messages more effective. Marketing approaches include sponsored content and influencers (trusted characters or celebrities), persuasive design, and gamified ads. These newer forms of advertising in mobile, interactive media, and smart technologies are harder to identify, as they are often integrated into the content. Children are marketed unhealthy foods, tobacco and e-cigarettes, alcohol, marijuana, and products about body appearance and self-image. Digital literacy is essential for children, teenagers, and parents to navigate these marketing approaches and protect themselves from potential harm (Radesky, 2020).

Digital Media and Well-Being

Digital media and especially social media provide an important context that has the potential to influence development as children navigate important developmental tasks and challenges, ranging from making friends to learning, and developing an identity. Adolescence is a particularly sensitive period because of biological, cognitive, and socioemotional changes that take place. The use of digital media has the potential to support or undermine children's well-being. There are several challenges in understanding the relationship between media use and well-being, however. Researchers have used various methods to assess media use such as exposure to media, importance of exposure, number of media platforms used, dependency or addiction to media, actual postings of media, number of likes one receives, responses to posts, and number of followers or friends. Moreover, different indices of well-being have been used such as social capital, psychological difficulties, friendships, loneliness, self-esteem, and life satisfaction. Lastly, the relationship between social media and outcomes is bi-directional or dependent on a third factor that may explain it. Despite these challenges, there are trends in the literature worth noting.

What the Children Say: Positive and Negative Outcomes

First, it is important to examine the children's perceptions of the effects that media use has on them because such perceptions may actually influence outcomes. The Responsible Innovation in Technology for Children (RITEC) is a project sponsored partially by United Nations Children's Fund (2022) with the goal to solicit children's ideas about well-being indicators in their digital experiences. Participants were 300 children from 13 countries, ranging in age from 7 to 18 years. The children reported that engaging socially with friends and family online provided them with a sense of belonging. When the parents and teachers also engaged positively with the children, the children viewed their relationship with them more positively. Children acknowledged safety risks such as encountering unwanted or shocking information online and wished for safeguards in relation to advertising, time-management, dealing with trolls, and interacting with people of their age. Children also mentioned that digital experiences could lead to boredom, isolation, and negative affect. A survey from the Pew Research Center (Anderson & Jiang, 2018) showed that US teens reported that social media has helped them connect with family and friends (40%), find others with similar interests (15%), access information and news more easily (16%), find entertainment (9%), and express themselves (7%). However, the same group of adolescents also reported negative effects of social media, such as bullying and spreading rumors (27%), damaging relationships (17%), fostering unrealistic life expectations (15%), addiction and distractions (14%), and peer pressure (12%; Anderson & Jiang, 2018). Similar results are reported from teenagers in the UK who were asked what they thought about social media (O'Reilly et al., 2018). While some participants acknowledged the potential positive effects of social media on well-being, the majority pointed to negative effects. The analysis revealed three major themes: 1. social media leading to stress, depression, low self-esteem, and suicidal ideation; 2. exposure to bullying and trolling on social media; and 3. viewing social media as addictive, often affecting sleep. Despite these negative perceptions, adolescents' self-reported social media use remained extensive (O'Reilly et al., 2018). In conclusion, it seems that even young children acknowledge the areas that they are vulnerable and need support from adults. Regarding the specific effects of media use, adolescents can identify positive and negative outcomes, but it is unclear the degree to which they relate to them. It is possible that they simply acknowledge the effects they hear adults talk about.

What the Research Says: Positive and Negative Outcomes

Research evidence shows that media use for children under 2 years of age has limited educational benefits and in-person interactions with parents are much more effective for learning. Even though interactive media via touchscreens allow apps to provide scaffolding to build skills at the child's level of competence, children do not transfer what they learn from touch screens to the real 3-dimensional world. Among preschoolers, high-quality TV programs can improve cognitive, linguistic, and social outcomes but excessive media use in early childhood has been linked to cognitive, language, and social/emotional delays, as well as obesity and cardiovascular risk. An earlier onset of media use, greater cumulative hours of media use, and low-quality content are significant predictors of poor executive functioning and theory of mind deficits in preschoolers. Unfortunately, many educational apps tend to have low educational potential because they are not based on established curricula (Chassiakos et al., 2016). According to Oswald et al. (2020), who conducted a review of studies from 2000 to 2019, there is a negative association between young children's screen time and deficits in cognitive functions, language, and communication as well as a positive association with behavior problems. Therefore, the consumption of digital media by children younger than 5 appears to be mostly maladaptive.

For schoolchildren, Oswald et al. (2020), showed inconsistent findings, with several studies showing no significant associations. Studies with significant results revealed associations with poor psychological functioning. In early adolescence, screen time exposure was linked with lower quality of life, lower self-esteem, poorer school functioning, and lower academic achievement. In late adolescence, studies with significant results primarily showed screen-time connections with poor mental health and lower positive psychological outcomes (Oswald et al., 2020). Indeed, additional studies reveal that the risks of media use in school-aged children and adolescents are multifaceted and include in addition to mental health concerns, lower happiness and life satisfaction, health and sleep problems, exposure to risky behaviors, and privacy concerns, cyberbullying, and sexting.

Van Den Eijnden et al. (2018) found that addiction to gaming among Dutch 7th and 8th graders was predictive of lower life satisfaction and social competence. Frequency of social media use was predictive of lower grades and higher perceived social competence (among boys) but addiction to social media, like gaming addiction predicted lower life satisfaction. McDool et al. (2016) found that spending 1 hour a day on social media reduced the probability of reporting overall life satisfaction by 14% and had a stronger effect on girls. All domains of life satisfaction, except for friendships, were negatively affected by social media use. Twigg et al. (2020) showed that spending more than 4 hours a day on social media was associated with lower life satisfaction among UK children aged 10–15 years, but only for girls. However, social media did not contribute to the overall decline in life satisfaction that took place over time; rather family characteristics like income explained the downward trend in life satisfaction in adolescence. Moreover, unhappiness may lead to stronger social media use. In one study, negative childhood experiences predicted increased unhappiness, which in turn predicted social media addiction among 10th and 11th graders, according to Demir (2021). Others suggest that it is passive social media use that is associated with declines in well-being and life satisfaction, whereas active use by interacting with others and posting content does not lead to such declines (Chassiakos et al., 2016).

Social exclusion from social media is linked to negative emotions. Timeo and colleagues' (2020) study demonstrated a significant connection between social media exclusion and negative emotions among Italian adolescents. In an experimental scenario, participants were asked to create a profile and post on a new social media platform. The researchers then manipulated the situation, giving only one like to those in the experimental group, while the control group received five likes. The goal of this manipulation was to induce feelings of exclusion among the participants. As predicted, the adolescents who believed they were excluded reported more sadness, pain, and anger, and lower levels of happiness. They also felt that their self-esteem, sense of belonging, and meaningful existence were threatened. However, when allowed to think of a special person close to them, these negative emotions and threats lessened. These findings highlight the importance of considering the impact of social media exclusion on well-being and the significance of relationships outside of the digital realm in promoting positive mental health among children and adolescents.

A U-shaped association between Internet use and depression has been observed, indicating heightened risks for depression at both high and low levels of Internet usage (Chassiakos et al., 2016). This means that both high-intensity and passive engagement with the Internet is maladaptive. Chiang et al. (2019) demonstrated that high social networking site usage among 5th graders in Taiwan predicted depression which then increased the propensity for addiction within a year. These results held even after accounting for parental education, income, and family type. How children engage with the media is also important to consider when understanding the relationship between media and depression. For example, among 10- to 12-year-old users of YouTube, Instagram, and Snapchat, making frequent appearance comparisons, perceiving others as more attractive, and engaging in appearance investment activities were found to be significant predictors of reduced body satisfaction, increased eating pathology, social anxiety, and depressive symptoms. Interestingly, making more appearance comparisons on social media was linked to increased depressive symptoms in girls and decreased depressive symptoms in boys. Frequent appearance comparisons were associated with less body satisfaction only in girls (Fardouly et al., 2020).

Because media addiction is strongly related to depression it is worth understanding how it may develop. Given the high use of smartphones among adolescents, smartphone addiction may be the primary cause of social media addiction. Additionally, the relatively new concept of Fear of Missing Out (FoMO) may also play a role. In a study with high school students, these variables explained 28% of the variance in social media addiction (Aygul & Akbay, 2019), with smartphone addiction being the strongest predictor of the two. Furthermore, high schoolers who reported great social media addiction also perceived themselves as less competent both socially and academically. Other factors that may lead to smartphone addiction are loneliness and failure to emotionally self-regulate. In a study of Indian adolescents, these variables accounted for 12% of the variance in smartphone addiction. Consequently, smartphone addiction accounted for 37% of the variance in academic performance, 31% of family conflict, and 34% of personal conflict (Mahapatra, 2019).

Research has shown that excessive use of digital technology can have negative impacts on physical well-being, including musculoskeletal strain, myopia, headaches, and skin irritation (Meates, 2021). It is calculated that high school students spend an additional 43,000 hours in improper posture. One common musculoskeletal concern is the development of a "text neck," which is more challenging for younger children whose heads are bigger in proportion to their bodies (Meates, 2021). In addition, screen time has been linked to decreased physical activity, with a 2-hour increase resulting in a 30-minute reduction in activity time among 11- to 15-year-olds in Europe and the US (OECD, 2018). Decreased physical activity is associated with lower subjective well-being and school grades (see Chapter 5). Furthermore, the use of smartphones before bedtime emitting blue light can lead to delayed sleepiness, later bedtimes, and shorter sleep durations, particularly in adolescents who use social media 30–120 minutes before bedtime (Chassiakos et al., 2016; Hamilton et al., 2020). This can result in reduced sleep quality, which has been shown to have a negative impact on overall mood and well-being. Generally, it is important to consider the negative impact of excessive digital technology use and to prioritize healthy habits, such as reducing screen time before bedtime and engaging in physical activity, to promote both physical and mental well-being. Lastly, a study of Australian 10- to 12-year-olds found that users of YouTube, Instagram, and Snapchat expressed greater concerns about their body image and displayed more disordered eating behaviors than non-users (Fardouly et al., 2020).

Additionally, privacy risks associated with social media use are a concern, with adolescents varying in their understanding of privacy practices, and even among those who do know how to set privacy settings, many choose not to do so. Cyberbullying presents new challenges, such as anonymity, the rapid spread of information, and the fluidity with which bully and target roles can switch in the online world. Victims of cyberbullying often report lower grades and other academic problems because of the experience and are at higher risk of both suicidal ideation and suicide attempts (Chassiakos et al., 2016). In a sample of Japanese adolescents (12–18 years), cyberbullying predicted psychological distress, and low self-esteem, but having emotional competence (i.e., understanding and regulating emotions) tempered the relationship between cyberbullying and distress (Urano et al., 2020). Sexting, the electronic transmission of nude or seminude images as well as sexually explicit text messages, is related to behaviors indicative of psychosocial challenges and risky sexual behavior for some youths. It is also associated with symptoms of depression, impulsivity, and substance use. Sexting may precede sexual intercourse, and addressing risky sexual behaviors and psychological symptoms associated with sexting through education and guidance should help to promote wellness and responsibility within adolescent populations (Chassiakos et al., 2016). Research has shown that exposure to alcohol or tobacco use or risky sexual behaviors in TV or movies is associated with the initiation of these behaviors. Similarly, several studies have illustrated that adolescents' displays on social media frequently include the portrayal of risky health behaviors, such as illegal alcohol use or overuse, illicit substance use, high-risk sexual behaviors, and harmful behaviors, such as self-injury and disordered eating. Exposure to this content creates the impression these behaviors as normative and desirable (Chassiakos et al., 2016).

Lastly, media multitasking is negatively associated with cognitive abilities, scholastic achievement, and behavior. Media multitasking among girls of 8–12 years was negatively related to social success, feeling normal, sleeping difficulties, and having parents who think that friends are a bad influence (Pea et al., 2012). In addition, increased media multitasking in adolescence was associated with poor academic performance, lower working memory capacity, and increased impulsive behavior. Moreover, media multitasking was linked to worse statewide standardized test scores in math and English (Cain et al., 2016). However, the researchers caution that it is difficult to establish causality, and simple interventions to regulate media multitasking may not necessarily improve test scores. Further research is needed to explore this link.

Despite the threats that digital media pose to children's subjective well-being and mental health, research supports some positive outcomes. For example, media use in older children and teenagers can increase collaboration, tolerance, and empathy. Social media platforms can provide tools for communication and engagement, as well as raise awareness of current events and promote civic engagement. Health benefits of social media may include enhanced access to valuable support networks for those with ongoing illnesses or disabilities, as well as promoting social inclusion among children who might otherwise feel excluded. For those with disabilities, technology-aided interventions through assistive and interactive digital media can improve learning and communication (Chassiakos et al., 2016). Social media offer unique opportunities for adolescent identity development, allowing teens to experiment with interests, self-presentation, and creative expression. During the COVID-19 pandemic, when teens had limited opportunities to explore the world, social media provided them autonomy and space to control what they shared and with whom. With more free time, many teens were able to explore new ideas and hobbies, using social media as a creative outlet. Platforms like TikTok enabled teens to share videos and ideas easily, fostering creativity. Social media also helped develop intellectual ideas and activism as teens became more aware of global issues and policies that affected them (Hamilton et al., 2020).

Social media offer a sense of community and belonging and give a place for self-disclosure. Craig et al. (2021) revealed that young adolescents who self-identified as LGBTQ+ individuals, sought out social media to find emotional support (i.e., feel accepted, liked, and supported), entertainment (i.e., deal with boredom), and specific information about LGBTQ+ questions they had. Results from a UK study showed that over half of the children (9–13 years of age) used at least one social networking site like Facebook for communication and children who used these sites had higher feelings of belonging compared to non-users. Among boys, the intensity of use was linearly related to their feeling of belonging, implying that online interactions may provide a comfortable environment for boys to practice self-disclosure and offer socially anxious boys a place to communicate and enhance their social skills (Quinn & Oldmeadow, 2013). Similarly, a substantial number of adolescents from Bermuda (aged 13–18) found it easier to discuss personal feelings online compared to offline. Casual exchanges online helped adolescents maintain a sense of connection and belonging with their closest friends, while intimate exchanges provided unique opportunities for self-disclosure. This was truer for older adolescents (Davis, 2012).

Lastly, social media can be instrumental for academic success beyond receiving assistance on homework from a friend. Wohn et al. (2013) found that first-generation students benefited from information about college applications offered on Facebook. Compared to non-first-generation students, these adolescents reported having lower college application efficacy, receiving lower emotional support from their parents, and having close friends who were less focused on school and attending classes. For first-generation students, instrumental support from Facebook friends and college-related information were associated with better confidence in the application process. For non-first-generation students, confidence was not linked to social media use. Thus, offering application help via social media can be particularly helpful for aiding first-generation students, who generally lack instrumental and emotional support.

What the Future Holds

The literature provides ample evidence of both positive and negative associations between the consumption of digital media and the overall well-being of school-age children and adolescents. Given the correlational nature of the evidence and the variety in the methodologies used across studies, it is challenging to frame these findings in a conceptual framework that would explain them. Yang et al. (2021) addressed the need for a theory to understand media effects on well-being by proposing a model consisting of three components. They suggest that children's activities, motives, and communication partners determine the outcomes of digital media consumption. Active (e.g., posting) and interactive (e.g., texting) activities may enhance the perception of social support. Passive browsing, on the other hand, may increase one's self-confirmation but also cause anxiety if this browsing leads to critical self-comparisons. Children who are motivated to use digital media to maintain their relationships may experience more belonging. Children who are motivated by FoMO, escapism, or need to create new relationships are not likely to enhance their well-being. Lastly, communicating with people they already know is more rewarding and beneficial than communicating with strangers. Stavropoulos et al. (2021) also proposed a model to better understand the different layers of factors that determine whether the consumption of digital media enhances or impedes well-being. Stavropoulos et al.'s multi-level cyber-developmental framework (CDF) takes into consideration the children's characteristics, and developmental challenges, as well as the bi-directional relationship between online and offline contexts. The children's characteristics include their biological, psychological, personality, and socio-demographic traits. This differential susceptibility can lead to different responses to the same digital media, either beneficial or adverse, depending on the user. The cyber layer includes virtual presence, level of engagement, and how the real self-representation mixes with the virtual self-representation. The interaction between the children's personal characteristics and the cyber layers is particularly crucial at junctions in development that are challenging such as puberty and transition to middle school. The interactions between multiple systems determine adaptive or maladaptive outcomes. Adaptive outcomes include digital competence, digital acculturation, and digital resilience, which involve effective functioning in both real and digital worlds, and the ability to manage challenges associated with digital media use. Maladaptive outcomes relate to problematic and addictive use of digital media that leads to distress and impairment in daily functioning.

Adaptively using current and future technologies requires changes in how new technologies are designed and in how children are socialized to use them. Parents too may have to change their own way of interacting with digital media to be a positive and supportive influence on their children. Parents, technology developers, and policymakers need to work together to create a safe digital environment. To be beneficial, children's digital experiences should contribute to their competence (e.g., learning how to solve a problem), emotional regulation (e.g., providing opportunities to de-stress and focus), self-actualization (e.g., providing activities that enhance a sense of purpose), empowerment (e.g., providing opportunities that build autonomy through mastery and decision making), social connection (e.g., enhancing social connections with significant others), creativity (e.g., nurturing curiosity), safety and security, and lastly to diversity, equity, and inclusion (i.e., all children can participate; United Nations Children's Fund (2022).

The American Academy of Pediatrics (AAP) recommends that parents a. build digital savviness (e.g., know what the children access and help them be informed consumers; demand better-designed digital products); b. enhance and monitor privacy settings on devices, apps, social media, virtual assistants, and wireless networks; c. create a family media use plan; d. teach children to analyze ads, identify algorithms, understand data collection, and recognize persuasive intent in technology design; e. talk to school administrators and teachers about the digital privacy of the technology tools they use; and f. engage in open and critical discussions about media with their children from a young age to encourage digital literacy and align media use with family values (Radesky, 2020). Parents should also be aware of how they model media use to their children and avoid negative experiences such as distractions from parent-child interactions and exposure to inappropriate media. Pediatricians can use the AAP Family Media Use Plan to help families develop individualized rules and guidelines for healthy media use and provide information about the benefits and risks of media use. Pediatricians can also screen for problematic Internet use and Internet gaming disorder and provide referrals to community resources if needed. Digital products for young children should be appropriately engaging, but not distracting and designed to be used by both parent and child to facilitate family participation in media use and modeling of more effective social and learning interactions (Chassiakos et al., 2016). Overall, parents and healthcare providers should engage in open and critical discussions with children about media to encourage digital literacy and align media use with family values.

References

Anderson, M., & Jiang, J. (2018). *Teens, social media, and technology*. Pew Research Center. Retrieved May 13, 2023, from https://www.pewresearch.org/internet/2018/05/31/teens-social-media-technology-2018/

Auxier, B., Anderson, M., Perrin, A., & Turner, E. (2020). *Children's engagement with digital devices, screen time*. Pew Research Center. Retrieved May 13, 2023, from www.pewresearch.org/internet/2020/07/28/childrens-engagement-with-digital-devices-screen-time/

Aygul, T. A., & Akbay, S. E. (2019). Smartphone addiction, fear of missing out, and perceived competence as predictors of social media addiction of adolescents. *European Journal of Educational Research*, *8*(2), 559–566. https://doi.org/10.12973/eu-jer.8.2.559

Buijzen, M., & Valkenburg, P. M. (2003). The unintended effects of television advertising: A parent-child survey. *Communication Research*, *30*(5), 483–503. https://doi.org/10.1177/0093650203256361

Cain, M. S., Leonard, J. A., Gabrieli, J. D., & Finn, A. S. (2016). Media multitasking in adolescence. *Psychonomic Bulletin & Review*, *23*, 1932–1941.

Chan, K. (2006). Exploring children's perceptions of material possessions: A drawing study. *Qualitative Market Research: An International Journal*, *9*(4), 352–366. https://doi.org/10.1108/13522750610689087

Chaplin, L. N., & John, D. R. (2007). Growing up in a material world: Age differences in materialism in children and adolescents. *Journal of Consumer Research*, *34*(4), 480–493. https://doi.org/10.1086/518546

Chaplin, L. N., John, D. R., Rindfleisch, A., & Froh, J. J. (2019). The impact of gratitude on adolescent materialism and generosity. *The Journal of Positive Psychology*, *14*(4), 502–511. https://doi.org/10.1080/17439760.2018.1497688

Chassiakos, R., Linda, Y., Radesky, J., Christakis, D., Moreno, M. A., Cross, C., Hill, D., Ameenuddin, N., Hutchinson, J., Levine, A., Boyd, R., Mendelson, R., & Swanson, W. S. (2016). Children and adolescents and digital media. *Pediatrics*, *138*(5). https://doi.org/10.1542/peds.2016-2593

Chiang, J. T., Chang, F. C., Lee, K. W., & Hsu, S. Y. (2019). Transitions in smartphone addiction proneness among children: The effect of gender and use patterns. *PLoS One*, *14*(5), e0217235. https://doi.org/10.1371/journal.pone.0217235

Christopher, A. N., Lasane, T. P., Troisi, J. D., & Park, L. E. (2007). Materialism, defensive and assertive self–presentational tactics, and life satisfaction. *Journal of Social and Clinical Psychology*, *26*(10), 1145–1162. https://doi.org/10.1521/jscp.2007.26.10.1145

Craig, S. L., Eaton, A. D., McInroy, L. B., Leung, V. W., & Krishnan, S. (2021). Can social media participation enhance LGBTQ+ youth well-being? Development of the social media benefits scale. *Social Media+ Society*, *7*(1). https://doi.org/10.1177/2056305121988931

Davis, K. (2012). Friendship 2.0: Adolescents' experiences of belonging and self-disclosure online. *Journal of Adolescence*, *35*(6), 1527–1536. https://doi.org/10.1016/j.adolescence.2012.02.013

Demir, Y. (2021). Relationships among childhood experiences, happiness, and social media addictions in adolescents. *Educational Process: International Journal*, *10*(1), 13–27. http://dx.doi.org/10.22521/edupij.2021.101.2

Dittmar, H., Bond, R., Hurst, M., & Kasser, T. (2014). The relationship between materialism and personal well-being: A meta-analysis. *Journal of Personality and Social Psychology*, *107*(5), 879. https://doi.org/10.1037/a0037409

Fardouly, J., Magson, N. R., Rapee, R. M., Johnco, C. J., & Oar, E. L. (2020). The use of social media by Australian preadolescents and its links with mental health. *Journal of Clinical Psychology*, *76*(7), 1304–1326. https://doi.org/10.1002/jclp.22936

Flouri, E. (2004). Exploring the relationship between mothers' and fathers' parenting practices and children's materialist values. *Journal of Economic Psychology*, *25*(6), 743–752. https://doi.org/10.1016/j.joep.2003.06.005

Froh, J. J., Emmons, R. A., Card, N. A., Bono, G., & Wilson, J. A. (2011). Gratitude and the reduced costs of materialism in adolescents. *Journal of Happiness Studies*, *12*(2), 289–302. https://doi.org/10.1007/s10902-010-9195-9

Gasiorowska, A., Chaplin, L. N., Zaleskiewicz, T., Wygrab, S., & Vohs, K. D. (2016). Money cues increase agency and decrease prosociality among children: Early signs of market-mode behaviors. *Psychological Science*, *27*(3), 331–344. https://doi.org/10.1177/0956797615620378

Hamilton, J. L., Nesi, J., & Choukas-Bradley, S. (2020). *Teens and social media during the COVID-19 pandemic: Staying socially connected while physically distant*. Retrieved May 13, 2023, from https://doi.org/10.31234/osf.io/5stx4

Jaspers, E. D., & Pieters, R. G. (2016). Materialism across the life span: An age-period-cohort analysis. *Journal of Personality and Social Psychology*, *111*(3), 451. https://doi.org/10.1037/pspp0000092

Kasser, T., Rosenblum, K. L., Sameroff, A. J., Deci, E. L., Niemiec, C. P., Ryan, R. M., Árnadóttir, O., Bond, R., Dittmar, H., Dungan, N., & Hawks, S. (2014). Changes in materialism, changes in psychological well-being: Evidence from three longitudinal studies and an intervention experiment. *Motivation and Emotion*, *38*, 1–22. https://doi.org/10.1007/s11031-013-9371-4

Lapierre, M. A. (2016). Emotion regulation and young children's consumer behavior. *Young Consumers*, *17*(2), 168–182. https://doi.org/10.1108/YC-11-2015-00566

Lenka, U., & Vandana. (2015). A review on impact of socialization agents in breeding consumerism among children. *Global Business Review*, *16*(5), 867–878. https://doi.org/10.1177/0972150915591654

Mahapatra, S. (2019). Smartphone addiction and associated consequences: Role of loneliness and self-regulation. *Behaviour & Information Technology*, *38*(8), 833–844. https://doi.org/10.1080/0144929X.2018.1560499

Manolis, C., & Roberts, J. A. (2012). Subjective well-being among adolescent consumers: The effects of materialism, compulsive buying, and time affluence. *Applied Research in Quality of Life*, *7*(2), 117–135. https://doi.org/10.1007/s11482-011-9155-5

McDool, E., Powell, P., Roberts, J., & Taylor, K. (2016). *Social media use and children's well-being* (IZA Discussion Paper No. 10412). Retrieved May 13, 2023, from https://ssrn.com/abstract=2886783

Meates, J. (2021). Problematic digital technology use in children and adolescents: Impact on physical well-being. *Teachers and Curriculum*, *21*(1), 77–91. https://doi.org/10.15663/tandc.v21i1

Mikeska, J., Harrison, R. L., & Carlson, L. (2017). A meta-analysis of parental style and consumer socialization of children. *Journal of Consumer Psychology*, *27*(2), 245–256. https://doi.org/10.1016/j.jcps.2016.09.004

Nairn, A., Ormrod, J., & Bottomley, P. A. (2007). *Watching, wanting and well-being: Exploring the links-a study of 9- to 13-year-olds*. National Consumer Council.

OECD. (2018). *New technologies and 21st century children: Recent trends and outcomes*. https://doi.org/10.1787/e071a505-en

Opree, S. J., Buijzen, M., & Valkenburg, P. M. (2012). Lower life satisfaction related to materialism in children frequently exposed to advertising. *Pediatrics*, *130*(3), e486–e491. https://doi.org/10.1542/peds.2011-3148

O'Reilly, M., Dogra, N., Whiteman, N., Hughes, J., Eruyar, S., & Reilly, P. (2018). Is social media bad for mental health and well-being? Exploring the perspectives of adolescents. *Clinical Child Psychology and Psychiatry*, *23*(4), 601–661. https://doi.org/10.1177/1359104518775154

Oswald, T. K., Rumbold, A. R., Kedzior, S. G., & Moore, V. M. (2020). Psychological impacts of "screen time" and "green time" for children and adolescents: A systematic scoping review. *PLoS One*, *15*(9), e0237725. https://doi.org/10.1371/journal.pone.0237725

Pea, R., Nass, C., Meheula, L., Rance, M., Kumar, A., Bamford, H., Nass, M., Simha, A., Stillerman, B., Yang, S., & Zhou, M. (2012). Media use, face-to-face communication, media multitasking, and social well-being among 8- to 12-year-old girls. *Developmental Psychology*, *48*(2), 327–336. https://doi.org/10.1037/a0027030

Piko, B. F. (2006). Satisfaction with life, psychosocial health, and materialism among Hungarian youth. *Journal of Health Psychology*, *11*(6), 827–831. https://doi.org/10.1177/1359105306069072

Quinn, S., & Oldmeadow, J. A. (2013). Is the igeneration a 'we' generation? Social networking use among 9-to 13-year-olds and belonging. *British Journal of Developmental Psychology*, *31*(1), 136–142. https://doi.org/10.1111/bjdp.12007

Radesky, J., Chassiakos, Y. L. R., Ameenuddin, N., & Navsaria, D. (2020). Digital advertising to children. *Pediatrics*, *146*(1). https://doi.org/10.1542/peds.2020-1681

Richins, M. L. (2017). Materialism pathways: The processes that create and perpetuate materialism. *Journal of Consumer Psychology*, *27*(4), 480–499. https://doi.org/10.1016/j.jcps.2017.07.006

Rose, G. M., Dalakas, V., & Kropp, F. (2003). Consumer socialization and parental style across cultures: Findings from Australia, Greece, and India. *Journal of Consumer Psychology*, *13*(4), 366–376. https://doi.org/10.1207/S15327663JCP1304_04

Schaeffer, K. (2019). *Most U.S. teens who use cell phones do it to pass time, connect with others, learn new things*. Pew Research Center. Retrieved May 13, 2023, from www.pewresearch.org/fact-tank/2019/08/23/most-u-s-teens-who-use-cellphones-do-it-to-pass-time-connect-with-others-learn-new-things/

Schor, J. B. (2004). *Born to buy: The commercialized child and the new consumer cult*. Scribner.

Stavropoulos, V., Motti-Stefanidi, F., & Griffiths, M. D. (2021). Risks and opportunities for youth in the digital era. *European Psychologist*. https://doi.org/10.1027/1016-9040/a000451

Sweeting, H., Hunt, K., & Bhaskar, A. (2012). Consumerism and well-being in early adolescence. *Journal of Youth Studies*, *15*(6), 802–820. https://doi.org/10.1080/13676261.2012.685706

Timeo, S., Riva, P., & Paladino, M. P. (2020). Being liked or not being liked: A study on social-media exclusion in a preadolescent population. *Journal of Adolescence*, *80*, 173–181. https://doi.org/10.1016/j.adolescence.2020.02.010

Twigg, L., Duncan, C., & Weich, S. (2020). Is social media use associated with children's well-being? Results from the UK Household Longitudinal Study. *Journal of Adolescence*, *80*, 73–83. https://doi.org/10.1016/j.adolescence.2020.02.002

United Nations Children's Fund. (2022). *Responsible innovation in technology for children: Digital technology, play and child well-being*. Retrieved May 13, 2023, from www.unicef-irc.org/publications/pdf/RITEC_Responsible-Innovation-in-Technology-for-Children-Digital-technology-play-and-child-well-being.pdf

Urano, Y., Takizawa, R., Ohka, M., Yamasaki, H., & Shimoyama, H. (2020). Cyberbullying victimization and adolescent mental health: The differential moderating effects of intrapersonal and interpersonal emotional competence. *Journal of Adolescence*, *80*, 182–191. https://doi.org/10.1016/j.adolescence.2020.02.009

Valkenburg, P. M., & Cantor, J. (2001). The development of a child into a consumer. *Journal of Applied Developmental Psychology*, *22*(1), 61–72. https://doi.org/10.1016/S0193-3973(00)00066-6

Van Den Eijnden, R., Koning, I., Doornwaard, S., Van Gurp, F., & Ter Bogt, T. (2018). The impact of heavy and disordered use of games and social media on adolescents' psychological, social, and school functioning. *Journal of Behavioral Addictions*, *7*(3), 697–706. https://doi.org/10.1556/2006.7.2018.65

Vogels, E., Gelles-Watnick, R., & Massarat, N. (2022). *Teens, social media, and technology*. Pew Research Center. Retrieved May 13, 2023, from www.pewresearch.org/internet/2022/08/10/teens-social-media-and-technology-2022/

Wohn, D. Y., Ellison, N. B., Khan, M. L., Fewins-Bliss, R., & Gray, R. (2013). The role of social media in shaping first-generation high school students' college aspirations: A social capital lens. *Computers & Education*, *63*, 424–436. https://doi.org/10.1016/j.compedu.2013.01.004

Yang, C. C., Holden, S. M., & Ariati, J. (2021). Social media and psychological well-being among youth: The multidimensional model of social media use. *Clinical Child and Family Psychology Review*, *24*, 631–650. https://doi.org/10.1007/s10567-021-00359-z

Yang, Z., Fu, X., Yu, X., & Lv, Y. (2018). Longitudinal relations between adolescents' materialism and prosocial behavior toward family, friends, and strangers. *Journal of Adolescence*, *62*, 162–170. https://doi.org/10.1016/j.adolescence.2017.11.013

12 Poverty, Physical Environment, and Discrimination

> Flint is a small town in Michigan, populated predominantly by African American residents, and has 40% of its population living in poverty. The town made national news when high levels of poisonous lead were discovered in the water because of temporarily switching the water supply to the contaminated Flint River. Residents quickly raised concerns about the water's quality, particularly its color, smell, and taste. Despite these complaints, city, and state officials dismissed the issue for several months but advised residents to boil the water. The city eventually reverted to its previous water source, but the damage to the pipes that have corroded and kept leaking lead was irreversible. Four percent of children under 5 had elevated levels of lead in their blood. Lead is particularly detrimental to children and pregnant women, potentially leading to learning difficulties, behavioral issues, and cognitive impairment, according to the World Health Organization (Kennedy, 2016). Indeed, the cases of children who qualified for special education services in Flint doubled four years after the switch, putting the school district in crisis.
>
> (*Green, 2019*)

Where children are raised, including their geography, socioeconomic status (SES), and cultural context, is a powerful determinant of their physical and psychological well-being. The biggest threat for each individual child depends on a range of factors. According to the American Academy of Pediatrics (2019), some common threats to children's well-being that have been identified by researchers and child advocacy organizations, include poverty, child abuse and neglect, exposure to violence, lack of access to quality healthcare, and educational disparities. Poverty influences several other contexts that affect the ability to be happy and successful. Directly, poverty can hinder children's health and learning abilities due to inadequate nutrition and increased stress. Indirectly, it can affect the family environment, parenting styles, and maternal responsiveness. Poverty also impacts the quality of schools, access to financial resources for supplementary learning, and the safety of neighborhoods. Moreover, poverty can limit students' exposure to positive role models and mentors, as well as professional connections that could help them envision a future in higher education and professional careers (Olszewski-Kubilius & Corwith, 2018).

DOI: 10.4324/9780429356414-16

This chapter focuses on the effects that poverty has on physical health and psychological functioning and the pathways that link poverty with negative outcomes, primarily through lower parental investment, decreased parenting quality, elevated chronic stress due to challenging environments, and children's cognitions about poverty (e.g., stereotype threat). The cumulative effect of multiple negative influences impacts the ability to cope with adversity and has long-lasting effects on childhood that even reach adulthood. Negative outcomes associated with poverty include poor self-regulation, deficits in executive functions, altered neurodevelopment, increased psychopathology, and disparities in academic achievement and educational attainment. Although inter-related to poverty, special emphasis is given to the physical environment (e.g., toxins and pollutants), the role of nature, and the association of racial discrimination with children's well-being. Lastly, the chapter presents some ideas about how to protect the well-being of children raised in poor contexts.

Understanding Poverty and Its Effects

The federal poverty line (FPL) is an income threshold decided by the US government to determine who is living in poverty. The specific threshold varies depending on the number of people in a household, but for the year 2021, the FPL for a single-person household is an annual income of $12,880, while for a family of four, it is $26,500. According to the most recent data from the U.S. Census Bureau, in 2019, approximately 3.6 million children under the age of 6 were living in poverty in the United States. This represented 15.7% of all children in this age group. When considering children under the age of 18, approximately 10.5 million of them lived below the federal poverty line in the United States. This represented 14.4% of all children in the country. Moreover, approximately 18.1 million children under the age of 18 lived in families with incomes between 100% and 199% of the federal poverty line in the United States. This represented 24.8% of all children in the country. In addition, about 3.8 million young adults between the ages of 18 and 24 were living below the federal poverty line in 2019, representing 16.2% of all young adults in that age group (U.S. Census Bureau, 2020). According to the most recent data from the United Nations Children's Fund (UNICEF), as of 2020, an estimated 385 million children were living in extreme poverty (i.e., living on less than $1.90 a day) around the world. This represents approximately 1 in 5 children globally. Additionally, UNICEF estimates that a total of 1.2 billion children (or around half of all children in the world) are living in poverty when measured by a higher poverty line of $3.20 per day. It is worth noting that the COVID-19 pandemic has had a significant impact on global poverty rates, with an estimated additional 150 million children being pushed into poverty due to the pandemic (UNICEF, 2021). Poverty rates can vary significantly by race and ethnicity in the United States, with children and adolescents from Black and Hispanic/Latino communities experiencing poverty at higher rates than their White counterparts. Poverty is an intricate and multidimensional construct. It can be characterized not only by financial factors such as family income but also by other indicators of social and economic disadvantage, like low parental education and occupational level. The degree and duration of poverty also play a role in its impact. Researchers have used slightly different approaches when measuring poverty. Some use the income-to-needs ratio which reflects the ratio of the child's family income and FPL, others use the term low SES to include those who have an income double the FPL, and others use the term economically disadvantaged to include those who live in absolute deprivation or relative lack of resources (i.e., the family possesses fewer or worse resources than others; children qualify for free school lunches; Heberle & Carter, 2015).

Evans and Kim (2013) identified three complementary pathways in the literature that show how psychological processes explain the negative effects of childhood poverty on human development. First, poor children experience lower parental investment. They often live in less cognitively stimulating environments with fewer resources like print media, age-appropriate toys, informal learning venues, and educational digital materials. They also experience impoverished language environments with fewer spoken words and less frequent reading by parents. Second, poor children experience lower parenting quality. Lower-income parents tend to engage in harsher and less responsive interactions with their children. Because of greater conflict and hostility in their lives, they are more likely to use corporal punishment. Less responsive parenting in disadvantaged families involves reduced attention and support for children's emotional needs and less instrumental assistance, such as helping with schoolwork or providing information and material support. Third, poor children experience elevated chronic stress. Disadvantaged children face numerous stressors that strain and eventually harm their biological and psychological regulatory systems, according to Evans and Kim (2013). This chronic stress model of childhood poverty has two major components: harmful effects caused by elevated environmental demands that strain biological response systems, and damage to self-regulatory capacities that help children manage these demands. Childhood poverty is stressful for children due to the challenging environments they grow up in. These environments are often characterized by family conflict, turmoil, family dissolution, maternal depression, exposure to violence, harsh parenting, and reduced parental responsiveness. Additionally, poor children tend to live in chaotic homes with structural issues, noise, crowding, toxins, and allergens. Their neighborhoods often have less social capital, higher exposure to pollutants, crime, street traffic, and limited access to physical activity and healthy foods (Evans & Kim, 2013).

Heberle and Carter (2015) proposed another mediator that additionally explains the effects of poverty. They argue that children's cognitions such as beliefs, attitudes, and stereotypes about poverty should also be considered. For example, children who hear their parents complain about their low-paid jobs and feel their parents' stress may develop a belief that work is unrewarding, further leading to low self-efficacy. Children who are aware that they are poor may experience prejudice which then compounds their stress levels. Therefore, considering how children experience poverty is important. The authors further propose that beginning in kindergarten children can discern poverty as a phenomenon and recognize the socio-economic group they belong to. In middle childhood, they are also aware of the stereotypes related to being poor. The authors cite research showing that children in middle childhood regardless of their own SES, believe that poor children are more likely to be rejected by their peers, perform worse academically because teachers dislike and discriminate against poor children, and are less likely to obtain their professional goals because they lack personal qualities needed to achieve such goals (Heberle & Carter, 2015). Whether children apply these beliefs to themselves and whether these beliefs cause stress is not clear in the literature, but it is worth exploring the effects of this stereotype threat which may be amplified by the child's race and gender.

Evans and colleagues (2013) propose that exposure to multiple stressors is a key feature of childhood poverty and has far-reaching consequences. When combined, the cumulative risk factor has a greater negative impact on development than a single risk. In the United States, 41% of children younger than 6 live in families that experience one or two risk factors, and 20% live in families that experience three or more (Evans et al., 2013). Early childhood adversity can predict adult morbidity in most chronic diseases, regardless of later upward social mobility. Poverty can influence physical disease through elevated chronic physiological stress that results from exposure to multiple stressors. Compared to their more advantaged peers, low-income children exhibit higher sympathetic nervous activity, hypothalamic-pituitary-adrenal (HPA) axis activity, metabolic dysregulation, and inflammation. These income-related changes in chronic stress markers can begin early in life. Allostatic load, a cumulative indicator of chronic stress, is also elevated in poor children. Additionally, adversity in early childhood may affect the expression of genes involved in chronic stress responses, thereby moderating children's vulnerability to the chronic physiological stress associated with poverty (Evans & Kim, 2013).

Low-income children experience elevated chronic physiological stress, partly due to higher levels of cumulative risk factors they encounter. Evans and Cassells (2014) provided longitudinal evidence of the effect of cumulative risk associated with poverty on psychological functioning. They followed a group of 9-year-olds until they reached emerging adulthood. They assessed cumulative risk at age 13 by accounting for noise exposure (decibel meter during a two-hour home visit), crowding (ratio of people in the family to the number of rooms), housing problems (e.g., poor maintenance), family turmoil, separation from family, and exposure to violence. The portion spent in poverty during childhood predicted externalizing problems and learned helplessness but not internalizing problems. Furthermore, the accumulated risk at age 13 fully mediated the relationship between the duration of poverty and externalizing problems. Cumulative risk partially mediated the relationship with learned helplessness.

Childhood poverty not only increases stress levels but also disrupts children's ability to manage environmental demands, affecting self-regulation and coping. Self-regulation relies on various processes, such as attention control, working memory, inhibitory control, delay of gratification, and planning, which can be compromised by chronic stress. Low-income children often exhibit deficits in self-regulation, but those with better self-regulatory skills tend to be more resilient to adverse psychological outcomes. Childhood poverty is also linked to maladaptive coping strategies in older children and adolescents. Low-income adolescents are more likely to use disengagement coping strategies, leading to increased internalizing, externalizing, and social difficulties. However, those who use engagement coping strategies show fewer adverse psychological symptoms (Evans & Kim, 2013).

Poverty's impact on children's educational achievement begins at birth, with children from higher-income families being exposed to greater child-directed speech than those from low-income families. Meta-analytic evidence suggests that low SES children hear 500 words per hour less than children from high SES families (Dailey & Bergelson, 2021). Vocabulary differences between higher and lower SES children appear as early as 18 months and continue to grow, significantly affecting cognitive development and school readiness. According to Olszewski-Kubilius and Corwith's review (2018), although national achievement gaps between the wealthiest and poorest students have narrowed between 1998 and 2010, they still exist at the start of kindergarten and are closing at such a slow pace that it would take a century for these students to begin school on equal footing. Children with more educated mothers and no welfare assistance exhibit higher math and reading skills upon entering kindergarten. Similarly, significant gaps in science knowledge persist between lower and higher SES children, mainly due to differences in informal exposure to the natural world by parents. Data from the National Assessment of Education Progress (NAEP) program since 1990, cited in Olszewski-Kubilius and Corwith (2018), have consistently shown large and enduring achievement gaps between students who qualify for the federal free and reduced lunch program and those who do not. Moreover, these gaps in mathematics and reading remain relatively stable. Achievement gaps are wider for persistently poor children, as they score significantly lower in math achievement compared to students who were never or only occasionally eligible for free and reduced lunch.

In their review, Olszewski-Kubilius and Corwith (2018) report that low-income students are significantly underrepresented in gifted programs of 2,000 US school districts with 50% of these districts reporting much lower percentages of low-income students compared to their representation in the district population. Furthermore, the level of poverty also affects excellence gaps, with a smaller percentage of students qualifying for free or reduced lunch reaching advanced levels in both math and reading compared to students not qualifying for subsidized lunch. High-achieving but low-income students were less likely to remain in the high-achieving group by 5th grade. In middle school, the high achieving low-income students were more likely to attend schools that did not track their academic performance and did not adequately prepare them for the challenges in high school. Moreover, when they began 9th grade, they were less likely to be placed on more challenging academic tracks that would have led to admission to more selective colleges. Additionally, they were less likely to pass advanced placement courses. Achievement and excellence gaps were also influenced by the unequal access to extracurricular activities, out-of-school programs, and informal learning opportunities at home and in students' communities. About two-thirds of the achievement gaps between low-income and high-income students in grade 9 could be attributed to differences in summer learning opportunities that accumulated over time. These opportunities included both formal summer programs and informal experiences like family vacations and museum visits. Research has shown that these gaps in informal learning opportunities, particularly concerning the natural world, contributed to early and long-lasting disparities in science achievement between low-income and higher-income children (Olszewski-Kubilius & Corwith, 2018). The findings highlight the disparities in educational achievement and opportunities for excellence among students from different socioeconomic backgrounds. These effects unfortunately are sustained across generations and are accentuated by race. Research shows that African American and Hispanic young adults are less likely than Asian Pacific Islanders and Non-Hispanic White counterparts in surpassing their parents in terms of achieving higher income, education, and occupation status (Ryabov, 2020).

During early childhood, family and home environments have a strong influence on neurodevelopmental processes that support cognitive, social, and emotional skills. However, research on the links between SES and neurodevelopment in early childhood is limited due to practical difficulties in acquiring brain imaging data in young children, as well as socioeconomic barriers faced by individuals from lower-resourced communities. Despite these challenges, some studies have shown associations between SES and neurocognitive outcomes in preschool children. Olson et al. (2021) conducted a review to examine the available evidence for neural correlates of SES in early childhood, including whether they are general or specific to certain brain regions or functions. The findings suggested observable associations between SES and brain development in early childhood, with certain brain structures and functions being more sensitive to socioeconomic contexts than others. Regions and circuits supporting language processing and executive function were particularly sensitive to SES. The studies examining SES relationships with brain structure revealed lower indices of cortical maturation in lower-SES children compared to higher-SES children. The findings on SES associations with fMRI measures were generally consistent across the age range studied, from infancy through early childhood. However, there was greater variability in the findings on EEG measures of brain function as related to SES, and there were some contradictory results. The review did not determine whether brain structure or function was more susceptible to SES-related alterations in brain development.

In conclusion, the negative effects of childhood poverty on development can be explained through several complementary pathways as identified by Evans and Kim (2013) and Heberle and Carter (2015). First, poor children experience lower parental investment, leading to less cognitively stimulating environments and impoverished language environments. Second, they also experience lower parenting quality, which involves harsher interactions, less responsiveness, and reduced attention to emotional needs. Third, they experience elevated chronic stress due to challenging environments characterized by factors such as family conflict, turmoil, maternal depression, and exposure to violence. Heberle and Carter (2015) added children's cognitions as another mediator, highlighting the importance of understanding how children experience poverty and the beliefs they form about it. A considerable percentage of young children in the United States live in families experiencing multiple risk factors. The cumulative risk factor may have a more profound negative impact on development than a single risk. Longitudinal evidence shows that cumulative risks associated with poverty impact psychological functioning, with childhood poverty predicting externalizing problems and learned helplessness. Childhood poverty also disrupts self-regulation and coping, as low-income children often exhibit deficits in self-regulation, leading to compromised attention control, working memory, inhibitory control, delay of gratification, and planning. Furthermore, low-income adolescents are more likely to use disengagement coping strategies, resulting in increased internalizing, externalizing, and social difficulties. Poverty significantly impacts children's educational achievement from birth, with disparities in language exposure, cognitive development, and school readiness evident between children from higher and lower socioeconomic backgrounds. Research has also identified associations between SES and neurodevelopment in early childhood, suggesting that socioeconomic context has far-reaching implications for children's brain development during a sensitive period that impacts their learning abilities throughout life.

The Physical Environment: Housing, Neighborhoods, and Access to Nature Settings

Because the immediate physical environments that poor families reside in are their homes and neighborhoods, researchers have sought to identify their characteristics that predict well-being, hoping to also figure out interventions that combat some of the effects of poverty. In an earlier study, Homel and Burns (1989) investigated how housing characteristics, street type, and neighborhood relate to children's perceptions of life satisfaction and their assessments of emotional (e.g., feeling anger, unhappiness, fear, worry) and social adjustment (e.g., having friends, support from peers and adults). The researchers evaluated the quality of housing characteristics by accounting for the floor occupied (e.g., ground, or above ground), housing upkeep, occupancy (rental or own), and availability for play space. The street types were identified as either residential, industrial, or commercial, and the quality of the neighborhood was determined by the number of stressors, crime, and employment rate. The researchers also controlled for several family characteristics such as occupational status, paternal and maternal education, employment status, cultural background, religion, number of children in the family, and family income. In this sample of 9- to 11-year-olds from Australia, the researchers discovered several interesting findings. The neighborhood score accounted for 3.3% of the variance in overall satisfaction. As neighborhood issues increased, satisfaction levels decreased. Housing upkeep was another significant predictor, contributing 3.2% to the variance, with individuals expressing lower satisfaction in poorly maintained homes. Occupancy type explained 2.4% of the variance, with children in rental accommodations reporting lower happiness within their families. When accounting for environmental and family variables, the explained variance in overall satisfaction score was 23.6%, with environmental factors accounting for 6.1% of this figure. The results demonstrated that the anticipated disadvantages stemming from low income were further intensified by residing in primarily nonresidential streets, many of which were situated in inner-city areas with high social problems.

Moreover, children residing in non-residential streets consistently experienced heightened levels of worry, anger, and unhappiness. Substandard housing was also linked to adverse outcomes, particularly an increase in anxiety. The environmental factors explained 5.7% of the variance in emotional adjustment out of a total variance of 25.4% explained by all factors. The most influential environmental factor was the street type. Again, the results highlight that the challenges of financially disadvantaged families are exacerbated by living on undesirable streets. For instance, the researchers reported that the most fearful children were found to reside in nonresidential streets in high social problem areas and had fathers with unskilled occupations, limited education, and low incomes. Lastly, social adjustment was significantly influenced by neighborhood social problems, street type, and the availability of play spaces. As neighborhood quality deteriorated, children's perceptions of their classmates worsened. Those living on commercial streets were most likely to identify themselves as lonely. Moreover, children without accessible play areas tended to spend less time with friends outside of school. However, this pattern of social restriction was primarily evident in neighborhoods with exceptionally high social problems, commonly found in deteriorating inner-city areas. Children residing in the low-risk areas, characterized by spacious and relatively new housing developments on the city's outskirts with access to a wide variety of out-of-school activities, demonstrated above-average social adjustment. These children were particularly more likely to report having multiple close friends.

Additional evidence of the housing and neighborhood effects is provided by Ferguson and colleagues (2013) who conducted an international review of studies to include not only information from Western Europe and the US but also countries of the southern hemisphere. Regarding housing type, Ferguson et al. found that research in affluent countries has mainly examined the developmental implications of high-rise housing for children, with some studies founding links between living in high-rise buildings and lower academic achievement and increased behavioral disorders in children. In the global South, the authors found that housing type was closely tied to housing quality, with many low-income families in urban areas living in informal housing that lacked basic amenities such as access to clean water and was usually unstable, leading to frequent residential mobility. Children in informal housing were more susceptible to injury, exposed to toxins, and less likely to attend school due to the lack of a formal address. Homelessness and living in informal settlements can negatively impact children's school performance, socioemotional well-being, and self-esteem. Expanding on the findings by Homel and Burns (1989), Ferguson and colleagues found that independent of SES, children living in substandard housing had lower academic competency and greater psychological distress in Western societies. These effects were further amplified by the duration of exposure to substandard housing. Poor quality housing placed additional stress on low-income parents, potentially reducing their ability to be warm and responsive caregivers. Unsafe home environments might have constrained play activities, which negatively impacted children's cognitive and socioemotional development (Ferguson et al., 2013).

Another characteristic of housing is its density. People per room is a key metric for measuring crowding and its impact on psychological functioning. Research from various cultural contexts, including the US, India, Thailand, Egypt, Hong Kong, South Africa, and Jamaica, showed similar developmental effects of crowding in residential and school settings. Children in the global South tended to live in more crowded homes compared to those in North America and Western Europe. Studies show that crowding negatively affected cognitive functioning (reading comprehension, IQ), school achievement, and socioemotional well-being (e.g., disruptions in children's exploration and play). Residential crowding also hindered parent-child interactions, with parents talking less and using simpler language with their children. Crowded environments strained family relationships, leading to increased aggression and withdrawal, and contributed to psychological distress in children. In educational settings, crowding has been associated with reduced cooperative play and more off-task time.

As discussed earlier, the location of the neighborhood and the level of cumulative stressors (e.g., employment rates, occupational status, violence) are associated with psychological well-being in children (Homel & Burns, 1989). Research with young adults reveals that the educational status of the neighborhood and how engaged youth are with the community predicts the intergenerational transmission of socio-economic status. In neighborhoods with high educational status and less disconnected youth, young adults were more likely to surpass their own parents in terms of educational attainment, income, and occupational prestige (Ryabov, 2020).

Another neighborhood characteristic that is often overlooked is its level of noise. Ferguson et al. (2013) reported that numerous studies in high-income countries have shown that chronic noise exposure during early childhood negatively influenced reading acquisition. Evidence from cross-sectional, as well as longitudinal studies, suggests a dose-response relationship that is mediated by cognitive deficits, such as impaired long-term memory, altered attentional strategies, and deficits in auditory discrimination, which is essential for speech perception and reading acquisition. Noise exposure may also affect caregiving behaviors related to reading acquisition as parents may engage in less conversation and reading with their children. Research on noise exposure and children's cognitive development in countries outside the US and Europe is limited. However, available evidence suggests that children exposed to noise may experience stress, irritation, annoyance, and elevated physiological stress indicators, such as blood pressure and stress hormones.

The physical quality of neighborhoods matters as well. Most children in the global South live in neighborhoods with poor physical quality, characterized by high levels of pollution, inadequate waste collection, poor sanitation, and limited access to resources such as green spaces, schools, and hospitals. These neighborhoods are often unsafe due to high traffic and insufficient street lighting. However, research on the impact of neighborhood physical conditions on children's cognitive and socioemotional development is limited, even in high-income countries (Ferguson et al., 2013). Parents of 9- to 12-year-olds in two Canadian cities reported higher psychological distress for their children in neighborhoods with lower physical quality. In Zurich, parents living near busy streets restricted their children's outdoor play, resulting in reduced social and motor skills among preschoolers. Similarly, high levels of street traffic in San Francisco neighborhoods were linked to less social interaction among neighbors. The quality of the neighborhood is enhanced by access to natural settings for children such as play areas and green parks. Researchers have specifically examined the role of natural environments on children's well-being. Based on the review by Ferguson et al. (2013), having access to natural outdoor play spaces lessened the reactions to stressful events and increased children's executive functioning. Being close to open green space was partially responsible for the inverse relationship between household income and childhood obesity and making schoolyards greener related to better academic achievement and psychological well-being.

In a large multi-wave study, Feng and Astell-Burt (2017a) followed the psychological adjustment of 4- to 13-year-old children from Australia in relation to the quantity and quality of green spaces. The quantity was determined by the percentage of land that was designated as green space. The quality was assessed by how great the parents perceived the parks and playgrounds in their neighborhood. As the quantity and quality of green space increased, the scores for socioemotional adjustment also increased while internalizing and externalizing problems declined. For all measures of psychological well-being, living in an area with 21–40% green space was optimal. In addition, for internalizing problems, there was a dose-response relationship with the quality of green spaces. Parents who lived in larger green areas tended to perceive them of higher quality and this was the case regardless of SES. Furthermore, children who lived in areas where more than 21% of it was designated as green were less likely to have suboptimal health as perceived by the parents (Feng & Astell-Burt, 2017b). In addition to the quality and quantity of green spaces, time spent in greenspace was a positive predictor of well-being as it was found to correlate with happiness and life satisfaction in a sample of 11- to 14-year-olds from New Zealand (Ward et al., 2016).

Another way to investigate the role of nature settings on well-being is to assess children's perceived connections to nature. Using data from the representative Australian study called the New South Wales Child Development Study, Whitten et al. (2018) demonstrated that children (12 years of age) who reported that being in nature makes them feel peaceful and have a sense of oneness with the natural world also reported higher life satisfaction and engagement with prosocial behaviors. The effect of connectedness to nature was smaller compared to the effect of having social support and socioeconomic advantage but was unique and significant. Similarly, Barrera-Hernández et al. (2020) demonstrated a positive correlation between subjective happiness and connectedness to nature in a sample of 9- to 12-year-old children from Mexico. Moreover, they revealed that connectedness to nature made children more likely to engage in sustainable behaviors, like recycling, which in turn increased happiness. Access to nature settings may contribute to psychological benefits through increased physical activity, which has been consistently linked to outdoor recreational spaces (Ward et al., 2016). Some evidence suggests that physical activity mediates the relationship between proximity to green space and children's moods and feelings (Nordbø et al., 2020).

The association between nature, psychological functioning, and well-being is well supported in the literature, but it is not clear how this relationship is moderated by features of the physical environment that disadvantaged children tend to reside in. Theoretically, the effect of nature on well-being should be consistently observed regardless of varying circumstances. Based on the *biophilia* hypothesis, proposed by E.O. Wilson, humans have an instinctive connection with nature for evolutionary reasons. Nature has provided the resources needed for survival and adaptation. This innate affinity further draws people to nature and other forms of life, thus enhancing their psychological well-being (Keltner et al., 2017). Evidence suggests that this is the case even when engagement with nature is achieved through immersion in natural history content. Participants, ages 16 to 24 years, reported greater awe, wonder, calmness, joy amusement, curiosity, and less anxiety, fear, stress, loneliness, and fatigue after they watched Planet Earth videos compared to a group that watched a popular drama (Keltner et al., 2017). Future research should explore how the benefits of connecting with nature generalize in poor contexts. Some evidence suggests that improving greenery was related to increased physical activity in adolescents living in deprived neighborhoods in Norway, but the effect of perceived greenery on depression only trended significant (Gubbels et al., 2016). Furthermore, future research should address whether the protective role of access to nature can buffer disadvantaged children from the effects of their impoverished physical environments.

In conclusion, the immediate physical environment, including home and neighborhood characteristics, has a significant impact on the well-being of children living in poverty. Environmental factors such as housing upkeep, occupancy type, street type, and neighborhood quality contribute to children's overall satisfaction and emotional and social adjustment. Housing type and quality, as well as residential density, influence children's academic achievement, socioemotional well-being, and self-esteem, with additional negative effects on caregiver-child interactions in crowded households. The neighborhood's educational status, level of cumulative stressors, and noise levels also play a role in shaping children's psychological well-being and cognitive development. Access to natural settings such as play areas and green parks has a significant positive connection with children's well-being. The quality and quantity of green spaces in children's environments are associated with improved psychological well-being and reduced internalizing and externalizing problems. Additionally, spending time in green spaces is linked to higher happiness, life satisfaction, and increased engagement in prosocial behaviors. Physical activity in green spaces may also contribute to psychological benefits. The biophilia hypothesis suggests that the connection between nature, psychological functioning, and well-being should be consistently observed across varying circumstances. However, more research is needed to investigate the buffering effect of nature in deprived neighborhoods.

Discrimination, Happiness, and Success

According to the United States Census Bureau, as of 2020, there were approximately 73.9 million children under the age of 18 in the United States. Of those, an estimated 50.8% were part of a minority race or ethnic group. Importantly the US population has become more racially diverse in the last decade, with the non-Hispanic White consisting 57.8% of the total population. The remaining self-identify as either Hispanic or Latino (18.7%), Black or African American (12.4%), Asian (6%), Native American or Alaska Native (0.9%), Native Hawaiian or Pacific Islander (0.2%), or multiracial/other (4%; U.S. Census Bureau, 2021). Despite the increasing diversity, 64% of the population considers racism a significant problem in the US (Pew Research Center, 2020). Furthermore, a 2019 report by the National Center for Education Statistics found that students of color, particularly Black and Hispanic students, were more likely to attend schools with higher rates of poverty and fewer resources than their White peers (National Center for Education Statistics, 2019). Evidently, SES interacts with race/ethnicity causing double jeopardy for disadvantaged youth. Black and Hispanic adolescents who are poor experience less self-worth and increased hyperactivity and depression than White adolescents who are also poor (McLeod & Owens, 2004). Moreover, African American and Hispanic adolescents report lower life satisfaction compared to their non-Hispanic White peers (Zullig et al., 2005), and Asian American adolescents (6–12 grades) report lower life satisfaction compared to their Black and Latino peers (Greene et al., 2006). Data from the UK also point to a similar trend toward decreased life satisfaction, yet reduced anxiety, among the youth of Black/African/Caribbean/Black British origin compared to their White counterparts (Department for Education, 2019).

The racial differences in well-being may be attributed to discrimination that minorities experience and therefore research has examined the psychological correlates of discrimination, particularly in adolescence. During this period, adolescents understand the social stratification and discrimination that goes with it in more abstract terms. As this is the period during which they are actively engaged in identity formation, experiencing discrimination may be particularly harmful. This can be more challenging as more mature coping strategies are still in the process of development. Benner et al. (2018) conducted a meta-analysis of 214 studies to determine the effect of perceived discrimination (e.g., frequency) on indicators of social-emotional stress (e.g., depression anxiety, loneliness, somatic complaints), positive well-being (e.g., life satisfaction, self-control), scholastic achievement (e.g., GPA, academic motivation), and engagement in risky behaviors (e.g., substance use, connection to deviant groups). A small to moderate effect size (.24) was found between discrimination and socioemotional distress. When considering specific indices of social-emotional stress, the strongest correlations were found between discrimination and depression (.26) and between discrimination and internalizing symptoms

(.26). The relationships between perceived racial/ethnic discrimination and positive well-being (−.14) and self-esteem (−.17) were of smaller effect size. A small effect size (−.10) was also observed between discrimination and academics. When examining the connection between perceived racial/ethnic discrimination and specific aspects of adolescents' academic performance, the effect sizes were small but significant for GPA (−.09), school engagement (−.14), and motivation (−.11). Lastly, the overall correlation between discrimination and risky behaviors was of moderate effect size (.20). The strongest correlation was found between discrimination and externalizing behaviors (.24). Smaller correlations were observed for the relationship between discrimination and substance use (.13), deviant peer affiliations (.15), and risky sexual behaviors (.16). Moreover, the researchers examined the potential moderator effect of multiple variables. The negative association between discrimination and social-emotional stress was higher among Asian and Latino adolescents than those of African descent, and the connection between racial discrimination and academic outcomes was stronger in the group of Latino descent than African descent, and this was even stronger among male adolescents of Latino descent. The authors suggested that African American parents are more likely to employ socialization strategies that prepare their children for coping with discriminatory experiences. Lastly, the association with social-emotional stress was higher in the US than in other countries but the negative association with academics was more prominent in countries other than the US and specifically in Australia. Younger adolescents were more likely to experience social-emotional stress in relation to racial discrimination than older adolescents and the period of transitioning to high school increased the negative association between academics and discrimination. Presumably, not having developed mature coping strategies or facing challenging transitions moderated the impact of discrimination. Lastly, having more specific experiences with discrimination was a more important moderator than cumulative perceived discrimination over the years.

Having a strong racial/ethnic identity has been considered a protective factor against the effects of discrimination. Chavous et al. (2008), for example, reported that during the transition to high school racial centrality moderated the relationship between discrimination and academic performance. Other researchers have examined the protective role of a strong ethnic identity against personal and group discrimination. In a group of immigrant adolescents, Stevens and Thijs (2018) found that personal discrimination was associated with worse self-esteem while group discrimination was associated with internalizing and externalizing problems, thus supporting the idea that group discrimination is threatening and damaging. Moreover, those with a weak ethnic identity and high perceived group discrimination reported more internalizing problems. Identifying strongly with the group may be a protective factor because being a part of the group produces feelings of belonging, connectedness, and pride in adolescents. Bratt (2015) expanded this research by examining the role of belonging to small groups (like family and friends) as well as large groups (ethnic and national) in the well-being of minority adolescents. Participants were 8th to 10th graders from Norway and belonged to various ethnic groups (Turks 18%, Pakistanis 10%, Vietnamese 9%, Indians 7%, other Asian ethnic groups 15%, Albanians 7%, Iraqis 9%, Nordic 5%, and from other European countries 14%). Well-being was indicated by measures of self-esteem, mental health problems, and life satisfaction. The findings supported that identification with small groups, especially family, predicted self-esteem, life satisfaction, and mental health outcomes in a longitudinal design, whereas ethnic and national identity had no causal effects despite correlating with well-being dimensions. These findings imply that small-group identities are potential covariates of ethnic identity. Future longitudinal studies may further explore the predictors of the well-being of minority children.

While several factors moderate the association between racial/ethnic discrimination and well-being outcomes, the specific mechanisms that explain the link are less clear. The relationship may be mediated by stress. Some evidence indicates that discrimination-related stress partially mediates the link between encountering discrimination and depression among Black middle schoolers (Lanier et al., 2017). Discrimination-related stress may derive from other sources as well because social stratification and differential treatment can occur across multiple levels and social markers (e.g., gender, poverty, obesity, and sexual minority). Adolescents' social identities often overlap and can result in greater marginalization and mistreatment. However, psychological research has not sufficiently recognized the fact that many youths possess multiple, intersecting social identities that make them vulnerable to stigmatization. The cumulative or nuanced effects of intersecting identities are still an open question.

In conclusion, research shows that perceived discrimination is associated with negative socioemotional outcomes, such as depression, anxiety, low self-esteem, decreased life satisfaction, as well as reduced academic achievement, and increased engagement in risky behaviors. The effect of discrimination on mental health varies across different racial and ethnic groups, with some groups experiencing stronger negative associations between discrimination and well-being. Factors such as age, gender, socialization strategies, and the development of coping mechanisms can moderate the impact of discrimination on an individual's mental health. Additionally, identification with specific ethnic or social groups may serve as a protective factor for some minority adolescents, providing a sense of belonging and connectedness. While the role of stress caused by discrimination has been partially explored, the specific ways in which racial prejudice impacts mental health are still not fully understood. Moreover, the research has not yet adequately addressed the psychological well-being of adolescents with complex, intersecting social identities.

Protecting Well-Being in Poor Contexts

Childhood poverty has profound effects on physical and psychological health. Addressing socioeconomic disparities is important to provide children from all backgrounds with equal opportunities for healthy development, educational achievement, and happiness. Interventions should target not only academic support but also address the broader socioeconomic context to help children develop the necessary cognitive, social, and emotional skills for happiness and success. Attempts to address achievement gaps and other disparities have included interventions that build psychological strengths, such as character development and social-emotional learning skills. Programs that build self-regulation, optimism, and persistence improve both life satisfaction and academic performance. Social-emotional learning interventions train parents and teachers to improve their management style, make fewer critical statements, and support the social-emotional needs of their students. One such program, called ParentCorps (Mihalic, 2016), was designed to enhance self-regulation skills in children from disadvantaged backgrounds. The program sought to increase parental involvement in the children's education, provide effective behavior management strategies, and encourage positive behavior support for parents and teachers. Research shows that children in schools using the ParentCorps program had higher kindergarten achievement scores and teacher-rated academic performance compared to children in control schools. Additionally, parenting knowledge, behavior support, and teacher-related parent involvement were improved (Allee-Herndon & Roberts, 2019). These results suggest that a universal family-centered intervention like ParentCorps has the potential to improve academic achievement for children living in poverty or disadvantaged urban neighborhoods. Lastly, early interventions are critical. Beginning with kindergarten, programs aiming at improving self-regulation and executive function had positive effects on reasoning, attention control, and stress levels, and led to improvements in reading, vocabulary, and math skills that persisted into 1st grade. The effects were particularly strong in high-poverty schools, suggesting that such interventions could help close the achievement gap for disadvantaged students (Allee-Herndon & Roberts, 2019).

Improving the physical environment children are raised in requires advanced planning. According to Forsyth (2020), communities that support healthy development should address the rights of children for protection, health care, education, safe neighborhoods, places to play and meet with others, green spaces to grow plants and interact with animals, unpolluted air and water, and equal access to all services regardless of background and family of origin. The research reviewed here points to the importance of accessing green spaces as means to improve psychological adjustment, happiness, and life satisfaction. At the very least, all communities should provide green recreation areas such as parks and safe paths and crossings leading to such areas.

Children can discern poverty and their SES from a young age, and they may be aware of stereotypes related to being poor, which could potentially impact their stress levels and self-perception. Poverty-related stereotype threats are amplified by race and gender. Empowering children to deal with discrimination is at the hands of parents, teachers, and child practitioners. Conversations about racism and discrimination may be different depending on the child's age, but it is recommended that they start early regardless of the family's racial or ethnic background. Children notice differences and treatment disparities from an early age, and discussing these topics can help them appreciate diversity and recognize discrimination. Conversations about diversity and discrimination are particularly crucial for children who are more likely to be targets of discrimination, as it can prepare them to cope with related stress. Children under 5 years of age can be taught to recognize differences as beautiful variations in human existence. Parents and teachers may introduce children to diverse cultures and people, and enjoy their food, stories, and films. Adults should promptly and comfortably answer young children's questions about race and talk about the unfairness, a concept they grasp, in racism. For children in middle childhood, conversations can relate to children's own experiences with discrimination, whether they are personal or not. Children can discuss stereotypes and racial bias portrayed in the media with trusting adults. Everyone should be mindful of racial bias in books and films and choose ones with varied representation. Teachers and parents may engage children to address racism at school and explore history together to understand the present. These activities are appropriate for adolescents as well who may additionally be encouraged to take action to promote awareness and stop discrimination. For adults to be effective, they need to reflect on their own biases and ensure that their actions challenge racism, demonstrate kindness, and promote dignity and respect for all (UNICEF, 2020). Celebrating race and skin color from a very young age supports positive self-esteem and builds the foundation for a strong racial/ethnic identity that plays a supportive role in adolescence when children understand discrimination as a multilayered concept (e.g., historical, psychosocial).

In conclusion, addressing socioeconomic disparities and providing interventions that target not only academic support but also the broader socioeconomic context and physical environment are crucial for providing children from all backgrounds with equal opportunities for healthy development, happiness, and educational achievement. Programs that build psychological strengths and improve self-regulation skills, along with access to green spaces, can positively impact children's physical and psychological health. Additionally, empowering children to deal with discrimination through conversations about diversity and racism from a young age can prepare them to cope with related stress and promote positive self-esteem and a strong racial/ethnic identity.

References

Allee-Herndon, K. A., & Roberts, S. K. (2019). Poverty, self-regulation, and executive function, and learning in K-2 classrooms: A systematic literature review of current empirical research. *Journal of Research in Childhood Education, 33*(3), 345–362. https://doi.org/10.1080/02568543.2019.1613273

American Academy of Pediatrics. (2019). The lifelong effects of early childhood adversity and toxic stress. *Pediatrics, 129*(1), e232–e246. https://doi.org/10.1542/peds.2011-2663

Barrera-Hernández, L. F., Sotelo-Castillo, M. A., Echeverría-Castro, S. B., & Tapia-Fonllem, C. O. (2020). Connectedness to nature: Its impact on sustainable behaviors and happiness in children. *Frontiers in Psychology*, 276. https://doi.org/10.3389/fpsyg.2020.00276

Benner, A. D., Wang, Y., Shen, Y., Boyle, A. E., Polk, R., & Cheng, Y. P. (2018). Racial/ethnic discrimination and well-being during adolescence: A meta-analytic review. *American Psychologist, 73*(7), 855. https://doi.org/10.1037/amp0000204

Bratt, C. (2015). One of few or one of many: Social identification and psychological well-being among minority youth. *British Journal of Social Psychology, 54*(4), 671–694. https://doi.org/10.1111/bjso.12105

Chavous, T. M., Rivas-Drake, D., Smalls, C., Griffin, T., & Cogburn, C. (2008). Gender matters, too: The influences of school racial discrimination and racial identity on academic engagement outcomes among African American adolescents. *Developmental Psychology, 44*(3), 637. https://doi.org/10.1037/0012-1649.44.3.637

Dailey, S., & Bergelson, E. (2021). Language input to infants of different socioeconomic statuses: A quantitative meta-analysis. *Developmental Science, 25*(3). https://doi.org/10.1111/desc.13192

Department for Education. (2019). *State of the nation 2019: Children and young people's well-being*. Department for Education. Retrieved April 23, 2012, from https://files.eric.ed.gov/fulltext/ED601921.pdf

Evans, G. W., & Cassells, R. C. (2014). Childhood poverty, cumulative risk exposure, and mental health in emerging adults. *Clinical Psychological Science, 2*(3), 287–296. https://doi.org/10.1177/2167702613501496

Evans, G. W., & Kim, P. (2013). Childhood poverty, chronic stress, self-regulation, and coping. *Child Development Perspectives, 7*(1), 43–48. https://doi.org/10.1111/cdep.12013

Evans, G. W., Li, D., & Whipple, S. S. (2013). Cumulative risk and child development. *Psychological Bulletin, 139*(6), 1342. https://doi.org/10.1037/a0031808

Feng, X., & Astell-Burt, T. (2017a). Do greener areas promote more equitable child health? *Health & Place, 46*, 267–273. https://doi.org/10.1016/j.healthplace.2017.05.006

Feng, X., & Astell-Burt, T. (2017b). Residential green space quantity and quality and child well-being: A longitudinal study. *American Journal of Preventive Medicine, 53*(5), 616–624. https://doi.org/10.1016/j.amepre.2017.06.035

Ferguson, K. T., Cassells, R. C., MacAllister, J. W., & Evans, G. W. (2013). The physical environment and child development: An international review. *International Journal of Psychology, 48*(4), 437–468. https://doi.org/10.1080/00207594.2013.804190

Forsyth, A. (2020). What is a healthy place? Models for cities and neighborhoods. *Journal of Urban Design, 25*(2), 186–202. https://doi.org/10.1080/13574809.2019.1662718

Green, E. (2019, November 6). Flint's children suffer in class after years of drinking the lead-poisoned water. *The New York Times*. www.nytimes.com/2019/11/06/us/politics/flint-michigan-schools.html

Greene, M. L., Way, N., & Pahl, K. (2006). Trajectories of perceived adult and peer discrimination among Black, Latino, and Asian American adolescents: Patterns and psychological correlates. *Developmental Psychology, 42*(2), 218–236. https://doi.org/10.1037/0012-1649.42.2.218

Gubbels, J. S., Kremers, S. P., Droomers, M., Hoefnagels, C., Stronks, K., Hosman, C., & de Vries, S. (2016). The impact of greenery on physical activity and mental health of adolescent and adult residents of deprived neighborhoods: A longitudinal study. *Health & Place, 40*, 153–160. https://doi.org/10.1016/j.healthplace.2016.06.002

Heberle, A. E., & Carter, A. S. (2015). Cognitive aspects of young children's experience of economic disadvantage. *Psychological Bulletin, 141*(4), 723. https://doi.org/10.1037/bul0000010

Homel, R., & Burns, A. (1989). Environmental quality and the well-being of children. *Social Indicators Research, 21*(2), 133–158. https://doi.org/10.1007/BF00300500

Keltner, D., Bowman, R., & Richards, H. (2017). *Exploring the emotional state of 'real happiness': A study into the effects of watching natural history television content*. Retrieved

April 22, 2023, from https://cms.bbcearth.com/sites/default/files/2022-04/bbcw-real-happiness-white-paper-final-v2–58ac1df7_2.pdf

Kennedy, M. (2016, April 20). Lead-laced water in Flint: A step-by-step look at the makings of a crisis. *NPR*. Retrieved May 17, 2023, from www.npr.org/sections/thetwo-way/2016/04/20/465545378/lead-laced-water-in-flint-a-step-by-step-look-at-the-makings-of-a-crisis

Lanier, Y., Sommers, M. S., Fletcher, J., Sutton, M. Y., & Roberts, D. D. (2017). Examining racial discrimination frequency, racial discrimination stress, and psychological well-being among Black early adolescents. *Journal of Black Psychology*, *43*(3), 219–229. https://doi.org/10.1177/0095798416638189

McLeod, J. D., & Owens, T. J. (2004). Psychological well-being in the early life course: Variations by socioeconomic status, gender, and race/ethnicity. *Social Psychology Quarterly*, *67*(3), 257–278. https://doi.org/10.1177/019027250406700303

Mihalic, S. (2016). *ParentCorps*. Retrieved May 17, 2023, from www.blueprintsprograms.com/program-costs/parentcorps

National Center for Education Statistics. (2019). *Status and trends in the education of racial and ethnic groups 2018*. Retrieved May 17, 2023, from https://nces.ed.gov/pubs2019/2019038.pdf

Nordbø, E. C. A., Raanaas, R. K., Nordh, H., & Aamodt, G. (2020). Disentangling how the built environment relates to children's well-being: Participation in leisure activities as a mediating pathway among 8-year-olds based on the Norwegian Mother and Child Cohort Study. *Health & Place*, *64*, 102360. https://doi.org/10.1016/j.healthplace.2020.102360

Olson, L., Chen, B., & Fishman, I. (2021). Neural correlates of socioeconomic status in early childhood: A systematic review of the literature. *Child Neuropsychology*, *27*(3), 390–423. https://doi.org/10.1080/09297049.2021.1879766

Olszewski-Kubilius, P., & Corwith, S. (2018). Poverty, academic achievement, and giftedness: A literature review. *Gifted Child Quarterly*, *62*(1), 37–55. https://doi.org/10.1177/00169862177380

Pew Research Center. (2020). *Amid protests, majorities across racial and ethnic groups express support for the Black Lives Matter movement*. Retrieved May 17, 2023, from www.pewresearch.org/social-trends/2020/06/12/amid-protests-majorities-across-racial-and-ethnic-groups-express-support-for-the-black-lives-matter-movement/

Ryabov, I. (2020). Intergenerational transmission of socioeconomic status: The role of neighborhood effects. *Journal of Adolescence*, *80*, 84–97. https://doi.org/10.1016/j.adolescence.2020.02.007

Stevens, G. W., & Thijs, J. (2018). Perceived group discrimination and psychological well-being in ethnic minority adolescents. *Journal of Applied Social Psychology*, *48*(10), 559–570. https://doi.org/10.1111/jasp.12547

UNICEF. (2020). *Talking to your kids about racism*. Retrieved April 24, 2023, from www.unicef.org/parenting/talking-to-your-kids-about-racism

UNICEF. (2021). *Child poverty*. Retrieved May 17, 2023, from https://data.unicef.org/topic/child-poverty/

U.S. Census Bureau. (2020). *Income and poverty in the United States: 2019*. Retrieved May 17, 2023, from www.census.gov/library/publications/2020/demo/p60-270.html

U.S. Census Bureau. (2021). *Annual estimates of the resident population by sex, age, race, alone or in combination, and Hispanic origin for the United States: April 1, 2020, to July 1, 2021*. Retrieved May 17, 2023, from www.census.gov/data/tables/time-series/demo/popest/2020s-national-detail.html

Ward, J. S., Duncan, J. S., Jarden, A., & Stewart, T. (2016). The impact of children's exposure to greenspace on physical activity, cognitive development, emotional well-being, and ability to appraise risk. *Health & Place*, *40*, 44–50. https://doi.org/10.1016/j.healthplace.2016.04.015

Whitten, T., Stevens, R., Ructtinger, L., Tzoumakis, S., Green, M. J., Laurens, K. R., Holbrook, A., & Carr, V. J. (2018). Connection to the natural environment and well-being in middle childhood. *Ecopsychology*, *10*(4), 270–279. https://doi.org/10.1089/eco.2018.0010

Zullig, K. J., Valois, R. F., Huebner, E. S., & Drane, J. W. (2005). Associations among family structure, demographics, and adolescent perceived life satisfaction. *Journal of Child and Family Studies*, *14*, 195–206. https://doi.org/10.1007/s10826-005-5047-3

Part 4

Conclusions

13 Pillars of Happiness and Success

The INSPIRE Model

Happiness and success are integral parts of well-being.

The purpose of this book was to unravel what makes children happy and successful by taking a holistic and developmental approach. The book posited that the journey toward happiness and success is a lifelong endeavor in which children must actively participate to realize their optimal functioning. Adults need to address children's needs and teach them how to become happy and successful despite individual and contextual influences. In doing so, the book considered primarily the research that has utilized children and adolescents as informants to give voice to their perspective on happiness, life satisfaction, and success. These variables were measured by instruments that tapped into global assessments of how one feels at the moment but also cognitive appraisals about one's life. Additionally, studies that focused on other variables of positive functioning like self-esteem and prosocial behaviors were also included. References to psychopathology such as internalizing (e.g., anxiety, depression, fear) and externalizing (e.g., defiance, aggression) symptoms were mentioned when research on positive outcomes was lacking or when studies included both positive and negative indices of well-being.

The studies reviewed in the book tested concepts from the adult psychological model of happiness and research on children's socioemotional and academic functioning to identify the factors that are indeed related to children's happiness and success. This chapter presents the book's findings regarding the contributions to happiness and success of the following factors: relationships, positive emotions, flow, spirituality, physical well-being, self-control, mindsets, executive functions, personality, intelligence, consumerism, materialism, digital media, poverty, physical environment, and discrimination. These conclusions are then evaluated in light of the PERMA plus model, which partially inspired this book, and the self-determination theory (Deci & Ryan, 2012), a theory of well-being that is referenced several times in the book. This evaluation leads to a new conceptual model of happiness and success to better reflect the elements of well-being that emerged from the literature. The proposed model is called INSPIRE and is based on seven pillars: Individual strengths

DOI: 10.4324/9780429356414-18

and traits, Nurturing relationships, Self-regulation, Physical health, Independence, Realizing competence, and Engagement.

The research reviewed in *Chapter 1: Relationships* supported the significance of relationships in self-perceptions of happiness and life satisfaction. Beginning in the preschool period, children recognized their family as a source of happiness and highlighted the need to fulfill needs and achieve personal goals to feel happy. Older children were able to identify the characteristics of interactions with others and the nature of the relationships that contributed to their well-being. The research showed that children and adolescents believed that supportive parents, teachers, and peers were a great source of their happiness. Strength-based parenting, specifically, was related to life satisfaction, increased positive affect, and decreased negative affect in adolescents because such parenting promoted autonomy, competence, and positive relationships with others.

Regarding the role of positive emotions discussed in *Chapter 2: Feeling Good*, research showed that experiencing gratitude, hope, and being optimistic by nature were linked to happiness and positive self-appraisals in school-age children. Furthermore, nurturing an optimistic explanatory style protected from depression. Positive emotions were essential in building positive relationships. Gratitude, for example, made relationships feel more fulfilling. Optimism and hope were supported by a strong sense of agency and in turn further supported a strong autonomous self. Research showed that teaching children emotional awareness and cognitive strategies to regulate emotions allowed them to engage in goal-directed behaviors that enhanced life satisfaction and positive affect, and down-regulated negative affect.

Chapter 3: Solitude and Flow showed that evidence of engagement in the form of flow experiences was limited in young children although it was expected that children have the capacity for deep engagement in enjoyable activities. Research revealed that most children and adolescents did not think favorably of solitude although adolescents acknowledged its benefits for promoting autonomy and identity formation. Children were more likely to benefit from solitude if they had positive attitudes towards solitude, were socially competent, and did not feel lonely in their personal relationships. The evidence further suggested that children and adolescents who had self-control and confidence were more likely to experience flow and that parents with adaptive control and unconditional love created opportunities for flow experiences. In turn, flow was linked to increased happiness and greater accomplishments.

In *Chapter 4: Spirituality*, the review demonstrated that the most significant forms of spirituality connected with happiness were the personal and communal types. Children who have a sense of identity, love for life, and sense of meaning in life, as well as children who are oriented towards others and exhibit respect, trust, and forgiveness, tended to be happier and reported higher life satisfaction. Having a sense of wonder and unity with the world related to happiness in children who spent time in nature. As children moved into adolescence, all forms of spirituality, as well as religiosity, connected with well-being. Practicing mindfulness as a secular form of spirituality seemed beneficial. In school settings, mindfulness interventions reduced externalizing and internalizing symptoms. Mindfulness built self-awareness and supported self-regulation by decreasing emotional reactivity and activating cognitive mechanisms that fight rumination and intrusive thoughts. Therefore, mindfulness and other spiritual experiences were encouraged in families and schools. Specifically, the literature suggested that spirituality was nurtured by unconditional love at home and respectful and caring relationships at school.

Chapter 5: Sound Body, Sound Mind reviewed the effects that physical health had on happiness and success. There was undeniable evidence that physical activity, health, and sleep were all significant influences. Moderate to vigorous activity was related to reduced stress, increased happiness, life satisfaction, and positive affect. Physical activity also improved cognition and academic outcomes, especially as children got older. Perceived health predicted life satisfaction and global happiness. Dietary behaviors that promoted health were also related to subjective well-being. Lastly, adequate sleep duration, high quality of sleep, and fewer sleep problems predicted global ratings of happiness in middle childhood and adolescence.

The book additionally explored factors that in the literature appear to affect academic outcomes and life accomplishments and hence, it examined developmental research on self-control, cognitive control, and children's theories about their abilities. *Chapter 6: The Power of Thinking Right* showed that children's ideas about their successes and failures influenced their accomplishments and perceptions about their competence. Research supported the existence of two mindsets, the growth and the fixed. While children might have a growth mindset in one area and not another, inducing a growth mindset encouraged greater effort and persistence on academic tasks. Research did not show the benefits of the growth mindset compared to the fixed mindset if students were confident in their abilities, but growth mindset intervention resulted in small benefits in academic outcomes compared to no intervention. Moreover, the effect that a growth mindset had on mental health was twice as high as the effect of a growth mindset on academic performance. There was increasing agreement that the growth mindset better explained recovery from setbacks than academic achievement. A concept related to a growth mindset is grit, which combines perseverance and passion in the pursuit of long-term goals. Some evidence supported that grit related to improved academic outcomes, higher life satisfaction, positive affect, and decreased negative affect and depression, at least in adolescence.

Chapter 7: Self Control identified several trends about self-control and success despite the diversity in definitions and measurements. The review in this chapter included studies that considered self-control as the ability to control impulses in favor of more desired responses. In tasks where impulsive emotion had to be controlled such as in delay of gratification tasks, there was a clear association between time of delaying and academic outcomes. However, the association was stronger in tasks that required control of impulsive movement. Moreover, pure impulse control (without deployment of cognitive processes) in preschool provided an academic boost in adolescence. Evidence from self-reports and behavioral tasks demonstrated that the relationship between self-control and academic and social competence began in the preschool period and stretched into adolescence. Better dispositional control of impulses in early childhood protected adults' physical and mental health problems. In adolescence, self-control was compromised by reward-seeking tendencies and impulsive adolescents were more likely to engage in risk-taking. Self-control ultimately supported children's autonomy because it allowed them to optimize their opportunities and direct their skills and motivations toward goals of their own choosing.

In *Chapter 8: Cognitive Control*, the review focused on executive functions and their associations with academic outcomes. There was indeed a strong connection as improvements in executive functions were accompanied by gains in academic performance, while deficits in executive functions were linked to learning difficulties and mental health problems. Evidence from cross-sectional and longitudinal studies supported these relationships in the preschool and school-age periods. Evidence also suggested that deficits in generalized and specific executive functions were considered risk factors for emotional, behavioral, and psychotic disorders. There was strong evidence that exposure to childhood adversity negatively impacted children's executive functions by increasing their stress levels and interfering with their brain development. The negative effects of stress on executive functions may be higher in younger children, while older children may experience a stress inoculation effect. Poverty was a major risk factor that can have lasting effects on children's ability to succeed, with parental care, maternal sensitivity, and home enrichment being significant mediators between low socioeconomic status and executive functions in affluent countries, while stunting was a significant mediator in low-income countries. Mindfulness, physical activity, and cognitive behavioral interventions improved executive functions. Moreover, opportunities for unstructured time and independent thinking and action supported executive functions in children.

This book extended the review to the influences of individual and contextual characteristics on happiness and success in children. *Chapter 9: Individual Differences Matter* explored the connection that personality characteristics and intelligence have with happiness and success. Beginning with temperament, effortful control, which is a precursor to conscientiousness, consistently emerged as a major predictor of academic performance, competence, and adjustment. Negative emotionality, a likely precursor to neuroticism, negatively correlated with academic outcomes and school adjustment and positively with internalizing and externalizing problems. Moderate levels of agreeableness and extraversion and high conscientiousness were positive predictors of academic achievement. The effects of conscientiousness and agreeableness were also powerful predictors of academic attainment, behavior conduct, social competence, and health-related outcomes. Personality traits that enhance self-efficacy like low neuroticism and high extroversion related also to higher positive affect and life satisfaction. Chapter 9 also revealed that individual differences in intelligence were critical in predicting academic performance and long-term success. Heredity plays a significant role in determining individual variations in intelligence, with studies showing that genetic makeup accounted for about half of the variability in children's intelligence scores. Meta-analytic studies consistently demonstrated a strong correlation between IQ scores and academic performance, especially in math, science, and reading. This correlation increased during childhood and adolescence, reflecting the growing importance of intelligence in education and the development of abstract reasoning, processing speed, and executive functions. In addition, the general intelligence factor (factor g) had been shown to be a stronger predictor of academic outcomes than specific subtest scores, validating the use of overall intelligence scores for diagnosing academic or learning difficulties. Intelligence also had a long-term impact on socioeconomic success in adulthood, with childhood and adolescent IQ scores correlating with occupational status, income, and educational attainment.

In line with Aristotle's theory of happiness that stipulates living a virtuous life is a happy life (Ross et al., 2009), *Chapter 10: Character Matters* explored character strengths that included moral virtues such as justice but also sets of skills and abilities that are learned, taught, and practiced, like temperance. In early childhood, prosocial behaviors like kindness and sharing were associated with happiness in children. In school age, hope, gratitude, and love were predictive of subjective well-being. Zest, perseverance, love of learning, hope, teamwork, social intelligence, and self-regulation predicted academic outcomes and school functioning. Furthermore, interventions that developed character strengths improved subjective well-being whether they focused on socioemotional learning or moral development. Character strengths also empowered children to avoid risky behaviors but in excess, some could put children at risk. Therefore, temperance emerged as an important character strength to cultivate.

Expanding the factors to cultural values and contextual characteristics, the book reviewed how consumerism, materialism, consumption of digital media, poverty, the physical environment, and discrimination relate to subjective well-being. *Chapter 11: Consumerism, Materialism, and Digital Media* showed that consumerism was linked to lower self-esteem, increased depression, and anxiety although emotion regulation moderated this relationship. Materialism was associated with emotional and behavioral problems, lower goal-directedness, lower academic performance, higher envy, and reduced prosocial behaviors. These results pertained to school-age children and adolescents. Consumption of digital media was also associated with numerous negative outcomes that intensified when consumption reached the level of addiction. In early childhood, behavior problems and deficits in cognitive function, language, and communication were observed. At school age, negative outcomes included lower life quality, lower self-esteem, poor school functioning, and lower academic achievement. In adolescence, the negative outcomes included poor mental health, lower happiness and life satisfaction, health and sleep problems, exposure to risky behavior, privacy concerns, cyberbullying, and sexting. The review demonstrated some potential positive outcomes as digital media could be tools for communication and engagement, advocacy, gaining information, finding a community, and a place for self-disclosure. Theories speculated that outcomes can be positive or negative depending on how children use digital media, their characteristics, developmental challenges, and the relationship between real and cyber self-representations.

Lastly, *Chapter 12: Poverty, Physical Environment, and Discrimination* explored the impact of contextual risk factors on well-being and the capacity to experience happiness and success. The review revealed that a considerable percentage of young children in the United States live in families facing multiple risk factors. Longitudinal evidence showed that cumulative risks associated with poverty impacted psychological well-being, with childhood poverty predicting externalizing problems and learned helplessness. Childhood poverty also disrupted self-regulation and coping, as low-income children often exhibited deficits in self-regulation, leading to compromised attention control, working memory, inhibitory control, delay of gratification, and planning. Furthermore, low-income adolescents were more likely to use disengagement coping strategies, resulting in increased internalizing, externalizing, and social difficulties. Poverty significantly impacted children's educational achievement from birth, with disparities in language exposure, cognitive development, and school readiness being evident between children from higher and lower socioeconomic backgrounds. Research also identified associations between low socioeconomic status and neurodevelopment in early childhood, suggesting that a poor context has far-reaching implications for children's brain development during a sensitive period that may impact their learning abilities. The review in Chapter 12 also revealed that the immediate physical environment, including home and neighborhood characteristics, had a significant influence on the well-being of children living in poverty. Environmental factors such as poor housing maintenance, rental occupancy, commercial street types, and low neighborhood quality negatively contributed to children's overall life satisfaction and emotional and social adjustment. Housing type and quality, as well as residential density (e.g., crowed households), influenced children's academic achievement, socioemotional well-being, self-esteem, and parent-child interactions. The neighborhood's educational status, level of cumulative stressors, and noise levels also played a role in children's psychological well-being and cognitive development. Access to natural settings such as play areas and green parks had a significant positive connection with improved psychological well-being and reduced internalizing and externalizing problems. Additionally, spending time in green spaces was linked to higher happiness, life satisfaction, and increased engagement in prosocial behaviors. Lastly, Chapter 12 illustrated how perceived discrimination was associated with depression, anxiety, low self-esteem, decreased life satisfaction, increased risky behaviors, and reduced academic achievement. Factors such as age, gender, socialization strategies, and the development of coping mechanisms moderated the impact of discrimination. Additionally, identification with specific ethnic or social groups served as a protective factor for some minority adolescents, providing a sense of belonging and connectedness.

The conclusions resulting from this book, as just outlined, render support for applying the PERMA plus model (Seligman, 2011) of adult subjective well-being to understand the factors that make children happy and successful. The evidence implies that relationships, positive emotions, flow experiences, physical health, spirituality, and character strengths are sources that optimize living across the life span. Taking a developmental perspective, the book demonstrated that the centrality of these factors in well-being varies due to children's ongoing development.

For instance, gratitude as a positive emotion was not understood and appreciated until children have more advanced perspective-taking and introspection skills. Solitary activities and flow as meaningful experiences developed more in adolescence although children had the capacity for deep immersion in their interests. The book unveiled that positive relationships and physical health played a central role in children's well-being from a young age. In addition, the book identified mindsets, personal characteristics, and regulatory processes as important factors that support accomplishments in the form of academic outcomes and beliefs about competence.

The evidence here also supports the self-determination theory (Deci & Ryan, 2012) which postulates that well-being derives from fulfilling three innate psychological needs of relatedness, competence, and autonomy. Relatedness refers to a feeling of being connected to others, having a sense of belonging, and being cared for. This component is similar to the element of relationships in the PERMA plus model and was supported by the evidence in this book. The component of competence in the self-determination theory is a feeling that one is effective and capable and is similar to the element of accomplishments in the PERMA plus model, which was also supported in this book. The component of autonomy refers to being self-directed and having a sense that actions are self-endorsed and aligned with one's values. This component is not highlighted in PERMA plus, but it is a significant element that emerged in this book. For example, preschoolers recognize the importance of agency in accomplishing goals and older children state that parenting that supports autonomy contributes to their happiness and life satisfaction. In addition, the book revealed the central role that regulatory processes played in achieving happiness and success, and therefore this factor deserves a stronger acknowledgment. The self-determination theory considers self-regulation as an outcome of the interaction between its components. It is speculated that when children meet their needs for competence, autonomy, and relatedness they are more likely to accept behavior standards and apply them to regulate thoughts, emotions, and behaviors. As this may be the case, recognizing regulatory processes such as self-control and executive functions offers a path to parents and adults who work with children to support these processes and optimize children's functioning. Lastly, this book identified several individual characteristics whether they are personality traits, intelligence, or characters strengths that influence perceptions of happiness, life satisfaction, academic outcomes, and other successes.

The conclusions presented in this book regarding what makes children happy and successful may better be organized under a new conceptual framework that emphasizes the main roles of relationships, engagement, physical health, autonomy, competence, and individual characteristics and provides a straightforward approach for parents, educators, and child practitioners to enhance well-being. The proposed model is called INSPIRE derived from the initials of its seven pillars: *Individual traits and strengths*, *Nurturing relationships*, *Self-regulation*, *Physical health*, *Independence*, *Realizing competence*, and *Engagement*. The INSPIRE model integrates the main elements of PERMA plus and the self-determination theory but also highlights the unique characteristics of the child and puts physical health and self-regulation at the foreground. The seven pillars of happiness and success are described in detail here.

Individual Traits and Strengths. This component highlights that each child is unique, with a specific set of inherited and acquired traits (e.g., conscientiousness and agreeableness), character strengths (e.g., perseverance or grit), and vulnerabilities (e.g., high negative emotionality). It encourages parents to discover, acknowledge, and nurture the individual traits and strengths of their children to promote personal growth and well-being.

Nurturing Relationships. This part of the model emphasizes the importance of relationships in a child's life, from parents, siblings, and extended family, to friends, teachers, and the broader community. Beginning with a secure attachment, infants who receive responsive parenting develop a sense of connectedness and personal effectiveness that provide the foundation of future relationships and self-regulation. Having faith in the effectiveness of one's actions to fulfill personal needs instills determination, persistence, and flexibility. Approaching challenges with assurance from people empowers children to overcome obstacles. When combined, these attitudes enable children to succeed even when confronted with adversity. Relationships with others are a great source of fun, pleasure, and laughter but also hope, love, gratitude, and other positive emotions that add meaning to life, enrich children's confidence in themselves as relational partners, and enhance perceived happiness.

Self-Regulation. This component refers to the developing regulatory processes including impulse control, cognitive control, and emotion and behavior regulation, as they were discussed in this book. The model acknowledges that to some extent, regulatory processes are non-volitional and depend on temperamental dispositions inherent to the child. During early childhood, with increasing emotional understanding, parents transition from controlling their children's emotional responses to teaching emotion regulation strategies. Preschoolers rely heavily on social support to regulate emotions and make some attempts to problem-solve or distract themselves. Controlled, voluntary, and intentional regulatory processes like cognitive appraisal rely on executive functions that develop more fully in middle and late childhood. Emotion coaching, social-emotional learning, and executive function interventions support self-regulation. Self-regulation processes play a significant role in optimizing functioning.

Physical Health. This element recognizes that physical wellness in the form of physical activity, health, and healthy dietary and sleep habits is a major contributor to subjective well-being and success. For example, physical activity enhances happiness, academic performance, cognitive skills, and other positive indices of well-being such as self-esteem and self-control.

Independence. Fostering independence or autonomy allows children to successfully pursue specific goals and feel successful. These goals may be relational or aim at self-improvement thus enhancing relationships and growth. Preschoolers recognize the role of agency in feeling happiness and older children identify parenting that supports their autonomy as a source of happiness and life satisfaction. Promoting optimism as an explanatory style and teaching hope promote independence and subjective well-being.

Realizing Competence. This component refers to the development of ideas and beliefs about the self and its effectiveness when pursuing goals. Perceiving the self as competent is related to positive psychological functioning and is considered essential to realizing the full human potential in varied settings. Enhancing a growth mindset and grit is likely to build self-efficacy and positive appraisals of the self. Because children and adolescents are consumers of digital media, realizing competence in virtual settings is also significant. Additionally, parents may consider how value systems like materialism may negatively affect positive self-evaluations.

Engagement. This element refers to the way children and adolescents engage with the world and the transcendent to create meaningful, immersive, creative, and emotionally impactful experiences. Flow experiences and actions that generate positive emotions such as prosocial acts belong to this pillar. Spiritual experiences that connect children with others, nature, and the transcendent enhance happiness and success. These types of engagement are abundant sources of positive emotions like gratitude and hope which promote happiness.

The INSPIRE model acknowledges that each child's journey toward happiness and success is unique and influenced by many factors. This model aligns with a strength-based approach, accentuating the potential of every child and the need for supportive environments that can nurture their capacities and skills. The INSPIRE model is also sensitive to children's emerging capabilities as they grow. It recognizes that children gradually identify factors contributing to their well-being. As children evolve into more introspective and reflective beings, their self-awareness and autonomy naturally expand. This progression fosters their ability to independently navigate their lives, thereby cultivating their potential for happiness and success. Children nurtured in families that place importance on and encourage the components highlighted in the INSPIRE model are likely to be equipped with the capacity to pursue their personal happiness and success continually throughout their lives.

Furthermore, fostering the elements encapsulated by the INSPIRE model could equip children with the resilience and capability to attain happiness and success, even in the face of adversity. Research shows that happiness in a form of feeling pleasure is relatively independent of life conditions associated with socioeconomic status and life events that affect it. Consequently, this form of happiness, possibly derived from simple activities like playing with friends, may provide a degree of resilience amidst adversity (Shmotkin, 2005). However, the INSPIRE model offers more comprehensive strategies to mitigate the effects of adversity and attain enhanced levels of functioning through social-emotional learning and executive function interventions. Targeted interventions promoting engagement, nurturing relationships, and improving physical health also play an instrumental role in safeguarding and advancing well-being. Nonetheless, addressing socioeconomic disparities and implementing interventions that enhance the physical environment remain crucial. These strategies ensure that children from all backgrounds are afforded equal opportunities for healthy development, happiness, and educational accomplishment.

It would be important to stress the interplay between the seven pillars. For example, perceptions of self-competence and efficacy often emerge within the context of early positive relationships with caregivers. Physical activity can be an excellent means to foster independence and autonomy, and the experience of independence can enable successful pursuit of specific goals and bolster self-competence. Personality traits may intersect with intelligence, with research suggesting a negative link between neuroticism and intelligence and a positive association between conscientiousness and cognitive flexibility (Johann & Karbach, 2022). Future research could determine the relative significance of each of these elements in predicting well-being, but it is expected that each child might have a different constellation of sources for happiness and success. Parents, educators, and child practitioners may utilize the strategies identified in this book to foster optimal functioning based on the individual understanding of a specific child. All children regardless of their challenges can learn how to become happy and successful.

References

Deci, E. L., & Ryan, R. M. (2012). Self-determination theory. In P. A. M. Van Lange, A. W. Kruglanski, & E. T. Higgins (Eds.), *Handbook of theories of social psychology* (pp. 416–436). Sage Publications Ltd. https://doi.org/10.4135/9781446249215.n21

Johann, V. E., & Karbach, J. (2022). The relations between personality, components of executive functions, and intelligence in children and young adults. *Psychological Research, 86*(6), 1904–1917. https://doi.org/10.1007/s00426-021-01623-1

Ross, W. D., Aristotle, & Brown, L. (2009). *Nicomachean ethics (Oxford world's classics)*. Oxford University Press.

Seligman, M. E. (2011). *Flourish: A visionary new understanding of happiness and well-being*. Simon and Schuster.

Shmotkin, D. (2005). Happiness in the face of adversity: Reformulating the dynamic and modular bases of subjective well-being. *Review of General Psychology, 9*(4), 291–325. https://doi.org/10.1037/1089-2680.9.4.291

Index

Taylor & Francis Group
an informa business

For Product Safety Concerns and Information please contact our EU representative GPSR@taylorandfrancis.com
Taylor & Francis Verlag GmbH, Kaufingerstraße 24, 80331 München, Germany

www.ingramcontent.com/pod-product-compliance
Ingram Content Group UK Ltd.
Pitfield, Milton Keynes, MK11 3LW, UK
UKHW020148200926
475702UK00016B/2614

* 9 7 8 0 3 6 7 4 0 4 9 9 4 *